MELVILLE

Andrew Delbanco is the Julian Clarence Levi Professor in the Humanities and Director of American Studies at Columbia University; a Fellow of the American Academy of Arts and Sciences; and a trustee of the National Humanities Center and the Library of America; and has served as Vice President of the PEN American Center. His most recent books are *The Real American Dream*, *Required Reading: Why Our American Classics Matter Now*, and *The Death of Satan*, which won the Lionel Trilling Award. His essays appear regularly in the *New York Review of Books*, the *New Republic*, the *New York Times Book Review*, and other journals. He and his wife have two children and live in New York City.

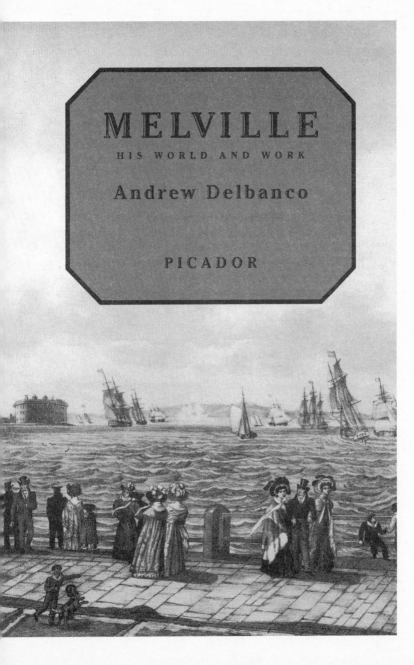

MELVILLE

HIS WORLD AND WORK

Andrew Delbanco

PICADOR

First published 2005 as a Borzoi Book by Alfred A. Knopf, Inc., New York, and
simultaneously in Canada by Random House of Canada Limited, Toronto

First published in Great Britain 2005 by Picador

This corrected edition first published in Great Britain 2006 by Picador
an imprint of Pan Macmillan Ltd
Pan Macmillan, 20 New Wharf Road, London N1 9RR
Basingstoke and Oxford
Associated companies throughout the world
www.panmacmillan.com

ISBN-13: 978-0-330-37108-7
ISBN-10: 0-330-37108-8

The acknowledgements on page 416 constitute an extension of this copyright page.

1 3 5 7 9 8 6 4 2

A CIP catalogue record for this book is available from
the British Library.

Printed and bound in Great Britain by
Mackays of Chatham plc, Chatham, Kent

Title page illustration: Detail of *New York Harbor from the Battery*,
lithograph by Thomas Thompson, 1829 (see page 33).

FOR DAWN

CONTENTS

ILLUSTRATIONS

PORTRAITS OF HERMAN MELVILLE

EXTRACTS
(supplied by a Sub-Sub-Sub-Librarian)

*He is very backward in speech & somewhat slow in comprehension, but you will
find him as far as he understands men & things both solid & profound, & of a
docile & amiable disposition*

—ALLAN MELVILL (MELVILLE'S FATHER),
ABOUT YOUNG HERMAN, AGE SEVEN,
C. 1826

Years ago I looked into Typee *and* Omoo, *but as I didn't find there what I am
looking for when I open a book I did go no further. Lately I had in my hand* Moby
Dick. *It struck me as a rather strained rhapsody with whaling for a subject and
not a single sincere line in the 3 vols of it.*

—JOSEPH CONRAD TO HUMPHREY MILFORD,
JANUARY 15, 1907

*I bought the Origin of Species yesterday for 6d and never read such badly written
catlap. I only remember one thing:* blue-eyed cats are always deaf *(correlation of
Variations). I finished* Vanity Fair *and* Cunt Pointercunt [Aldous Huxley's Point
Counter Point]. *A very pains talking work. The only thing I won't have forgotten
by this day week is Spandrell flogging the foxgloves. I bought* Moby Dick *to-day for
6d. That's more like the real stuff. White whales & natural piety.*

—SAMUEL BECKETT TO THOMAS MACGREEVY,
AUGUST 4, 1932

Through Melville, Moby Dick *has been absolved of mortality. Readers of* Moby-
Dick *know that he swims the world unconquered, that he is ubiquitous in time
and place. Yesterday he sank the* Pequod; *within the past two years he has
breached five times; from a New Mexico desert, over Hiroshima and Nagasaki,
and most recently, at Bikini atoll.*

—HOWARD P. VINCENT, *THE TRYING-OUT OF
MOBY-DICK*, 1949

T. E. Lawrence ranked Moby Dick *alongside* The Possessed *or* War and Peace. *Without hesitation, one can add to these* Billy Budd, Mardi, Benito Cereno, *and a few others. These anguished books in which man is overwhelmed, but in which life is exalted on each page, are inexhaustible sources of strength and pity. We find in them revolt and acceptance, unconquerable and endless love, the passion for beauty, language of the highest order—in short, genius.*

> —ALBERT CAMUS, 1952 (TRANSLATED FROM THE FRENCH BY ELLEN CONROY KENNEDY)

There is a Melville whom one scarcely knows whether to call the discovery or invention of our time, our truest contemporary, who has revealed to us the traditional theme of the deepest American mind, the ambiguity of innocence, "the mystery of iniquity," which we traded for the progressive melodrama of a good outcast (artist, rebel, whore, proletarian) against an evil bourgeoisie.

> —LESLIE FIEDLER, 1952

If you had met the three of us along the road you would have seen a peculiar sight: we looked like two sardines guiding an unsteady Moby Dick into port.

> —FRED ALLEN DESCRIBING HIMSELF AND HIS BROTHER, IN 1910, FLANKING HIS FATHER ON THEIR WAY HOME FROM SUNDAY DINNER IN CAMBRIDGE, MASSACHUSETTS, FROM *MUCH ADO ABOUT ME*, 1956

He goes to getting ready for bed, pulling off his clothes. The shorts under his work pants are coal black satin covered with big white whales with red eyes. He grins when he sees I'm looking at the shorts. "From a co-ed at Oregon State, Chief, a Literary major." He snaps the elastic with his thumb. "She gave them to me because she said I was a symbol."

> —KEN KESEY, *ONE FLEW OVER THE CUCKOO'S NEST*, 1962

There was ease in Ahab's manner as he stepped into his place,
There was pride in Ahab's bearing and a smile on Ahab's face;
The cheers, the wildest shoutings, did not him overwhelm,
No man in all that crowd could doubt, 'twas Ahab at the helm.

. . . .

And now the white-fleshed monster came a hurtling through the air,
While Ahab stood despising it in haughty grandeur there!
Close by the sturdy harpooner the Whale unheeded sped—
"That ain't my style," said Ahab. "Strike! Strike!" Good Starbuck said.

. . . .

With a smile of Christian charity great Ahab's visage shone,
He stilled the rising tumult and he bade the Chase go on.
He signalled to the White Whale, and again old Moby flew.
But still Ahab ignored it. Ishmael cried, "Strike! Strike, Man!" too.

. . . .

The sneer is gone from Ahab's lips, his teeth are clenched in hate,
He pounds with cruel violence his harpoon upon his pate.
And now old Moby gathers power, and now he lets it go.
And now the air is shattered by the force of Ahab's blow!

Oh, somewhere on the Seven Seas, the sun is shining bright,
The hornpipe plays yet somewhere and somewhere hearts are light;
And somewhere teachers laugh and sign, and somewhere scholars shout.
But there is no joy in Melville—mighty Ahab has Struck Out.

—RAY BRADBURY, "AHAB AT THE HELM,"
1964

"Future Broadway Musicals Based on Famous Literary Classics," MAD Magazine, *January 1966*
(MAD #100 © 1966 E. C. Publications, Inc. All Rights Reserved. Used with Permission.)

*Call me, Ishmael. Feel absolutely free to. Call me any hour of the day or night at
the office or at home and I'll be glad to give you the latest quotation with price-
earnings ratio and estimated dividend of any security traded in those tirelessly
tossing, deceptively shaded waters in which we pursue the elusive whale of Wealth,
but from which we come away at last content to have hooked the twitching bluegill,
solvency. And having got me call me anything you want, Ish baby. Tickled to death
to be of service.*

—PETER DE VRIES
OPENING LINES OF
THE VALE OF LAUGHTER, 1967

*Melville, it happened, was Bech's favorite American author, in whom he felt
united the strengths that were later to go the separate ways of Dreiser and James.
Throughout dinner, back at the hotel, he lectured Petrescu about him. "No one,"
Bech said—he had ordered a full bottle of white Rumanian wine, and his tongue*

felt agile as a butterfly—"more courageously faced our native terror. He went for it right between its wide-set little pig eyes, and it shattered his genius like a lance." He poured himself more wine. The hotel chanteuse, who Bech now noticed had buck teeth as well as gawky legs, stalked to their table, untangled her feet from the microphone wire, and favored them with a French version of "Some Enchanted Evening."

"You do not consider," Petrescu said, "that Hawthorne also went between the eyes? And the laconic Ambrose Bierce?"

"Quelque soir enchanté," the woman sang, her eyes and teeth and earrings glittering like the facets of a chandelier.

"Hawthorne blinked," Bech pronounced, "and Bierce squinted."

—JOHN UPDIKE, *BECH: A BOOK*, 1970

"Call me Smitty."

—PHILIP ROTH, OPENING SENTENCE OF *THE
GREAT AMERICAN NOVEL*, 1973

Why write? Where does writing come from? . . . These are questions to ask yourself . . . The writing professor this fall is stressing the Power of the Imagination. Which means he doesn't want long descriptive stories about your camping trip last July. He wants you to start in a realistic context but then to alter it . . .

Tell your roommate your great idea, your great exercise of imaginative power: a transformation of Melville to contemporary life. It will be about monomania and the fish-eat-fish world of life insurance in Rochester, New York. The first line will be "Call me Fishmeal," and it will feature a menopausal suburban husband named Richard, who because he is so depressed all the time is called "Mopey Dick" by his witty wife Elaine. Say to your roommate: "Mopey Dick, get it?" Your roommate looks at you, her face blank as a large Kleenex. She comes up to you, like a buddy, and puts an arm around your burdened shoulders. "Listen, Francie," she says, slow as speech therapy. "Let's go out and get a big beer."

—LORRIE MOORE,
"HOW TO BECOME A WRITER," 1984

Anyone who has read **Moby-Dick** *would find it irresistible now to extrapolate from that great novel to the real world, to see the American empire preparing once again, like Ahab, to take after an imputed evil.*

—EDWARD SAID, JANUARY 12, 1991, IN *THE
GUARDIAN*, ON AMERICAN PREPARATIONS
FOR THE FIRST GULF WAR

You'd have to be Melville to transmit the full strength of Stanley's will.

> —MICHAEL HERR, SPEAKING OF STANLEY
> KUBRICK, 1999

As we now know, Al Gore was on his way to make his concession speech when an aide's pager went off telling him that the Bush margin of victory was collapsing by the minute in Florida as the final votes came in. Al Gore clung to the wreckage with the ferocity of a Captain Ahab. He phoned George Bush to say that he was not conceding after all.

> —BBC NEWS, NOVEMBER 13, 2000

Herman Melville, who was born on Pearl Street in Lower Manhattan, had a pivotal moment as a young man, according to papers shown to this column by an unpublished Melville biographer. A neighborhood store owner overcharged him by mistake. When he discovered the error, the shopkeeper, who happened to be Jewish, apologized and said, "Call me a schlemiel."

Melville was enchanted by that sentence. But he was unfamiliar with Yiddish, and didn't quite get it right when he used it years later for the opening line of Moby-Dick.

> —CLYDE HABERMAN, *NEW YORK TIMES,*
> FEBRUARY 3, 2001

(At the dinner table at Meadow's apartment)

FINN: *Did you like* Billy Budd*?*

A.J.:   *It was OK. My teacher says it's a gay book.*

CARMELA: *. . . Oh, that is ridiculous! . . . I'm sorry, but* Billy Budd *is not a homosexual book.*

MEADOW: *Actually, it is, Mother.*

CARMELA: *I saw the movie, Meadow, with Terence Stamp.*

COLIN (MEADOW'S ROOMMATE):   *Terence Stamp was in* Priscilla, Queen of the Desert.

CARMELA: *I don't know about that. But* Billy Budd *is the story of an innocent sailor being picked on by an evil boss—*

MEADOW: *—who's picking on him out of self-loathing, caused by homosexual feelings in a military context.*

CARMELA: *Oh, please!*

ALEX: *Actually, Mrs. Soprano, there is a passage in the book where Melville compares Billy to a nude statue of Adam before the fall.*

A.J.:   *Really?*

TONY: *I thought you read it.*

CARMELA: *So it's a Biblical reference. Does that make it gay?*

. . .

TONY: *Must be a gay book. Billy Budd's the ship's florist, right?* (Laughter)

MEADOW: *Leslie Fiedler has written extensively on gay themes in literature since the early 60s*—Billy Budd *in particular.*

CARMELA: *Well, she doesn't know what she's talking about.*

MEADOW: *She's a he, Mother, and he's lectured at Columbia, as a matter of fact.*

CARMELA: *Well, maybe* he's *gay, you ever thought of that?*

—*THE SOPRANOS*, SEASON FOUR, EPISODE 12,
DECEMBER 1, 2002

I've been thinking about "Bartleby" lately. . . . The mess in Iraq presents two seemingly unacceptable possibilities: stay and having our soldiers killed daily, or leaving and ushering in chaos. . . . In today's world of bleak alternatives . . . Bartleby's story is a sobering reminder that what life requires is remaining engaged—preferring, and acting on those preferences.

—ADAM COHEN, *NEW YORK TIMES*,
AUGUST 29, 2003

Adam Cohen's "Bartleby" isn't mine. "I would prefer not to" is good existential philosophy. President Bush should have employed it in Iraq.

—GUS FRANZA, LETTER TO THE EDITOR, *NEW
YORK TIMES*, AUGUST 30, 2003

"Maybe I'm becoming like Captain Ahab with bin Laden as the white whale. Maybe you need someone less obsessive about it."

—RICHARD CLARKE TO CONDOLEEZZA RICE,
AS RECALLED IN CLARKE'S BOOK, *AGAINST
ALL ENEMIES*, 2004

Mayor Michael Bloomberg's obsession with building a football stadium on the Far West Side of Manhattan is in danger of leaving other development projects in its shadow—including the rebuilding of ground zero. Since Lower Manhattan is where Melville began the saga of Moby-Dick, *it seems appropriate to wonder whether Mr. Bloomberg is turning into a modern-day Ahab, pursuing his great white elephant of a stadium as the former World Trade Center site sinks into trouble.*

—*NEW YORK TIMES*, LEAD EDITORIAL
("MANHATTAN'S MAYOR AHAB"),
MAY 2, 2005

Few novels . . . captured the imagination of hedge-fund managers quite like Moby-Dick *. . . says Mr. Reiferson of Americus Capital, because money managers like to give the impression that they are being Ahab-like in "maniacally pursuing their goals." Mr. Reiferson says he planned to name his fund after Bildad, a character who helped finance the whaling expeditions. But in the end, he felt the reference as "too obscure, unless I could raise money from Melville scholars."*

—*THE WALL STREET JOURNAL*,
FEBRUARY 16, 2006

PREFACE

Why write about a writer's life? For me, the reason has to do with a feeling that we all live by some unknowable combination of free will and fate. This feeling tends to grow as one gets older, and so there is a certain comfort in watching someone make something beautiful and enduring out of the recalcitrance and fleetingness of life.

There is a problem, though, with bringing this motive to bear on Herman Melville. As he said about the title character of his haunting story "Bartleby, the Scrivener," who responds alike with maddening silence to compassion or coercion, "no materials exist for a full and satisfactory biography of this man." Only about three hundred Melville letters, many of them perfunctory, have survived, as compared, say, to twelve thousand letters by Henry James. As for letters received, he was in the "vile habit" (as he called it) of destroying them, and most of his manuscripts, left behind in 1863 when he moved out of his Berkshire home, probably went up in flames in a house-cleaning bonfire set by the new owners. His journals were brief and few, and since he was not famous for long in his own time, no Boswell followed him into the taverns to write down his table talk.

The "business" of the biographer, Henry James says, is "detail," and so any conventional biography of Melville is a business bound to fail. The incidents of his daily life—his flirtations and quarrels, his jokes and rants at the family table—have slipped beyond the reach of even informed conjecture, and most attempts to tell his life are notable for the discrepancy between the vividness of what he wrote and the vagueness of the figure who appears in writings about him. Today, despite the immense surge in his prestige, he remains so murky that when a photograph was discovered a few years ago showing a heavily bearded man with top hat standing on a Staten Island pier that Melville was thought to have visited, there was great excitement that it might be him, even though the photo shows little more than a featureless silhouette.

Now and then, thanks to some friend or relative who mentions him in a letter, this "fabulous shadow," as Hart Crane called him, comes into focus. We see him eating with his brother in a Manhattan steakhouse, driving his sleigh in a Berkshire snowstorm, or taking his granddaughter to Madison Square Park to see the tulips and then, after sitting on a bench for a while,

Herman Melville [?] on Staten Island

walking back to his house alone, having forgotten her. But these faint trails lead only to the edge of his inner life. When (or if) he left the child and walked out of the park, was he distracted by a pleasant daydream or lost in an old man's confusion? Or did the incident take place at all?

It is impossible to know, and sooner or later the question arises whether one should even try. Melville once wrote that "on a personal interview, no great author has ever come up to the idea of his reader," and since biography ought to be a kind of interview, this comment contains an admonition to leave him in his self-concealment. He wrote, after all, with special sympathy about "isolatoes" who barricade themselves against the gadding world and live alone with their demons and dreams—as when he described, in *Moby-Dick*, how the thundering minister Father Mapple climbs into his pulpit by means of a rope ladder, then leans over the rail "deliberately [to] drag up the ladder step by step, till the whole was deposited within, leaving him impregnable in his little Quebec." Melville, too, withdrew, especially in later life, when he would sometimes hang a towel over the doorknob inside his study so that no one could see him through the keyhole. He ensured that the man whom we barely glimpse in the historical record will always be incommensurate with the genius whom we meet in the works.

A few summers ago, I had an experience that left me feeling hesitant to invade his posthumous privacy. I was in the reading room of the Houghton Library, holding in my hands a note from a former shipmate who had written to Melville to tell him he had named his son after him, and to beg him for a visit or a keepsake. Turning the pages of this letter that Melville himself had once removed in surprised anticipation from an envelope bearing the name of a friend from whom he had not heard in years, I felt that I was eavesdropping, like a tourist in a church who comes upon a worshipper kneeling in prayer.

In trying to find a right relation with this figure whom one might call Melville the Problem (he once likened his eminent friend Nathaniel Hawthorne to a closed "black-letter volume in golden clasps, entitled 'Hawthorne: A Problem' "), I owe an enormous debt to the biographical researches of many scholars. My own chief aim, however, has not been to add to the store of facts about Melville's life; and though I hope here and there to have done so, my emphasis is on his writing, and on its complex connections to the intellectual and political context in which he lived and worked. There is, therefore, a good deal in this book about what was going on in the United States during his lifetime. My hope is that the reader might thereby gain what Hawthorne called a "home-feeling with the past"—with, that is, the past that Melville experienced as the present.

Finally, I take seriously D. H. Lawrence's remark that Melville "wrote from a sort of dream-self, so that events which he relates as actual fact have indeed a far deeper reference to his own soul, his own inner life." Since the route to that inner life can only be through his own words, this book is above all an attempt to reconstruct that virgin moment when, long before we knew anything about whether Melville was a gentle or harsh husband, an opponent or proponent of this or that idea, it was his *words* that seized and dazzled us. The critic Richard Poirier reminds us of what can happen when we drift away from the words:

> Most of us, when we are away from the text, tend to maunder on in a clubbable way about inexactly remembered scenes or characters or bits of phrasing . . . when we remember good ol' Proust he becomes not in any important way different from good ol' Tolstoy, even though the two could never have been mistaken for each other when we first met them in their writings.

Anyone who reads Melville's words will know what Emerson meant when he wrote in his journal that, while reading Shakespeare, "I actually shade my eyes." My hope for this book is that it will convey something of the tone and texture of Melville's time while giving some sense of why, in our time, the glare of his genius remains undimmed.

ANDREW DELBANCO
NEW YORK CITY, MAY 2005

It had always been one of the lesser ambitions of Pierre,
to sport a flowing beard, which he deemed the most
noble corporeal badge of the man, not to speak
of the illustrious author.

—*HERMAN MELVILLE,*
PIERRE, OR THE AMBIGUITIES,
BOOK 17

c. 1846/47. Oil painting by Asa Twitchell

1860

1861

1868

1870. Oil painting by Joseph Eaton

1885

MELVILLE

INTRODUCTION
MELVILLE:
FROM HIS TIME TO OURS

1.

When Melville was born in 1819 in New York City, it was a town of about a hundred thousand people with streets lit dimly by oil lamps as if by so many lightning bugs. The best way of sending a message was via a wax-sealed letter carried by a messenger on a horse. Such giants of the revolutionary generation as Thomas Jefferson and John Adams were still alive, while the political institutions they had invented remained fragile and, according to many putatively sage observers, unlikely to endure.

By the time he died in New York in 1891, its population had grown to over 3 million, the Brooklyn Bridge was carrying traffic, as was the Second Avenue Elevated Railway, and the city was forested by so many telegraph, telephone, and electricity poles that live wires falling into the street were a hazard of urban life. Slavery, which still existed in New York when Melville was born, had been abolished in every state of the Union. Reconstruction had been tried and abandoned in the South, and the great wave of immigration was at full tide in the cities of the North. In short, during Melville's childhood, the rhythm of American life was closer to medieval than to modern, but by the time he grew old, he was living in a world that had become recognizably our own.

These changes in how Americans lived were matched, and probably exceeded, by changes in how they thought about their lives. Perhaps the most important intellectual event of Melville's early years was the publication in 1836 of Emerson's *Nature,* which declared that "the moral law lies at the center of nature and radiates to the circumference" of a natural world that is the "incarnation of God." In 1890, about a year before he died, Melville borrowed from the New York Society Library the latest novel by William Dean Howells, *A Hazard of New Fortunes,* a book written in the shadow of Darwin, who had long since destroyed Emerson's romantic view of creation

LEFT: *New York City, 1817*

OPPOSITE: *New York City, 1890*

and replaced it with a vision of the natural world created by chance and filled with brutality.* The protagonist of that novel looks down from the Second Avenue El upon a "lawless, Godless" world in which "the play of energies [is] as free and planless as those that force the forest from the soil to the sky."

We tend to think of Melville as having been a practicing fiction writer for much of the century through which he lived, but in fact he devoted only twelve of his seventy-two years (from 1845 to 1857) to prose that was published in his lifetime. His early years were unpromising—"until I was twenty-five," he wrote to Nathaniel Hawthorne, "I had no development"—and from the age of forty until his death he wrote mainly poems, some of which were never published, and those that did make it into print were scarcely read. In this respect, the shape of his career—a decade of fiction followed by a turn to poetry—resembles that of his younger contemporary Thomas Hardy. At the end of his life, he returned for one last effort at prose fiction: the exquisite short novel *Billy Budd,* still in manuscript when he died. When the death notices appeared, even people who had known him were surprised; as one of the obituary writers put it, "his own generation has long thought him dead."

Melville began his career auspiciously when, after cruising the Pacific by whaleship and warship as a young man, he came home to upstate New York and started to write down (and embellish) his experiences. His first book,

*The entry in the charge ledger is preserved at the library's current home on East Seventy-ninth Street.

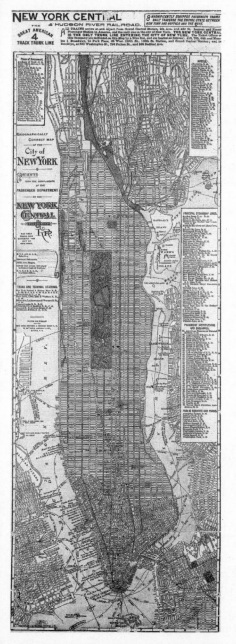

Typee, appeared in 1846, and the public liked it. They liked the "labial melody" of the native girls he claimed had held him in "indulgent captivity." They liked the picture of an American lad lying like a god recumbent on the warm sand, sucking coconut under the tropical moon. They also liked his winks and hints that all was not quite right with the not-so-noble savages who waited on him. In between the banquets and orgies, he worried that he would be forcibly tattooed and that, were he ever to make it back home, he would be received as a freak. And since he suspected that his captors were cannibals, his pleasure at being pampered was mixed with anxiety that he was being prepared like the fatted calf for a tribal feast.

Those early books (*Typee* was followed a year later by a sequel, *Omoo*) were sunny and charming, dappled only here and there with shade and sorrow. But Melville's ambition outgrew them, and when he turned outward in his next books (*Mardi, Redburn,* and *White-Jacket*) to comment on such issues as slavery, urbanization, and immigration, he began to lose his public, who wanted to hear more about the sirens and savages of Polynesia. It did not help that he turned inward as well, toward what he later called "the tornadoed Atlantic" of his being. *Mardi* was a book of "depths," as Hawthorne put it, ". . . that compel a man to swim for his life," and most prospective readers declined to take the plunge. The clock had run out on Melville's fifteen minutes of fame.

One of the paradoxes of this life is that just when he was being forgotten by his contemporaries, Melville wrote the book for which he would be remembered by posterity. He was in his early thirties, a time when many men feel that the chance for untried things is slipping away. It was the summer of 1850. With his money worries growing and his audience shrinking, he was working on yet another young-man-goes-to-sea story when the new book began, as the phrase goes, to write itself. It became the story of a "moody stricken" captain, bent on vengeance against a great white whale that had dashed his boat to splinters on a previous voyage and ripped him half to death. At first this peg-legged captain, named Ahab for an apostate Israelite king, keeps himself hidden belowdecks just as he had been submerged in Melville's mind. Only after the Nantucket pilot has steered the ship to the edge of the open ocean does Ahab reveal himself, and the moment he does, we recognize in him that rarity in literature—a truly original character who, "like a revolving Drummond light, raying away from itself," so lights up the world that it is as if we are seeing it for the first time.

Melville had thought that *Moby-Dick* would be done before the end of that summer. But it outran his intentions, and he found himself experimenting with how best to represent the ebb and flow of the unconscious, the quasi-erotic excitement of killing, and the psychodynamics of demagoguery. Partly, perhaps, out of the fear that every writer feels at exposing his work to public appraisal, he resisted the idea that he would ever finish it. "This whole book," he wrote with a self-serving sexual pun, "is but a draught—nay, but the draught of a draught; small erections may be finished by their first architects; grand ones, true ones, ever leave the copestone to posterity. God keep me from ever completing anything." His immense ambition matched the scale and swagger of the young nation whose multitude of voices he wanted to comprehend in prose with the same bear-hug comprehensiveness that Walt Whitman was bringing to poetry. His book became a meditation on that species of madness that, in Melville's day, was known as "monomania"—as the mutilated Captain Ahab, in his "frantic morbidness," blames an unreasoning animal for "not only all his bodily woes, but all his intellectual and spiritual exasperations."

When *Moby-Dick* finally appeared at the end of 1851, it did not restore its author's reputation. It was really two books—a going-to-sea story, and a daring metaphysical adventure—and when the second swallowed the first, it swallowed it whole, leaving it intact like Jonah in the belly of the beast. During Melville's lifetime, *Moby-Dick* never came close to selling out its first edition of 3,000 copies, and when, in December 1853, the unsold copies burned up in a fire in the publisher's warehouse, few noticed and fewer cared.

Melville managed three more novels that were published under deteriorating contractual terms—*Pierre*, about a fanatic who destroys his world while trying to reform it; *Israel Potter*, about an old soldier discarded by his country; and *The Confidence-Man*, a "masquerade" of disguise and deceit set aboard a Mississippi steamboat. But *Moby-Dick* had tested (and *Pierre* exhausted) the patience of his public, and he was forced to retreat into writing for the new monthly magazines such as *Harper's* and *Putnam's*. In 1856, he collected several of these pieces, including two masterworks, "Bartleby, the Scrivener" and *Benito Cereno*, in a volume entitled *The Piazza Tales*, which was greeted by the editor George W. Curtis with this accurate prediction: "He has lost his prestige—and I don't believe the *Putnam* stories will bring it up." Melville's subsequent works were written in verse—a collection of Civil War poems, *Battle-Pieces and Other Aspects of the War*, published in a small edition in 1866, followed at wide intervals by three books of poetry printed privately with the help of subventions from relatives who thought the discipline of meter and rhyme might have some therapeutic value for him.

After failing in a brief attempt at lecturing, he withdrew from public life. In 1866, he took a job with the U.S. Custom Service in Manhattan, having earlier traveled to California, Europe, and the Middle East. The following year, he and his wife suffered the worst calamity that can befall any parent: at age eighteen, their firstborn son, Malcolm, shot himself in his bedroom at home. Some twenty years later, their second son, Stanwix, died alone in a San Francisco hotel at the age of thirty-five. Melville never wrote directly about these events, but they cast a shadow over his later writings, and are felt at the heart of his valedictory masterpiece, *Billy Budd*.

2.

Since the present book is mainly concerned with Melville's work in the context of his life and times, it tells a symmetrical tale of artistic triumph and public failure about a writer who earned little more than $10,000 over his lifetime, counting all his sales in Britain as well as America. Something, therefore, should be said about his posthumous success.

Over the course of the twentieth century, Melville became an American

Mastodon CD, Leviathan,
by Paul Romano, 2004

icon to a degree unmatched by any other writer. Today, there is a journal named *Leviathan* devoted solely to his work, a thriving Melville Society, and there are academic conferences galore. As one literary scholar puts it, in a formulation that seems poised somewhere between irritation and satisfaction, *Moby-Dick* is today "the unavoidable centerpiece of the American tradition." Ever since the 1930s, when the poet and avid Melvillean Charles Olson searched out the surviving volumes from Melville's personal library (some were donated by his granddaughter to Harvard; others had been sold by his wife to a Brooklyn bookseller), scholars have tried to track down every check mark, underlining, and marginal jotting in every book whose pages Melville may have turned. In Olson's day, when comments in the margins were found to be erased, the only recourse was to turn the paper to and fro so that different rakings of light might reveal to the naked eye (aided, at best, by a magnifying glass) indentations left by the erased pencil. More recently, Melville's personal copy of a book he consulted while writing *Moby-Dick,* Thomas Beale's *The Natural History of the Sperm Whale,* was laid out at Harvard like the Shroud of Turin under an infrared camera capable of discerning microscopic graphite traces left by Melville's pencil after he—or, more likely, someone else—had rubbed away the marks and annotations.

If he has become a fixture in "high" culture, Melville has also found a place in popular culture, abroad as well as at home. Hardly a town in America within ten miles of a tourist beach lacks a "Moby Dick" fish restaurant, and as far away as Tehran there is a popular kebab place called "Moby Dick."

Melville in Belgium

Melville's great book has been the subject of marathon readings, spin-offs, sequels and prequels, adaptations for television, stage, film, painting, and performance art, comic books, cartoons, even dinnerware decorated with images of Ahab and the hated whale. At Yale, students refer to the college hockey rink, designed by the modernist architect Eero Saarinen, as "Moby Dick," in honor of its undulating form. The *New York Post* recently offered its readers a "Moby Dick coupon" toward the purchase of a hardback edition sold exclusively at a deli one door down from the *Post*'s offices on Eighteenth Street. In 2004, the heavy metal rock band Mastodon released an album, *Leviathan,* devoted to themes ("Seabeast," "Aqua Dementia," "I Am Ahab") from *Moby-Dick,* and in Denmark one can tour Copenhagen's canals aboard the sightseeing boat *Moby Dick.* Outside the medieval Belgian city of Ghent, there is a brothel with the intriguing name "Moby Dick Fun Pub."

A few years ago in New York, a "floor-length periwinkle Grecian gown" with Melville's words inscribed in the seams was offered for sale at just under $2,000; and today, for considerably less, one can take a boat ride at an Ohio theme park amid sounds of surf with background voices reciting *Moby-Dick* along with selections from Eskimo poetry. And if the first words of the book ("Call me Ishmael") have become universally familiar, its last words ("then all collapsed, and the great shroud of the sea rolled on as it rolled five thousand years ago") have currency too: a reporter for Slate.com quoted them recently to describe the breasts of a formerly buxom actress after her implants were removed.

The New Yorker,
November 21, 1988,
cartoon by
Gahan Wilson

Herman Melville Wonders If His Agent Has
Oversold Spinoffs from "Moby Dick"

What does it all mean? A "literary text acts as a kind of mirror," one the-
orist has said, and surely no text written by an American has been as power-
fully reflective as *Moby-Dick*. Melville himself considered the phenomenon
of reflection in "The Doubloon" chapter of *Moby-Dick,* in which Ahab nails
a gold coin to the mast as a reward for the first sailor to catch sight of the
white whale. Inscribed on that coin are the images of three mountain peaks:
one with a tower on top, the next with a flaming volcano, the last with a crowing cock. Ahab stares into the burnished gold and, in his narcissistic frenzy,
concentrates his mind upon the only subject that interests him: "The firm
tower, that is Ahab; the volcano, that is Ahab; the courageous, undaunted,
and victorious fowl, that, too is Ahab; all are Ahab; and this round gold is but
the image of the rounder globe, which, like a magician's glass, to each and
every man in turn but mirrors back his own mysterious self."

Few readers in Melville's time wished to look deeply into a book about
common sailors who stab to death majestic animals and chop their bodies
into bloody broth in order to deliver such luxuries as skirt hoops and canes
made of whalebone, hair-dressings and perfume made of whale oil, to people
like themselves. *Moby-Dick* was last reprinted during Melville's lifetime in
1876; ten years later, it went out of print. While there were stirrings of interest soon after he died (it was published in a new edition in 1892), and, in an
article entitled "The Best Sea Story Ever Told," one critic wrote in 1899 that
Moby-Dick had "an Elizabethan force and freshness and swing," as late as
1917 Melville was still getting only a brief mention in the *Cambridge History*
of American Literature, mainly in the chapter on "Travel Writers."

His rediscovery was a joint Anglo-American operation. In England, the novelist Viola Meynell led the way with her introduction to the 1920 reissue of *Moby-Dick* in the Oxford World's Classics series. Gradually, the affable travel writer gave way to a writer who had anticipated James Joyce's literary innovations, and who, in the relishing phrase of one of the leaders of what came to be known as the Melville revival, had "sinned blackly against the orthodoxy of his time." This was the beginning of Melville's reclamation as a protomodernist writer fed up with prudery and priggishness, sexually mobile (his biographers suspecting that he enjoyed native boys as well as native girls), and unconstrained by the respectabilities of life or art. Writing in 1919, the American critic Frank Jewett Mather, Jr., reported that reading Melville was "like eating hasheesh"; and in England, D. H. Lawrence, writing in 1921, discovered in him "a futurist long before futurism," whose work makes one feel "the sheer naked slidings of the elements."

As the critic and novelist Frank Lentricchia says of *Moby-Dick*, "Melville desires, before Joyce, that the something that his writing is about be the writing itself pouring onto the pages . . . without structural confinement, inspired by the library of his mind." He jumped from omniscient to first-person to choral narration, mixing the proper speech of well-bred officers with the dirty songs of illiterate sailors. With his ambulatory style—always digressive, never consecutive—he was happier to wander than to go straight. Restlessly experimental, he was by turns playful, ironic, somber, and uproariously funny, sometimes dropping into bawdy comedy, sometimes soaring into soliloquies worthy of *King Lear.* To those who discovered him in the 1920s, it seemed as if they had come upon a prophet of the Jazz Age. And though he wrote his major works while living in the Berkshire Hills, his sensibility, like that of all the major modernist writers, had been formed by a city—specifically by New York City, where he learned to write with the miscellaneous profusion of a magazine, sending out in divergent directions short chapters that spill onto each other like the overlapping advertising posters on an urban wall.

In the 1930s, Melville's reputation continued to grow, but on a new basis. Along with his precocious modernity, his preoccupation with the human capacity for hate and treachery and atavistic violence now touched a nerve. To borrow a phrase from one of his best readers, Walker Percy, Melville seemed to know in advance the great secret of the twentieth century—that "only the haters seem alive." Already by 1927, E. M. Forster was hearing in *Moby-Dick* a "prophetic song" about a man whose "knight-errantry turns into revenge," and two years later, on the verge of what was to be the most hideous decade in Western history, Lewis Mumford described *Moby-Dick* as a book about a man who, "in battling against evil . . . becomes the image of the thing he hates."

By the 1940s, it was impossible to read about Ahab without feeling his kinship to the jackbooted tyrants who were dragging a whole continent into an orgy of hate. "That inscrutable thing," Ahab says of the whale, "is chiefly what I hate . . . and I will wreak that hate upon him"; and in Ahab's mismatched confrontation with his decent but weak first mate, Mr. Starbuck (now of coffee-bar fame), there seemed a prescient anticipation of Yeats's twentieth-century lament that "the best lack all conviction, while the worst / Are full of passionate intensity." Like those horrific charismatics—the *Generalissimo,* the *Führer,* and *Il Duce*—Ahab had his private squad of secret police, five "dusky phantoms" chosen for their proficient delight in killing, whom he keeps hidden and hungry, as if they are a pack of carnivores left to starve in their cage. Once released, they leap to the chase whenever he spies a breeching whale that might be the one he is looking for. By the early 1950s, the Trinidadian writer C. L. R. James could describe *Moby-Dick* as "the biography of the last days of Adolf Hitler."

Yet *Moby-Dick* was not a book for a particular moment. It is a book for the ages. What gives it its psychological and moral power is that, freakish as he is, Ahab seems more part of us than apart from us. Like all great literary representations of evil, he is attractive as well as repulsive. And so Melville emerged in the twentieth century as the American Dostoevsky—a writer who, with terrible clairvoyance, had been waiting for the world to catch up with him.

Ever since, he has routed his rivals in the competition for readers. Emerson, once regarded as a dangerous infidel, remarked in his journal that "I hate goodies," but he strikes many readers as something of a goody himself. That other New England worthy, Emerson's neighbor and friend Henry D. Thoreau, tells us in *Walden* that he is seized by the desire "to devour" a woodchuck raw, but it seems a good bet that Thoreau cooked his meat thoroughly. These writers are kept alive mainly as classroom assignments; but Melville is different: he is a living presence in the larger culture. Among his contemporaries, he is today by far the largest, having combined Whitman's New York bluster with Hawthorne's New England gravity into a sensibility that created, in *Moby-Dick,* the one nineteenth-century American classic (possibly along with *Huckleberry Finn*) that remains morally powerful without having come to seem moralistic. To paraphrase the historian Dominic LaCapra, many writers are good for thinking about, but only a few, after their own time has passed, continue to be good for thinking with. Melville belongs to that select company.

Since he "arrived" in the mid-twentieth century, there has been a steady stream of new Melvilles, all of whom seem somehow able to keep up with the preoccupations of the moment: myth-and-symbol Melville, countercultural

Melville, anti-war Melville, environmentalist Melville, gay or bisexual Melville, multicultural Melville, global Melville. As for how he will fare in our "postmodern" (or is it already post-postmodern?) age, the early signs suggest that he remains as current as ever. In the immediate aftermath of that terrible day now known as 9/11, Captain Ahab was suddenly everywhere. For some, he was a symbol of America's obsession with hunting down bin Laden. Writing in *The Observer* in London a few days after the attack, Edward Said remarked that

> Osama bin Laden's name and face have become so numbingly familiar to Americans as in effect to obliterate any history he and his shadowy followers might have had before they became stock symbols of everything loathsome and hateful to the collective imagination. Inevitably, then, collective passions are being funnelled into a drive for war that uncannily resembles Captain Ahab in pursuit of Moby Dick, rather than what is going on, an imperial power injured at home for the first time, pursuing its interests systematically in what has become a suddenly reconfigured geography of conflict.

For others, with perfect symmetry, Captain Ahab was a prescient model of Osama bin Laden's hatred of America—a "demagogue [who] can fuse his personal need for vengeance with the popular will by promising his followers a huntable enemy [the United States] in which evil is 'made practically assailable.' " One scholar has enumerated citations of Melville in the weeks following the terror attacks—in the Scottish *Sunday Herald, The Australian, The Washington Post,* the *San Francisco Chronicle,* the *Los Angeles Times, The Atlantic Monthly, The New York Review of Books, Counter-Punch, Daily Nexus,* and the University of Wisconsin's *Badger Herald.* This is, no doubt, a partial list. The community of Melville critics has lately come to include figures ranging from former Senator Gary Hart to the Hollywood actor Richard Gere, both of whom likened President George W. Bush to Ahab in his determination to attack Iraq.

In all these respects and more, Melville seems to renew himself for each new generation. Even before the last vestiges of what William James called "tender-minded" faith in "the great universe of God" drained out of nineteenth-century thought, Melville had surveyed with twentieth-century suspicion all claims of metaphysical warrant for any idea or ideology. Long before the existentialist movement, he composed what Albert Camus called an "Odyssey beneath an empty sky," in which there came forth, out of "endless darkness . . . the visages of foam and night"—not only in *Moby-Dick* but in a series of works that seemed to anticipate the angst of modern life. He doubted the existence of what his contemporaries called God and post-modernists call "presence"; a doubt that gave rise, in that great chapter of *Moby-Dick*, "The Whiteness of the Whale," to a meditation on the whale's whiteness as a symbol of the "voids and immensities of the universe." Yet, as his friend Hawthorne knew, he could "neither believe, nor be comfortable in his unbelief." He never stopped looking for traces of God, as when, in the beautiful "Grand Armada" chapter, he describes Ishmael staring through the clear water at a school of nursing mother whales whose suckling infants "calmly and fixedly gaze away from the breast . . . as if . . . still spiritually feasting upon some unearthly reminiscence."

"I love all men who *dive*," Melville once said of Emerson, whom he counted among the "corps of thought-divers, that have been diving & coming up again with blood-shot eyes since the world began." But writing of those (including himself) who dream of penetrating to the depths of things, he gave vent to a feeling somewhere between eulogy and mockery that marks him as a fellow traveler in our post-theistic world. Consider this passage from *Pierre*, which can be read as a retort to the Romantic faith—still very much alive in Melville's time—that at the core of each of us there is some germ or spark or trace of God, if only we could find it:

> [As] far as any geologist has yet gone down into the world, it is found to consist of nothing but surface stratified on surface. To its axis, the world being nothing but superinduced superficies. By vast pains we mine into the pyramid; by horrible gropings we come to the central room; with joy we espy the sarcophagus; but we lift the lid—and no body is there!—appallingly vacant as vast is the soul of a man!

There is in that last sentence an antic, even cruel view of man driving himself through an arduous quest only to discover at the climactic moment that in fact there is nothing to be unearthed—nothing but more mud, rock, and dust—and that the self, like the universe, is devoid of meaning except for the meanings we project into it for the sake of reassuring ourselves.

3.

In writing Melville's life, it is tempting to regard everything in his early years as leading up to *Moby-Dick*, and everything afterwards as falling away from it. This view is not exactly wrong, but it is a distortion, and it may be helpful to bring out of the shadow of *Moby-Dick* a number of works that today seem utterly fresh and urgent: *Pierre,* with its themes of sexual confusion and transgression; *Benito Cereno,* with its account of the multiple horrors of race hatred; "Bartleby," about the loneliness of modern urban life; and *Billy Budd,* with its perennially and, today, particularly salient theme of conflict between individual rights and the safety of the state.

At least since the 1920s, when the failure of Melville's contemporaries to recognize his genius began to be redressed, every generation has felt a need to come to terms with him in its own way. This continually renewed present-ness is the mark of a great writer. For some readers today, the Melville who counts is the corrosive critic of America, the writer who represents the United States in *Moby-Dick* as a bloodthirsty killing machine with the teeth of killed whales inserted in her bulwarks—a "cannibal of a craft," a "thing of trophies" decked out in "the chased bones of her enemies." With fires burning to melt whale blubber into marketable oil, the *Pequod* is a "red hell," and her criminally cruel captain beyond appeal from a passing ship whose captain begs for help in finding a man—his own son—lost overboard.

But if Melville warned against America's violence and hubris, he also wrote with delirious passion about America's promise. A decade after John L. O'Sullivan coined the now notorious term "Manifest Destiny," Melville wrote in *White-Jacket* about—and with—the missionary zeal of the United States:

> We Americans are the peculiar, chosen people—the Israel of our time; we bear the ark of the liberties of the world. . . . God has given to us, for a future inheritance, the broad domains of the political pagans, that shall yet come and lie down under the shade of our ark, without bloody hands being lifted. God has predestinated, mankind expects, great things from our race; and great things we feel in our souls. . . . Long enough have we been skeptics with regard to ourselves, and doubted whether, indeed, the political Messiah had come. But he has come in us, if we would but give utterance to his promptings. And let us always remember, that with ourselves—almost for the first time in the history of earth—national selfishness is unbounded philanthropy; for we cannot do a good to America but we give alms to the world.

This passage has properly become one of the touchstone passages of our literature. When Melville wrote it, it expressed the ideals of a nation that saw itself as the last best hope of earth in the wake of the failure of the European democratic revolutions of 1848. By the turn of the twentieth century, it seemed to anticipate the jingoism with which the United States seized, in the name of liberty, Spanish imperial possessions from Cuba to the Philippines. A century after it was written, when our literature was being deployed in the 1950s as a weapon on the cultural front of the Cold War, it seemed an expression of self-serving generosity in the spirit of the Marshall Plan. By the Vietnam era, it was widely cited as an exhibit of national arrogance—a sort of naive companion text to Norman Mailer's novel *Why Are We in Vietnam?*—in which one could see America in all its fatal pride. Today, amid images of the invasion and occupation of Iraq, it has again become a passage of great power and unsettling ambiguity.

Herman Melville was one of those writers whom Lionel Trilling described as "repositories of the dialectics of their times" in the sense that they contain "both the yes and no of their culture." In coming to terms with him, we are free to choose the prose-poet of our national destiny who imagines a world of grateful converts to the American Way, or the writer who saw the ship of state sailing toward disaster under lunatic leadership as it tries to conquer the world. In this respect he was—and is—as vast and contradictory as America itself.

CHAPTER 1
CHILDHOOD AND YOUTH

1.

He was born on August 1, 1819, into good circumstances. But his parents lacked the money to stay there, and so they turned frequently, at no small cost to their dignity, to their elders for help. On his mother's side, the benefactor had been Maria's late father, Peter Gansevoort, a towering man (six foot three in an age when six-footers were rare) famous for having commanded the defense of Fort Stanwix, an outpost guarding the trade route from the Great Lakes, during the British siege of 1777. There is a tendency today to think of the Revolutionary War as a dispute among bewigged gentlemen who sent men into battle with inaccurate guns to the martial music of fife and drum; in fact, it was a brutal war whose combatants literally tasted sweat and blood flung from the bodies of their enemies as they slashed at each other with bayonets. It was not uncommon for wounded soldiers to be stabbed through and left to bleed to death "like sieves," or to have their brains dashed out with "barbarity to the utmost" by the musket butts of the advancing enemy. Melville was to write about this war in the novel *Israel Potter,* in which he described the Yankee defenders at Bunker Hill gripping their muskets by the barrel and beating back the British assault by "wielding the stock right and left, as seal-hunters on the beach, knock down with their clubs the Shetland seal."

Melville's Gansevoort grandfather was known for his valor in the face of superior numbers of enemy troops. At Fort Stanwix, having refused to receive a verbal message from the officer in charge of the British assault, he was presented with a written ultimatum to surrender "exhibiting in magnificent terms . . . the strength of the [British] army . . . and the hopeless situation of the garrison," to which he replied with formal contempt:

Sir:—In answer to your letter of today's date, I have only to say, that it is my determined resolution, with the forces under my command to defend this fort, at every hazard, to the last extremity, in behalf of the United American States, who have placed me here to defend it against all their enemies.

> I have the honor to be, Sir,
> Your most obedient and humble servant,
> Peter Gansevoort, Col.,
> Commanding Fort Stanwix

This immovable eighteenth-century gentleman lived out his years in Albany. Upon his death in 1812, seven years before his grandson Herman was born, Peter Gansevoort's assets were passed on to his son Peter Junior, along with the obligation to look after his sister Maria and her unborn children.

On the Melville side, too, there was a modest fortune, and Herman's father, Allan, did his best to tap it. Allan's father, Major Thomas Melvill, was also a celebrated veteran of the Revolution, accustomed to being greeted on the streets of Boston with bows of deference.* In 1831, when the deference was turning to pity, Dr. Oliver Wendell Holmes made a little verse sketch of him called "The Last Leaf":

> *My grandmamma has said—*
> *Poor old lady; she is dead*
>   *Long ago—*
> *That he had a Roman nose,*
> *And his cheek was like a rose*
>   *In the snow*
>
> *But now his nose is thin,*
> *And it rests upon his chin*
>   *Like a staff,*
> *And a crook in his back,*
> *And a melancholy crack*
>   *In his laugh.*

One basic fact linked the lives of Melville's grandfathers: both had been born British and had become, by violence, American. On childhood visits to Boston, Herman heard war stories directly from Thomas Melvill, who still wore his "old three-cornered hat, / And the breeches, and all that," and

---

*The surname was usually spelled without the final "e" until Maria added it after her husband's death.

LEFT: General Peter Gansevoort, *oil painting by Gilbert Stuart, c. 1794*
RIGHT: Thomas Melvill, *c. 1834*

proudly showed his grandson the vial containing tea leaves brushed from his clothes after he had taken part in the Boston Tea Party dressed in Indian garb and warpaint. Though he never knew his maternal grandfather, Herman learned about "the hero of Fort Stanwix" from his mother and uncles, and doubtless had him in mind for the portrait, in *Pierre,* of "grand old Pierre Glendinning"—a massive man who, "during a fire in the old manorial mansion, with one dash of his foot . . . had smitten down an oaken door," and "in the wilderness before the Revolutionary War . . . had annihilated two Indian savages by making reciprocal bludgeons of their heads."

If Melville's grandfathers were holdovers from the glorious past, his father lived in a fanciful future. Born in Boston, Allan Melvill wooed his bride from a venerable Dutch patroon family in Albany, then moved to the fast-growing city of New York. Having made the Grand Tour of Europe as a young man, he became an import merchant specializing in what today we would call accessories—a "deluxe Mr. Micawber," as James Wood has aptly called him—with the groundless optimism of someone proficient at deceiving himself. He was always counting on this or that "*confidential Connexion*" to deliver a windfall, or assuring his creditors that some long-pending deal was about to close. "My prospects brighten," he wrote in 1820 to his own father when Herman was not yet a year old, "& without being over sanguine, I may be allowed to indulge, under the blessing of Heaven, anticipations of eventual success."

LEFT: Allan Melvill, *watercolor by John Rubens Smith, 1810*
RIGHT: Maria Gansevoort Melvill, *oil painting by Ezra Ames, c. 1820*

Allan was being over-sanguine, and everyone knew it—though for a time his bravado almost convinced the world that his failures were temporary and his successes deferred. By all accounts, he had an eye for quality. An advertisement he placed in 1824 in a New York newspaper gives an idea of his inventory: "Fancy Hdfks. and Scarfs . . . Elastic and Silk Garters, Artificial Flowers, Cravat Stiffners, &c. Also in store . . . rich satin striped and figured blk Silk Vestings, Gros de Naples Hdkfs, Belt and Watch Ribbons, 7–16 & 7–22 Silk Hose . . . Horse Skin Gloves . . . Cologne and Lavender Waters, &c." He could switch easily into the visitor's native language when a Frenchman entered his store, and he furnished his home with mementoes of his European travels, whose provenance he loved to detail for friends over a glass—or two—of old cognac.

But the yield from his talents was meager. Year by year, Allan turned his life into an almost sordid tale of reckless borrowing and groveling appeals for cash to carry him through to the next promised bonanza. He never became at ease in the increasingly impersonal system whereby European exports were sold in bulk to American auction houses, from which they were bought by wholesalers and distributed to the retail trade—a business in which good taste and personal charm counted for less than the ability to anticipate rising markets by buying low and falling prices by selling high. Following the trade agreements with Britain that settled the War of 1812, something like the frantic rhythm of modern commodities markets developed, and Allan Melvill was unprepared. Nearly forty years later, aspects of Allan turn up in his son's portrait, in *White-Jacket,* of an effete Commodore's secretary who looks like an "ambassador extraordinary from Versailles," and whose prized possessions include "enamelled pencil-cases" and "fine French boots with soles no thicker than a sheet of scented notepaper."

If Melville's father was always off on some flighty new venture, his mother was a woman of gravity. Daughter of a respected family with roots in the quasi-feudal aristocracy of the Hudson Valley, Maria Gansevoort had grown up speaking Dutch with her parents, who provided her with the years of music and dancing lessons essential to a young lady of breeding who was expected to make herself gracious and decorative. But she was trained as well in the severe Protestantism of her ancestors, and remained wary all her life of placing too much faith in the things of this world lest they be snatched away. Especially in the months after giving birth, which she did eight times, she was given to moodiness, and though she wanted her own children to master such worldly arts as penmanship and deportment, she was at pains to prepare their souls for deprivation and death.

It was from Maria that Herman received the rudiments of a religious education. Although she chastised him well into adulthood for his spotty church attendance, and he was never what we would call "observant," the ultimate questions posed by religion never lost their hold on his imagination. Maria, who knew the Bible in Dutch as well as English, brought biblical stories, exempla, and precedents into the lives of all her children, and for her second son characters from the Bible always remained as vividly alive as the worthies and villains of his own time. Ishmael, Bildad, Ahab, and Elijah are just a few of the names in *Moby-Dick* by which he invests characters with a priori allegorical significance before they begin to act in his invented world. He ends his great story "Bartleby, the Scrivener" with a quotation from the Book of Job (Bartleby sleeps "with kings and counselors"); and in his final work, *Billy Budd,* he gives the music of the Bible in a telling variation to Captain Vere, who quotes Acts 17:28, reminding his officers that the "element in which we move and have our being" is not God, but the sea. The pioneer scholar Nathalia Wright counts 250 biblical allusions in *Moby-Dick* alone. Melville knew the Bible so well, she writes, that "he could smell the burning of Gomorrah, and the pit; hear the trumpet in the Valley of Jehoshaphat and . . . taste Belshazzar's feast."

In the early years when he heard travelers' tales from his father and Bible stories from his mother, Herman was too young to understand the toxic mixture of gratitude and resentment that both his parents felt because of their continued dependence on their own parents. But the anxieties of childhood stayed with him. "Ah, fathers and mothers!," he wrote in the self-mocking style of *Pierre*, ". . . give heed! Thy little one may not now comprehend the meaning of those words and those signs, by which, in its innocent presence, thou thinkest to disguise the sinister thing ye would hint. Not now he knows; not very much even of the externals he consciously remarks; but if, in after-life, Fate puts the chemic key of the cipher into his hands; then how swiftly and how wonderfully, he reads all the obscurest and most obliterate inscriptions he finds in his memory. . . ." When childhood memories do turn up in Melville's writing, they tend to be "shadowy reminiscences," such as his allusion in *Moby-Dick* to the workmen he saw on visits to Boston, pushing wheelbarrows of dirt down Beacon Hill for the landfill that would become Back Bay. Tensions in his parents' home in New York and summer visits to his Boston grandfather left impressions that became, over time, fragmentary memories tinged with sadness—as when he recalls, in *Redburn,* the melancholy longing provoked by the miniature glass ship displayed in his grandfather's curio case, or when, in *Pierre,* he draws a portrait of a smothering mother whose compulsive demands on her son are a form of displaced rage.

Among the strains between his parents were their religious differences. Although Allan habitually spelled the word GOD with capital letters, he adopted his own father's mild Unitarianism, which, according to more pious members of the family, including his wife, tended to diminish the majesty of God in favor of the dignity of man. Maria not only took her churchgoing more seriously but was warmly committed to the Calvinist creed to which her family had subscribed in its Dutch Reformed version. After Herman was born, she managed to persuade her pastor, the Reverend J. M. Mathews, to make an exception to the church rule against home baptism. When Mathews came to the Melvill house on Pearl Street in August 1819 to baptize the new baby, he asked both parents to acknowledge the hard truth that "children are . . . born in sin, and therefore are subject to all miseries, yea to condemnation itself," and to promise that they would instruct their child "to the utmost of your power" in the shame of its sinfulness. Allan made sure that these affirmations were followed by a reception featuring a strong rum punch.

One thing at which Allan Melvill was adept was living beyond his means, and so his children grew accustomed to comfort and even to a touch of opulence. The family always employed several servants—housekeeper, cook, nurse, and waiter—and Allan did not cut back on expenses as he descended into debt. On the contrary, he increased them by moving from address to address, each an improvement in space and prestige on its predecessor—from No. 6 Pearl Street, just a few steps from the waterfront, a year later to larger quarters on Courtlandt Street (on the future site of the World

Trade Center), to a still grander house on Bleecker Street, and finally, in 1828, to Broadway, between Bond and Great Jones streets.

Tracing the Melvills' movements northward in Manhattan reveals a family trying to disguise the fact that its fortunes were declining. Their migration away from the noise and smell of the waterfront exemplified their plight: even as Allan moved up in the world of appearances, he was losing touch with the source of his livelihood. "In this republican country," as Nathaniel Hawthorne wrote years later, "amid the fluctuating waves of our social life, somebody is always at the drowning-point"—and Allan Melvill was one of the drowning.

2.

How well he hid this truth from his second son is impossible to know. But we do know that on a stormy October night in 1830, his business in ruins, and owing several months of back rent on his house, Allan Melvill, accompanied by eleven-year-old Herman, fled New York City via steamboat for Albany, where his wife and the rest of the children had preceded him. Two months later, he presented the undignified spectacle of a middle-aged man and father of eight begging his own father for help: "I am destitute of resources and without a shilling," he wrote to the old Major on December 4, and "may soon be prosecuted for my last quarters rent . . . without immediate assistance I know not what will become of me. . . ." He had become, in effect, the ward of his brother-in-law, Peter, the Gansevoort son and heir, who generously agreed to cover his "daily expences" with loans.

It was the end of Allan Melvill's hopes and of his son's boyhood. "I had learned to think much and bitterly before my time," Herman was to write nearly twenty years later in the voice of the fictional narrator in *Redburn*. "I must not think of those delightful days, before my father became a bankrupt . . . and we removed from the city; for when I think of those days, something rises up in my throat and almost strangles me." The memory of cowering with his beaten father in that ship as it pitched and rolled at anchor while the storm blew through New York left its trace in *Moby-Dick* when, speaking through the voice of Father Mapple, Melville writes of Jonah "lying in his berth" while his mind "turns and turns in giddy anguish."

The move to Albany brought no relief. As Allan continued to lose his battle against bankruptcy, he fell into that "ambiguous condition," as Elizabeth Hardwick has described it, in which "the remembrance of things past created by birth, prosperity, [and] an honorable reputation" shades into anger at their loss and the old "feeling of entitlement [becomes] a treacherous companion that encourages debt." Meeting old debts with new loans, he took a job as a clerk in the local branch office of a cap and fur concern. In December 1831, returning from a discouraging trip to New York during which he had tried to pacify his creditors, he was forced by ice in the Hudson River to disembark from the steamboat at Poughkeepsie. He continued north for the final seventy miles by open carriage through subzero temperatures over two days and nights until, at the village of Greenbush, he crossed the frozen river on foot to rejoin his family at Albany.

Allan had become, as his son was to write a quarter century later in a story, "Jimmy Rose," about a ruined New York merchant, "a pauper with wealth of polished words; a courteous, smiling, shivering gentleman" whose "creditors, once fast friends, pursued him as carrion for jails." Not yet fifty years old, he had been brought so low by fortune "that the plummet of pity alone could reach him." Still, he was a proud man, and after the grueling trip up the Hudson he thought he could shake off the ensuing cough. Even when he turned feverish with pneumonia he persisted in his work, spending long days at the store, sleeping fitfully at night or not at all.

Early in January 1832, he began to show signs of delirium, and his brother Thomas, the old Major's eldest son, was summoned from his Berkshire farm to Allan's bedside, where he found him in a terrible state. "Hope is no longer permitted of his recovery in the opinion of the attending Physicians," Thomas wrote to a family friend, "and indeed—oh, how hard for a brother to say! I *ought not* to hope for it—for—in all human probability—he would live, *a Maniac!*" Herman, having been withdrawn from school, was probably at home much of the time during Allan's final harrowing days. Years later, with the cries of his bedridden father in his memory, he wrote about the maimed Captain Ahab "raving in his hammock."

Allan Melvill died a few days after his brother had given up hope. In the wake of his death, it was no longer financially feasible for the two older boys, Gansevoort and Herman, to return to school. Herman had spent four years at the New York Male High School, where the teaching techniques were rote and humiliation, followed by barely a year at the grammar school of Columbia College; then, after the flight from New York, he had entered Albany Academy. But even in relatively flush times, the expense of Herman's schooling had struck his parents as a dubious investment, and it was now out of the question. Throughout his childhood, they had fretted about his penmanship, and, as anyone knows who has glanced at his manuscripts—even allowing for the relatively loose standards of correctness that prevailed in the

Gansevoort
Melville, *c. 1836*

nineteenth century—he never really mastered spelling. As part of the family's retrenchment, he was now taken out of school and put to work as an errand boy in the New York State Bank at its Greek Revival headquarters on Albany's Market Street.*

It was the eldest son, Gansevoort, who earned accolades at school and was, according to his father, a boy of "tenacious memory and glowing fancy," while Herman, the second son and third child out of eight, was "less buoyant in mind" and "backward in speech & somewhat slow in comprehension." Gansevoort was slender and poised; Herman was stocky and ruddy. Before the family finances collapsed, Gansevoort had been expected to go off to Harvard; now he was compelled instead to try his hand at the cap and fur business, and by the summer of 1834 he was doing well enough to hire his brother as his assistant, sending Herman's wages straight into their mother's account.

But the family's string of bad luck had not yet run out, and their half-repaired life began to unravel again. Like those of his father, Gansevoort's prospects proved illusory. The first blow came in 1835, when fire destroyed the store and most of the stock; then, in 1837, a national financial panic made credit scarce and customers wary. The Melvilles (Maria had by now added the "e" to her married name—perhaps to signify her hopes for a fresh start)

*He was to enroll for a short time in 1835 at the Albany Classical School, and, in the fall of 1836, briefly once more at the Academy, where he apparently acquired some Latin.

had been going back and forth between Albany and Thomas Melvill's farm near Pittsfield in western Massachusetts, where the children were sent in summer to escape the periodic cholera outbreaks in town.

In May 1838, more dependent than ever on the charity of her brother, Maria moved with the younger children and, apparently, with Herman—who had briefly held a teaching job near his uncle's Berkshire farm—to the village of Lansingburgh, ten miles north of Albany (today part of the city of Troy), where the cost of living and the conspicuousness of their failure would be smaller. When the Connecticut clergyman Timothy Dwight had visited the area thirty years earlier, he noted depressed real estate values in what had once been a center of trade and shipbuilding; and while there had been some revival with the opening of the Erie Canal in 1825 and more recently because of tourist interest in a local botanical garden, the heyday of the neighborhood was past. The Melvilles' retreat was now complete: from the metropolis, to a provincial city, and finally to a village where their neighbors included other wellborn families who had never ventured out or else, like them, had been routed in their encounter with the wider world.

3.

It is dispiriting—this tale of a genteel family beset by money woes. Maria suffered from headache and depression, and the children were shocked by the loss of their father and the spectacle of his derangement. "In our cities," Herman was to write twenty years later in *Pierre*, "families rise and burst like bubbles in a vat." But there is a disjunction in tone between his later writings about his early sorrows and the high-spirited bits of juvenilia that survive from his youth. An alert teacher at the Albany Classical School had recognized the boy's facility in writing "themes"; and Herman's first appearances in print, in February and March 1838, as the pseudonymous author of three letters to the editor of the *Albany Microscope*, were playful and exuberant. His election as president of the local literary society had caused a brouhaha when the defeated candidate cried foul in a letter to the newspaper—perhaps sincerely, or perhaps as a plot premeditated jointly by winner and loser to gain attention for their club. In his replies, Melville issued an alliterative blast at the sore loser for trying to "palm upon the public a palpable misrepresentation of the facts," used a strategic abbreviation to express his indignation ("you published . . . a vile calumny upon the Ass"), and concluded with an invitation to carry on their mutual pursuit of the truth: "N.B. Your incoherent ravings may be continued if you choose; they remind me of the croakings of a Vulture when disappointed of its prey."

On the basis of these over-the-top performances, no one could have predicted a major literary career, but as befits the Greek name of the literary club, the Philo Logos Society, they do reveal the boy's instinctive pleasure in wordplay. When the family moved to Lansingburgh, more effusions followed, again in the form of pseudonymous letters to the local paper, this time the Lansingburgh *Democratic Press,* in which Herman published two "Fragments from a Writing Desk" (May 4 and May 18, 1839). This two-part story, its prose overheated in the manner of Poe, with sexually charged echoes of Byron and *The Arabian Nights,* is a vague allegory of a young man obsessed by a ravishing beauty and longing for "one long, long kiss upon her hot and glowing lips." Beseeching her to declare her love, he discovers at what should be the climactic moment that she, being deaf and dumb, cannot respond.

There may have been something self-therapeutic in these literary exercises, a kind of verbal muscle flexing that relieved the enervating effect of being his mother's captive confidant. Perhaps there was an uncompleted love affair behind the story (apparently, Herman had courted a local belle without success), or more likely it registered his early education, obtained through witnessing his father's decline, in the futility of quests and dreams. "Cursing the ignus fatuus, that danced so provokingly before me," this first of Melville's quasi-fictional narrators writes from close acquaintance with the cost of self-deception. "Absurd conceits . . . infested my brain."

The fledgling writer was a little wild himself—darkly handsome now, long-haired, unkempt, and given to bouts of drinking. In the fall of 1838, at the urging of his uncle Peter, who was losing patience with the prolonged dependence of his sister and her children, Herman took some training in engineering at a local academy. But despite his uncle's commendation to business friends involved in the construction of the Erie Canal, he failed to land a surveying job there, possibly because he struck his prospective employers as flighty or truculent.

Finally, in the spring of 1839, he decided to make an escape, or at least an experiment. Following the example of one of his cousins, he arranged to sail as a cabin boy aboard a merchant ship that plied the route between New York and Liverpool carrying cotton and a few passengers. "Herman is happy but I think at heart he is rather agitated," his mother wrote to Gansevoort about his brother's decision, adding that "I can hardly believe it & cannot realize the truth of his going." On June 5, 1839, after the downriver trip from Albany to the city of his father's disgrace, Melville sailed for England aboard the merchant vessel *St. Lawrence.* He was not quite twenty. His name was mistakenly entered on the crew list as Norman Melville, probably as a consequence of his unimproved penmanship.

4.

With this first embarkation, Herman Melville entered a phase of life we can follow only by means of his fictional recollections written years later—in this case, in his novel published in 1849, *Redburn,* whose subtitle was *His First Voyage: Being the Sailor-Boy Confessions and Reminiscences of the Son-of-a-Gentleman, in the Merchant Service.* Except for this deferred work of fiction, there is no documentation of his three months at sea, or of the month ashore at Liverpool. All that remain are a few tantalizing mentions of letters that have since disappeared, as when his mother wrote to her youngest son, Allan Junior, in July 1839 that Herman, in a letter just received, "says he would give all the sights of Liverpool to see a corner of home."

In *Redburn,* Melville recalled this first ocean voyage as his leap from boyhood to manhood—an association between going-to-sea and coming-of-age that in antebellum America was almost formulaic, yet for many young men proved nonetheless to be true. Here, as recorded in a crude yet touching poem left in manuscript by one Norman Knox Wood, who had made the round trip between New York and Liverpool as a working seaman a year before, is the same mixture of envy and contempt toward paying passengers that gives *Redburn* its authenticity:

> *Now our ship with foaming spray,*
> *Over the ocean takes her way,*
> *Around her bows the dolphins play,*
> *As we sail*

> *I have left my peacefull home*
> *On the Oceans depth to roam*
> *And be wet by briny foam*
> *Let landsmen rail*

We listen to the Oceans roar
They shivering about the open door
And call for blankets half a score
  Almost froze to death

While we watch on deck do walk
Under the bulwarks take a caulk
Or eat a piece of good fat pork
  & warm our fingers with our breath

In *Redburn,* ten years after the fact, Melville reconstructed his own journey as the first time in his life that he was neither pampered nor pressured by adults who placed high hopes in him, but was ordered about as just another hired hand. "Let to rove / At last abroad among mankind," he found himself amid rough men who had no interest in his pedigree except as a subject for mockery. In Liverpool, he was struck by the sight of black men embracing willing white women, and of people dying or dead in the gutter while pedestrians passed by unfazed as if the bodies were trash awaiting disposal by the street sweepers.

The Melville we know from these early years is a young man retrospectively imagined by his older self as an angry brooder wrestling with his sense of grievance. There is a scene in *Redburn* in which the boy, having ventured for the first time from home carrying a fowling piece and wearing pants patched by his mother, steels himself aboard the Hudson River steamboat for the moment when he must tell the ticket collector that he can produce only half the two-dollar fare. With a mixture of shame and insolence, he refuses the clerk's order to relinquish his cabin seat and go out on deck in the sleet and wind, then spends the rest of the trip glaring at the paying passengers who, fearful that this boy with a musket might be crazy, sneak worried looks back at him. In describing the boy's distress, Melville was surely recalling his own feelings as a boy of twenty:

Talk not of the bitterness of middle-age and after life; a boy can feel all that, and much more, when upon his young soul the mildew has fallen; and the fruit, which with others is only blasted after ripeness, with him is nipped in the first blossom and bud. And never again can such blights be made good; they strike in too deep, and leave such a scar that the air of Paradise might not erase it. And it is a hard and cruel thing thus in early youth to taste beforehand the pangs which should be reserved for the stout time of manhood, when the gristle has

become bone, and we stand up and fight out our lives, as a thing tried
before and foreseen; for then we are veterans used to sieges and battles,
and not green recruits, recoiling at the first shock of the encounter.

Yet even as he pitied himself, Melville sensed opportunity in his misfor-
tune. When he later remarked—in the voice of Ishmael in *Moby-Dick*—that
"a whaleship was my Yale College and my Harvard," he was looking back
with both resentment at his loss of a privileged life and relief at having
escaped it. Perhaps he did blame his father for squandering the family
money and good name; but he also understood that a father's failure can create a son's freedom. He was beginning to feel the exhilaration of being
untethered. There was no more cap and fur business, no more of Allan's surviving associates to whom he needed to prove himself, and, perhaps most
important, no hovering mother fretting about his future. He had become a
young man at large, if not at ease.

But the thrill of being at liberty did not last. As soon as he returned to
New York aboard the *St. Lawrence,* on the last day of September 1839, he
was sucked back into family troubles. Maria was all but frantic now with
money worries, and by October her brother Peter was writing "with the
most painful feelings" to Judge Lemuel Shaw that "by the failure in business,
some time since, of her son Gansevoort, Mrs. Melville has become entirely
impoverished—mortgages are foreclosing upon her real estate & as I have
just heard, the furniture is now advertised for sale." After a recreational day
or two in Manhattan, Herman was back upstate, where he landed a teaching
job in Greenbush (the same village from which his father had crossed the
frozen river on his last voyage home) and was promising his mother that she
could expect from him at least $150 to $200 a year—the equivalent of $5,000
or $6,000 in today's dollars. Since he hiked to Albany on Friday nights to
pick up the mail before going on to tend to his mother at Lansingburgh, one
of his aunts called him, a little cruelly, the "family post-man." Years later, in
Pierre, he was to describe how the widow Mrs. Glendinning tries to turn her
son, who is "strangely docile to the maternal tuitions in nearly all things,"
into a surrogate husband.

A few surviving documents suggest Melville's state of mind while he
marked time as schoolteacher and dutiful son. A sketch called "The Death
Craft," signed "Harry the Reefer," and published in *The Democratic Press,*
has been attributed to him—another bit of Gothic fluff, about a young man
terrified by a vision of a ship with a bloody human head hanging from the
jib-boom and skeletons from the yardarms, only to wake from his dream in
the arms of his bride. There is also a peculiar note in Melville's hand
appended to a letter written by his mother on December 7, 1839, to his

younger brother Allan, who was clerking in Albany. Melville signed this note "Tawney," perhaps in ironic acknowledgment of names he was being called by people mocking him for the suntan he had acquired at sea. (Nearly a decade later, in *White-Jacket,* he would recall "an old negro, who went by the name of Tawney . . . a staid and sober seaman, very intelligent, with a fine, frank bearing, one of the best men in the ship, and held in high estimation by everyone.") The sound of the speech he had heard aboard the *St. Lawrence* from black and Cockney shipmates had stayed with him, and now found its way into what may have been a coded message conveying to Allan what today we would call the feeling of being infantilized:

> How is you? Am you very well? How has you been?—As to myself I haint been as well as husual. I has had a very cruel cold for this darnation long time, & I has had and does now have a werry bad want of appetisement.

Too much ought not to be made of this odd bit of baby talk, but there is reason to read it as an expression of his restiveness in the extended childhood that seemed his lot. Effects of the economic contraction of 1837 were still being felt, among them the failure of the school at Greenbush to meet its payroll. "Money has not for many years been more scarce than it is at present," Uncle Peter wrote to Maria, who eventually replied that Herman "thinks of going far-west, as nothing offers for him here." He was itching to get out—out of the domestic enclosure in which he felt stifled, out of the shadow of Gansevoort, who while in New York trying to establish himself in the law wrote to reprimand him for "that laziness which consists in an unwillingness to exert oneself in doing at a particular time, that which ought then to be done." This kind of aphoristic chiding is hard for a younger brother to take, and one can imagine Herman muttering as he runs another errand for his tongue-clucking mother: What, exactly, "ought . . . to be done"?

Nearly fifty years later, in his copy of a translation of Balzac's novella *The Two Brothers* (1887), Melville underscored and checked a passage that must have sent him back in memory to his boyhood feelings of drift and deficiency:

> Agathe [the mother] believed that the purely physical resemblance which Philippe [her older son] bore to her carried with it a moral likeness; and she confidently expected him to show at a future day her own delicacy of feeling, heightened by the vigor of manhood. . . . Joseph, three years younger, was like his father, but only on the defective side. In the first place, his thick black hair was always in disorder, no matter what pains were taken with it; while Philippe's, notwithstanding his

vivacity, was invariably neat. Then, by some mysterious fatality, Joseph could not keep his clothes clean; dress him in new clothes, and he immediately made them look like old ones. The elder, on the other hand, took care of his things out of mere vanity. Unconsciously, the mother acquired a habit of scolding Joseph and holding up his brother as an example to him. Agathe did not treat the two children alike; when she went to fetch them from school, the thought in her mind as to Joseph always was, "What sort of state shall I find him in?" These trifles drove her heart into the gulf of maternal preference.

Balzac's family romance held up a retrospective mirror in which Melville recognized his incorrigible younger self in the shadow of his impeccable older brother.

As dreamy as he was slovenly (all his life he remained, as Hawthorne later remarked, "a little heterodox in the matter of clean linen"), he settled now into that mood of longing to be evoked so often in his writing—beginning with the portrait in *Typee* of his melancholy friend Toby gazing over the bulwarks of the ship at anchor just out of reach of the beckoning islands, and continuing in the opening paragraphs of *Moby-Dick*, in which he describes the scene in lower Manhattan along the Battery:

> Posted like silent sentinels all around the town, stand thousands upon thousands of mortal men fixed in ocean reveries. Some leaning against the spiles; some seated upon the pier-heads; some looking over the bulwarks of ships from China; some high aloft in the rigging, as if striving to get a still better seaward peep. But these are all landsmen; of week days pent up in lath and plaster—tied to counters, nailed to benches, clinched to desks. How then is this? Are the green fields gone? What do they here?

In Melville's world, men ashore gaze to sea and men at sea gaze to shore. The deck, as much as the ground, burns beneath their feet.

5.

So he went adventuring again, this time in his own country. In June 1840, in hopeful partnership with his friend Eli Fly, but with no plan in mind beyond

"There now is your insular city of the Manhattoes. . . . Right and left, the streets take
you waterward. Its extreme down-town is the Battery, where that noble mole is
washed by waves, and cooled by breezes, which a few hours previous were out of sight
of land. Look at the crowds of water-gazers there." Moby-Dick, *chapter 1*
New York Harbor from the Battery, *lithograph by Thomas Thompson, 1829*

the notion that his rudimentary knowledge of surveying and his friend's clerical skills (Fly was a good copyist) would find them work, he headed west, joining a stream of migrants who felt stymied in the East. Some were sons who had inherited little or nothing—or nothing but debt—from their fathers; others were artisans out of work or farmers struggling to compete with larger farms to the west whose goods could now be transported east quickly and cheaply via the Erie Canal. Like many of their contemporaries, Melville and Fly anticipated help in the form of lodging and introductions from relatives who had preceded them. They pinned their hopes on Herman's uncle Thomas, who had left the failing family farm in the Berkshires a couple of years earlier to make a fresh start in Galena, Illinois. But as it turned out, Thomas Melvill was reprising the family theme, with the variation that he was courting legal as well as financial disaster. Not long before Melville and Fly arrived, he had been caught embezzling, and avoided a jail term only because his employer decided not to press charges. The wave of loan recalls and foreclosures that had begun in the East had spread westward, and by the time the young seekers arrived in Illinois they found nothing to do but knock about as low-budget tourists in depressed frontier towns.

Unaware of what awaited them, the pair made their way to Buffalo through the Erie Canal, coasting slowly in boats pulled by horse teams slogging along a towpath that ran beside the four-feet-deep waterway, passing "billiard-room and bar-room" along "one continual stream of Venetianly corrupt" life. From Buffalo they continued to Chicago by steamboat over the Great Lakes, whose "ocean-like expansiveness" stirred them. Melville stored the memory and, ten years later in *Moby-Dick,* combined his personal recollection of Indians encamped on the shore with his secondhand knowledge of such historic events as Commodore Perry's victory over the British on Lake Erie during the War of 1812. The result was a prose-poem on America's inland sea:

> In their interflowing aggregate, those grand fresh-water seas of ours,— Erie, and Ontario, and Huron, and Superior, and Michigan,—possess an ocean-like expansiveness, with many of the ocean's noblest traits; with many of its rimmed varieties of races and of climes. They contain round archipelagoes of romantic isles, even as the Polynesian waters do; in large part, are shored by two great contrasting nations, as the Atlantic is; they furnish long maritime approaches to our numerous territorial colonies from the East, dotted all round their banks; here and there are frowned upon by batteries, and by the goat-like craggy guns of lofty Mackinaw; they have heard the fleet thunderings of naval victories; at intervals, they yield their beaches to wild barbarians, whose red painted faces flash from out their peltry wigwams; for leagues and leagues are flanked by ancient and unentered forests, where the gaunt pines stand like serried lines of kings in Gothic genealogies; those same woods harboring wild Afric beasts of prey, and silken creatures whose exported furs give robes to Tartar Emperors; they mirror the paved capitals of Buffalo and Cleveland, as well as Winnebago villages; they float alike the full-rigged merchant ship, the armed cruiser of the State, the steamer, and the birch canoe; they are swept by Borean and dismasting blasts as direful as any that lash the salted wave; they know what shipwrecks are, for out of sight of land, however inland, they have drowned full many a midnight ship with all its shrieking crew.

After the fruitless visit to Galena, Melville and Fly resumed their journey downriver by steamboat on the Mississippi, possibly as far south as Cairo, Illinois. Then they made their way home via the Ohio River to somewhere in the Alleghenies, whence they traveled by foot, stage, and possibly rail through Pittsburgh and Philadelphia to New York, and finally by riverboat back upstate to the doldrums from which they had fled. Like the journey to Liverpool, the trip is undocumented except in scattered fragments in Melville's later writings—in the paean in *Moby-Dick* to the Great Lakes, in glimpses of down-and-out characters boozing "in the groggeries along the towpath" of the Erie Canal, or in allusions to Niagara Falls ("if you travel away inland into his deep and noble nature," he wrote of Hawthorne, "you will hear the far roar of his Niagara"), which Melville probably saw on a detour from Buffalo just when it was first becoming a tourist attraction. If he had gone west to test the rumor that there was easy money to be made on the frontier, he came home having learned something about his credulity.

By late summer or fall of 1840, still in the company of Fly, he fled again, this time to New York City, with no idea of what to do with himself. Gansevoort, whose worry about his younger brother's future grew in proportion to Herman's aimlessness, set him up in a cheap boardinghouse and took him for meals to the popular tavern Sweeney's, where a barker outside the door called out the house specialties—"Rosebeefrosegoosemuttonantaters!"—in one amazingly extended breath. Melville liked the buzz and tumult of the place. Having let his hair grow since he had given up schoolteaching for pioneering, he was looking wild again, and from Gansevoort's reports one imagines him eating with canine urgency, as if he fears that his food will be snatched away by some equally ravenous creature hovering near and ready to pounce.

Fly found work as a copyist, but officework seemed to Melville a soul-killing business, and in any case his poor spelling and penmanship made him an unlikely candidate. Besides, he had other interests. The trip to Liverpool had stirred his curiosity to see the world, and "far inland," possibly during the abbreviated trek west, he had read James Fenimore Cooper's swashbuckling sea romance *The Red Rover;* not long afterwards he read Richard Henry Dana, Jr.'s gripping account of life as a common sailor, *Two Years Before the Mast,* and felt himself "tied and welded . . . by a sort of Siamese link of affectionate sympathy" to its Boston Brahmin author.

There was, as well, a family history of roving. One cousin, Guert Gansevoort, had sailed the Pacific aboard a warship; another had died in a shipwreck; a third had recently returned from a whaling cruise to New Zealand; and yet another, while Herman was still groping toward his future, had embarked on a naval expedition charting unexplored islands. "The Melville family," according to his cousin Julia, "resemble the Jews in one particular, they are to be found in every part of the globe." With these precedents in mind—both ominous and encouraging—and with small prospects in a city swarming with job seekers, Herman left New York to spend Christmas in Lansingburgh and to tell his mother what he had decided.

After the farewell visit, he headed off for the whaling port of New Bedford in search of a ship that would sign up a deckhand with only a few weeks' merchant marine experience. Gansevoort went along to see him off. "It is a great consolation to me," Gansevoort wrote a few weeks later to their brother Allan, "that I have done my duty towards him, thoroughly and conscientiously in this his last cruise upon land." In their last hours ashore, they went to a shop where Herman exchanged his coat for "duck shirts, etc.," since, as Gansevoort put it, "shore toggery is of no use to a sailor."

Writing a few days later to her daughter Augusta, Maria recounts how the two brothers parted. After a sunny description of Herman's mood, she takes note of Gansevoort's brotherly attentiveness in a sentence that, with little emendation, could be a description of a deathbed vigil:

> Last week I received a long letter from Herman, who has embarked for a long Voyage to the Pacific, under the most favorable auspices, and feeling perfectly happy. Gansevoort was with him to the last and assisted with his more matured Judgement in supplying him with every comfort.

It was a mother's way of acknowledging, with mixed satisfaction and foreboding, that her second son had broken free.

CHAPTER 2
GOING NATIVE

1.

On January 3, 1841, aboard the whaleship *Acushnet*, Herman Melville embarked on a journey that, for purposes of biography, might as well have been to the far side of the moon. For young men who found themselves without prospects, the Pacific beckoned, as Charles Olson once remarked, like "another West, prefigured in the Plains." Cruising this vast half-charted territory and tracking down its wild beasts was a great adventure that conferred on the hunters a certain glamour and even sexual prestige; on Nantucket, center of the American whaling industry, there was talk among young women that the most satisfying husbands were those who had proved their virility by going to sea to kill whales.

Whaling also offered the more practical reward of paid room and board. Since compensation was calculated according to a system by which each crew member contracted to receive an assigned fraction, or "lay," of the revenue the ship brought in, there was little prospect of earning much. In *Moby-Dick*, Ishmael signs up for the three hundredth lay (0.3 percent), while his Polynesian friend Queequeg, after demonstrating his skill with a harpoon, does better: he gets the ninetieth lay, or a little more than 1 percent. These were meager wages, and, like sharecroppers later in the century, whalemen typically saw most of their promised profit evaporate in interest payments on "loans" received at the outset of their service in the form of clothing, tools, bedding, and the like.

Something like two thirds of whaleship crews deserted at one stopover port or another, forfeiting what little pay they could expect if they had seen the voyage through, so that the shipmates with whom a whaleman set sail were unlikely to be the same with whom he came home. Of the twenty-five men who embarked in 1841 with Melville aboard the *Acushnet*, eleven returned on the same ship in 1844. In *Typee*, when Melville tells how he deserted one whaleship and, after a few weeks of beachcombing, joined the crew of another, he was describing a common pattern of what amounted to hitchhiking through the Pacific.

Owners and officers, on the other hand, stood to make a tidy sum. In New Bedford and Nantucket, veteran captains and even mates were known to retire to grand houses overlooking the harbor from which they once had sailed. In the fast-expanding American market, whaling was big business. Before the discovery of petroleum in Pennsylvania in 1859 made the whaling industry almost instantly obsolete, the clean and bright-burning oil produced by whale blubber was in high demand as fuel for household lamps, streetlights, lighthouses, locomotive headlights, and just about every form of artificial illumination. It supplied lubricant for factory machinery, sewing machines, and clocks. The whale's hairy bristle was used in brooms and brushes; and before the invention of artificial plastics, whalebone—which becomes flexible when heated and retains its formed shape upon cooling— was used for such everyday items as canes, corset stays, and umbrella ribs. Already during the eighteenth century, the pearly white wax (spermaceti) extracted from the sperm whale's head had been refined for use in hair-dressings as well as in superior candles, of which Benjamin Franklin was an early champion. "You will find," he wrote to a friend in 1751, "that they . . . may be held in the hand, even in hot weather, without softning; that their Drops do not make Grease spots like those from common candles; that they last much longer, and need little or no Snuffing." But the greatest treasure was to be found in the whale's gut: ambergris, a foul black liquid that oxidizes when exposed to air and becomes a pleasant-smelling wax that, once refined, was used as a fixative for perfume.

The world of whaleships was a world of pent-up longings—a tale told in sailors' songs and even in the scrimshaw objects that whalemen whittled during long nightwatches. Toothpicks, whistles, and pipe-tampers were carved out of whale teeth in the form of a woman's leg, which the user could suck or fondle in the absence of the real thing. Into whale's teeth were carved images of women with legs invitingly spread; ships were adorned with female figureheads whose bare breasts jutted toward the sea, and sailors wrote in their journals about how they loved to "ride" the ship, "in raptures with her . . . motions . . . as she plunges and rears her proud head." In *Moby-Dick*, Melville alludes to the frustration of men with women much on their minds but nowhere to be seen. "Where's your girls," demands one sailor miserably alone at night. "Who but a fool would take his left hand by his right, and say to himself, how d'ye do? Partners! I must have partners!" Fed up with the substitutional satisfactions of masturbation, this fellow

LEFT: *A whaler's walking companion*

RIGHT: *Scrimshaw Fantasy: "What's my juicy little pear at home doing right now? Crying its eyes out?—Giving a party to the last arrived group of harpooneers, I dare say."* Moby-Dick, *chapter 29*

wishes that "all the waves were women, then I'd go drown, and chassee with them evermore! There's naught so sweet on earth—heaven may not match it!—as those swift glances of warm, wild bosoms in the dance, when the over-arboring arms hide such ripe, bursting grapes." When one veteran of an actual whaling voyage, whose memoir Melville read in 1849, wrote of "the deprivations peculiar to whalemen in long voyages," he was not talking about dietary restrictions. The sperm whale, after all, was so named because of the milky fluid contained in its head, which, in its color and viscosity, resembled semen.

Though not exactly a closed-shop business—the ships were open to blacks and Indians and others shut out from trades closer to home—whaling had a certain inbred intimacy, as if the few thousand whalemen cruising the world at any one time had been dispersed from a handful of villages where everyone knew everyone else.* Many whalemen were really boys. In fact, as one historian has written, "New England mothers sent their sons to kill whales in the Pacific Ocean at an age when modern parents would think twice about letting them have the car for a weekend." Among

*Although there is little documentation of wage discrimination aimed against blacks and other minorities in the whaling industry, blacks were more likely to be found in service occupations such as cook and steward than in more skilled roles such as carpenter, blacksmith, or boatsteerer. Lee A. Craig and Robert M. Fearn, "Wage Discrimination and Occupational Crowding in a Competitive Industry: Evidence from the American Whaling Industry," *Journal of Economic History* 53, no. 1 (March 1993): 124.

Nantucket families there was a "clannish commitment to the hunt," and though shipowners by 1850 more often recruited crews by using professional contractors than by relying on local word of mouth, "there were still skippers [able] to remember the days when they knew the father of every man in their crew."

But if whaling was a family affair, it was also the first international industry dominated by the United States. With a characteristic flourish, Melville declared in *Moby-Dick* that "Yankees in one day, collectively, kill more whales than all the English, collectively, in ten years." This was an inflated claim, but according to a survey published in *Hunt's Merchants' Magazine & Commercial Review* in 1849, two thirds of the worldwide fleet of about 1,000 whaleships were, in fact, American, of which 249 vessels sailed out of New Bedford and another 69 out of Nantucket. As Melville remarks, the whaling fleet replicated the labor system by which America's canals and transcontinental railroad were being built. "The native American"—by which he meant native-born whites—"liberally provide the brains, and the rest of the world as generously supplying the muscles." During his whaling years, the officers to whom Melville owed obedience were sometimes men of social rank comparable to his own, while the men with whom he worked, ate, and slept included semiliterate sailors, as he put it in *Moby-Dick,* from "all the isles of the sea, and all the ends of the earth."

In fact, Melville and his shipmates were among the last men to hunt and kill whales by drawing close to the animal, piercing it with a thrown harpoon, then stabbing at it till it bled to death. Whaling could be as dangerous as war. A male sperm whale, which can weigh as much as 60 tons and reach a length of over 60 feet, can hold its breath for up to 90 minutes, dive to depths of 3,000 feet, and propelled by its gigantic tail (respectful whalers called it "the hand of God") reach swimming speeds of 20 knots. And since the public had a romantic sense of whale killing as it often has of war, the men who dared to hunt these creatures became a species of culture hero. Their images appeared on the covers of books of maritime tales and poems and their exploits were celebrated in traveling stage shows, as when Captain E. C. Williams toured the country in the 1850s presenting his "Illustrated and Muscular Lecture . . . on the Leviathan Hunt in the South Seas," complete with rigged whaleboat, painted ocean panoramas, and actors performing the hunt while mood music played in the background. Like the Wild West shows that became popular later in the century, these celebrations were memorials to a vanishing world.

Although whaling continued in something like its traditional form until the early twentieth century, within a few years of the publication of *Moby-*

Dick it had already become less hazardous and glamorous since whaleships were increasingly equipped with harpoon guns that could deliver an explosive charge at a range of 50 meters. Well aimed, such a missile killed upon impact, leaving the whaleman mainly with the inglorious job of dissecting the shattered corpse into its edible and salable parts.

2.

After six months at sea, while the *Acushnet* lay at anchor in early July in Nukuheva harbor in the Marquesan Islands in the South Pacific, Melville deserted with a shipmate and spent about a month among the inhabitants of the Typee Valley in what he later called "indulgent captivity." The island of Nukuheva (as the Polynesian name is usually spelled in English transliteration) is shaped something like a Bundt cake: a circular landmass ringed by steep hills that rise straight out of the sea and then drop sharply into an interior cavity. Ancestors of the island's inhabitants, who numbered about eighty thousand when Melville landed there, had probably arrived some two thousand years before the Spanish, in a bloody raid, made the place known to Europeans in 1595. The next recorded encounter, under the English captain James Cook, would not take place until 180 years later.

Dispersed among villages along the inlets and bays that penetrate the coastal hills, as well as farther inland in tribal groupings, the native population of Nukuheva depended for sustenance on rain blowing in on the trade winds from the southeast. There are no freshwater springs, but in times of ample rainfall the water flows down from higher elevations in streams and waterfalls. In times of drought, the natives lived on stores of breadfruit, and were known to invade the villages of neighboring tribes for the purpose of sacrificing captives to the rain gods.

These mutually hostile people spoke a common Polynesian dialect comprehensible to one another and to the natives of Tahiti and Hawaii, but they possessed no written language. Warriors of the Typee (or Taipi) Tribe were rumored to practice cannibalism on their enemies and known for their ferocity—a temperament suggested in the frightful human faces that stare out of multiple eyes carved on both sides of the bludgeoning end of their war clubs. As marks of martial achievement, they decorated themselves with tattoos so dense and intricate that untinted flesh was hardly visible on veteran war-

Marquesan war club. On a visit to Nathaniel and Sophia Hawthorne in 1851, Melville, according to the Hawthornes' son, Julian, gave a vivid account of "a fight which he had seen on an island in the Pacific, between some savages . . . performed with a heavy club." And now "where is that club," Sophia wanted to know.

riors, who wore earrings made of whale teeth and arranged their hair in tufts that looked to Western eyes like the devil's horns.

In what is sometimes considered the first act of American imperialism, Captain David Porter, while conducting raids on the British Pacific whaling fleet as part of a harassment campaign during the War of 1812, had sailed into Nukuheva harbor and claimed the island for the United States. But Porter's claim was never formalized by Congress, and it went unacknowledged by the British and French, for whom Nukuheva remained a contested, if minor, prize. Just weeks before Melville's arrival aboard the *Acushnet,* the island had been reclaimed for Louis Philippe of France by Admiral Dupetit-Thouars, and Melville witnessed French warships lobbing shells ashore in order to put down any acts, or thoughts, of resistance.

When Melville came ashore on this beckoning and threatening island, he brought with him his shipmate Toby Greene, with whom he had struck up a friendship around the "cordial detestation" they shared for the ship's captain. Toby was to become an important figure in Melville's life because he not only accompanied him on his first island adventure but also, five years later, while working as a sign painter in Buffalo, came to Melville's defense when the first reviewers of *Typee* charged his friend with having made up his stories out of whole cloth. "Leaning . . . against the bulwarks and buried in thought," Toby was a brooder who regarded the world with a "dry, sarcastic humor," as when he assigned the name "Jack Nastyface" to a crewman whose skin (in Greene's phrase) was as "rough as a MacAdamized road."

But if Toby Greene had a role to play in Melville's future, he was reticent about his own past. He was "one of that class of rovers you sometimes meet at sea, who never reveal their origin, never allude to home, and go rambling

Toby Greene

over the world as if pursued by some mysterious fate they cannot possibly elude." Having discovered their affinities during long nights on deck, the two young men made a pact to desert together at the first opportunity, which arrived in the form of a day of liberty ashore. They then fled quickly into the hills in order to elude any search party that might be sent after them, expecting to hack their way through to one of the reputedly friendly villages of the Happar Tribe. But the brush and brambles were so thick that they could sometimes measure their progress only in inches, and after several exhausting days, having lost their bearings and much of their morale, they found themselves among the dreaded Typees.

To make matters worse, Melville injured his leg during the climb. As his condition deteriorated, the two agreed that Toby should return by canoe to Nukuheva harbor in hopes of bringing back help from any Westerners they could find, even at risk of being caught by agents of the *Acushnet*. As it turned out, four years would pass before Melville again saw Toby Greene, who, when they met in upstate New York in the summer of 1846, claimed he had reached the beach, found a few white men with boats and guns, and hired one of them, an Irishman "who had resided on the Island for some time," to go back and bring Melville out. This scoundrel apparently had pocketed the money and done nothing in return. Melville, meanwhile, having regained his mobility and sensing that his hosts had no intention of letting him go, lingered for a few weeks before breaking away and returning to his starting point on his own. There, on August 9, he resumed his journey on the Australian whaler *Lucy Ann,* which had dropped anchor at Nuku-heva while the captain looked for men with whom to replenish his own crew depleted by desertions. Such, in bald summary, was the experience that Melville was to draw upon for his first book, *Typee: A Peep at Polynesian Life.*

3.

A "small, slatternly looking craft," the *Lucy Ann* proved to be even less comfortable than the *Acushnet.* When the ship reached Tahiti for resupply in mid-September 1842, Melville, having joined another crew revolt, was briefly imprisoned ashore as a mutineer under authority of the British con-sul. During the day, supervision was lax in the "calabooza," as the makeshift prison was called; but at night he and his fellow inmates were compelled to sleep with their legs locked in stocks by the ankles, though their native guards allowed them to lie on piles of leaves and furnished them with wooden headrests of the kind they themselves used for pillows. After a cou-ple of weeks of halfheartedly enforced incarceration, he was released to wan-der Tahiti and the neighboring island of Eimeo, where he worked as a field hand. His new employers were a New Englander and a Londoner trying to make money by supplying whaleships with sweet potatoes and other fresh produce that sailors relied on for preventing scurvy and rickets.

Melville's second book, *Omoo: A Narrative of Adventures in the South Seas,* picks up the story aboard the *Lucy Ann,* which he calls the *Julia.* After recounting the mutiny, the imprisonment, and what was, in effect, his second desertion, he recalled with affection the pair of expatriate entrepreneurs who set him to hoeing and lugging potatoes in his new island refuge: Zeke, who spoke with "a twang like a cracked viol" acquired in the backwoods of Maine; and the Cockney companion Melville called Shorty, who "clipped the aspirate from every word beginning with one." But the charm of working for Zeke and Shorty soon wore off in the tropical sun, and in November 1842 Melville moved on again. This time he shipped aboard the *Charles and Henry,* a whaleship out of Nantucket, which after months of fruitful hunting arrived in April 1843 at the port of Lahaina, West Maui, in what was then known as the Sandwich Islands and today is called Hawaii. Along with a copy of *The Child's Robinson Crusoe,* the ship's library was stocked with wholesome books, including an anti-gambling tract called *Victims of Gam-ing* and *A Lecture to Young Men on Chastity* by Sylvester Graham, inventor of the cracker that still bears his name and that was promoted in the nineteenth century for its anti-aphrodisiac properties.

It is doubtful whether Graham crackers—or anything with comparably calming effects—were available. From Lahaina, Melville made his way to Honolulu, a town of some ten thousand inhabitants where prostitutes were more plentiful than missionaries in what was a favorite port of call for the nineteenth-century equivalents of sex tourists. There he stayed three months, working at odd jobs including a stint as a bowling pin setter. (In *White-Jacket,* he was to describe a sailor's triumphant performance in a shipboard theatrical as a "ten-stroke.") On August 17, 1843, he enlisted as an ordinary seaman in the U.S. Navy and shipped aboard the frigate *United States,* landing at Boston nearly fourteen months later, on October 3, 1844.

This was the rough itinerary that supplied Melville with the experiences he was eventually to tap for the outburst of work that included *Typee, Omoo, Mardi,* and *White-Jacket* (for *Redburn,* he returned for his material to his earlier voyage to Liverpool), and that culminated in the publication of *Moby-Dick* some seven years after his return home. Melville's four years at sea were the seedtime for his imagination. But there survives only a single scrap actually written during this time, and the most we can glean from it is that, despite the fact (as he wrote in *Omoo*) that "a man of any education before the mast is always looked upon with dislike," he was evidently held in favor by his fellow sailors. During the troubles at Tahiti, one of them, an illiterate man named Henry Smyth, asked him to write a message to a sick friend imprisoned aboard a nearby French frigate for his role in a mutiny:

On Board the Lucy Ann
September 25th 1842

Dear George,

On arriving here the other day I was sorry to hear that you were verry ill on board the French Frigate.—I should like verry much to go and see you but I cannot possibly as I can not be allowed to:—so I take the liberty to write you a few lines.—You know we all agreed to hang out on your account when we came aboard from the Corvette—but it so happened that those who talked loudest were the first to return to their duty. I was the last one that went forward, and would not have turned to at all, but that I found it was of no use,—so after being in double irons some time I thought it best to go forward & do my duty as usual

You must remember me to Peter

I do not know that I have any thing further to say to you

I often think of you & I & Young Smith have often talked about
you during the night watches at sea

—Good bye
My Dear George
Hoping you will be soon at liberty
I remain Yours & c
Henry Smyth

We shall never know how faithfully this letter transcribes Smyth's
words, but it affords a glimpse of Melville as an amanuensis with characteris-
tically uncertain spelling. Perhaps the dashes mark pauses when he held his
pen poised while Smyth pondered how to express himself to his absent
friend. Besides a few mentions in family correspondence of letters sent to or
received from Herman (since lost), this bit of ventriloquism is the only trace
we have of him during his nearly four years before the mast.*

4.

When Melville jumped ship at Nukuheva, he brought with him, along with
Toby Greene, a wad of tobacco and a roll of cloth that he stuffed into his
trousers for use as barter with the natives. He was also equipped with a few
ideas about what kind of people the Pacific islanders would turn out to be.

When he and Toby scrambled through the brush to the top of a coastal
hill and made the arduous descent into the valley, they were going to a place
visited previously by only a few Westerners, some of whom had never come
back. According to sailors' lore, those men had stayed on because they had
found there a paradise of sexually compliant women from whom no sane
man would wish to escape; according to other reports, they did not return
because they had been murdered and eaten. Melville was never one of those
"students versed more in their tomes / Than life" (as he described them

---

*There is a tantalizing reference in the September 4, 1844, issue of the Honolulu paper *The
Friend of Temperance and Seamen:* "If Mr. Herman Melville, formerly officer on board Am. W.S.
Acushnet, is in this part of the world, and will call upon the seamen's chaplain, he may find several
letters directed to his address." Since Melville had left Hawaii aboard the *United States* a year ear-
lier, he never saw those letters, which have not been located. See Lynn Horth, ed., *The Writings of
Herman Melville: Correspondence* (Evanston and Chicago: Northwestern University Press and the
Newberry Library, 1993), p. 565.

much later, in his poem *Clarel*), and it was not till after he had returned home that he did any systematic reading about the South Seas—so these kinds of stories, both enticing and frightening, were just about all he knew about where he was going. They had the effect of urging him on to see for himself what "the olden voyagers had so glowingly described."

The two men hatched their plan out of nervous hopes in which curiosity competed with fear. What they hoped for were "naked houris" (Melville was required by his publisher, John Wiley, to change this phrase in the manuscript of *Typee* to "lovely houris") and "groves of cocoa-nut—coral reefs—tattooed chiefs—and bamboo temples; sunny valleys planted with bread-fruit trees—carved canoes dancing on the flashing blue waters." What they feared were "cannibal banquets" and "savage woodlands guarded by horrible idols—*heathenish rites and human sacrifices.*" These "strangely jumbled anticipations" had come to them not only from old salts and young braggarts aboard ship but also from popular magazines, lectures, and even schoolbooks they had studied as children. It was a time, as the historian Michael Rogin has put it, when "the contrast between 'savagery' and 'civilization' dominated the . . . American imagination." Press and pulpits poured forth a steady stream of commentary on the nature of savages—mostly provoked by the problem or plight (depending on one's point of view) of Indians, who were victims of a process that today we would call "ethnic cleansing" but that in those days was called "removal."

A few people in antebellum America spoke, without much effect, of white conquerors as "pseudo . . . civilized" plunderers, who wanted to steal land from people weaker than themselves; but the official line was that the white man's expansion first across North America and then, by the 1840s, into the Pacific, was literally a godsend: a divinely ordained step leading humankind out of darkness into light. As for those who, like Melville, left home to encounter primitive peoples in remote corners of the earth—whether they were missionaries, military men, traders, whalers, or glorified pirates—they took with them, as one scholar puts it, "their lives . . . in their baggage." And so it is useful to inspect Melville's "baggage" in order to get a sense of what he left behind and what he brought home with him.

Melville's firsthand knowledge of so-called primitive people was very small. Like others who made the voyage out, he was inclined to conflate the attitudes and practices of one exotic people with those of another, and there is a sense in which, despite his ignorance, he thought he knew where he was going. Many writers before him had noted among North American Indian tribes "the wondrous custom of offering maidens of the village to distinguished visitors," a custom that sailors to the Pacific had reason to hope would be honored in whatever culture they encountered. As for Melville himself, he had glimpsed only a few Indians here and there: Indian men working as longshoremen on the docks where his father had done business, Indian women working in New York or Albany as seamstresses, servants, or prostitutes. On his trip west in 1840, he had seen Ojibways and Winnebagos walking the streets of Buffalo and encamped along the shores of Lake Erie; in *White-Jacket* he reports seeing a Sioux warrior displaying the severed hands of recently scalped enemies. These were borderland Indians struggling to survive by hawking skins, flints, baskets, or, in some cases, themselves to the very people who had destroyed their former existence.

The process of destruction seemed irreversible, though one pretext for the removal of Indians was the illusory assurance that they would find sanctuary in the west. If he is "to be found in any of his savage grandeur," James Fenimore Cooper wrote as early as 1828, "the Indian must now be chiefly sought west of the Mississippi." "The West" has always been the place to which Americans try to banish their problems, and Indians certainly qualified as one. In Cooper's novels, written between the late 1820s and early 1840s, there are essentially two types of Indians: degraded descendants of ancient warlike Indians who slink around the edges of white settlements, and noble prairie Indians, who have a Roman stoicism and dignity. Cooper likens the former to dogs feeding on scraps from the master's table and celebrates the latter as people who live as their forebears had lived, wild and free, beyond the reach of white settlement, if only for the moment.

By heading into the Pacific, Melville was taking the ultimate trip west— to a place where uncontaminated savages could be witnessed at first hand, as was hardly possible any longer in the continental United States, at least not for a young man who needed to get paid en route. When he left, the expulsion of Indians from their ancestral lands along the eastern seaboard was in its final stages, justified by the claim, as a Vermont lawyer put it in 1839, that "Indians' bones must enrich the soil before the plough of civilized man can open it." Efforts to resist, from Indians and whites alike, proved of little avail. The most conspicuous instance was that of the Cherokee Tribe, whose rights to lands in Georgia, Mississippi, and Alabama had been affirmed and reaffirmed by treaties and courts, but who were forcibly removed westward in the 1830s to join their tribesmen "already established in prosperity" (the words of the commanding officer, Winfield Scott) beyond the Mississippi. Among the Cherokee, the route of their "emigration" (also General Scott's term) came to be known as "the Trail of Tears."

Melville had no more than a boy's glancing awareness of these events, or of their prevalent explanations; but he could hardly look at a newspaper without catching some reference, anointed with crocodile tears, to the removal of primitive peoples as the price to be paid for the spread of civilization. While a few public figures expressed more than ritual regret about what was happening—"it is impossible to conceive of a community more miserable, more wretched," Henry Clay said of the Cherokee on the Senate floor in 1835—most seemed to agree that their relocation was not only inevitable but for the best. And since some self-exculpating theory is always useful to justify self-interested actions, Americans in Melville's time were full of talk about their superiority to the various dark peoples whom they felt entitled to displace. In the later 1840s, even opponents of the imperialist war with Mexico (in this case, the liberal Boston minister Theodore Parker) did not doubt "the superior ideas and . . . better civilization" of the "Anglo-Saxon race," though Parker preferred that Mexico be civilized "by the schoolmaster [rather] than the cannon."

This attitude of racial superiority continues to flicker in our own time, but by the mid-twentieth century, when it became disreputable among educated people, it was rarely stated openly or frankly. Conventional in Melville's time, it was shared by religion and science, by the educated and the ignorant, by advocates and opponents of Indian removal and slavery, in both the North and the South.

According to the most advanced students at that time, the human species was distributed among five races: American Indian; Caucasian (a term coined by the German ethnologist Johann Blumenbach in 1781); Mongolian; Ethiopian; and Malay. Although it was customary to associate differences of color and feature among the races with corresponding mental and moral differences, the Bible taught "that of one blood God had made all the nations" (Acts 17:26). And since the biblical story of Creation precluded the notion that human beings derived from multiple origins, even the most resolute racialists of Melville's day had to fall back on some sort of environmental explanation for human difference. There was, in other words, a kind of agnosticism in the air on the theoretical question of whether the differences between civilized and savage people, however stark, were written into their respective natures or were attributes that could be learned and unlearned.

In practice there was considerable agreement about who stood where in the hierarchy of cultures. If, for example, pro-slavery southerners such as William Gilmore Simms believed that the Ethiopian, or Negro, was designed to be nothing more than an "implement in the hand of [white] civilization," the anti-slavery New Englander Ralph Waldo Emerson was no less convinced, at least as a young man, that "nature has plainly assigned different degrees of intellect to . . . different races, and [that] the barriers between them are insurmountable." In Melville's America, there were differences in the intensity with which these platitudes were expressed and in the political lessons drawn from them; but the hierarchy itself—which in fact hardened as slavery came under pressure from humanitarian reformers—was almost universally accepted.

5.

These ideas were among the items that Melville packed in his baggage for his visit to the "Malay" race, but the trip triggered a debate within his mind over what they were worth. What he expected to encounter was a race of savages little better than children, people stuck—to use a psychoanalytic term that came into currency much later—in a state of arrested development. Though they did not yet possess this vocabulary, Melville's immediate predecessors, and most of his contemporaries, understood the history of mankind as a universal process of advancement that moved at different speeds in different places, and that somehow skipped over certain peoples and left them mired in the primitive past. Commentators of a naturalist bent counted the effects of climate and terrain among the reasons for human disparities, while others more religiously inclined looked to divine design as the sole and total cause. Some believed that primitive peoples could be lifted into civilization by education and training. Others doubted it. Whatever the putative cause or remedy, there was general agreement that certain races were equipped for advancement and others were not.

Civilization, in other words, was the process by which human beings suppress their instincts and turn into self-controlled citizens. "Savage" was the name for people incapable of self-suppression ("Tahitians," as Melville wrote rather casually in *Omoo*, "can hardly be said to reflect; they are all impulse"), people who continued to live in a scavenger's relation to nature, under the open sky or in portable shelters, plucking their daily needs from whatever grew or roamed in the wild. As one of Melville's contemporaries, Horace Bushnell, put it in a speech to the Home Missionary Society in 1847, Indians are "a wild race of nomads," who "think it no degradation to do before the woods and wild animals what in the presence of a cultivated state they would blush to perpetrate." They make no distinction between public and private. They have no science, only superstition, and so their "fireside stories," as Francis Parkman wrote in 1851, are full of "wild recitals of necromancy and witchcraft—men transformed to beasts, and beasts transformed to men, animated trees, and birds who spoke with human tongue." They cultivate nothing. The relation between the idea of cultivation and the emerging notion of "culture" (a word used increasingly in Melville's time as a synonym for civilization) was strong since, as the horticultural metaphor implies, human beings require fertilization and pruning no less than do livestock or crops.

For Europeans, such discussions were parlor talk. The practice of enslaving "inferior" peoples had been formally abolished in the British Empire in 1833, and even while it lasted, slavery was, for its beneficiaries in the home country, little more than an unpleasant rumor. By the time an English gentleman stirred sugar into his tea or had his servant fold his linen, the role of some faraway slave in producing these luxuries had been forgotten— or, more likely, had never been much thought about. As for that vaunted invention of the Enlightenment mind, the Noble Savage, if he existed at all, he was a distant colonial subject of whom a few examples had been brought back from the tropics and put on exhibition in London or Paris.

For Americans, however, even in Melville's day, the idea of the primitive cut closer to home. The savage past did not seem superseded, as Europeans lost no opportunity in pointing out, and Americans could never be quite sure where they stood in the continuum that ran from savage to civilized. When Captain David Porter, for example, recorded his voyage to the Marquesas in his journal—which Melville read while working on *Typee*—he complained that France "attached to us no more merit than [it] would have given to one of the natives for being born there."

A good example of the classic Enlightenment account of how the civilizing process was supposed to work may be found in a book by an eighteenth-century Scotsman named James Monboddo that was still widely read in Melville's time. *The Origin and Progress of Language* (1773) described how, as history advances, the "will and pleasure" of individuals gradually submits to "public wisdom":

> First, we see men living together in herds, like cattle or horses . . . carrying on some common business, such as fishing or hunting. . . . Next, we see them submitting to government, but only upon certain occasions; and particularly for the purpose of self-defense. . . . The next stage of civil society . . . is that of the Indians of North America, who have a government in time of peace as well as war. . . . The last stage of civil society, in which the progression ends, is that most perfect form of polity, which, to all the advantages of the governments last mentioned, joins the care of the education of the youth, and of the private lives of the citizens; neither of which is left to the will and pleasure of each indi-

vidual, but both are regulated by public wisdom. Such was the government of antient Sparta, and such were all the plans of government
devised by Plato and other philosophers.

Reading this account of how man evolves from "frugivore to a cannibal
to a civilized being" is like walking through the Hall of Man in an old-style
Museum of Natural History, with its sequence of dioramas that starts with a
caveman in animal skins and ends with astronauts in pressure suits. It has the
tableau quality of an exhibition behind glass; it is disconnected from the
viewer, to be admired from behind the rope and concluded with a visit to
the souvenir shop. It is about a process that was finished long ago. Still, in
spite of itself, there are hints of self-questioning: If man had reached his
highest point of development in the ancient past, at Sparta and Athens, what
has happened since? Does civilization move steadily upward, or reach and
then stall on a plateau? Or might it be a cyclical affair of rise and fall?

Here, composed some fifty years later, is another version of the same
universal human history—this one by an American, namely, Thomas Jefferson, who wrote it in a letter to a friend near the end of his life, in 1824, when
Melville was five years old:

> Let a philosophic observer commence a journey from the savages of the
> Rocky Mountains, eastwardly, towards our sea-coast. These he would
> observe in the earliest stage of association living under no law but that
> of nature, subsisting and covering themselves with the flesh and skins
> of wild beasts. He would next find those on our frontiers in the pastoral
> state, raising domestic animals to supply the defects of hunting. Then
> succeed our own semi-barbarous citizens, the pioneers of the advance
> of civilization, and so in his progress he would meet the gradual shades
> of improving man until he would reach his, as yet, most improved state
> in our seaport towns. This, in fact, is equivalent to a survey, in time, of
> the progress of man from the infancy of creation to the present day.

For Americans of restive temperament, this little essay in universal history
was an invitation to time travel. It held that to travel west is tantamount to
going back to the beginning of time—like entering the Hall of Man at the exit
and moving against the traffic toward the entrance.

Melville himself had gone a short distance in that direction on his
aborted journey with his boyhood friend Eli Fly, and now, on the *Acushnet*,
he was going further. He had skipped the continental route and was headed
straight to an encounter with the Beginning of Man.

6.

Yet, amid all the self-congratulating, a growing number of dissenters were not so sure how much celebration the so-called civilizing process really deserved, and as Melville headed inland with Toby, he became one of them. A question was forming in his mind—the same question that Walt Whitman posed in *Leaves of Grass* a few years after Melville returned from his trip:

> *The friendly and flowing savage, who is he?*
> *Is he waiting for civilization, or past it and mastering it?*

Though Melville had as yet no clear plan to become a writer, this question was to become the theme of his first book.

Long before Melville began seriously to think about the question, it was already a recurrent theme for writers whom we tend to group under the rubric "Romantic"—writers who doubted that civilization in the sense of technological advancement and self-suppression was all boon and benefit. From the pioneer physician Benjamin Rush (a contemporary and friend of Jefferson's), who speculated that sedentary life leads to insanity by weakening blood circulation to the brain, to Melville's contemporary Thomas Wentworth Higginson, who declared his "constitutional affinity for undeveloped races," and recommended athletic exercise as a means for restoring the zest of savage life, a strong countercurrent ran against the Enlightenment idea of civilization as linear progress. The ethnologist Henry Schoolcraft, for example, who traveled in the 1820s among the Indians of Minnesota and Wisconsin, envied their "primitiveness and freshness of fancy belonging only to the mind in its incipiency." And though he knew much less than Schoolcraft about Indian languages, Cooper praised Indians for the "sententious fulness" of their language, for drawing "metaphors from the clouds, the seasons, the birds, the beasts, and the vegetable world," and for their ability to "express a phrase in a word, and convey different significations by the simplest inflexions of the voice." This mythic Indian—ancestor of the Hollywood Indian who speaks in monosyllables like "Uggggh" and "How"—is more body than mind, and has a quasi-erotic relation to the world. His speech is uncorrupted by irony, euphemism, or any other form of self-consciousness. Emerson, too, admired him—remarking that "children and savages use only nouns or names of things, which they convert into verbs. . . . As we go back in history, language becomes more picturesque, until its infancy, when it is all poetry." Civilization, in other words, comes with a price: it weakens the imagination.

Behind these celebrations of the imaginative, and imaginary, primitive lay a body of Romantic writing that, starting at the end of the eighteenth century, had exalted eloquent innocence as the highest achievement of human culture. History was coming to be understood as a story of degeneration rather than of progress—a theme that Melville was to put in the form of a question in his long philosophical poem, *Clarel:* "Prone, prone are era, man, and nation / To slide into a degradation?" Terms such as "primitive" and "illiterate" were losing their pejorative connotation and becoming terms of praise—a transformation rooted in the ideas of European Romanticism. The German scholar Friedrich Wolf, for example, in a book published in 1795 that had considerable influence on American intellectual life, proposed that the poet of the *Iliad* and *Odyssey,* known as Homer, had actually been a bard who sang his tales, which were redacted by later scribes into written form. The German philosopher Johann von Herder celebrated the intuitional directness of the Old Testament stories in *The Spirit of Hebrew Poetry* (1782–83), which was not translated into English until 1833 (by the Vermont transcendentalist James Marsh), and was one of many contributions to the celebration of feeling and spirit, as opposed to reason and argument, as the ultimate source of morality and wisdom.

Melville had no special interest or even awareness of these scholarly and philosophical developments, but by the time he embarked on his travels, a new and strongly pejorative meaning of the term "civilization" (which Newton Arvin remarks is what Melville "called what revolted him") was displacing the older, honorific sense of the word. "What a contrast," Emerson wrote in 1839,

> between the well-clad, reading, writing, thinking American, with a watch, a pencil and a bill of exchange in his pocket, and the naked New Zealander, whose property is a club, a spear, a mat and an undivided twentieth of a shed to sleep under! But compare the health of the two men and you shall see that the white man has lost his aboriginal strength. If the traveler tell us truly, strike the savage with a broad-axe and in a day or two the flesh shall unite and heal as if you struck the blow into soft pitch, and the same blow shall send the white to his grave.

It was a view with which Melville concurred, but usually with a dose of self-mocking irony that shows him doubting the cogency of the new Romantic dissent as well as of the old orthodoxy. "Among savages," he wrote almost parodically in *Mardi*, "severe personal injuries are, for the most part, accounted but trifles. When a European would be taking to his couch in despair, the savage would disdain to recline."

As the vaunted superiority of civilization came into question, intellectuals had also begun to speak not of one universal form of civilization but of plural civilizations—thereby acknowledging no singular means of organizing life to which humankind ought to aspire. In 1838, a pungent writer named Abner Kneeland, who earned the distinction of being the last man in New England to be tried for the crime of blasphemy (in a trial presided over by Melville's future father-in-law, Judge Lemuel Shaw), had this to say about the idea of civilization as a normative value:

> A Parisian will be surprised to hear that the Hottentots cut out one of the testicles of every little boy; and a Hottentot will be surprised to hear that the Parisians leave every little boy two. Neither the Parisian nor the Hottentot is astonished at the practice of the other because he finds it unreasonable, but because it differs from his own.

This kind of cultural relativism had been adumbrated centuries before by Montaigne in his famous essay *Of Cannibals*, which Melville read with delight not long after returning from the Pacific. It had more recent advocates as well: in the 1780s, Benjamin Franklin reflected that "savages we call them because their Manners differ from ours, which we think the Perfection of Civility; they think the same of theirs." Melville was drawn to this kind of relativism, as when he described in *White-Jacket* a naked Polynesian named Wooloo. The binary balance of his sentences creates a seesaw feeling not very different from what one feels when reading a late twentieth-century postmodern writer like Jacques Derrida or Paul de Man:

> [Wooloo] seemed a being from some other sphere. His tastes were our abominations: ours his. Our creed he rejected: his we. We thought him a loon; he fancied us fools. Had the case been reversed; had we been Polynesians and he an American, our mutual opinion of each other would still have remained the same. A fact proving that neither was wrong, but both right.

While Melville cruised the Pacific, this kind of cultural comparison was becoming the subject of formal discussion at meetings of the American Ethnological Society, founded in New York in 1842. The members (several of whom belonged to Melville's circle when he moved to New York in the late

1840s) held lectures and debates on such topics as the place of missionary work that aimed to convert "primitive" peoples versus disinterested investigation that promised to leave them alone. By the end of the decade, the *American Whig Review* was describing ethnology as "the science of the age." In short, although we tend to think of Melville's America as a nation bursting with jingoistic confidence in itself, countervailing voices were being raised against the presumption of conflating the here and now with the high and good.

Ethnological history, which tends to deal with peoples waning or already lost, encourages the view that civilizations follow an inevitable rhythm of rise and fall. And in the nineteenth century, most educated persons had read at least some Thucydides and Gibbon, from whom they learned that power was transient, that every nation follows a parabolic arc, beginning its descent at just the point where it reaches its height (Melville read them—though probably not till after his return from the Pacific). In the late 1830s, the Hudson River School painter Thomas Cole captured this theme in a sequence of paintings that Melville saw in 1846 in New York in a gallery on Chambers Street. In the four large canvasses of *The Course of Empire,* Cole depicted a city, complete with neoclassical columned temples, going through a four-stage cycle of rise, triumph, decline, and decay—from pastoral beginnings, through civic flowering, into decadence, and ultimate destruction. In the first panel we see the city rise out of raw nature, and then we follow it, phase by phase, as it falls back into ruins overgrown by weeds and vines.

Recalling his visit to Pompeii in the 1820s, another contemporary, Theodore Dwight, described the entire expanse of the known world as "a mass of bones and ashes . . . a melancholy shore, which the waves of time have strewed with the wrecks of nations." And in 1831, in one of the most delicately ruminative poems composed in America before the Civil War, William Cullen Bryant (whom Melville was to meet in New York in 1847) mused on the recent discovery in the Mississippi Valley of what were thought to be burial mounds constructed by a prehistoric people who had once roamed the American plains.

> *The prairie-wolf*
> *Hunts in their meadows, and his fresh-dug den*
> *Yawns by my path. The gopher mines the ground*
> *Where stood their swarming cities. All is gone:*
> *All—save the piles of earth that hold their bones . . .*

How much in this vein Melville had read before his Pacific voyages is not known. But in germinal form, these themes of relativism and transience were present in his mind; and on his homeward journey, they grew to the verge of expression, as when he heard a song "chanted, in a low, sad tone, by aged Tahitians"—or so he claimed. In fact, Melville lifted the song from a book called *Polynesian Researches,* written by the English missionary William Ellis in 1833. But whether he actually heard it, or stole it from another writer, the fact that he was drawn to it tells us something about his mood:

> *"A harree ta fow,*
> *A toro ta farraro,*
> *A mow ta tararta."*

> *The palm-tree shall grow,*
> *The coral shall spread,*
> *But man shall cease.*

A few years later, in a similar mood, he was to conclude *Moby-Dick* with the sinking of a whaleship that stays stubbornly afloat as the fatal ocean pours in, until finally "all collapsed, and the great shroud of the sea rolled on as it rolled five thousand years ago," obliterating all except the memory of a lone survivor.

In a letter to Hawthorne written in 1851, Melville dismissed his Pacific years as time wasted, remarking that "until I was twenty-five, I had no development at all." This self-assessment should be doubted. It was during his time at sea, between the ages of twenty-one and twenty-five, that he awakened from the lethargy by which he had often been touched and sometimes enveloped. Here is his soulmate D. H. Lawrence, imagining Melville's mood as he planned his escape with Toby: "He was mad to look over horizons. Anywhere, anywhere out of our world. To get away. To get away, out! . . . To cross a horizon into another life. No matter what life, so long as it is another life."

If Melville's mind came alive in the Pacific, so, too, did his senses. He experienced many new physical sensations—from the stench of rotting whale carcasses to the fragrance of fresh-split coconuts, from numbing cold to heat so fierce that he felt his brain being steamed in the equatorial sun. The tales he was eventually to tell about his South Seas adventures came from a young man savoring the memory of all sorts of physical responses more intense than anything he had felt before, from the choking nausea of his first days at sea to the giddy delight of learning how to climb the rigging in the open air or the electric touch of a beautiful Marquesan girl or boy. His eyes had been pleased by the sight of naked native bodies, his ears treated to the "labial melody" of Polynesian women crooning as they squatted down to bathe him. Here was savagery to be savored!

What Melville found at sea was what other writers have found in war: a feeling of *contact* with the world that shocked him equally with moments of desire and dread. He gave up on notions and theories learned from books and became at last an engaged participant in life—even, as Lawrence lovingly called him, a "gallant rascally epicurean eating the world like a snipe, dirt and all baked into one *bonne bouche*."

CHAPTER 3
BECOMING A WRITER

1.

When he shipped from Honolulu aboard the naval frigate *United States* in August 1843, Melville began a long voyage home that retraced his outbound route, docking at Nukuheva too briefly to allow shore leave, and at Tahiti, where the ship took on provisions while anchored tantalizingly close to the beach. It must have been strange to see this alien shore again, still foreign yet now familiar, stirring memories rather than anticipations. Perhaps it was one of those experiences that lay behind the many images in Melville's writing of things desired that seem near enough to reach for, yet too distant to grasp. After a few days at rest, the *United States* proceeded east, then north along the coast of South America, making stops at Valparaiso, Lima, and, for a period of ten weeks, Callao. There the men were again denied shore leave and mustered twice a day to stand at attention in honor of Commodore Catesby Jones, whose flagship *Constellation* was anchored nearby while he and his officers were rowed about the harbor to inspect the fleet.

During his months of naval service, Melville witnessed things he had never seen in the whale fishery or the merchant marine. He saw burials at sea conducted with military honors, as well as a good deal of flogging, which was the standard punishment meted out in doses calibrated to the seriousness of the culprit's offense. He saw, literally in the flesh, what he had read about in Dana's *Two Years Before the Mast*—men bleeding from gashes in their backs but with little or no idea of what they had done to merit them. Here is Dana quoting one Captain Thompson as he dances around the object of his ministration, "swinging half round between each blow" to get the torque he needs for full effect:

> If you want to know what I flog you for, I'll tell you. It's because I like to do it! Because I like to do it! It suits me! That's what I do it for!

When the flogged man cries out, "Jesus Christ! O Jesus Christ!," his captain offers some advice: "Don't call on Jesus Christ . . . *He can't help you. Call on Frank Thompson!* He's the man! He can help you! Jesus Christ can't help you now!"

There were also happier sights and sounds. Melville took dreamy pleasure in the "St. Domingo melodies" sung by the man-o'-war's cook to the accompanying "clattering [of] . . . soap-stones against the metal" as the mess assistants scoured the copper vats in which beef was boiled into a kind of salty porridge. He loved such culinary words as "dunderfunk" (the sailors' name for a hard-baked cake of indefinite ingredients) and "burgoo" (a syrupy slop sweetened with molasses) that eluded the better-spoken officers, to whom such words were nothing more than mystifying slang. His initiation into sailor talk had an enduring effect on a writer who inclined toward formality and sometimes slipped into sententiousness. The years Melville spent at sea helped to save him from a certain stuffy earnestness, as he suggests in *White-Jacket,* when he turns the bulky coat, in which the boy narrator struts about at first like a prig in a tux, into a metaphor for haughtiness. At the climax of that book, he pitches the boy overboard and makes him tear off the coat to save himself from drowning, in effect, in himself.

His predecessors in the gentleman-goes-to-sea genre, including Dana, had never quite got beyond the tone of the Brahmin slumming among the hoi polloi, but Melville opened himself to the sailor's life and became genuinely part of it. He shed his pretensions. He discovered that at sea competence counts more than breeding. He learned to live at a constant pitch of sentry alertness, since a split second of drowsiness or reverie could kill him. This was to be the theme of that memorable chapter in *Moby-Dick,* "The Mast-Head," in which Ishmael reflects on how easy it would be to slip from his height and be dashed to death on the deck below, or, if the ship were listing, to disappear with a quiet splash into the sea. In *White-Jacket,* in a sentence both reportorial and allegorical, Melville remarks that "Sailors, even in the bleakest weather . . . never wear mittens aloft; since aloft, they literally carry their lives in their hands, and want nothing between their grasp of the hemp and the hemp itself."

For part of each day, Melville manned a lookout post some seventy feet above the deck. In this "airy perch" he was removed from the cruelties below and shaded from the sun by the mainsails above, and it was there that he befriended Jack Chase, captain of the maintop—the nautical name for the "spacious and cosy" platform, complete with railing, that formed "a kind of balcony" affixed high aloft the mainmast. Near the end of his life, Melville was to dedicate *Billy Budd* to Chase, whose exuberant wit and charm he remembered with love undiminished by time, thinking back to their long talks some forty years earlier about life and literature ("Jack had read all the verses of Byron, and all the romances of Scott, talked of Rob Roy, Don Juan . . . Macbeth and Ulysses") while they "looked down upon the land-lopers below, sneaking about the deck, among the guns."

There were other friends, too, who shared his interest in reading, among them the brooding "man-of-war hermit" Oliver Russ, named Nord in *White-Jacket,* who mostly kept to himself but one night lowered his reserve and, with Melville as companion, "scoured all the prairies of reading, dived into the bosoms of authors, and tore out their hearts." It was an occasion of such lasting significance to Russ that, sixteen years later, he gave his son the com-memorative name Herman Melville Russ. And there was a fellow New Yorker named Ephraim Curtiss Hine—probably the model for another recluse whom Melville, in *White-Jacket,* called Lemsford—who snatched every moment he could to write poetry.* Fearful that his poems would be dis-posed of in one of the bouts of sweeping and scrubbing at which the crew was periodically set to work, Hine stuffed his manuscript for safekeeping into a ship's cannon by ramming it in with the "tompion," a sort of plunger kept in place in the barrel to keep out the sea spray. When the ship fired a vol-ley in return to a salute from a shore battery somewhere off South America, he arrived too late at the sheltering gun to save his work-in-progress, which had been blown out to sea in shreds. Jack Chase, whose name Melville retained in *White-Jacket,* consoled him with words that were later to register on Melville, whose own publishing career was to have its share of misfires:

> Never mind, my boy, no printer could do the business for you better. That's the way to publish . . . fire it right into 'em; every canto a twenty-four-pound shot; *hull* the blockheads, whether they will or no. And mind you, . . . when your shot does the most execution, you hear the least from the foe. A killed man can not even lisp.

Ashore, on a brief leave that allowed him just enough time for a tour of Callao and a dash into Lima, Melville saw dogs and vultures feeding on human corpses amid the rubble of buildings that had fallen to ruin over cen-turies or—he could not be sure which—that had collapsed during the earth-quake that had struck the city not long before, in 1828. These sights were to stay with him, along with his memory of the tarnished silver altar in the cathedral, crowds of cigar-smoking men drinking *chicha* in the cafés, and dark-eyed women cruising the alleys in cloaks as enticing as they were con-

---

*In 1848, Hine's *The Haunted Barque* was privately printed at Auburn, NY.

Lemuel Shaw

cealing. Two years later, in *Typee,* he was to compare the "diminutive" feet of a naked Polynesian girl to those that "peep from below a Lima lady's dress." Later still, he was to use Lima as the setting for the gruesome last scene of his great novella *Benito Cereno,* in which the severed head of a mutinous slave is impaled on a pike, his dead eyes staring at the cathedral and, across the Rimac bridge, the monastery of Mount Agonia in the distance.

After alternating for months between tedium and diversion, Melville landed in early October 1844 in Boston, where he may have spent a few days "lingering or malingering" (Elizabeth Hardwick's nicely inconclusive phrase) and possibly a few nights lodging at the home of Judge Lemuel Shaw, Chief Justice of the Supreme Judicial Court of Massachusetts. Shaw was prosperous, portly, and nothing if not proper. The executor of Allan Melvill's estate, he embodied, as Dana remarked, "the social and political respectabilities of Boston." His stout character twice had been tested by the death of women he loved: he had been engaged to Allan Melvill's sister, Nancy Wroe Melvill, who died in 1813, while their wedding was being planned; five years later, he married Elizabeth Knapp, who died in 1822 giving birth to a daughter whom he named for her.

When Melville landed in Boston in 1844, Elizabeth Shaw was an eligible young woman still living at home with the judge and his second wife, Hope Savage Shaw. During Herman's years at sea, she had become friendly with his sisters Helen and Augusta. On the premise that Herman remembered her from childhood, one biographer speculates that he sought out Elizabeth now with the urgency of a sailor returning to a sweetheart, and that she thrilled to the stories that tumbled from the "bearded lips of a brilliant, dark, muscular, handsome young man." Perhaps. Or perhaps she was out of town. Or he may never have visited the Shaws at all.

But even if he only glanced up from Boston Harbor toward Beacon Hill, where the Shaws' four-story brick house with its pillared brownstone entrance stood on Mount Vernon Street, he must have felt a twinge of envy, or at least resigned awareness of his own family's fall. As a child he had walked on that street with his eminent grandfather, whom passersby greeted with bows and salutes; now, for lack of alternatives, he was headed west to a rented house in Lansingburgh ruled by his mother. Whatever detours he may have taken en route, he prepared for the homecoming with mingled feelings of relief and dread. "The flood-gates of the wonder world" that had opened for him during his years at sea were shutting down. There was no reason to believe that his mother had become less importuning during his absence. The correspondence among his sisters is filled with complaints about her, as when Helen, writing to Augusta in 1841, reported that their mother "scanned the page with a critical eye, pronounced the chirography beneath contempt, and insisted upon my copying the document" until it met her stenographic standard.

We cannot know whether Maria spared Herman this kind of pestering when he came home. What we do know, on the authority of Gansevoort's friend Nathaniel Parker Willis, is that he fought off his feelings of deflation by telling and retelling what he had seen and done. When autumn had passed, the young traveler "beguiled the long winter hours of his own home circle" with stories of his adventures, and was encouraged by family and friends to write it all down.

2.

Melville's "home circle" was made up now mainly of women. With Gansevoort and Allan off in New York trying to advance their careers in politics and law, the household consisted of four sisters under Maria's supervision— Helen (twenty-seven) and Augusta (twenty-three), who were occasionally away themselves husband-hunting in Albany or Boston, along with Kate (nineteen), Fanny (seventeen), and Herman's fourteen-year-old brother, Tom. If we can apply to Herman the musings of young Redburn, he had a "vague prophetic thought that I was fated, one day or other . . . just as my father used to entertain strange gentlemen over their wine after dinner . . . [to] be telling my own adventures to an eager auditory." Aside from his wish to break the cycle of shuttling between a tedious job and a thankless mother, he had gone to sea with the half-formed intent to become a storyteller, and he came home brimming with tales to be disgorged to listeners he hoped would be held rapt by the telling.

Entertaining them was Melville's rehearsal for a literary career at a time when a fiction writer's commercial prospects depended largely on the ability to please female readers who, as James Fenimore Cooper lamented in 1849, were likely to find that sea fiction has "the odor of bilge-water" and induces the "*maladie de mer.*" Against these odds, Melville had to learn to amuse his sisters—to titillate without quite scandalizing them; an apprenticeship that left its mark on his early work, as in *Omoo* when "he managed," as the literary scholar William Charvat has noted, "a detailed description of a wildly phallic native dance without seeming to be in the middle of it." There is something wonderfully incongruous about the Melville family scene in that fall of 1844: the randy young globe-trotter up in the attic reliving his escapades, while his mother and virgin sisters bustle about below tending to household business. He felt cooped up in a different kind of "indulgent captivity," or so one might glean from an early review of his first book. "If he meets a native female Islander," this reviewer complained, "she is a goddess;—if a missionary's wife, she is a blowzy looking, red-faced, fat oppressor of the poor native—reducing him to the station of drudge." Was there a touch of Maria in his portrait of Mistress Missionary? How, for the "family post-man," could there not have been?

One can only imagine how Melville's mother and sisters reacted to hearing about the Polynesian girls applying tropical oil with their "soft palms" to his "whole body" and then competing "with one another in the ardor of their attentions." No wonder he had looked forward "with transport" during his days in the Marquesas to his nightly body rub, which gave him, he was sure, "such sensations" as no sultan in the seraglio had ever enjoyed. But it is a long way from raconteur to author, and most who try to make the transition fail to go the distance. Many young men, Elizabeth Hardwick points out, "have held forth over their schnapps and received a like urging to proceed from the conversation to the blank white page," but in the cold light of morning they find that writing is a more arduous business than spinning tales in the night.

It is the rare young writer who does not fall in love with the idea of becoming famous, and Melville was no exception. When he remarked years later to Hawthorne that no man "who is wise, will expect appreciative recognition from his fellows," he was reproving his younger self for having craved it. In *Omoo,* he sketches a character, based on the steward of the *Lucy Ann,* John Troy, in whom there are also touches of self-portraiture: the voluble Dr. Long Ghost, a charlatan posing as a physician who carries in his head great swatches of poetry that come pouring out at the slightest prompt. This charming scamp ("a man of humorous desperation," D. H. Lawrence called him, "throwing his life ironically away") was for Melville simultaneously a model to be mimicked and shunned; debonair and decadent, he was a drifter who took pleasure in the attention of his native hosts, yet he was full of contempt for them. The more he delights in his own cleverness, the more one feels a dark belligerence in his charm, an oddly affable hatred toward those whom he deems inferior to himself, heightened by his resentment that he has been sentenced, after some "unfortunate affair that set him a-roving," to pass his days among them.

Dr. Long Ghost anticipates the sort of character one meets in the novels of Joseph Conrad or Graham Greene, a man self-exiled to some remote colonial outpost, to which he has brought feelings of both superiority and failure. He is an early version of the cosmopolitan raconteur to whom, years later, Melville was to devote the second half of *The Confidence-Man,* a man for whom "life is a pic-nic *en costume,*" in which "one must take a part, assume a character, stand ready in a sensible way to play the fool." A not-so-distant cousin of Goethe's Mephistopheles, he was a figure who haunted Melville's imagination and to whom he would return near the end of his life in *Billy Budd* in the person of John Claggart, whose unfathomable hatred is disguised by his "low musical voice" as he spreads his poison with a sinister smile.

Did Melville himself have something of Dr. Long Ghost's desperation disguised as antic spirits? No one who heard him hold forth in Lansingburgh or, later, in New York left more than a fragmentary account of the experience, though there is evidence in his writing that he had an instinct for performance—as when he writes, in *White-Jacket,* about the "difficult art" by which a good comic performer keeps a straight face, "preserving the utmost solemnity," while setting his audience "all in a roar." We get a further hint of Melville's histrionic power from Sophia Hawthorne, wife of Nathaniel, who reported that "when he describes any thing with the living voice . . . it is there, it is here, just as he says it, & he himself is each several person of the tale."

Yet despite—or perhaps because of—their urgency and vividness, Melville's tales were greeted with incredulity. In a book published in 1884, while Melville was still alive, Sophia and Nathaniel's son, Julian Hawthorne, reconstructed an evening his parents had spent with Melville in the summer of 1851, when he came over to their Berkshire cottage to deliver one of his tall tales. It was the story of "a fight which he had seen on an island in the Pacific, between some savages, and of the prodigies of valor one of them performed with a heavy club." After their talkative guest had gone home for the night, Sophia wondered aloud—probably with a little edge in her voice but also with affection ("a man with a true warm heart," she later called him, ". . . with life to his fingertips")—" 'Where is that club with which Mr. Melville was laying about him so?' " As for her husband, "Mr. Hawthorne thought he must have taken it with him; Mrs. Hawthorne thought he had put it in the corner; but it was not to be found." To resolve the matter, "the next time Melville came, they asked him about it; whereupon it appeared that the club was still in the Pacific island, if it were anywhere."

At first, the young traveler's audiences were all aglow with eagerness to hear him. "With his cigar and his Spanish eyes," as his brother's friend Nathaniel Willis later described him, he "*talks* Typee and Omoo, just as you find the flow of his delightful mind on paper." But as the stories grew familiar, Melville's confidence that he was being admired led to worry that he was being indulged. Years later, he was to play with this theme in "The Town Ho's Story," the chapter of *Moby-Dick* in which Ishmael recalls a stopover in Lima where he had once entertained "a lounging circle of my Spanish friends . . . smoking upon the thick-gilt tiled piazza of the Golden Inn." For a while, Ishmael manages to hold his audience with his tale of shipboard violence and mutiny, but he soon finds himself peppered with skeptical questions: "Tell me," says one of the listeners, ". . . if your story is in substance really true? It is so passing wonderful! Did you get it from an unquestionable source?" Ishmael, indignant, calls for a copy of the Bible, upon which he will swear to his veracity.

When Melville moved from telling tales to friends and family to trying to write for the public, he found that he had to defend his truthfulness against the skepticism of prospective publishers. Sometime in late 1844 or early 1845, he joined his brothers in New York City, where he stayed on and off over several months, "writing something," as his younger brother Allan put it, "about his adventures among the cannibals." By summer, he had completed his first manuscript under the title *Typee* and submitted it to Harper Brothers, the leading New York publishing firm. When rejection came on the grounds that "it was impossible that it could be true," Gansevoort offered to help.

Gansevoort Melville had been dabbling in politics, giving speeches on behalf of Democratic candidates that were, according to the editor of the *New York Tribune,* Horace Greeley, full of "gas and glory"—especially his anti-British tirades delivered to cheering crowds of Irish immigrants who hated the English and wanted them out of the Oregon Territory, which

Britain and the United States had occupied jointly for decades. As the number of American settlers rose in the Willamette Valley and farther north (in present-day Washington State) around Puget Sound, Democrats grew increasingly belligerent, and Gansevoort Melville became closely associated with the party's campaign slogan—"Fifty-four forty or fight!"—calling for Britain to relinquish its claims to the territory south of the 54°40′ parallel. Some historians even credit him with coining the nickname "Young Hickory" for the Democratic presidential candidate, James A. Polk, which identified Polk as heir to Andrew Jackson, known as "Old Hickory" for his unbending resolve against those he deemed enemies of "the people," especially bankers, Indians, and Old World imperialists.

Soon after Herman's return from the Pacific, Polk was elected, in November 1844, on an expansionist platform, and Gansevoort commenced a campaign for himself—not for elective office, but for a patronage position. After months of lobbying, he succeeded in getting an appointment as secretary to the American legation in London. Before departing for his new post in the summer of 1845, he learned that his brother's book had been rejected by Harpers and offered to take the manuscript with him to see what could be done in what was, after all, still the literary capital of the English-speaking world. By December, he had found a taker. The English publisher John Murray, though he too "scented the forbidden thing—the taint of fiction," agreed to bring out the book on condition that excisions be made "on the score of taste."

After placing the manuscript with Murray, Gansevoort continued to work on Herman's behalf, reading aloud from the page proofs one morning over breakfast to a distinguished visitor, Washington Irving, who liked what he heard and commended the book to his own American publisher, G. P. Putnam, one of the Harper brothers' rivals. Putnam, in turn, found the book so absorbing that it "kept him from church," and without delay he contracted with Gansevoort, to whom Herman had given power of attorney, to bring it out under the Wiley & Putnam imprint in New York.

3.

Melville's first book appeared in February 1846, bearing the title *Typee* and a dedication—"To Lemuel Shaw, Chief Justice of the Commonwealth of Massachusetts, this Little Work is Affectionately Inscribed by the Author"—

that was both ingenuous and strategic. The book was a quick, if modest, success. "Get it and read it by all means," recommended the *New York Illustrated Magazine*, and enough people complied so that *Typee* sold roughly six
thousand copies in its first two years; not a best seller, but a more than
respectable showing for a first book by an unknown author.

It told of Melville's flight from the despotic captain into a tropical island
of perils and pleasures. It told how, after jumping ship, he and Toby clawed
their way inland through the brush to escape the pursuing search party, then
encountered a naked native boy and girl with whom they tried to communicate in pantomime. Taken back to their village, Melville (he calls himself
Tommo) is fussed over by men and pampered by women, especially the
beautiful Fayaway, whose very name (one consonant removed from "faraway") suggested her dreamy remoteness from everything he had known till
then.

Typee took place at an island spa where the only item on the menu was
lotus; it was Melville's prose equivalent to Tennyson's poem "The Lotos-
Eaters" (1832) about Odysseus surrendering to luxury in the land of the
poppy, "a land / In which it seemed always afternoon . . . where all things
always seem'd the same," where life is one long easeful sleep. He gave his
book the structure of the ancient tale of world-weary man transported to paradise; but if Tennyson had imagined his exhausted mariners relieved to be at
ease, Melville told of a young man whose restlessness gets the better of his
self-indulgence. Before long, he grows fearful that he has fallen captive to
cannibals awaiting a convenient moment to eat him, and once his fear overwhelms the compensatory pleasures, he plans and executes his escape, pursued to the last by one of his enraged captors with a knife in his teeth.

This story, and the way Melville wrote it, made for irresistible reading.
In reviewing *Typee* for the *Salem Advertiser* in March 1846, Hawthorne
expressed delight at its "voluptuously colored" descriptions of native girls,
and found himself swept up by a young writer endowed with what the English critic William Hazlitt, whom Melville was soon to read with admiration, had called "gusto." Hazlitt used this word to describe how Titian
represents female flesh in paint. It is a word exactly apt for Melville's word
paintings in *Typee* of Polynesian beauties, whose bodies, as Hazlitt had
observed of Titian's nudes, seem "sensitive and alive all over; [having] not
merely . . . the look and texture of flesh, but the feeling in itself . . . the limbs
of his female figures have a luxurious softness and delicacy, which appears
conscious of the pleasure of the beholder."

Melville was not free to write about sex with the directness we expect
today, and so he sometimes smuggled it into his writing in the form of snig-

gering jokes—from an aside in *Typee* about a ghostly vessel "tacking . . . somewhere off Buggery Island" (a phrase that his wife listed after his death among those he had wanted deleted from future editions) to the celebration of the sperm whale's penis (as long as a man is tall) as "grandissimus" in "The Cassock" chapter of *Moby-Dick*. He lived at a time when it was indelicate for gentlemen to refer in the presence of ladies to the leg of a table or chair (the proper term was "limb") and when, as a guidebook published in 1841 "for the use of young ladies at home, and at school" made clear, modesty was required at every moment of every day:

> Do not suffer your hand to be held or squeezed, without showing that it displeases you by instantly withdrawing it. If a finger is put out to touch a chain that is round your neck, or breast-pin that you are wearing, draw back, and take it off for inspection. Accept no unnecessary assistance in putting on cloaks, shawls, overshoes, or anything of the sort.

Among the few contemporary writers who got close to candor about sexual pleasure was Nathaniel Hawthorne, who in *The Scarlet Letter* described Hester Prynne as having "a radiant and tender smile that seemed gushing from the very heart of womanhood" and was followed, after intimacy with her lover, by a "crimson flush."

In this context of coyness, *Typee* was a daring book. One reason Hawthorne appreciated it was its sensuous directness, as when Melville describes the "free pliant figure" of Fayaway, whose skin is "inconceivably smooth and soft":

> Her complexion was a rich and mantling olive, and when watching the glow upon her cheeks I could almost swear that beneath the transparent medium there lurked the blushes of a faint vermilion. The face of this girl was a rounded oval, and each feature as perfectly formed as the heart or imagination of man could desire. Her full lips, when parted with a smile, disclosed teeth of a dazzling whiteness; and when her rosy mouth opened with a burst of merriment, they looked like the milk-white seeds of the "arta," a fruit of the valley, which, when cleft in twain, shows them reposing in rows on either side, imbedded in the red and juicy pulp. . . .

Melville was introducing his readers here to a new kind of woman—new, at least, within the boundaries of permissible literary description. In most respectable books of the day, female characters tended to be chaste daughters or virtuous mothers, though in some underground fictions such as *Mary Ann Temple: Being an Authentic and Romantic History of an Amorous and Lively Girl, of Exquisite Beauty, and Strong Natural Love of Pleasure!* (1849) or George Thompson's *New-York Life* (also published in 1849), women are portrayed as furtive masturbators who "scarcely pass a day without some secret violation of the laws of chastity." Contrary to the cliché of Victorian prudery, women's capacity for strong sexual pleasure was well recognized; but since female orgasm was thought to be seated in the ovaries and necessary for conception, and was therefore approved as a natural part of the reproductive process, it was also deliberately limited as a form of birth control.

Fayaway, as the phrase goes, was another story. Open and inviting, yet somehow with nothing lewd in her invitation, she was an unself-conscious promise of reciprocal pleasure. She was Melville's embodiment of a secret about which decent writers were expected to be reticent: that women could be sexually exciting—and excited—without being wanton. She offered, as the literary historian Ann Douglas has written, "exactly what the American Victorian lady would deny her male counterpart: unmoralized pleasure," and Melville wrote about her with the recollected passion of a now distant lover whose lovemaking had been spiced by the knowledge that their time together was fast running out.

By the time he reached Nukuheva, long overdue for a "warm, wild" reception, Melville was suitably grateful when he got it. "I have more than one reason," he says with a wink, "to believe that tedious courtships are unknown" in Polynesia. Upon arriving among the Typees, he met with no delay in getting "on the very best terms possible" with Fayaway, his "peculiar favorite," who introduced him to a new world of sexual frankness. Marquesan girls do not dance modestly in *Typee.* They "dance all over, as it were; not only do their feet dance, but their arms, hands, fingers, ay, their very eyes, seem to dance in their heads . . . they so sway their floating forms, arch their necks, toss aloft their naked arms, and glide, and swim, and whirl, that it was almost too much for a quiet, sober-minded modest young man like myself." Almost, but not quite.

Even in his earliest work, Melville converted the tact required by the literary norms of his time into a means to charge his writing with sexual energy: on the Pacific isles, the winds blow "like a woman roused . . . fiercely, but still warmly, in our face." He was later to remember the very landscape as tumescent, the orange trees "spreading overhead a dark, rustling vault, groined with boughs, and studded here and there with the ripened spheres, like gilded balls." Looking back on his time among the Typees, he describes Nukuheva harbor as a glistening aperture set within a row of swelling hills. When he explored an adjacent bay, he "plunged into the recesses of the first grove that offered," as if his whole body had become an engorged extension of his penis, and he found himself "floating in some new element, while all sort of gurgling, trickling, liquid sounds fell upon my ear." The wad of cotton cloth with which he stuffed his trousers in hopes of trading it for the natives' favor created an unconcealable "protuberance in front."

With its lubricious accounts of oil rubs and orgies, *Typee* gave its author a measure of fame and even attracted to him the nineteenth-century equivalent of a rock star's groupies: "You dear creature," one woman beseeched him in a feverish fan letter, "I want to see you so amazingly." What immunized him against the hazards of early fame was his awareness of the gap between what he had done and what he still hoped to do. Melville's self-confidence was large, but his demands upon himself were larger. His writing had the sort of brashness—as in *Typee*'s take-the-reader-by-the-collar opening, "Oh! ye state-room sailors . . . what would ye say to our six months out of sight of land?"—that is usually associated with his contemporary Walt Whitman. But in the realm of self-promotion Melville did not come close to matching Whitman, who shamelessly turned private letters of praise from notable persons into unauthorized blurbs, and even reviewed (anonymously) his own books. What Melville felt was not so much enchantment with himself as surprise at the vitality of what he had created, and a drive to do more.

During this first flush of literary celebrity, he had begun to see more of Elizabeth Shaw. The preceding May, while he was deep in his South Seas reminiscences, she had been in Lansingburgh, putatively to visit his sisters; and now, in March 1846, he went to see her in Boston. The number of intervening contacts—letters, visits, messages carried by his sisters—is uncertain, but later that year, Lizzie, as she was known to family and friends, came to Lansingburgh again, this time for two months. Before the end of the year, they had promised themselves to each other.

Lizzie Shaw was a steady young woman of no exceptional beauty, but even in the spare historical record there are hints of a certain flair that helps to account for why she was drawn to the young adventurer, and he to her. Soon after her first appearance as a bridal candidate on the Boston social scene, she wrote a thank-you note in the form of a biblical parody to the hostess of a Beacon Hill ball:

1. And Lemuel said unto Hope, Come, let us go up to the house of Aunt Dow—and the number of them that went was three.

2. And Hope and Elizabeth took counsel together saying, what shall we wear? And wherewithal shall we array ourselves? And Hope said, ask thy cousin Jane concerning the matter, and whatever she says that shalt thou do.

3. And when Elizabeth could not go to her for reason of a great storm that arose, she sent a man servant to enquire concerning the matter.

4. And after this manner spake Jane unto her. Thou shalt wear thy blue silk with a bare neck, and in no wise shalt thou wear white muslin.
 . . .

6. And when Elizabeth heard the words of the messenger which she had sent, she said within her heart, this will I do, I will wear the blue silk, and the sleeves thereof shall be made short. And it came to pass that she did so, according to the words which she had spoken that day.
 . . .

8. And as they drew nigh unto the house, they heard the sound of music and dancing, and they said one to another, behold it proceedeth from the Brass band, and verily it was so.
 . . .

10. And they tarried there a goodly time until it waxed late, and the hour of departure drew nigh. And Lemuel arose and spoke thus unto Elizabeth, my daughter behold the night is well nigh spent, and thy mother is weary and sorely vexed with her cold. Come now, put on thy thick apparel, and return with us unto thine own home.

11. And when Elizabeth heard the words of her father she was exceeding sorrowful and said unto him, peradventure they will dance again, and if I may not join them it will be a grievous thing unto me; for I have danced but five times, nevertheless, as thou sayest, that will I do.

There is an appealing capacity for self-mockery here, and an awareness of the gap between personal wishes and daughterly duties. Herman Melville, a magnetic young man whose sisters she had befriended and of whose family her father approved, now became the leading candidate to satisfy both Lizzie's desires and her obligations.

While working on *Typee,* and in the optimistic aftermath of its publication, Melville had gone from being a boy unencumbered with responsibilities to a man thinking about marriage to a willing bride. In that spring of 1846 he was already working on a sequel that he called *Omoo,* his transliteration of a Polynesian word meaning "Wanderer." He was, in other words, becoming a professional writer. Having started out as an unacceptable publishing risk, he had gained bargaining power with the success of *Typee,* so that in the fall, Harper Brothers offered a relatively generous contract for *Omoo,* including a

$400 advance. Yet he had no illusions that he could support himself with his pen. In the spring of 1847, he was in Washington knocking on the doors of senators and representatives looking for a government job. Fortunately, he did not find one.

4.

For Lizzie Shaw, her proper father, Melville's chronically anxious mother, and, not least, himself, there remained the question of how he was to turn his talent and ambition into a means for making a living. *Typee* was a promising start, but the number of Americans in the mid-1840s who could expect even a subsistence income from their writing was extremely small. Melville's literary hopes marked him as a prospective member of what one contemporary, in 1845, referred to as a "brood of unfortunates, called American authors."

One reason was the absence of an international copyright law, which meant that American publishers were free to keep all earnings derived from unauthorized reprints of books by foreign authors. In the case of an American reprint of a British book, since publishers had no obligation to pay the author anything at all, they could offer high discounts to retail booksellers—sometimes as much as 50 percent—which, in turn, gave retailers an incentive to push sales. When Charles Dickens came to the United States on a speaking tour in 1842, he complained at every stop that he had never earned "sixpence from an enormous American sale of all my books," and resolved to "whisper in your ear two words, International Copyright."

The whispering campaign got Dickens nowhere. What we would call "pirated" British titles continued to dominate American newspaper advertisements and subscription lists (the nineteenth-century equivalents of the front table in Barnes & Noble), while American authors were consigned, in effect, to the back of the store. From the point of view of fledgling American writers like Melville, publishers were deliberately stunting the size of their audience. From the publishers' point of view, the public was getting what it wanted: English books.

If we take the long view, we can see that while American writers griped and whined, a market for books was at last forming, along with a functional system for distribution and sales—developments that eventually worked to the benefit of American as well as foreign authors. But writers generally are not interested in long-term trends to be discerned by future historians; they

are interested in earning a living. Forty years earlier, the Philadelphia novelist Charles Brockden Brown had explained the situation from the point of
view of publishers reluctant to publish him:

> Here have I a choice of books from England, the popularity of which is
> fixed and certain, and which will cost me nothing but the mere
> expences of publication; whereas, from you, I must purchase the privi-
> lege of printing what I may, after all, be unable to dispose of, and which
> therefore may saddle me with the double loss of the original price and
> the subsequent expences.

This was a frankly economic explanation—probably franker than what
authors actually heard from publishers—of why authorship in America
remained more a hobby than a profession.

There were also cultural reasons. For one thing, as Thomas Jefferson
wrote to an English correspondent in 1825, "Literature is not yet a distinct
profession with us. Now and then a strong mind arises, and at its intervals of
leisure from business emits a flash of light. But the first object of young societies is bread and covering." For another thing, the antebellum United States
was still a very Protestant country whose few novelists had to contend with
what Henry James was later to call "the old evangelical hostility" to the art of
fiction. As late as 1850, in *The Scarlet Letter,* Hawthorne imagines his
"black-browed" Puritan ancestors shaking their heads over him as a "degen-
erate . . . writer of story books!"

To make matters worse, although it had been fully seventy years since
the Revolution, New World readers retained a filial interest in Old World
subjects. The children of the revolutionary generation, such as Melville's
parents, had grown up as British subjects in cultural attitude if not political
allegiance. More than likely, their childhood homes had been decorated with
prints and engravings imported from England or, if executed by American
artists, depicting English country villages or London cityscapes. The flutes
and harpsichords they learned to play as children tended to come from England, as did the teachers who gave lessons in how to play them. In prosperous families, an itinerant decorator—probably an English artisan working
temporarily in America—might have been hired to paint landscape murals
above the mantelpiece that "were merely slight transformations of English
works . . . with a few details changed to suggest the colonial locality." In
short, in the first half of the nineteenth century the props, accoutrements,
and manners of an American household with any claim to refinement imi-
tated English models. As late as 1852, Lizzie's stepmother wrote to her son
traveling in England, seeking advice on a matter of deportment: "You know I

am apt to swing my arms," she acknowledged, so "I wish you to write me how the English ladies walk . . . how they place theirs to prevent motion that is visible." There is no record of his response.

The same kind of nervous emulation characterized American literary culture, such as it was. In 1820, soon after Melville was born, a leading Boston publisher estimated that fully three quarters of the books bought by Americans were written in England; in the same year, the editor of the *Edinburgh Review* posed a sneering rhetorical question—"Who reads an American book?"—to which he gave a plain and largely accurate answer: no one. More than twenty years later, in 1842, when Melville was soaking up experience for his attempt at a literary career, the biggest event of the literary season in the United States was Dickens's lecture tour.

A general observation by Jacques Barzun sheds light from another angle on the unpromising professional prospects of a young American writer. A "wide-awake youngster," Barzun points out, ". . . begins to be aware of the wide world in his or her early teens. By then, knowledge of the recent past has also been absorbed automatically: it was 'the present' for the parents, who keep referring to it. Its striking events and startling notions come through this hearsay to seem part of the youth's own experience." For Melville's parents, born in the 1780s, the "recent past" and "striking events" that they passed on to their children in the form of family lore had been the Revolution and the formation of the new nation—their fathers' military heroics, the presidency of George Washington (who appointed Thomas Melvill Inspector of Customs at Boston and signed Peter Gansevoort's membership certificate in the Society of the Cincinnati, a hereditary organization of Revolutionary War officers). Then, just as Allan and Maria Melvill reached adulthood, English troops returned to sack the capital of the upstart nation during the War of 1812. As Herman grew up, stories of recurrent war against Britain were the stuff of family table talk.

His parents, in other words, belonged to a generation peculiarly divided. They were provincials hobbled by their sense of inferiority to Old World culture, so much attached to European customs and standards that, as Melville put it in *Pierre,* they could be "satirically said to have thought of importing European air for domestic consumption." But they were proud of, even boisterous about, their fathers' part in throwing off the Old World master whom they had reason to hate. What they felt toward Europe and England, and doubtless imparted to their children, was a mixture of nostalgia and resentment, and they never quite knew whether to remake themselves into Yankee democrats or to defend their parents' quasi-aristocratic Old World tastes. All Americans who aspired to culture in the honorific sense of the word were split within themselves over this question, and tried, as we would say, to "have it both ways"—as when, in 1831, a patriotic divinity student set new words to the old tune of "God Save the King" and called his hymn "America" (better known today as "My Country 'Tis of Thee").*

But writing new lyrics for old music is, at best, a half-creative act—and here, in miniature, was the dilemma for would-be writers and artists in the young country: How was one to express American ideas and sentiments through European forms? On his trip through America in that same year, Alexis de Tocqueville noted the unpopularity of the "small number of men in the United States who are engaged in the composition of literary works," which are "English in substance and still more so in form," and by which they try to "transport into the midst of democracy the ideas and literary fashions that are current among the aristocratic nation they have taken for their model." One of Melville's signal contributions to our literature was to help destroy Old World forms and supplant them with something new and essentially American. "Long enough," as he wrote in *White-Jacket*, "have we been skeptics with regard to ourselves."

As Melville grew up under these conditions of divided cultural allegiance, the scale of literary production in the United States began to grow as well. The call for literary independence became a refrain not only in the salons and magazines but also in theaters, where, by the 1830s, there was brisk competition for a $300 prize to be awarded to "an original comedy whereof an American should be the leading actor." Slowly, the idea of a distinctive American literature was taking hold, and so was the evidence that such a literature was actually in the making. Between 1820 and 1830, only about a hundred novels by American writers were published in the United States; in the next decade, the number rose above three hundred, and in the 1840s, it leapt toward a thousand. A few American writers, led by Irving and Cooper and followed closely by Emerson, even achieved recognition in Britain.

What had begun as a professional quarrel between workers and managers in the literary business had become, by the 1840s, a full-fledged national debate, not just about the rights of authors versus the interests of publishers but about whether a homegrown literature suited to "the peculiar nature and the need of those for whom it is made" was possible, and, if so, what kind of literature it should be. The discussion ran parallel to the earlier political debate between Federalists and Republicans over whether the national interest was best served by fostering industry at home or by preserv-

---

*The student, who went on to become a Baptist minister, was Francis Smith, a Harvard classmate of Oliver Wendell Holmes, Sr. (class of 1829), and an acquaintance of both the Melvills and the Shaws.

ing the rural purity of the United States and relying on imports from Europe for finished goods.

Melville joined the discussion belatedly. "Believe me, my friends," he wrote in 1850, "men not very much inferior to Shakespeare, are this day being born on the banks of the Ohio. And the day will come, when you shall say who reads a book by an Englishman . . . ?" By then the subject of what he called "literary flunkeyism toward England" was well worn and, in theory at least, the matter pretty much settled. Eminent New Englanders such as William Cullen Bryant (*Lectures on Poetry,* 1825), William Ellery Channing (*Remarks on National Literature,* 1830), and Emerson (*The American Scholar,* 1837), as well as, more recently, the leading southern man of letters, the South Carolinian William Gilmore Simms (*Americanism in Literature,* 1845), had all weighed in on behalf of "the expression of [the] nation's mind in writing."

By the time Melville made his own contribution to the discussion, the theoretical question was closed, and everyone agreed that Americans needed a literature of their own—including the British, who chided them for not having produced one. But the old practical questions remained: What kind of writing was called for? And who, if anyone, would pay to read it?

5.

Even under the best conditions, it is risky to bet one's future on literary success; but in starting out with a book whose truthfulness was open to question, Melville stacked the odds against himself. Chances were good that even if the first critical quarrels over his literary merit came out in his favor, someone unhappy with the verdict would wait for an opportunity to attack him again. *Typee* had given him a degree of renown. But it had also saddled him with a reputation for exaggeration that he never quite lived down, despite Toby Greene's testimony (published in the *Commercial Advertiser* in July 1846) backing up his version of what the two men had experienced together in the Marquesas. To shore up his credibility, Melville rushed off "The Story of Toby" to both his American and his English publishers, who added it to reprints of *Typee.*

Yet despite his and Toby's insistence that he had written "unvarnished truth," many readers still doubted him—and not without reason. Melville was a writer who delighted in what he called, near the end of his life, "literary sin." His tales were on the tall side, and stretching them was part of the "pleasure which is wickedly said to be in sinning." His hairsbreadth escapes from cannibal warriors (it is practically impossible that they could have run along a raw coral beach as described in the final chapter of *Typee*), the sexual profligacy of his shipmates, and his own combination of prowess and self-restraint were all claims that tested credulity.

Moreover, Melville's readers doubted that he had much grasp of the Polynesian languages—even of the sound of words he had heard and tried to pronounce himself. After Melville's death, Robert Louis Stevenson complained that the man possessed "no ear for [the Polynesian] language whatever." Stevenson liked to say that at Melville's christening "some influential fairy must have been neglected" among those handing out gifts to baby Herman. When the roll call of fairies was called to announce their donations, they spoke in order: " 'He shall be able to see,' " decreed the first. " 'He shall be able to tell,' 'He shall be able to charm,' " said the next and the next. " 'But he shall not be able to hear,' exclaimed the last."*

There was something to this charge. Whether one attends to Melville's garbling of Polynesian words or to his eyewitness accounts of tribal practices, no one is likely to mistake his early books for the work of a scrupulous field anthropologist. They are not reliable. They are willfully outrageous mixings of fiction and fact; their "unvarnished truth" was a melange of embellished memories, yarns he had heard from other sailors, and thefts from books (notably William Ellis's *Polynesian Researches,* from which he copied the melancholy Tahitian song) that he raided for anecdotes to supplement his own. He was greedy for anything he could use to attract an audience, and he sometimes fell into a certain coyness—a tone of "I'll show you only so much" of the sort one expects today from a "romance" novel, with its explicit accounts of foreplay that fade, as the climax approaches, into euphemism and innuendo. His scenes of sex and savagery tend to break off before they culminate. "He gets up voluptuous pictures," complained one reviewer who was undecided whether Melville went too far or not far enough, "and with cool deliberate art breaks off always at just the

---

*Some modern scholars defend Melville's ear, suggesting that Stevenson was misled by Melville's habit of spelling Polynesian names that end in a vowel sound, such as "Happa" (Melville spelled it "Happar"), with a terminal "r." For an English speaker with a mid-nineteenth-century Northeast American accent, the terminal "r" may have designated a preceding long "a" sound. This is as close as we are likely to get to hearing Melville's speaking voice: broad and open, not unlike the Boston accent (he probably pronounced the word "farther" the same way he said "father") that today has become a caricature of itself. See Harrison Hayford and Walter Blair, eds., *Omoo* (New York: Hendricks House, 1969), pp. 344–46.

"*Their jet-black tresses streaming over their shoulders, and half-enveloping their otherwise naked forms.*"
Typee, *illustration by Guido Boer, 1931*

right point so as without offending decency, he may stimulate curiosity and excite unchaste desire." Melville liked to step outside his narrative, reporting debaucheries—as when the island girls swim out naked to offer themselves to his bug-eyed shipmates—which, he claimed, he had declined to join.

And so the opening of *Typee* amounted to a dubious promise to arouse his readers while denying that he had been aroused himself. He describes the Marquesan girls performing a collective striptease: raising the curtains of hair (by winding it into coils) that screen their backs and buttocks, then stroking themselves with oily hands to prepare for what we would call group sex:

> These swimming nymphs . . . succeeded in getting up the ship's side, where they clung dripping with the brine and glowing from the bath, their jet-black tresses streaming over their shoulders, and half-enveloping their otherwise naked forms. There they hung, sparkling with savage vivacity. . . . Nor were they idle the while, for each one performed the simple offices of the toilette for the other. Their luxuriant locks, wound up and twisted into the smallest possible compass . . . the whole person carefully dried, and from a little round shell that passed from hand to hand, anointed with a fragrant oil.

But *Typee* was more than an invitation to leer at what went on in the pleasure groves of Polynesia. It was a work of intellectual precocity set in a half-imaginary Eden, where sexual repression (Melville did not have the word, but he grasped the concept long before Freud named it) was unknown. The "penalty of the Fall presses very lightly," he wrote, upon the inhabitants of this Edenic world, by which he meant that they had been spared the necessity of labor, and that they relished sex without guilt or shame. To Western eyes, they were no different from savages, as Bushnell had described them—people who "think it no degradation to do" in the open what in "a cultivated state they would blush to perpetrate," and their precocity was attested by the sight of barely pubescent girls nursing their own babies.

It was as if he had actually entered the prelapsarian world that earlier writers had only wanly or furtively imagined. He had come to a place where there were neither persons—at least not in the sense in which individual persons were understood to exist in the culture from which he was on furlough—nor property. "There was not a padlock in the valley, nor anything that answered the purpose of one." It was a place of which Europeans had dreamt from time immemorial, a place free of what he was later to call "social acerbities," without inhibition, jealousy, or rivalry. He knew that his readers would want to learn what an American lad experienced in this paradise, among voluptuaries with beautiful bodies ("bathing in company with troops of girls formed one of my chief amusements"), but he also knew that his readers' curiosity was more than merely prurient. He had touched in *Typee* the age-old longing to transport oneself, if only by the vehicle of imagination, out of worn pathways into places unmapped and unknown. "We dream all night of those mountain-ridges in the horizon," Thoreau was to write a few years later, "though they may be of vapor only, which were last gilded" by yesterday's sun. *Typee* was Melville's version of this American dream—not the dream of raising one's status in the world as it is, but the dream of starting over, getting out from under, and putting it all away to discover life anew.

6.

As a description of the culture into which its author had ventured, *Typee* is not to be taken seriously. Modern anthropologists have made clear that

Melville misunderstood the complex kinship relations of the Marquesan islanders as well as their system of marking off sacred from profane activities with taboo and purification rituals. He made no serious effort, as Stevenson complained, to learn their language. What he did was to conduct an irresponsible thought experiment—irresponsible, that is, with respect to trying to understand on its own terms what he had actually seen. He reimagined the Typee world as the inverse of his own, in a book that amounted to an extended rhetorical question: What would it mean to live in paradise?

In a remarkable chapter entitled "Producing Light à la Typee," Melville engaged this question by describing how Tommo's male attendant, Kory-Kory, strikes a spark for the purpose of igniting his master's pipe. The boy props a six-foot stick at a forty-five-degree angle against "some object" such as a rock or tree trunk, then straddles it, holding at crotch height a shorter stick with a pointed end that he rubs up and down against its longer partner. The friction creates a groove, at the bottom of which a little pile of wood shavings starts to gather:

> At first, Kory-Kory goes to work quite leisurely, but gradually quickens his pace, and waxing warm in the employment, drives the stick furiously along the smoking channel, plying his hands to and fro with amazing rapidity, the perspiration starting from every pore. As he approaches the climax of his effort, he pants and gasps for breath, and his eyes almost start from their sockets with the violence of his exertions. This is the critical stage of the operation; all his previous labors are vain if he cannot sustain the rapidity of the movement until the reluctant spark is produced. Suddenly he stops, becomes perfectly motionless. His hands still retain their hold of the smaller stick, which is pressed convulsively against the further end of the channel among the fine powder there accumulated, as if he had just pierced through and through some little viper that was wriggling and struggling to escape from his clutches. The next moment a delicate wreath of smoke curls spirally into the air, the heap of dusty particles glows with fire, and Kory-Kory almost breathless, dismounts from his steed.*

---

*In the surviving fragment of the *Typee* manuscript (now in the New York Public Library), Melville originally used the phrase "attains his climax" to describe Kory-Kory's exertion. Sometime before first publication, this phrase was changed to the more decorous "approaches the climax of his effort." See Robert K. Martin, *Hero, Captain, Stranger: Male Friendship, Social Critique, and Literary Form in the Sea Novels of Herman Melville* (Chapel Hill: University of North Carolina Press, 1986), p. 36.

Typee was a mirror of the world that Melville left behind—and so, true to the optics of reflection, everything in it was a reverse image of life at home. At home, lighting a fire is easy, but sex is fraught with difficulties. In *Typee,* sex is relaxed and free, but generating a spark for the visiting Westerner who wants his smoke is a chore. The Typees' garden needs no tools or tending, while "civilized" man channels his libidinal energy (Freud was to call the process sublimation) into tools far advanced over the native's stick and groove. It is the achievement of civilization that one need only reach into the drawer to find energy stored in the form of a match. But, Melville asked in *Typee,* to what end? And at what cost?

Here, as it were, was the rub: Melville's self-abrasive knowledge that he could find no lasting pleasure among the lotus-eaters. *Typee* reported his discovery that he was finally unfit for "long exile from Christendom and civilization," no matter how strong the enticements. More than anything—more, even, than his sporadic dread of being cannibalized—he feared that his hosts would mark him as a convert to their tribe by tattooing his face and forearms, those public parts of his body that, if decorated Marquesan-style, would forever define him at home as a freak.

He wanted to be a tourist, not an exile—a point well taken by D. H. Lawrence, who calls attention to the painful swelling in Melville's leg that begins to torment him as soon as he scrambles down the coastal mountain into the happy valley:

> We can't go back, and Melville couldn't. Much as he hated the civilized humanity he knew. He couldn't go back to the savages; he wanted to, he tried to, and he couldn't.
>
> Because, in the first place, it made him sick; it made him physically ill. He had something wrong with his leg, and this would not heal. It got worse and worse. . . . When he escaped, he was in a deplorable condition—sick and miserable, ill, very ill.
>
> Paradise!
>
> But there you are. Try to go back to the savages, and you feel as if your very soul was decomposing inside you.

From a writer of a temperament very like Melville's, these remarks go to the heart of the matter. The injured leg is a throbbing reminder of Melville's half-conscious estrangement from the land he has entered. At his first look "down into the bosom of [the] valley which swept away in long wavy undulations," a kind of vertigo engulfs him, and with time the abscess in his leg brings on fever and thirst. When relief appears in the form of a running brook, he kneels over it, pausing in order "to concentrate all my capabilities of enjoyment" on the imminent pleasure of drinking; but upon touching his lips to the water, he recoils with a taste like ash in his mouth and pulls back, spitting.

Amid such spells of sensory confusion, Melville and Toby brace themselves for their first encounter with people native to the island, but their preparations come to naught when they stumble upon a faint path worn through the jungle by human tread. "Robinson Crusoe," Melville reports, "could not have been more startled by the footprint in the sand" than he was at his first encounter with two figures, one male, one female, "partly hidden by the dense foliage." Equally terrified by the white-skinned invaders, the two natives stare at Toby and Tommo like deer poised to run. There is an Abbott-and-Costello-Meet-Tarzan-and-Jane absurdity to the scene as Melville and Toby break into a frantic pantomime of hopping and pointing by which they try to convey the benignity of their intentions. Half convinced, the Marquesan Adam and Eve lead them to the village elders, who inspect them by bending over them, nose to flesh, in order to sniff their skin.

Much of the charm of *Typee* is in this kind of self-mockery. Melville described himself not with the high self-regard that one finds in contemporary narratives by missionaries or explorers, but as a galumphing oaf in the country of the graceful. As his leg worsens, he submits to the ministrations of the tribal medicine man, who chants invocations and pounds the swollen leg, while his assistant holds down the patient writhing like "a struggling child in a dentist's chair." Whether by time or by magic, the leg heals, and Melville begins to wonder at the eagerness with which his hosts work at restoring him to wholeness. Are they planning to eat him?

A taste for human meat is not something the Typees willingly reveal, and Melville builds narrative tension by describing how their inadvertent hints lead him to fear that their cannibal appetite is the true reason for their solicitude. In Melville's time, the question of cannibalism was, as it remains today, a contested one. There were periodic reports of "survival cannibalism" at sea—incidents in which shipwrecked sailors resorted to eating the bodies of perished shipmates in order to stay alive. Not long after *Typee* appeared, news spread of the hideous experience suffered in the winter of 1846–47 by the Donner party—a group of emigrants who, trapped by early snows en route to California through the Sierra Nevada, were forced to subsist on the flesh of their comrades. But such incidents (Edgar Allan Poe had taken up the theme of survival cannibalism ten years earlier in his story "The Narrative of Arthur Gordon Pym") underscored the horror without confirming the existence of man-eating outside extreme circumstances. Although there were occasional speculations that beyond the civilized world cannibalism was a regular feature of life—as when a Fiji chieftain, brought to the United

States in 1842, died of what the *New York Herald* presumed was withdrawal from his usual diet of human flesh—it was an unproven premise, perhaps even a "fiction," as one scholar has put it, "of the nervous white mind." Therefore, any book that promised eyewitness proof was guaranteed an audience, rather the way a book promising to prove the existence of UFOs finds readers in our own time.

But even though Melville became known as "the man who lived among cannibals," he was coy about the question in *Typee*—full of hints without ever offering anything conclusive. The first clue comes the morning after a group of warriors has returned from battle with a neighboring tribe, and Melville notices that a wooden cooking vessel has appeared overnight in the village "piazza." Lifting the lid, he catches a glimpse of what seem "the disordered members of a human skeleton, the bones still fresh with moisture," before he is chased away with cries of "*Taboo! Taboo!*" We are left to surmise that what he has seen is the residue of a human stew consumed the night before, when the returning warriors had borne on their shoulders poles to which were strapped bundles wrapped in palm leaves—"green winding sheets," as he pointedly calls them—stained with blood. But he never quite establishes that these bundles are the oozing bodies of slain enemies, and he never sees anyone feast on them.

It is impossible to know how much Melville depended on his own memory for *Typee* and how much he played variations on books about the South Seas that he had hauled up to the attic in Lansingburgh or bought or borrowed in New York. There was no shortage of available accounts containing scenes similar to passages he included in *Typee*. Ellis, for instance, reports in *Polynesian Researches* (on secondhand evidence) that Polynesian warriors baked the bodies of slain enemies "in leaves of the hibiscus and plantain, as they were accustomed to wrap their eels or other fish." And though Melville was never charged with outright plagiarism, some critics doubted that his limited experience (he claimed to have stayed among the Typees for four months, but it had actually been less than four weeks) could have provided him with all the incidents he related. Before he sat down to write, according to one reviewer, what he "remembered of the Islands of the Pacific, had become a sort of confused mass in his own brain," and so he turned to other men's recollections as substitutes for his own.

Among his aids to memory may have been *Adventures in the Pacific,* published just the year before *Typee,* by an English physician, John Coulter, who writes with a self-exculpating squeamishness akin to Melville's own. "I must throw a veil," Coulter wrote about a cannibal feast, "as I had only one look at the beginning of it, and left the area sick to loathing." This kind of strategic reticence was conventional in the many accounts of primitive culture that poured off the presses in Melville's day—books in which the island world is seen through screens of foliage, glimpsed in moonlight or shadow, or inferred from the discovery of what look like gnawed human bones.

7.

So Melville was no anthropologist, but he had proven himself a writer who could hold an audience. The portrait of Fayaway was a hit with readers, for whom she became a successor princess to that sexually passionate mother-of-America, Pocahontas—primitive yet refined, dark yet saved from savagery by her natural modesty, as expressed in her capacity to blush. Among her many admirers was the poet Ellery Channing, whose tribute "The Island Nukuheva," which he sent to "bold / Adventurous Melville," noted with proper discretion that Fayaway "Moved like a creature wove of sanctity, / Fell like a sunbeam in that summer world." Channing did not mind at all that her customary dress was nothing more than "a slight belt of bark."

What Melville had done was to establish a connection with his audience. He cared less about misinforming them than about enthralling them. Years later, he put a check mark in his copy of Wordsworth and Coleridge's *Lyrical Ballads* beside the statement in the preface that "every Author, as far as he is great and at the same time *original,* has had the task of *creating* the taste by which he is to be enjoyed: so it has been, so will it continue to be." The young Melville felt constricted by prevailing standards of taste, and knew that in order to make a place for himself in the emerging American literary scene he would have to push his readers to expand their range of curiosity and tolerance.

For the revised American edition of *Typee*, he was forced to excise some of his harsher comments about missionaries. There, compared to what he would demand of his readers in later books, he inflicted only slight pressure; he was at that stage of life when a young man worries about how he is doing in the eyes of acknowledged practitioners and, even as he chafes within the rules, has an uncertain sense of what is required of him.

He had learned to be a writer by shutting himself up with his recollected emotions for the purpose of reliving them, becoming a student of his own senses. One imagines him swirling wine on the tongue to delay the swallow and prolong the taste, or postponing exhalation while holding tobacco smoke in his lungs. Years later, in the voice of Ishmael in *Moby-Dick*, he was to report that "when between sheets, whether by day or by night, and whether asleep or awake, I have a way of always keeping my eyes shut, in order the more to concentrate the snugness of being in bed." One imagines the young Melville, after his vitalizing years at sea, with eyes closed in the effort to recall this or that delicious sensation. While he wrote *Typee,* he was living again in a muffled world among guarded people from whom he could find refuge only in his memory and imagination.

The Melville who wrote *Typee* was not, as Elizabeth Hardwick has put it, "a painter of his own face in the mirror," but, as he himself wrote in 1850, "if you rightly look for it, you will almost always find that the author himself has somewhere furnished you with his own picture." To find Melville in *Typee,* it is best not to look for him in the young man frolicking among the natives—episodes doubtless embellished if not invented. We are more likely to find him before the story gets rolling, for example, on the beach at the Bay of Tior, where he had rowed over in one of the *Acushnet*'s whaleboats in order to witness the French admiral take possession of the place. Watching the admiral in "laced chapeau" being greeted by a "tattooed savage" chieftain, he stands to the side, peels back the skin of a banana, and chomps on it while he muses on the two men in their divergent decorations and symmetrical pride. This is Melville standing between two fantasies of the Western mind—the Noble Savage and the Enlightened Emissary of Europe—while giving his allegiance to neither. He is Melville as flâneur, loafing not in Baudelaire's city or Whitman's, but in the tropical jungle, refraining from all judgments, soaking up experience for the day when he would be ready—at his desk in Lansingburgh, alas—to pour it all out.

CHAPTER 4
ESCAPE TO NEW YORK

1.

With the success of *Typee* behind him and *Omoo* in progress, Melville was more than ready to give up village life. After returning from the Pacific, he had enrolled part time in that peerless school for the study of literary careerism, New York City, where he visited his brothers Allan and Gansevoort at their law firm in a neighborhood of taverns and coffeehouses south of City Hall. Since in the 1840s scheduled steamboat service linked New York to the river towns of the Hudson Valley, it was relatively easy to travel to the city for business or refreshment. Melville made the trip regularly, and by early 1845, he had become known as the "runaway brother," a familiar presence in the office sitting at a spare desk poring over a manuscript rumored to be a racy account of his adventures in the South Seas.

Up in the quiet country, he was an expansive young man trying unsuccessfully to contract himself. A family friend who saw him in Lansingburgh early in 1846 wrote to his sister Augusta that "his countenance spoke his thoughts" as he worked at "making himself agreeable" while waiting one Sunday morning for his mother and sisters to dress for church. But down in the city, he dispensed with restraint. "I would to God Shakspeare had lived later, & promenaded in Broadway," he remarked a few years later. "Not that I might have had the pleasure of leaving my card for him at the Astor [Hotel], or made merry with him over a bowl of . . . punch; but that the muzzle which all men wore on their souls in the Elizabethan day, might not have intercepted Shakspere's full articulations."

In January 1845, while in this unmuzzled city, Melville wrote to his sister Catherine, teasing her about her nickname, Kate:

> I don't know how it is precisely, but I have always been very partial to this particular appellative & can not avoid investing the person who

bears it, with certain quite captivating attributes. . . . Besides loveliness
of form & face, the Kates are always amiable, with fine feelings, a little
too modest at times, but wondrous sly, always in good-humor, sometimes in regular mad-cap spirits & once in a while (I am *sorry* to say it)
rather given to romping.

Melville's expertise about Kates ("They romp with such grace & vivacity,
that I verily believe they are more dangerous then") had been acquired by
studying the promenading beauties on Broadway. "Now, I saw a girl in
Broadway yesterday, & I'll lay you a rose-bud her name was Kate—Why, I'm
sure of it.—Did'nt she have . . . a merry smile, & even a kind of a merry little
walk?"

With coquettish girls on parade and young men openly sizing them
up, New York was a very different place from buttoned-up Boston, where
Melville courted Lizzie with due deference and his sisters felt safely at home.
The distinction was nicely caught in the writings of Nathaniel Willis, who
had left Boston a few years earlier to edit the *New-York Mirror*, which he dedicated to the proposition that "the country is tired of being *be-Britished*."
Willis liked to play on the differences between Boston, where churches were
points of origin from which the whole town had radiated outward, and New
York, where even landmark churches had become minor elements in the
cityscape squeezed between the proliferating shops and hotels. He loved the
opera (all the rage in New York while still considered a low taste by Bostonians), and especially such enchantresses as the French soprano Juliette Bourgeois, who in 1845 sang the title role in Rossini's *Semiramide* under the name
Eufrasia Borghese, delighting Willis with her "intoxicating way of crushing
her eyes up to express passion."

In his generically titled "City Lyric" (1843), Willis registered the New
York presumption that there is really only one place in America that merits
the term ".city":

> *Come out, love—the night is enchanting!*
> *The moon hangs just over Broadway;*
> *The stars are all lighted and panting—*
> *(Hot weather up there, I dare say!)*

>   .   .   .   .

> *What perfume comes balmily o'er us?*
> *Mint juleps from City Hotel!*
> *A loafer is smoking before us—*
> *(A nasty cigar, by the smell!)*

> *Oh Woman! thou secret past knowing!*
> > *Like lilacs that grow by the wall,*
> *You breathe every air that is going,*
> > *Yet gather but sweetness from all!*

> *On, on! By St. Paul's, and the Astor!*
> > *Religion seems very ill-plann'd!*
> *For one day we list to the pastor,*
> > *For six days we list to the band!*

The city Willis described in these slight but atmospheric poems was a place where chance encounters seem full of promise: not yet Whitman's "city of orgies," but a city of erotic opportunity where eyeing and being eyed by strangers is a permissible pleasure. Here, in 1844, he recalls his excitement at finding himself seated on a bus beside a young woman who dozes off as her kerchief grazes his leg:

> *And I have felt from out its gate of pearl*
> *Her warm breath on my cheek, and while she sat*
> *Dreaming away the moments, I have tried*
> *To count the long dark lashes in the fringe*
> *Of her bewildering eyes! The kerchief sweet*
> *That enviably visits her red lip*
> *Has slumber'd, while she held it, on my knee,—*
> > *And her small foot has crept between mine own—*

Willis was among the many New Yorkers, as E. B. White put it a century later, who had "pulled up stakes somewhere and come to town, seeking sanctuary or fulfillment." They had come to a place, as the novelist and editor Charles Briggs wrote with requisite obliqueness, where a young man could openly enjoy the viscous slipperiness of a meal of oysters, which "fills up [his] mouth, touches all the organs of taste at the same time, and leaves nothing to be desired."

2.

But if New York was a place of daring frankness, there were limits to be observed by respectable writers—and by the spring of 1846, at the request of his publisher John Wiley, Melville was arranging for an expurgated edition of *Typee*. Wiley himself had tinkered with the text before allowing typesetting to proceed for the first American version. He had struck out the description of the native queen who "threw up [her] . . . skirts" to reveal her tattooed buttocks, as well as a reference to "the unholy passions of the crew." But the *Morning Courier and New York Enquirer* still found the book "utterly incredible," and to the critic of the *New York Evangelist, Typee* seemed, despite Wiley's cleanings-up, best suited for those who liked "opera-dancers, and voluptuous prints." In a letter to the *Albany Argus,* Melville expressed his irritation at the tongue-cluckers: "*Typee* is a true narrative of events which actually occurred. . . . Although there may be moving incidents and hairbreadth escapes, it is scarcely more strange than such as happen to those who make their home on the deep."

In the midst of these exchanges he received an alarming letter from Gansevoort, sent off from London on April 3 with news of favorable English reviews. The letter was otherwise grim: "I sometimes fear that I am gradually breaking up," his brother wrote, and "it is becoming a toil to me to make the exertion necessary to dress to go out. . . . Man stirs me not, nor woman either. . . . The only personal desire I now have is to be out of debt." There was something terminal about Gansevoort's tone ("I never valued life much—it were impossible to value it less than I do now"), and even as the letter crossed the ocean, he was losing his sight, bleeding from the gums, and coughing blood. On May 29, Herman wrote back with buck-up encouragement: "I . . . think I see you opening this letter in one of those pleasant hamlets roundabout London, of which we read in novels. . . . At any rate I pray Heaven that such may be the case & that you are mending rapidly." Gansevoort never received that letter, having died on May 12. When the news reached the family in early June, Herman went down to New York to meet the coffin and brought his brother's body home to their mother.

Although no direct statement survives from Melville about his reaction to the news of Gansevoort's death, there is an entry (November 24, 1849), poignantly confused about the passage of time, in the journal that he kept during his own London trip three and a half years later: "No doubt, two years ago, or three, Gansevoort was writing here in London, about the same hour as this—alone in his chamber, in profound silence—as I am now. This silence is a strange thing. No wonder the old Greeks deemed it the vestibule to the higher mysteries." And in a strongly felt chapter of *White-Jacket,* also written in 1849, Melville related a vignette about a common sailor who learns that his brother, an officer aboard a supply ship, is due to come aboard after years of separation. Loath to be seen in his state of mean subservience, the sailor cannot bear to reveal himself. Melville writes the scene with great intensity (" 'How my heart thumped,' " says the sailor, " 'when I actually *felt* him so near me; but I wouldn't look at him—no! I'd have died first!' "), and one comes away with the feeling of having read a writer deeply aware of the inevitable mix of love and rivalry in the fraternal relation.

Gansevoort Melville left behind a burden of debt that pushed the family back into what Herman called "exceedingly embarrassed circumstances"—so close to insolvency, in fact, that covering the funeral expenses proved a strain for his survivors. Though Allan Junior was now the family's best financial hope, Herman tried to help by building on the success of *Typee*. In 1846, he was often in New York, cultivating literary contacts that Gansevoort had made for him and negotiating directly with prospective publishers of *Omoo,* the book he was working on from spring through the end of the year (he had gotten fed up with Wiley's tampering, and signed a contract with Harper & Brothers in December), in which he carried on the tale of his adventures through his time in Hawaii and Tahiti. When *Omoo* appeared in the spring of 1847 under the Harper & Brothers imprint, the critics divided again between praising and scolding. The *Sunday Times & Noah's Weekly Messenger* greeted *Omoo* as the work of the "De Foe of America," while Horace Greeley, in the *Tribune,* objected to its "racy lightness." Whatever the verdict, Melville had become a figure on the New York literary scene, and by the summer of 1847 he and his bride-to-be had decided to settle there.

In the months leading up to the wedding, Melville traveled the triangle between Lansingburgh (according to Maria, he was "restless and . . . lonely here without his intended"), Boston, where Lizzie busied herself with wedding preparations, and New York, where he and Allan (also recently engaged) planned to set up house together with their wives, two sisters, and, inevitably, their mother. Already at work on a new book, *Mardi, and a Voyage Thither,* which he was soon to describe as "continued from, tho' wholly independent of, *Omoo,*" Herman was now the senior Melville male. He was also a young man enjoying literary celebrity and looking forward to a stylish marriage.

On August 4, 1847, Herman Melville and Elizabeth Shaw were married in Boston, in a ceremony attended by troops of Beacon Hill worthies. The groom's fame was sufficient to merit an unconventional wedding notice in one New York newspaper, the *Daily Tribune,* on August 7:

BREACH OF PROMISE SUIT EXPECTED—Mr. HERMAN *TYPEE OMOO* MELVILLE has recently been united in lawful wedlock to a young lady of Boston. The fair forsaken FAYAWAY will doubtless console herself by sueing him for breach of promise.

*Elizabeth Shaw
Melville, c. 1847*

During their honeymoon trip, Lizzie discovered that she liked the French
sophistication of Montreal—a good sign for her capacity to adjust to life in
New York, which, remarkably enough, she had never visited, even briefly. In
October the four newlyweds, having pooled their resources (Allan's bride,
Sophia Thurston, came from a well-to-do family), moved into a house on
Fourth Avenue just behind Grace Church. With his New England affilia-
tions and Beacon Hill wife, Melville was still "half Bostonian" at a time when
the *Independent* newspaper, taking account of the number of New England
émigrés in town, described New York as "the capital of the universal Yankee
nation." According to Charles Briggs, who had spent his childhood on Nantucket, so many New Yorkers came originally from out of town that "it somehow or other happens that you rarely meet with a New Yorker born." Among
the city's literary lights, Willis came from Maine; Bryant (editor, since 1829,
of the *Evening Post*) from western Massachusetts; Greeley and his managing
editor at the *Tribune,* Charles A. Dana, from New Hampshire; and that flam-
boyant Virginian Edgar Allan Poe, Briggs's colleague at the *Broadway Journal,* had been born in Boston. (Like many New Yorkers, Poe was, as Yvor
Winters called him, a man "without a background.") Then as now, life in
New York was about forgetting the past and inventing the future.

Even before Melville took up full-time residence, the city had begun to
affect his tone. If *Typee* had a certain primness, the voice in *Omoo* moves
away from the family fireside and closer to barroom banter—especially when
he gets around to his old subject of sexually precocious girls. In body and

spirit, "the soft, plump" girls of *Omoo* are city girls of the sort whom Willis approved—not *"fleshy . . . exactly . . .* but large and full," and fulsomely frank. Consider one particularly instructive beauty, who while "dallying with her grass fan" is eager to help the young visitor improve his "knowledge of Tahitian." When asked if she is "mickonaree"—that is, converted to Christianity by missionaries—she laughs with confidential glee and points to her genitals, provoking Melville to recall a couplet from Pope's *Epistle to a Lady:*

> *A sad good Christian at the heart—*
> *A very heathen in the carnal part.*

This is a South Seas version of what Melville encountered in New York—not just the "Kates" romping on Broadway, but streetwalkers of the sort he was later to sketch in *Pierre,* standing by night in the "cross-lights of a druggist's window . . . a figure all natural grace but unnatural vivacity . . . horribly lit by the green and yellow rays" of the gaslight. Sex in *Typee* had been an innocent pleasure. In *Omoo,* it is a transaction.

3.

After settling in the city in the fall of 1847, Melville was to go on over the next two and a half years to write most of *Mardi,* all of *Redburn* and *White-Jacket,* and, in the early weeks of 1850, the first chapters of the book that was to become *Moby-Dick.* The New York literary scene that he joined was presided over by a pair of native-born brothers, Evert and George Duyckinck, who, like Melville's family on the Gansevoort side, were descended from old Dutch stock. Both Duyckincks were "very clerical looking," according to Whitman ("thin—wanting in body: men of truly proper style. God help 'em!"), but they made up in spark and savvy for what they lacked in body. In 1840, when *The Democratic Review* moved to New York from Washington, D.C., Evert became its literary editor, and over the next twenty-five years he edited, and sometimes bankrolled, a host of magazines, including the highbrow *Arcturus* (in *Mardi,* Melville named his ship *Arcturion,* and complained about the low literary level of its crew: "Ay, ay, *Arcturion!* thou wast exceedingly dull"), the broadly satiric *Yankee Doodle,* and the mass-market *Holden's Dollar Magazine.* Duyckinck's most significant venture was the weekly *Literary World,* to which Melville contributed reviews

Evert Duyckinck

and for which Duyckinck himself wrote a column, "The City Desk," that (along with Lewis Gaylord Clark's "The Editor's Table" in the rival *Knicker-bocker Magazine*) is recognizable as a forerunner of "Talk of the Town" in today's *New Yorker.*

Not yet thirty in 1846 when he first met the twenty-seven-year-old Melville, Evert Duyckinck was also the editor of Putnam's "Library of American Books" in which *Typee* had appeared. Though he, too, had doubts about the young author's veracity, he recognized Melville's talent and made an effort to promote him. A master at setting up raves for his friends and getting his enemies panned, he sent copies of *Typee* to Hawthorne and Simms and also arranged for the first chapter to run in the *Mirror.* Like many literary patrons before and since, Duyckinck and his younger brother George were dabblers—"elegant inutilities," one friend called them—with money and time to waste. Credited by no less an authority than James Russell Lowell with maintaining "the soul of a gentleman" through the rough-and-tumble of America's Grub Street, Duyckinck turned his house at 20 Clinton Street into New York's leading literary salon and made his extensive book collection available as a kind of lending library to friends, including Melville.

But if Duyckinck was adept at what Briggs called "the art of puffing," he was hardly the only player in town. Each of the new magazines had an aggressive editor who built up his own coterie of writers, who in turn made mutual genuflections in the pages of whatever journal was paying them at the moment. With the reading public expanding, editors were hungry for fresh material and willing to pay for it; but a young writer's aim was not so much the pay as the exposure, which he imagined might help the reception of his next book and, when that day of which every author dreams finally comes, turn into money.

Melville never quite threw himself into the fray. Even when his talent was budding and he was trying to sell himself, he stood in uneasy relation to the backscratchers and backbiters with whom he waited in line. In 1846, Poe described the literary scene in a merciless essay called "The Literati of New York City," published in a Philadelphia magazine whose readers could be expected to appreciate the attack on their rival city to the north. (There is no evidence that Melville and Poe ever met, though Melville was later to model a character after Poe in *The Confidence-Man.*) Poe understood that sheer bulldoggishness could get a tin-eared versifier or a humorless humorist published and noticed:

> The most "popular," the most "successful" writers among us, (for a brief period, at least,) are ninety-nine times out of a hundred, persons of mere address, perserverance, effrontery—in a word, busy-bodies, toadies, quacks. These people easily succeed in *boring* editors (whose attention is too often entirely engrossed by politics or other "business" matter) into the admission of favourable notices written or caused to be written by interested parties—or, at least, into the admission of *some* notice where, under ordinary circumstances, *no* notice would be given at all. In this way ephemeral "reputations" are manufactured which, for the most part, serve all the purposes designed—that is to say, the putting money into the purse of the quack and the quack's publisher; for there never was a quack who could be brought to comprehend the value of mere fame. Now, men of genius will not resort to these man-oeuvres, because genius involves in its very essence a scorn of chi-canery: and thus for a time the quacks always get the advantage of them, both in respect to pecuniary profit and what *appears* to be pub-lic esteem.

Melville was not immune to the blandishments of flattering editors, and his own contempt for the literati, though it eventually exceeded Poe's, was in part directed at himself. In *Pierre,* whose title character becomes a bad writer combining the swagger of Byron with the self-pity of Goethe's young Werther, he looked back to these New York years and, in recognizing how limited his achievement had been in *Typee* and *Omoo,* captured the absurdity of it all: "From the proprietors of the Magazines whose pages were honored by his effusions, [Pierre] received very pressing epistolary solicitations for the loan of his portrait in oil, in order to take an engraving therefrom, for a frontispiece to their periodicals." There was an allusion here to the Duyckincks' request for Melville's daguerreotype after they had acquired *Holden's Dollar Magazine.*

In retrospect, Melville's "petitioning and remonstrating literary friends" seemed to him men of small minds and large egos, their talent outstripped by their ambition. Yet for a time they were his exemplars and guides, from whom he learned that to live in New York was to live on the edge, as much for the sake of the risks as in spite of them. To succeed as a writer, you had to be able to look an editor in the eye and to accept a deadline that you know you will miss; and you had to have the gumption, when he comes back in anger to berate you, to laugh him off. The city, largely rebuilt since the "widespread and disastrous" fire of 1835 (as Melville describes it in *Pierre*), was no longer the same place through which Melville had walked with his father as a child. Yet in coming back to New York, he had returned in all essentials to his father's world—a place where a man's most valuable assets were the calm with which he made his promises and the charm with which he broke them.

4.

In and beyond New York, the Duyckinck circle was coming to be known as "Young America"—a term that had been in circulation for years ("If there is *la jeune France*," James Fenimore Cooper had declared in 1838, "there is also *la jeune Amérique*"), but that had lately become affixed in particular to the Duyckincks and their friends. They were proud, raw, and strident, less cerebral than the "transcendentalists" of New England and more comfortable with the populist rhetoric of the Democratic Party with which Gansevoort had become associated during the '44 campaign. "Young America" was a national movement, of which the New York branch was loudest and largest, made up of brooders and glib talkers, ideologues and idealists; some were green, others were seasoned, but all had a scrappy, streetfighter style, and could be counted on to blow up in indignation on behalf of their friends and to stoop to name-calling when provoked by their enemies. In a city that had become a "world capital of invective," they were short on niceties and long on insults. When Greeley attacked the *New York Herald* in 1841 as a scurrilous rag (which it was), the editor of the *Herald,* James Gordon Bennett, replied by calling him, in print, "Horace Greeley, BA and ASS," adding for good measure that one could "galvanize a New England squash, and it would make as capable an editor as Horace." One observer wrote that "the only way of securing exemption from [Bennett's] attacks" was "to advertise largely in the paper . . . or to send the editor presents in money or other direct bribes."

Bennett may have set the standard for vulgarity, but his was a difference in degree rather than kind. Another New York editor gleefully described the leading journal of New England, the *North American Review,* as a spittoon for over-the-hill Bostonians, a "superannuated dust-box into which old fogydom expectorates freely," and even the relatively genteel Duyckincks regarded Boston as a "country town of litterateurs and blue-stockings." Evert was delighted when he heard about a New York doctor who lost his temper with a patient afflicted with chronic bad breath and—presumably working on the homeopathic principle—advised him with New York bluntness to "Eat sh—t."

But there was another side—a "soft-focus" side, we might call it—to the local scene in which, by the late 1840s, Melville had become a presence. The same literary culture that produced Willis's bawdy sketches had also produced, as recently as 1830, such treacle as George Pope Morris's ballad "Woodman, Spare That Tree!" ("Touch not a single bough! / In youth it sheltered me, / And I'll protect it now") and, a little earlier, John Howard Payne's "Home, Sweet Home," a song that eventually migrated from his forgotten opera, *Clari, or, the Maid of Milan* (1823), into the collective American unconscious, from which it periodically erupts, as when Judy Garland clicks together her magic slippers in *The Wizard of Oz:* "'Mid pleasures and palaces though we may roam, / Be it ever so humble, there's no place like Home!" Such sentimental effusions were produced by would-be patrician authors nostalgic for a bygone era when people knew to which class they belonged and were, supposedly, content to stay there. This sort of thing was a protest against the fast pace, social mixing, and, in general, what we would call the *edge* of urban life. It was led by Washington Irving and his fellow "Knickerbockers"—writers who described a softer, gentler world that existed, of course, mainly in their imaginations, and who wrote with a fairy-tale charm that gave some of their writings an afterlife as children's stories (of which "Rip Van Winkle" has proven the longest-lasting).

By the time Melville joined the New York literati, most regarded it as a sin to be sappy or solemn or without a ready quip—a fact that James Russell Lowell turned into a rhyming couplet when he wrote of Briggs, "He's in joke half the time when he seems to be sternest / When he seems to be joking, be sure he's in earnest." Remarking on the New York impatience with anything prissy or provincial, Lowell pointed out to Briggs in 1844 that "You

Gothamites strain hard to attain a metropolitan character, but I think if you *felt* very metropolitan you would not be showing it on all occasions." Lowell was on to something. As their city outstripped its American rivals, New Yorkers were turning in a spirit of competitive emulation toward metropolitan Europe. This was not new. What was new was that by the 1840s New York had become a credible competitor.

Among those who had foreseen the ascent was Melville's father. Long before the rise of Young America, when Maria was pregnant with their second child in the winter of 1819, Allan Melvill had written with local pride to his Boston friend Lemuel Shaw that "New York the empress queen of this vast continent . . . will most unquestionably before the close of the present century, equal London in arms, commerce & population." It was a good prediction. By the time his son Herman moved to New York twenty-eight years later, the demand for European fashions had grown exponentially, as had the demand for "European style" restaurants complete with tablecloths and menus—places that seated customers at private tables and cooked meals to order rather than putting out a dish or two at communal tables at advertised times. Opera and gambling were regular features of New York nightlife, and the same shops that sold libretti for the evening's performance displayed lottery tickets in their windows. Reputable gentlemen openly kept mistresses, a "French" innovation to which American wives were not always reconciled, as in the notorious case of Mrs. Charles Astor Bristed, who broke up her husband's Parisian-style menage when she "clapper-clawed" her rival in public.

As life in New York became self-consciously sophisticated—a contradiction in terms, as Lowell was right to point out—its pace accelerated to something like what we know today. In 1851, one observer posted himself in front of City Hall in order to estimate the number of vehicles that passed by, and within an hour he counted more than twelve hundred. The noise level rose to what seemed to nineteenth-century ears a terrible din: the perpetual *clip-clop* of iron-shod horses on stone block, the whistle of steamboats running the ferry routes between Manhattan, Brooklyn, and New Jersey, the scrape and clang of rail trolleys equipped with bells and bellowing drivers, the rattle of carriages bumping over cobblestone. "A more ingenious contrivance for driving men mad through sheer noise was undoubtedly never invented," said Poe, himself a connoisseur of madness. Above the transit noise soared the ubiquitous newsboy's voice not yet deepened by puberty, rising "high above the city's din" with news of "accidents and casualties . . . and the murderous barbarities of savages, which were never perpetrated, except in his own teeming fancy." And then there were the hollering pushcart peddlers, each with his own style of navigating the crowded streets—some patient and careful, some reckless and careening—and the barkers in the fishmarkets, who "made considerable noise" in trying to pawn off "refuse pieces of stale halibut" on gullible shoppers.

Near the markets, and around the food stalls along the avenues, good odors—the aroma of smoked and fried eel still "with heads and skins on," as well as "tripe, pigs' feet, plates of boiled lobsters, crabs, and other delicacies" favored by the business-lunch crowd—competed with the stench of manure and rotting garbage. The rising level of filth was fast catching up with that of Europe's notorious slum cities, whose inhabitants, as Friedrich Engels wrote of Manchester in 1844, could not enter or leave their outside privies without "wading through puddles of stale urine and excrement." In the 1840s, horses were everywhere in New York and pigs still ran loose on Sixth Avenue, so the streets were coated by "mud" made of animal droppings mixed with rainwater; without a sewage system, the city was literally flowing with both animal and human shit.

No wonder, then, that when the "mud" dried in the sun, New Yorkers, as Briggs described them in his 1839 novel *The Adventures of Harry Franco,* "hurried through the streets, wrapped in their cloaks, and their hats drawn tightly over their eyes, and their heads bowed down to keep the dust out of their faces, as it met them in spiral eddies at the corners of the avenues." Shop doors were shut tight, and on the horse-drawn trolleys the boys whose job it was to open and close the doors kept their hands in their pockets, unwilling to let in blasts of fecal dirt.

When Melville relocated himself to this "babylonish brick-kiln" of a city, its tempo was already in his pulse. Ever since he had wandered out as a boy onto Broadway, the sound and sight of revelers had been "as natural" to him, as Lewis Mumford put it, "as the sound of rain or the play of sunlight." In New York, Mumford observed, Melville "simply could not forget the wideness of the world." Its human variety stirred him. It was already the city in which, as F. Scott Fitzgerald was to write some seventy-five years later, one feels the "satisfaction that the constant flicker of men and women and machines gives to the restless eye." Melville savored his childhood memories of watching belles and dandies stroll along the Battery and, hand in hand with his father, witnessing veterans of the Revolutionary War march by in full regimentals, or free blacks celebrate the African American festival "Pinkster's Day" in gold-edged scarves and bright bandannas. Years later, he caught the spectacle of the city in nautical analogies that registered a sense of freedom akin to what he had felt at sea—as when he wrote, in "Bartleby," of the "bright silks and sparkling faces . . . in gala trim, swan-like sailing down the Mississippi of Broadway."

By the late 1840s, New York had established itself as *the* American city,

New York Street Scene, Harper's Weekly, *1859*

a magnet not only for intellectuals and entrepreneurs but also for upcountry farmboys looking for work, and the greenhorn theme was already a motif in New York novels and stories. (Although his origin is never made clear, Melville's most memorable urban character, Bartleby, has the "pallidly neat, pitiably respectable" demeanor of an out-of-towner.) The originating book was Briggs's *Harry Franco,* which retold the ancient tale of young-man-comes-to-big-city-and-gets-fleeced. One of the most popular novels of its day, it included scenes that Melville likely had in mind while working, in 1852, on the New York chapters of *Pierre.* Harry's father sends him off with a pep talk: remember, he tells the boy as he leaves the family farm, that "men are but men, and there is no station whatever can make more of them." But it does not take long before the big-city sharks and schemers, Mr. Dooitt, Mr. Slobber, Mr. Bargin, and the portly Miss Rippletrump—like everyone else Briggs had been reading Dickens's *Pickwick Papers*—put this democratic faith to the test. Everyone in town seems to be out to extract something for nothing from the country rube, and they usually do.

With the influx of immigrants both domestic and foreign, housing grew scarce and dear, and boarders in the cheaper rooming houses were sometimes forced to live five or six to a room. Between 1840 and 1850, the number of residents in the city shot up from 400,000 to nearly 700,000, and though there were large open tracts north of Fourteenth Street, most New Yorkers still clustered at the southern tip of Manhattan, where they felt themselves living in a city of "crowded hotels, crowded streets, hot summers," as the landscape architect Andrew Downing put it in 1851. "Where is the quiet reverse side of this picture of town life?" Downing wondered, dreaming of "a green oasis for the refreshment of the city's soul and body"—an oasis that came into being a few years later when his student Frederick Law Olmsted designed and, by a political miracle not duplicated since, actually built a great public park north of Fifty-ninth Street.

When Melville came to town, it had as yet no "reverse side." It felt cramped and crammed—a mood he was to evoke in the opening pages of *Moby-Dick* (published in the same year as Downing's plea for air), where he writes of "crowds, pacing straight for the water, and seemingly bound for a dive," with their faces set toward the open sea and their backs to the "insular city." When the old Trinity Church was torn down in 1839 to make room for a larger church building, one New Yorker savored the break in the wall of buildings that allowed, for a few months, "an unobstructed view of the bright blue Western sky,—the only bright prospect left for the thousands who daily visit that street." In "Bartleby," when Melville described a law office separated from the adjacent building by an air shaft three feet wide, he was noting a fact of life as true for many New Yorkers then as it is for most New Yorkers now.

5.

Among the striking aspects of New York life has always been the proximity of poverty and wealth. In 1840, the horse pulling a rich man's carriage down Broadway could expect to sleep that night in better quarters than the man who knocks on the carriage door begging for a coin. Many of the poor were young. Of the city's roughly 600,000 inhabitants in 1845, nearly a third were children under the age of fifteen. Those lucky enough to have something like a real childhood could be seen trotting beside open gutters down which they guided toy boats made of folded paper or nutshells—anything that would float in the filthy water.* Others were orphans or vagrants working as ped-

---

*In such recent representations of antebellum New York as Kevin Baker's novel *Paradise Alley* (2001) or Martin Scorsese's film *Gangs of New York* (2002), we get a vision of a city where the gutters run not so much with water as with blood.

dlers, messengers, newspaper hawkers, or else petty criminals and prostitutes. By midcentury, New York's "Five Points" neighborhood, a cluster of
swampy alleys and rat-infested buildings near today's Foley Square and
Chinatown, was the most famous slum in the nation, if not the world. "The
gorgeous rainbow that spans the whirling torrent of metropolitan life," Greeley wrote on Christmas Day, 1845, "rests its base on . . . dark depths of misery and crime."

It has always been possible in New York to avert one's eyes from the
"dark depths," but when Melville lived there the screen that divided rich
from poor was wearing thin. Unofficial boundary lines broke up the city into
crazy-quilt patterns of rich neighborhoods bordering on poor ones, with no
transition or buffer between them. Fashionable shops illuminated by gaslight
gave some neighborhoods the luminous enchantment of Paris by night,
while a block or two away the only interruptions in the darkness were
smudgy spots of light from oil lamps.

Under these conditions, it was common for proper New Yorkers, as Margaret Fuller wrote in the *Tribune,* to "creep into a safe retreat, arrogantly to
judge, or heartlessly to forget, the others." Every crowd seemed potentially a
mob. Periodic outbreaks of cholera were blamed on the mainly Irish immigrants, who were widely held responsible for the squalor in which they lived.
As early as the 1820s, there were complaints about "worthless foreigners, disgorged upon our shores," as if the Old World were excreting its waste into the
New World, and broad agreement that "the inmates of [Europe's] Alms-
Houses . . . land as paupers, live as paupers, and have no ambition to live in
any other way." In 1844, even before the nativist and anti-Catholic "Know-
Nothing" Party emerged as a force in national politics, New Yorkers elected a
mayor who ran on the platform of "No Irish Need Apply," and everyone
blamed immigrants for the rising incidence of street crime. According to the
New England reformer Lydia Maria Child, who had moved to the city in 1841,
New York was "a sort of common sewer for the filth of nations." Later, in *Redburn,* Melville was to write about this human "filth"—in this case German—
just before it spilled ashore: "old men, tottering with age and little infants in
arms; laughing girls in bright-buttoned bodices, and astute, middle-aged
men with pictured pipes in their mouths," who, while at sea, sang "the songs
of Zion to the roll of the great ocean-organ."

When Melville moved to this increasingly immigrant city, the United
States was just entering its "take-off" stage,* and New York was the best

---

*The economist Walt Rostow, who coined that term and identified 1844 as the "take-off" year, was
named after that ultimate New York booster Walt Whitman.

place to feel the power of the young nation coiled for release. Yet beneath the ebullience was a sense of foreboding that the social problems accompanying industrialization—worker unrest, disease born of unsanitary conditions, predatory crime among the poor—were heading for America like a toxic cloud drifting in from Europe. Newspaper editors sent fast schooners to meet incoming ships miles out at sea in order to bring back the latest news from Paris or London ahead of the competition. By the late 1840s, the news was of socialist dreams, utopian experiments in communal living, and heady visions of a new international regime of democracy. Led by Giuseppe Mazzini, the Young Italy (*Giovine Italia*) movement sought to establish a Roman republic, and New Yorkers read about the struggle in the *Tribune*'s excited eyewitness letters from Greeley's European correspondent, Margaret Fuller (who, according to Elizabeth Barrett Browning, was "one of the out & out *Reds*"). By the late 1840s, the *Tribune* had become America's first truly international newspaper, featuring articles in translation from German and French sources, including a column on revolutionary events by a socialist sympathizer named Karl Marx.

By February 1848, the unrest had spread to France, and Europe seemed on the brink of conflagration. Mobs of workers and students in Paris tore up paving stones and pulled up trees in order to build barricades against the king's army. George Duyckinck, on a European tour, wrote to Evert that "every shop was shut . . . [and] doors, boards, carriages, whatever came to hand was pressed into the Barricade" by citizens "armed with rusty old swords, spits, hatchets and iron bars from the railings of the nearest church." Within weeks, Louis Philippe abdicated, and Austria and Germany had descended into civil war, while in England (where the French king sought refuge), four thousand policemen were deployed in battle-ready formation on the Thames bridges to keep mobs of jobless men at bay, as Queen Victoria and Prince Albert fled for safety to the Isle of Wight.

To the New York partisans of "Young America," what was happening in the Old World seemed a kind of backdraft from the New World—a democratic wind sweeping away the remnants of feudalism as humankind embraced the doctrine (as Melville was to call it in *Moby-Dick*) of "divine equality." Yet the prospect of political and social upheaval at home was growing as well. New technologies such as mechanized threshers were throwing agricultural workers out of work and swelling the flow of unskilled men to the cities even as the flow of immigrants across the Atlantic reached flood tide. By the mid-1840s, nearly half of New Yorkers were foreign-born, many living in wretched conditions, especially in winter, when frozen canals and sluggish ocean commerce reduced demand for packers and carters, leaving them no money for shelter just when they needed it most. In 1849, when Melville wrote in *Redburn* that "to be a born American citizen seems a guarantee against pauperism," he was writing wishfully.

As it became clear that this guarantee would not be honored, Young America came to believe that the only means of relieving the pressure of immigrants pouring into the city was to open the "safety-valve" of the frontier. Most of Melville's friends in the Duyckinck circle were both democratic idealists and avowed expansionists, but in the 1840s it became increasingly difficult to reconcile these two commitments. The first shock came in 1845, when the United States annexed the Republic of Texas by admitting it to the Union as a slave state. Already in 1844, when Gansevoort Melville had stumped for Polk, the strain between pro- and anti-slavery Democrats had grown severe, and Gansevoort tried to mediate between the anti-annexationist camp (still loyal to the venerable Martin Van Buren) and the Polk expansionists. At one point, the influential editor of the *Post,* William Cullen Bryant, proposed splitting the difference—secretly urging New York Democrats to vote for Polk but, in congressional contests, to support only candidates who opposed annexation. When fighting broke out in 1846 between the United States and Mexico over competing land claims, opposition to the war surged among anti-slavery northerners, both Whigs and Democrats, who opposed it as a ploy to enlarge the territory open to slavemasters. The battle cry of the Democratic Party, "Manifest Destiny," first used in *The Democratic Review* in 1845 by Duyckinck's friend John L. O'Sullivan, was coming to seem a pretext for an imperialist land grab.

Allowing for the imprecision of such analogies, it may be said that the political atmosphere in which Melville found himself during his New York years was a nineteenth-century preview of what twentieth-century Democrats were to experience in the 1960s. The Democrats of Melville's day, as well as progressive Whigs like Greeley, saw themselves as inheritors of Andrew Jackson's political struggle against that "class . . . who . . . hedge themselves round with exclusive privileges and elevate themselves at the expense of the great body of the people." Their literary program was populist and nationalist. They defined themselves as partisans of the New against the Old, of Youth against Age, of the Future against the Past. "Manifest Destiny" was their "New Frontier." ("Americanos! Conquerors! Marchers humanitarian!" Whitman wrote, trying to hold the ideas of conquest and liberation together in one poetic line.) But just as the Democrats of the 1960s saw the New Deal consensus weakened and ultimately destroyed by a war that drove them into bitterly opposed factions, Democrats of the 1840s split over the Mexican War, which exposed the dirty secret of the expansionist ideology— that it favored slavery. By the end of the decade, even as the editors of *The*

THE DEMOCRATIC FUNERAL OF 1848.

The Democratic Funeral of 1848. *Calhoun, wearing an iron collar labeled "Slavery,"
is at center carrying the stretcher bearing the bodies of Martin Van Buren (as a fox)
and Lewis Cass (as a gas bag). The body of retiring President Polk is borne on the
second stretcher. Cartoon published by Abel & Durang, Philadelphia, 1848*

Democratic Review insisted that "slavery in the South will never break up our
glorious Union," everyone could see that the Jacksonian consensus was coming apart. Greeley, though nominally a Whig, shared the Democratic enthusi-
asm for expansion, and coined the phrase "Go West, young man"; but he
moved to the left on the issue of slavery and eventually became a critic of
President Lincoln for moving too slowly toward emancipation. O'Sullivan,
champion of "Manifest Destiny," drifted to the right and ended his career as
a Confederate sympathizer. A fissure was opening up between men who had
once stood together on the platform of Democracy.

In the summer of 1847, Melville fell into the breach. Duyckinck asked
him to write something for *Yankee Doodle* about the hero of the Mexican War,
General Zachary Taylor, and Melville complied with "Authentic Anecdotes
of Old Zack," a series of sketches that recounts Taylor's habit of slapping his
buttocks whenever he wants to emphasize a point (which was often), thus
wearing down "the seat in his ample pants" until they become almost thread-
bare. Knowing how thin the cloth has become, a drummer boy puts a tack in
Zack's saddle, expecting that when the General jumps off his horse with the
pin in his ass, everyone will blame the Mexicans. The "Old Zack" sketches
were the closest thing that Melville ever did to hackwork, and yet they waver
between affection and contempt—tonal incongruities that tell us something
about his growing political confusion. Like his friends in the Duyckinck cir-

cle, he was unable to reconcile the messianic vision of "Manifest Destiny" (as late as September 1847, Walt Whitman could still refer to the Mexican War as "the best kind of conquest") with the increasingly manifest fact that America was making the world safe not so much for democracy as for slavery. Writing some twenty years later in *Clarel* about the mixed motives of medieval Crusaders, Melville remained persuaded that "in that age," no less than in his own, "Belief devout and bandit rage / Frequent were conjoined."

6.

In the summer of 1847, newly married and settled in the house on Fourth Avenue, Melville put punditry aside and resumed his career as a writer of books. Determined to free himself from his lingering reputation as an author who passed off fiction as fact, he announced that this time he was writing a pure "romance" in order to "see whether, the fiction might not, possibly, be received for a verity; in some degree the reverse of my previous experience." The new book, *Mardi,* took shape in his mind as yet another tale of a young man (Taji) who jumps ship with a friend, but it quickly left realism behind and became a fantasy tour of its author's imagination. In a letter of March 1848 to John Murray, the English publisher who had brought out *Omoo,* Melville explained about his new work that "proceeding in my narrative of *facts* I began to feel an incurable distaste for the same; and a longing to plume my pinions for a flight, and felt irked, cramped and fettered by plodding along with dull commonplaces,—So suddenly abandoning the thing alltogether, I went to work heart and soul at a romance." Murray balked, adopting what Melville called an "Antarctic tenor" in his reply, and *Mardi,* with its "peculiar thoughts & fancies of a Yankee upon politics & other matters," was eventually published in London in March 1849 by Murray's rival, Richard Bentley. In April, Harper & Brothers brought it out in New York.

Taji's object of desire in *Mardi* is a beautiful maiden who hails from "the Island of Delights, somewhere in the paradisiacal archipelago," about whom Melville wrote as if she were a goddess in some Ovidian allegory of love:

> Her name was Yillah. And hardly had the waters of Oroolia washed white her olive skin, and tinged her hair with gold, when one day strolling in the woodlands, she was snared in the tendrils of a vine. Drawing her into its bowers, it gently transformed her into one of its

blossoms, leaving her conscious soul folded up in the transparent petals.

Here hung Yillah in a trance, the world without all tinged with the rosy hue of her prison. At length when her spirit was about to burst forth in the opening flower, the blossom was snapped from its stem; and borne by a soft wind to the sea; where it fell into the opening valve of a shell.

The rest of the story—double the length of any of Melville's previous books—is taken up with Taji's search through the watery world for Yillah, who tantalizes him with tokens of her presence; but the book ends without ending, as "pursuers and pursued flew on, over an endless sea."

What Melville produced in *Mardi* was a wildly miscellaneous mix of lyrical writing and metaphysical disquisitions (mostly uttered by a babbling philosopher well named Babbalanja), but by the spring and summer of 1848, when he was deep into the book, political events once again seized his attention. In mid-March, Evert Duyckinck wrote to George, who was still in Paris, that "a walk in Broadway to-day is a thing of excitement, the news of the Revolution in Paris having imparted to every one that vivacity of eye, quickness of intelligence and general exhilaration which great public events extend to private ones." To press the analogy between Melville's time and ours, one may say that 1848 was the 1968 for his generation—a year of worker-student alliances and revolutionary manifestos promising the advent of a new age. Everyone was swept up by the high hopes. "I am fairly en rapport with the Revolution," Evert announced to his brother when, in France, the poet-statesman Alphonse de Lamartine (a "wondrous" man "of physical and moral courage," according to Whitman) briefly led the Second Republic. Everywhere in Europe, autocratic governments were teetering, and some fell.

But by the early summer of 1848, reaction had set in and the restorationists were gaining the upper hand. In France, the "great whale the French revolution," as Duyckinck called it, was already in its death throes; the brief period of republican rule came to a bloody end in June when government troops fought pitched battles in the streets of Paris against workers armed chiefly with sticks and stones. By the time the smoke cleared, more than four thousand French citizens had died, and in the aftermath hundreds more were hunted down and shot without trial or sent to labor camps in Algeria. Within weeks, Lamartine was gone and the general who had quelled the uprisings had assumed dictatorial power. Looking back two decades later on these events, again in his retrospective poem *Clarel,* Melville was to write:

What if the Kings in Forty-Eight
Fled like the gods? Even as the gods
Shall do, return they made; and sate
And fortified their strong abodes.

In *Mardi,* these events show up in digressive excursions into such half-imaginary countries as "Dominora" (England), where workers march for their rights; "Franko" (France), where the fires of revolution are still flaring; and "Vivenza" (the United States), where bag-of-wind politicians try to talk the slavery issue to death. In 1847, when Melville had begun work on *Mardi,* calls for revolution were just beginning to be heard; by the time he finished it in the fall of 1848, reaction and restoration were at hand; and in December, Louis Napoleon ascended to the throne once held by his uncle Bonaparte. A few American observers, such as Charles A. Dana of the *New York Sun,* saw the failed radicals of Europe as heroes who had tried valiantly, if too soon, to extend political rights to all citizens. But most Americans, including Melville, took a "plague on both their houses" attitude toward what amounted to a European civil war. "Evil," he wrote in *Mardi,* "is the chronic malady of the universe, and checked in one place, breaks forth in another."

Under the pressure of events, Melville had veered again into politics, but the cycle of revolution and reaction finally seemed to him a faraway piece of theater, and in most of *Mardi* he directed his attention inward. This was, as the Jungian critic Henry Murray has written, the book in which he discovered the unconscious and explored (in Melville's words) "the world of mind; wherein the wanderer may gaze round, with more of wonder than Balboa's band roving through the golden Aztec glades." Melville learned in this book to accede to his reckless moods ("better to sink in boundless deeps, than float on vulgar shoals; and give me, ye Gods, an utter wreck, if wreck I do") and to follow his "radiant young" muse wherever she might take him:

> far to the South, past my Sicily suns and my vineyards, stretches the Antarctic barrier of ice: a China wall, built up from the sea, and nodding its frosted towers in the dun, clouded sky. Do Tartary and Siberia lie beyond? Deathful, desolate dominions those; bleak and wild the ocean, beating at that barrier's base, hovering 'twixt freezing and foaming; and freighted with navies of ice-bergs,—warring worlds crossing orbits; their long icicles, projecting like spears to the charge. Wide away stream the floes of drift ice, frozen cemeteries of skeletons and bones. White bears howl as they drift from their cubs; and the grinding islands crush the skulls of the peering seals.

Mardi was published almost simultaneously in London and New York to mixed notices, ranging from an article in *Blackwood's* that dismissed it as "rubbishing rhapsody" to a long, respectful review by a French critic that Duyckinck ran in translation in *The Literary World*. Melville later remarked to Duyckinck that his book had been "stabbed *at* (I do not say *through*)— & therefore, I am the wiser for it." To his credit, Duyckinck recognized *Mardi* as "an onward development" for a writer working now in a mood of honeymoon eagerness, driven on, as Melville said of himself, by a "blast resistless." "Like a frigate," he wrote, "I am full with a thousand souls; and as on, on, on, I scud before the wind, many mariners rush up from the orlop below, like miners from caves; running shouting across my decks."

In a letter to her stepmother written in December 1847, Lizzie conveyed the heady mood of these New York days, making as clear as decency would permit that she and her "industrious boy" took domestic but still flirtatious pleasure in each other as she managed the household while he threw himself into his writing:

> We breakfast at 8 o'clock, then Herman goes to walk, and I fly up to put his room to rights, so that he can sit down to his desk immediately on his return. Then I bid him good bye, with many charges to be an industrious boy and not upset the inkstand, and then flourish the duster, make the bed, etc., in my own room. Then I go downstairs and read the papers a little while, and after that I am ready to sit down to my work— whatever it may be—darning stockings—making or mending for myself or Herman—at all events I haven't seen a day yet, without *some* sewing or other to do. If I have letters to write, as is the case to-day, I usually do that first—but whatever I am about, I do not much more than get throughly engaged in it, than ding-dong goes the bell for luncheon. This is half past 12 o'clock—by this time we must expect callers, and so must be dressed immediately after lunch. Then Herman insists upon my taking a walk of an hour's length at least. So unless I can have rain or snow for an excuse, I usually sally out and make a pedestrian tour a mile or two down Broadway. By the time I come home it is two o'clock and after, and then I must make myself look as bewitchingly as possible to meet Herman at dinner. This being accomplished, I have only about an hour of available time left. At four we dine, and after dinner is over, Herman and I come up to our room and enjoy a cosy chat for an hour or so—or he reads me some of the chapters he has been writing in the day. Then he goes down town for a walk, looks at the papers in the reading room, etc., and returns about half-past seven or eight. Then my

*Elizabeth and
infant Malcolm,
c. 1850*

work or my book is laid aside, and as he does not use his eyes but very little by candle light, I either read to him, or take a hand at whist for his amusement, or he listens to our reading or conversation, as best pleases him. For we all collect in the parlour in the evening, and generally one of us reads aloud for the benefit of the whole. Then we retire very early—at 10 o'clock we all disperse.

To help buy his share of this house in which he spent his days writing with breaks for meals, walks, and whist, Melville had been offered a $2,000 gift by Lizzie's father. But having insisted on regarding the gift as a loan, he found himself worrying about money, and with "duns all round him . . . looking over the back of his chair," he recognized, as he said of a character in *Mardi,* "the necessity of bestirring himself to procure his yams." It took him eighteen months to write *Mardi*—a slow earnings pace, considering that the $500 advanced by Harper Brothers was not payable till the end of 1848, though the situation was helped when Bentley advanced 200 guineas, in March 1848, for the English edition.

When their first child, Malcolm, was born in February 1849, Herman and Lizzie were at her parents' home in Boston, and the new father wrote to Allan (to whom a child had also just been born) an oddly arch letter:

When old Zack heard of it—he is reported to have said—"Mark me: That boy will be President of the United States before he dies." . . .

> The harbor here is empty:—all the ships, brigs, schooners & smacks
> have scattered in all directions with the news for foreign parts . . .
> & . . . the Devil roared terribly bethinking him of the lusty foe to sin
> born into this sinful world.—

The author of this letter was a man in high spirits, but also a man with a
growing awareness of his responsibilities.

Soon after *Mardi* was published, he bestirred himself to work faster.
After dashing off some reviews for *The Literary World,* he composed his
next two books, *Redburn* and *White-Jacket,* in quick succession in the
spring and summer. Even before they appeared (in November 1849 and
March 1850), he was denigrating them to his father-in law as "two *jobs* which
I have done for money—being forced to it as other men are to sawing wood."
After reading a laudatory review of *Redburn,* he was even harsher in his journal: "I, the author, know [it] to be trash, & wrote it to buy some tobacco
with."

7.

In fact, by comparison to the windy ramble of *Mardi,* both *Redburn* and
White-Jacket were deft and well paced. For *Redburn,* Melville reverted to the
autobiographical and realist mode, recounting his first ocean crossing of ten
years earlier, followed by his experiences in the "pestilent lanes and alleys" of
Liverpool, which he found "very much such a place as New York," and in
London, where his "lady-like" friend Harry Bolton shows him around the
bordellos and gambling dens. Young Redburn, equipped with a guidebook
inherited from his father, and having "impressed every column and cornice
in my mind" from the book's illustrations, had hoped to retrace his father's
route via "priory or castle" around Merrie Olde England. But time has oblit-
erated the picturesque past; and while looking in vain for his father's world,
he discovers instead an unmapped world of cruelty and corruption.

In a chapter worthy of Carlyle or Dickens, Melville described Redburn's
encounter with a woman dying in the gutter with "two shrunken things like
children" enfolded in her "blue arms." Unused to such sights and ill-
prepared by his father's tourist guide, he stands transfixed as one of the children, too feeble to cry, lifts her head and whimpers while he rushes off for
help. Everywhere he turns he is rebuffed—by passersby, loiterers, ragpick-

ers, even policemen ("It's none of my business, Jack . . . I don't belong to
that street")—and all he can do is throw down some bread and cheese,
at which one of the girls "caught . . . convulsively" but lacked sufficient
strength to chew or swallow. For a moment, Redburn wonders if he has the
courage to commit a mercy killing to end their suffering. After further
attempts to find help, he returns to the spot, from which there now wafts the
smell of rotting corpses. Going off to inform a policeman, he comes back
once more to find that this time the authorities have taken action: mother
and children are gone, and on the spot where they died is a pile of lime.

With an infant mortality rate among the poor of nearly two in three, versus less than one in five for the rich, Liverpool was a blighted Old World
city, and by 1849 Melville knew that New York had become the portal
through which such miseries were entering the United States. He still clung
to the idea that for the likes of those he had seen dying in the Liverpool gutter, America ("not a Paradise then, or now; but to be made so, at God's good
pleasure, and in the fullness and mellowness of time") could furnish refuge.
He had imbibed from his New York friends a messianic idealism, though
within a few years, in a story entitled "Poor Man's Pudding and Rich Man's
Crumbs," he was to write that the poor in America "suffer more in mind
than the poor of any other people in the world" because of "the smarting
distinction between their ideal of universal equality and their grindstone
experience."

In the concluding chapters of *Redburn,* Melville looked back to his
experience of sailing home from Liverpool on a ship carrying hundreds of
Irish emigrants packed in steerage as if in "dog-kennels." While struggling to
stay alive on bits of sea biscuit, they were tormented by rumors that they
were going to be sold en route as slaves in Barbary. *Redburn* was Melville's
unflinching rendition of what might be called the prehistory of these newest
New Yorkers, who endured weeks at sea huddled "'tween decks," where
clearance was too low for a man of average height to stand upright. Many had
been coaxed aboard by traffickers who, after renting storage space aboard
ship, made big profits by charging as much as twenty-five dollars each; and
those who survived the extortion and shipboard conditions were met at the
New York pier by slumlord runners who brought them under threat to
boardinghouses where they were forced to pay exorbitant rents.

Before the exodus from the Irish famine was over, more than a quarter of
Ireland's population had died or fled, including a million people who
crossed the Atlantic. Lydia Child, who had moved to New York from Boston
in order to edit an abolitionist newspaper, did not extend her sympathies for
Negro slaves to these desperate emigrants, whom she likened to dogs. But
Melville was moved by them: he describes in *Redburn* the stunned joy of an

old man who, on a brief escape to the deck, watches porpoises leap in the sea, and terrified children begging their empty-handed mothers for bread, while adults with typhus are dragged behind a screen to die out of sight. Melville was touched by how, to these emigrants, "America must have seemed as a place just over a river. Every morning some of them came on deck, to see how much nearer we were: and one old man would stand for hours together, looking straight off from the bows, as if he expected to see New York city every minute, when, perhaps, we were yet two thousand miles distant, and steering, moreover, against a head wind." *Redburn* was a rebuke to the xenophobes: "Let us waive that agitated national topic, as to whether such multitudes of foreign poor should be landed on our American shores; let us waive it, with the one only thought, that if they can get there, they have God's right to come; though they bring all Ireland and her miseries with them."

Like the other books that Melville produced at Mozartean speed during his New York years, *Redburn* was a book of old maritime memories overlaid by new urban experiences. Whether he was writing about emigrants at sea or about the "elbowing, heartless-looking crowd" ashore, he had become an urban writer. New York introduced him to a paradox of modern life: that one depends for psychic survival on a combination of high alertness and willed insouciance. In New York, Melville learned that to live in the modern world meant to live both widely and narrowly—widely in the sense of cultivating a cosmopolitan awareness of human variety, but narrowly in the sense of shutting out the specter of human desperation that presses against the consciousness from all directions all the time.

8.

In the summer of 1849, with *Redburn* "going thro' the press," Melville remained in the city in order to go over the proofs and to get started on his next book, which he dispatched in the amazingly short span of two months. The second of his two "*jobs,*" *White-Jacket, or the World in a Man-of-War* was another paean on behalf of democracy, this time in the form of an embellished memoir of his fourteen months of naval service aboard the frigate *United States,* which he hopefully called the *Neversink. White-Jacket* was as loose and baggy as the garment for which it is named—the many-pocketed coat that signifies the narrator's puffed-up pride. In its pacing, the book was closer to *Mardi* than to *Redburn*—organized as a series of illustrative vignettes that oscillate between dignity and cruelty as the men of the ship rise at once to defend one another in the face of arbitrary power and then, at the next moment, take pleasure in the unmerited punishment of a fellow sailor.

The crew of the *Neversink* included a number of stalwart democrats, notably the large-hearted Jack Chase, who treats every man as if he were a nobleman, with "a polite, courteous way of saluting you, if it were only to borrow your knife," and the dignified old Ushant, the "Nestor of the crew," who rather than obey the captain's order to shave his beard submits to a flogging and spends his last days aboard in the brig. But for every such paragon of dignity there is an abusive beast, led by the captain himself, whose favorite sport is flogging. The theme of *White-Jacket* was the co-existence in one society—and sometimes in one man—of the worst and best human impulses. Recalling the giddy feeling of working high aloft in the rigging, Melville's narrator sees the dream of equality realized in the sight of small human figures working cooperatively on the deck far below; but coming face-to-face with the same men in the depths of the ship he discovers a festering ugliness, personified by a "Troglodite" Yeoman who, "immured all day in such a bottomless hole, among tarry old ropes," keeps watch over the ship's stores while casting "goggle-eyes" at young sailors.

The strongest writing in *White-Jacket* comes when Melville describes the sight of men mangled by the strap and recalls his memory of fearing that he would be flogged himself. Here, as the narrator is arraigned at the mast for an infraction he has not committed, the boatswain's mate stands "curling his fingers through the *cat*," waiting for the captain to give the order:

> The Captain stood on the weather-side of the deck. Sideways . . . was the opening of the lee-gangway, where the side ladders are suspended in port. Nothing but a slight of sinnate-stuff served to rail in this opening . . . and though he was a large, powerful man, it was certain that a sudden rush against him, along the slanting deck, would infallibly pitch him headforemost into the ocean.

Awaiting his stripes, the boy invokes nature as justification for pitching the captain overboard:

> I but swung to an instinct in me—the instinct diffused through all animated nature, the same that prompts even a worm to turn under the heel. Locking souls with him, I meant to drag Captain Claret from this

earthly tribunal of his to that of Jehovah. . . . Nature has not implanted any power in man that was not meant to be exercised at times, though too often our powers have been abused. The privilege, inborn and inalienable, that every man has, of dying himself, and inflicting death upon another, was not given to us without a purpose. These are the last resources of an insulted and unendurable existence.

Then an officer steps forward in the nick of time, and the exonerated boy is thereby spared the lash.

Flogging in the Navy was abolished by act of Congress shortly after Melville's book was published, but flogging was already a safe issue on which to call for reform.* Yet informing the flogging scenes in *White-Jacket* was the more contentious issue of slavery. No one in America could read in 1850 about people living "an insulted and unendurable existence" without thinking of slaves, though Melville touched the issue only gingerly, allowing it into his book as a whispered analogy. When he says that for a flogged sailor, "our Revolution was in vain" and "our Declaration of Independence . . . a lie," he was unwittingly anticipating the words of former slave Frederick Douglass, who in 1852 would ask, with mordant irony, "What, to the American slave, is your 4th of July?"

As he had done in *Redburn,* Melville wrote into *White-Jacket* a displaced commentary on an ominous American reality—poverty in the former case, slavery in the latter. In a harrowing chapter, "Fun in a Man-of-War"— which Ralph Ellison may have had in mind for the account of the "Battle Royal" in his *Invisible Man,* in which young black men beat each other senseless before a delighted white crowd—Melville described how white sailors take sadistic pleasure in watching black men knock heads. "*Head-bumping,*" he explains, "consists in two negroes . . . butting at each other like rams." When the two black men get overzealous and start to fight in earnest, the captain, for whom such performances are "an especial favorite," reminds them that "I . . . permit you to *play* [but] I will have no *fighting.*" Naturally, he follows up the reprimand by having them flogged.

---

*In September 1850, Congress enacted a law abolishing flogging, and during the debates leading up to its passage, one writer for *The National Era* urged that Melville's book "be placed in the hands of every member of Congress." There is no evidence, however, that this was done. See Howard P. Vincent, *The Tailoring of Melville's White-Jacket* (Evanston: Northwestern University Press, 1970), p. 4, and Myra C. Glenn, "The Naval Reform Campaign Against Flogging: A Case Study in Changing Attitudes Toward Corporal Punishment, 1830–1850," *American Quarterly* 35, no. 4 (Autumn 1983): 408–25.

9.

"I have swam through libraries," Melville was soon to write about these immensely productive New York years, by which he meant both Evert Duyckinck's personal library on Clinton Street and the New York Society Library (located then on Broadway between Leonard Street and Catherine Lane, and still in operation today on East Seventy-ninth Street), which he had joined as a shareholding member in January 1848. More and more, Melville's writing bore the marks of wide and eclectic reading, which included Montaigne, Defoe, Coleridge, Dante, Schiller, Thackeray, and Seneca, as well as those seventeenth-century prose masters Robert Burton and Thomas Browne; he referred to the last as a "crack'd Archangel."

In *Mardi*, his range of reference had vastly expanded over that of *Typee* and *Omoo:*

> Like a grand, ground swell, Homer's old organ rolls its vast volumes under the light frothy wave-crests of Anacreon and Hafiz; and high over my ocean, sweet Shakspeare soars, like all the larks of the spring. Throned on my sea-side, like Canute, bearded Ossian smites his hoar harp, wreathed with wild-flowers, in which warble my Wallers; blind Milton sings bass to my Petrarchs and Priors, and laureats crown me with bays.

And for *White-Jacket* Melville pillaged many sea-voyaging tales, among them an obscure volume called *A Mariner's Sketches,* by Nathaniel Ames, in which he found a frightening account of a sailor's fall from the yardarm into the sea. He turned that passage into a near-death experience in which, tumbling toward unconsciousness, the narrator feels "soul-becalmed" until "of a sudden some fashionless form brushed my side—some inert, coiled fish of the sea" that shocks him back to life. Having reversed his fall and ascended to the surface just before he would have inhaled the fatal water, the sailor finds himself weighed down by the "placental" jacket until he rips it "up and down, as if I were ripping open myself."

While in the Pacific, Melville had never fallen from a mast—but in the oceanic city of New York he experienced just such a breakout into freedom. It was in this "metropolitan magnificence" that he divested himself of his last vestiges of pride and pretense, and it was here that his writing took on what Warner Berthoff has called its "distinct and original signature suggestive of some whole new apprehension." One feels the new style emerging in *Omoo,* and by the time of *Mardi* Melville had acquired an emphatic New York voice—as in this riff (spoken by Babbalanja) on the theme of smoking, in which pipes turn into symbols of fidelity and cigarettes into signs of mortality:

> Like a good wife, a pipe is a friend and companion for life. And whoso weds with a pipe, is no longer a bachelor. After many vexations, he may go home to that faithful counselor, and ever find it full of kind consolations and suggestions. But not thus with cigars or cigarrets: the acquaintances of a moment, chatted with in by-places, whenever they come handy; their existence so fugitive, uncertain, unsatisfactory. Once ignited, nothing like longevity pertains to them. They never grow old. . . . The stump of a cigarret is an abomination; and two of them crossed are more of a *memento-mori,* than a brace of thigh-bones at right angles.

The pipe is wife or friend, the cigarette a passerby, messenger in a hurry, or one-night whore; the passage catches the rhythm of a city in which "fugitive" chats occur a hundred times a day, where Melville moved between the "vexations" of the street and the comforts of his first post-bachelor home. Though not quite yet his mature voice, it has advanced far beyond what Charles Briggs or Cornelius Mathews or any of the established New York novelists of the day could do. Melville does not exactly write *about* the city, but the patter of images has the city's pulse and moves toward the rambling anthological prose of *Moby-Dick.*

In *The Confidence-Man,* written some six years after he left New York, Melville asked, and answered, a salient question: "Where does any novelist pick up any character? For the most part, in town, to be sure. Every great town is a kind of man-show, where the novelist goes for his stock, just as the agriculturalist goes to the cattle-show for his." This claim may seem odd coming from a writer in whose fiction—except for Harry Bolton in *Redburn,* and a handful of characters in *Pierre,* "Bartleby," and such minor stories as "Jimmy Rose"—the urban population is notably low. Yet it was not so much on Melville's plots or characters or settings that New York left its mark as in the nerve and sinew of his prose. It was here that he fulfilled Tocqueville's prediction that when America came of age, its literature would be "fantastic, incorrect, overburdened . . . loose . . . vehement and bold"; here that he moved through vehemence ("fire flames on my tongue") toward a kind of ecstatic blasphemy. His plethoric tables of contents (*Mardi* has 195 chapters,

White-Jacket 93, and *Moby-Dick* 135 plus the Etymology, Extracts, and Epilogue) look strikingly like those of the city magazines he was reading and for which he occasionally wrote. Here is an alphabetical sampling of articles in the 1847 issue of *Yankee Doodle* that ran one of Melville's "Old Zack" sketches:

An Amazed Author
The Battle of the Frogs and Mice
Cruelty to Seamen
Drawing the Line
Freeks of Feeling
Great Shakes
Highly Important
"I Drunk!"
New Melody
Poetry for the Million
Scenes in our Sanctum
Skeleton Found
Slang
Who asked you?
Zeal out running Discretion

And here is a sampling of chapter titles from *Moby-Dick,* which Melville began writing while in New York:

Loomings
Chowder
Merry Christmas
The Whiteness of the Whale
Hark!
The Hyena
Monstrous Pictures of Whales
Less Erroneous Pictures of Whales
Of Whales, in Paint, in Teeth, &c.
The Whale as a Dish
The Pequod Meets the Jeroboam. Her Story
Measurement of the Whale's Skeleton

Before his move to New York, Melville's prose had stayed pretty much within the limits of conventional narrative; but as he immersed himself in the city, his books became eclectic miscellanies, with innumerable tangents spoking out from the spine of the story, each one reaching for some new analogy that diverts our attention to some novel sensation, or topic, or fact. The city itself was a circulating collection of newspapers, leaflets, business cards, broadsides, tabloids, placards, magazines, banners, hired men walking the streets in sandwich boards, signs affixed to carriages (the nineteenth-century equivalent, as one historian has remarked, of bumper stickers), and Melville swam with pleasure through this outdoor collection en route to the indoor reading rooms where he went for more traditional literary plunder.

Moving clause by clause through Melville's New York prose is like strolling, or browsing, on a city street: each turn of phrase brings a fresh association; sometimes we are brought up short by a startling image requiring close inspection; sometimes a rush of images flickers by; but there is always the feeling of quickened pulse, of some unpredictable excitement, in aftermath or anticipation. And if New York broke open Melville's style, it opened his mind as well to the cosmopolitan idea of a nation to which one belongs not by virtue of some blood lineage that leads back into the past, but by consent to the as-yet-unrealized ideal of a nation comprehending all peoples ("our blood is as the flood of the Amazon," he wrote in *Redburn,* "made up of a thousand noble currents all pouring into one") in a future of universal freedom. New York was the birthplace of Melville's democratic imagination—both in substance and style.

With the exception of family trips upstate and to Boston, Melville was relatively stationary during the three years that he lived in New York, from

The Bill-Poster's Dream,
lithograph by B. Derby, 1862

the summer of 1847 till the summer of 1850. One extended absence was a four months' journey to London and the Continent in the fall and winter of 1849–50, undertaken mainly for the purpose of placing *White-Jacket* with an English publisher. He had become, by then, a city creature. In his London diary, we get a glimpse of his "vagabonding thro' the courts & lanes" (including the red-light districts), book buying, bar-hopping, theater- and museum-going, a man at ease with every aspect of urban life from the private gentlemen's clubs to the spectacle of a public execution. "The mob was brutish," he wrote in his journal about the howling crowd at a public hanging. (Charles Dickens was present, too, though the two men were unaware of each other.) These city years had deepened the ambivalence he had acquired at sea toward what he later called "ruthless democracy." In New York, in May 1849, when an anti-British mob attacked the theater at Astor Place to show their contempt for the English actor William Macready, Melville could hear from his house the roar of the crowd and the gunfire from troops called in to quell the rioting. It was an experience that chastened him and, as the scholar Dennis Berthold has cogently written, left him "struggling to understand . . . a world where . . . working-class people opposed abolitionism, immigration, and foreign culture, and where state militias murdered citizens," and thereby further estranged him from "unreflective nationalism." The energy of the city now felt but one step removed from anarchy, and the faraway revolutions of Europe seemed close to home.

Yet Melville is not usually thought of as an urban writer. He tends to be left out of discussions of the "New York School" in American writing—in which declamatory writers such as Whitman and Allen Ginsberg take up their places along with salon writers from Washington Irving to Calvin Trillin, whose cocktail-hour wit suits the small format of the New York magazine sketch. There has never been, however, an American writer more deeply affected, indeed *in*fected, by the tone and rhythm of the city. "Herman by birth & from his residence in the city of New York," his sister Augusta wrote in 1857, "is known as a New Yorker; all his books are published in that city; all his interests are there. . . ." Duyckinck, on the other hand, thought him more at home "in the fields and in the study, looking out upon the mountain . . . [where] he finds congenial nourishment for his faculties, without looking much to cities." They were both right.

The city impressed itself indelibly upon Melville's imagination. It gave his writing a new form, or rather, it liberated him to experiment with formlessness. As the *New York Times* critic A. O. Scott wrote in an evocative piece ("With Ishmael in the Island City") published shortly after September 11, 2001, Melville's work is filled with that New York "feeling of loneliness in the midst of bustle." He understood, as Scott says, that while "viewed

objectively, our lives are small and inconsequential [and] our choices nuga-
tory . . . they never feel that way, and we struggle to comprehend the nature
of the bonds, random or providential, that tether us to history." A few years
after he had moved away from New York (temporarily, as it turned out),
Melville remembered the city as a vanity contest:

> In towns there is large rivalry in building tall houses. If one gentleman
> comes next door and builds five stories high, then the former, not to be
> looked down upon that way, immediately sends for his architect and
> claps a fifth and a sixth story on top of his previous four. And not till the
> gentleman has achieved his aspiration, not till he has stolen over the
> way by twilight and observed how his sixth story soars beyond his
> neighbor's fifth—not till then does he retire to his rest with satisfaction.

He concluded this reflection with a pastoral suggestion: "Such folks, it
seems to me, need mountains for neighbors, to take this emulous conceit of
soaring out of them." This is the Melville who put New York behind him by
moving in the summer of 1850 to the Berkshire hills. But it was in New York
that he had turned his own incipient hubris into the bold and brawling prose
equivalent of Whitman's "barbaric yawp." Melville experienced the great
city as every true New Yorker has always experienced it—with a combustible
combination of love and hate, out of which his major work was starting to
take form.

CHAPTER 5
HUNTING THE WHALE

1.

The first glimpse we get of Melville in the grip of his masterpiece comes in a letter to Richard Henry Dana, Jr., on May 1, 1850, declaring that he was "half way" into "a strange sort of book" about a whaling voyage. There was nothing especially original or arresting about this choice of subject, since storms at sea, shipwreck, mariners lost, harbors bristling with mast and sail were all common themes in art as well as in the writing of the day. These subjects, and whaling in particular, were familiar fare at a time when most people still lived on or near the coast and felt a certain intimacy with the "watery part of the world." Yet Melville's drive to break the boundaries of literary form reflected his sense that neither he nor anyone else had yet found a way to adequately describe it.

Searching for models in art as well as literature, he had roamed the picture galleries during his trip to London, visiting the Dulwich and Vernon collections, the newly established National Gallery, the royal collections at Hampton Court and Windsor Castle, and the vast private collection of Samuel Rogers. He had seen seascapes by Canaletto and Claude Lorrain, and was particularly drawn to those of J. M. W. Turner, in which he saw intimations of what, in *Moby-Dick*, he was to call the "howling infinite." Early in his new book he describes a painting of an indistinct sea scene, consisting of "unaccountable masses of shades and shadows," that seemed to him an effort "to delineate chaos" itself. When he described this fictional picture, he may have had in mind Turner's vertiginous paintings, which Hazlitt had aptly described as "pictures of nothing . . . representations not so properly of the objects of nature as of the medium through which they are seen." In one of the books that Melville consulted while composing *Moby-Dick*, Thomas Beale's *Natural History of the Sperm Whale*, he wrote on the title page this high compliment: "Turner's pictures of whalers were suggested by this book."

But if Melville found oceanic truth in Turner, he had not encountered anything comparable in words—not even in Dana's *Two Years Before the Mast*. In 1847, he had reviewed for Duyckinck's *Literary World* a memoir by a ship captain entitled *Etchings from a Whaling Cruise,* finding it long on "unvarnished facts" but short on "the poetry of salt water." Having already written five maritime books himself, he knew what a writer was up against in trying to bring the subject to life for landlocked readers. "Blubber is blubber you know," he wrote to Dana, "tho' you may get oil out of it, the poetry runs as hard as sap from a frozen maple tree;—& to cook the thing up, one must needs throw in a little fancy, which from the nature of the thing, must be ungainly as the gambols of the whales themselves." These early remarks about his new work-in-progress have a chipper lightness, as if he is getting ready to rattle off another yarn, trying this, discarding that, smoothing the kinks out; he gives no hint of being engaged in something of an altogether different order from anything he had attempted before. By speaking about the new book in a tone somewhere between modesty and self-denigration, he was tamping down his own expectations.

Two months later, on June 27, we get another glimpse of *Moby-Dick* in the making, this time in a letter to his English publisher, Richard Bentley, to whom he expressed the hope that he would have the book done by fall. It will be, he says, "a romance of adventure, founded upon certain wild legends in the Southern Sperm Whale Fisheries, and illustrated by the author's own personal experience, of two years & more, as a harpooneer." In this bit of self-advertising, Melville was reverting to his old hyperbolics. The truth was less glamorous: the only ship on which he might have served as harpooneer was the *Charles and Henry,* on which he had lived and worked for not quite six months, from early November 1842 to mid-May 1843, and for which he had probably signed up as a boatsteerer.

As he issued these progress reports—embellished as they inevitably are when an author writes to an editor—he was still living in New York. His speed of composition had slowed from the astonishing pace at which he had poured out *Redburn* and *White-Jacket,* which between them had taken only four months. By June he had been in the city uninterruptedly (with the possible exception of an excursion to West Point) since his return from England in February, and he was ready for a break. Lizzie was suffering from her annual spring allergy, or "rose cold," and worried about being confined in the dusty town all summer. With the hot months approaching, Melville's thoughts turned to the Berkshires, where he had spent some of his happiest childhood days on his uncle's farm near Pittsfield—now owned by his cousin Robert, who, needing cash, had turned it into a boardinghouse that he advertised in the *Pittsfield Sun* as "unrivalled either for the beauty of its scenery or the salubrity of the air." The place proved appealing enough to attract poets (the Longfellows had come from Cambridge two summers earlier) and ex-presidents (John Tyler had been a guest the previous fall), and for Melville there was the added enticement of childhood memories. It was a place, he knew, that provided opportunities for both sociability and solitude, a convenient meeting ground for the literati of New York and Boston, being roughly equidistant from each.

By mid-July he was settled in, sharing the house with not only Lizzie and Malcolm but also Allan, Sophia, and their baby Maria, cousin Robert, his wife, children, and widowed mother, as well as a number of boarders, including a New York couple, John and Sarah Morewood, who, in fact, were in the process of buying the property from its financially pressed owner. Melville brought with him some books on whales and whaling that he had borrowed in New York for filling in factual details as he put the finishing touches—or so he thought—on his manuscript, which he somehow planned to polish off on summer holiday amid a gaggle of family and affable strangers.

But the book had its own plans. It slowed down. Or, rather, it paused before taking off in a new direction and toward a new form. More than a year was to go by before the final version was ready for the press, and when publication was finally at hand, in September 1851, Melville wrote to Sarah Morewood:

> Don't you buy it—don't you read it, when it does come out, because it is by no means the sort of book for you. It is not a piece of fine feminine Spitalfields silk—but is of the horrible texture of a fabric that should be woven of ships' cables & hausers. A Polar wind blows through it, & birds of prey hover over it.

A year earlier, when the evening air started to have an autumn bite, Melville had begun to turn his whaling adventure into the most ambitious book ever conceived by an American writer.

2.

In an expansive mood after sending off the upbeat letter to Bentley on June 27, he had come up to Pittsfield with Lizzie and little Malcolm, planning on a vacation of indefinite length. His comments on the jaunts he took with his cousin around the countryside in the third week of July are full of compliments ("Glorious place & fine old fellow") about the several hosts who fed and supplied them with drink and bed when they stopped for the night. At the end of the month he made a quick trip back to the city to tend to business and collect the books he needed. His mood was high, as the country pleased him so much that he had pretty much made up his mind to move his family there. Though he had missed the chance to negotiate for his cousin's place (a grand house, it has since been converted into the main building of the Pittsfield Country Club), he had his eye on a neighboring farm that he heard was coming on the market. This new prospect was more modest; yet, as Duyckinck later wrote, its "grounds would satisfy an English nobleman— for the noble maples and elms and various seclusions and outlooks and all for the price of a bricked city enclosure of 25 × 100!" Anticipating financial help from Lizzie's father, Melville moved quickly toward a deal (transfer of the deed came in September) to buy these 160 acres spread out below Mount Greylock. He called his new home "Arrowhead," in honor of the flint arrowheads that were dug up here and there around the property in planting season.

While in the city, he invited Duyckinck to come up to join him in his temporary lodgings and, in a burst of unauthorized hospitality on behalf of his cousin Robert, he asked the long-winded Cornelius Mathews to come up too. Melville may have read Mathews's bizarre romance ("as ridiculous a fanfaronade as the age produced," according to one estimate) entitled *Behemoth: A Legend of the Mound-Builders* (1839), about prehistoric mound-dwellers who kill a giant mastodon after tracking it to the seashore, where they find the "mighty Brute resting on the sea . . . presenting, in the grandeur and vastness of his repose, a monumental image of Eternal Quiet." In time for his thirty-first birthday on August 1 and his third wedding anniversary on August 4, Melville was back in Pittsfield, looking forward to a literary gathering planned for Monday, August 5, by a summer neighbor, the distinguished New York lawyer David Dudley Field.

Field had in mind a picnic walk up Monument Mountain, to be followed by afternoon supper at his house. Along with Duyckinck and Mathews, the guest list included summer residents Dr. Oliver Wendell Holmes and Nathaniel Hawthorne, who was renting a cottage near Lenox overlooking Stockbridge Lake. Duyckinck was enthralled. "The Poets have made no mistake," he wrote. "The air is balm." And when he got to the old Melvill mansion, to which the Morewoods were soon to give the aristocratic-sounding name "Broadhall" (possibly at the suggestion of Melville's sister Kate), it struck him as a splendidly Gothic inheritance from times past. "Quite a piece of mouldering rural grandeur," Duyckinck called it, as if he were visiting

Poe's House of Usher or Hawthorne's House of Seven Gables, and noted that "the family has gone down & this is their last season. The farm has been sold. Herman Melville knows every stone & tree & will probably make a book of its features. The old lady, his aunt, shows you a vial of the Boston tea, brought home by his grandfather in his shoes from the famous Boston tea party in the harbor."

The morning of the hike was misty, but for Melville it was to be a clarifying day. As thunderclouds rolled in and the other hikers scrambled to construct makeshift umbrellas out of branches and picnic cloths, he ventured "to seat himself," according to Duyckinck, "boldest of all, astride a projecting bow sprit of rock while little Dr. Holmes peeped about the cliffs and protested it affected him like ipecac." After Melville had finished showing off his crow's-nest cool on the edge of the precipice, the picnickers continued on, as the Boston publisher James T. Fields later recalled, "with merry shouts and laughter."

For the history of literature, the important occurrence on Monument Mountain was the immediate and intense connection established that day between Melville and Hawthorne. The older man (Hawthorne was forty-six) had reviewed *Typee* four years earlier, and his interest in Melville was now renewed by their meeting, which a local journalist reconstructed some thirty years later: "One day it chanced that when they were out on a pic-nic excursion, the two were compelled by a thunder-shower to take shelter in a narrow recess of the rocks of Monument Mountain. Two hours of enforced intercourse settled the matter. They learned so much of each other's character, and found that they held so much of thought, feeling and opinion in common, that the most intimate friendship for the future was inevitable." Within a few days, Hawthorne got hold of every book Melville had written and, as Sophia wrote to Duyckinck, read rapidly through them while lying "on the new hay in the barn."

Melville, too, turned to his new friend's writings (he had received a copy of *Mosses from an Old Manse* as a gift from his aunt) and, in the days following, wrote an excited review of *Mosses* expressing gratitude to Hawthorne for having "dropped germinous seeds into my soul." In Hawthorne he found a writer in touch with the dreamworld that he himself had begun to explore in *Mardi*—a writer who knew, as Hawthorne put it in one of the best stories of the collection, "The Birthmark," that "truth . . . finds its way to the mind close muffled in robes of sleep and then speaks with uncompromising directness of matters in regard to which we practise an unconscious self-deception during our waking moments."

That Melville was willing to take time off from his book testified not only to Hawthorne's startling effect on him but also to his confidence that his manuscript had reached the filling-in stage when, as he had done with *Typee* and *Omoo,* he stepped back from what he had written and added here and there some ballast of factual detail gleaned from other books. He was still telling friends that his work was nearing completion. Two days after the picnic, Duyckinck, who published Melville's Hawthorne review in *The Literary World* in two installments, on August 17 and 24, wrote to his brother George that "Melville has a new book mostly done,—a romantic, fanciful & literal & most enjoyable presentment of the Whale Fishery—something quite new." There is no telling how much of the manuscript Duyckinck had actually read, or whether he was merely transmitting the author's own account of it. "Romantic . . . fanciful . . . most enjoyable" are apt enough terms for the opening chapters (sometimes called "the land chapters") that rehearse once again Melville's trademark story of a young man in flight from his dreary life ashore in pursuit of something—though he knows not what— that might bring greater satisfaction. But the work that Duyckinck described is not the *Moby-Dick* we know, at least not the whole of it.

Sometime after the mountain hike, Melville found himself scrutinizing what he had written so far, getting so close to it that he entered into it and tore it up from within. "Revision" is too slight a term for what he now set out to do. Reading Melville's review of *Mosses from an Old Manse* today with the advantage of knowing that he was about to attack his own book anew, one discovers a writer whose ambition has risen beyond anything he had yet attempted. "You must have plenty of sea-room to tell the Truth in," he writes about Hawthorne (who did not write about the sea), and chides Americans for leaving "to future generations the glad duty of acknowledging him for what he is." Emboldened by Hawthorne's example and by the approval Hawthorne had expressed for his own early work, Melville proclaimed his blood brotherhood with "Nathaniel of Salem," whose "soft ravishments . . . spun me round about in a web of dreams" as they joined together in that fraternity where "genius, all over the world, stands hand in hand, and one shock of recognition runs the whole circle round."

The review of *Mosses* was Melville's announcement to the world of his own genius, registering not only his appreciation of Hawthorne in person and on the page but also his immersion in a number of great writers who now lifted him to a new level of epic ambition. There are echoes of Milton, as when he proclaims that it is "better to fail in originality, than to succeed in imitation" (Satan, in *Paradise Lost,* declares it "Better to reign in Hell, than serve in Heav'n"), and he had accrued a special debt to Virgil. In September 1849, just before his trip to England, he had bought on account Harper's Classical Library, which included John Dryden's translation of the *Aeneid.* In *Mardi,* he had mentioned "Virgil my minstrel," and in *White-Jacket,* the

sight of Jack Chase encouraging the poet Lemsford had put him in mind of
the Roman patron "Mecaenas listening to Virgil, with a book of the Aeneid
in his hand." But these pro forma nods toward the Roman poet had been
conventionally reverent; it was not until sometime in 1850 that Melville had
his true encounter with the *Aeneid* and found himself recapitulating Virgil's
story of a haunted mariner voyaging out to avenge a grievous loss.*

The men of *Moby-Dick* are Virgilian wanderers. They long for home
even as fate calls them away from "safety, comfort, hearthstone, supper, warm
blankets, friends, all that's kind to our mortalities." Early in the book, one
hears echoes of Virgil's account of the Trojan mariners preparing, after brief
respite, to set sail again with ships newly caulked as Queen Dido watches
them from a hilltop in Carthage. There is the same mood of fated, if futile,
human striving in Melville's account of New Bedford as a place where men
step briefly ashore before consigning themselves once more to the sea:

> New Bedford rose in terraces of streets, their ice-covered trees all glit-
> tering in the clear, cold air. Huge hills and mountains of casks on casks
> were piled upon her wharves, and side by side the world-wandering
> whale-ships lay silent and safely moored at last; while from others came
> a sound of carpenters and coopers, with blended noises of fires and
> forges to melt the pitch, all betokening that new cruises were on the
> start; that one most perilous and long voyage ended, only begins a sec-
> ond; and a second ended, only begins a third, and so on, for ever and
> for aye. Such is the endlessness, yea, the intolerableness of all earthly
> effort.

The writing here has a controlled intensity of which Melville had not been
previously capable. In the long second sentence, the range of alliterated initial consonant sounds mimics the "blended noises" of men laboring on the
docks: the words begin with an aspirate "h" ("Huge hills"), a hard "c" ("cask
on casks . . . carpenters and coopers"), a hard "s" ("side by side," "silent
and safely"), a "w" (world-wandering whale-ships), and an "f" ("fires and
forges" and "for ever and for aye")—seven pairs and one triplet of alliterated

---

*It seems likely that he had already read Dryden's *Aeneid* in a copy borrowed from some friend or
library before adding the book to his own collection—a lag consistent with his customary practice.
In other instances of his literary borrowing, for example, his allusion to Friedrich Schiller's poem
"The Veiled Statue at Sais" (also acquired in 1849) at the end of chapter 76 of *Moby-Dick,* he does
not seem to have marked the poem until years after first reading it. See the note in the annotated
edition of *Moby-Dick,* ed. Luther S. Mansfield and Howard P. Vincent (New York: Hendricks
House, 1952), p. 771.

words that perfectly convey the ceaseless repetition of the dockside work. And by prolonging the sentence with a vowel sound ("aye") as open-ended as a howl, Melville makes it feel as interminable as the work it describes, then ends the paragraph—but does not exactly conclude it—with a short sentence that reaches for some satisfying inference to be drawn from all that has gone before. He achieves here a mastery of verbal effects that one expects from only the most accomplished poetry.

In the rhymed couplets of Dryden's *Aeneid,* he encountered a poem full of images ("The Cables crack, the Sailors fearful Cries / Ascend; and sable Night involves the Skies; / And Heav'n itself is ravish'd from their Eyes") that stirred his own memories of life at sea, as when he wrote of "that direst of storms, the Typhoon" tearing the sails from the *Pequod*'s masts, leaving them briefly visible in blazes of lightning, "fluttering here and there with the rags which the first fury of the tempest had left for its after sport." When Melville has the narrator of *Moby-Dick* envision himself losing his balance in a dreamy moment and dropping "through that transparent air into the summer sea," he is retelling Book V of the *Aeneid,* in which the pilot Palinurus, having "clos'd his Swimming Eyes" under a spell from the god of sleep, plunges into the ocean and drowns.

And then there was *Frankenstein.* While in London, Melville had acquired from Bentley a copy of Mary Shelley's novel about an errant genius who hunts down the quasi-human monster he has created after it has turned against him and murdered the woman he loves. Having tracked the creature to the icy North, Frankenstein commandeers a scientific expeditionary ship headed to the Arctic and turns it into an instrument of his private vengeance. This story of obsession and revenge so captured Melville's imagination that when he read in Lamb's *Final Memorials* about William Godwin's (Mary Shelley's father) gift for creating characters "marvellously endowed with galvanic life," he wrote in the margin: "*Frankenstein.*" Here, in a speech that installed itself in Melville's mind, is Frankenstein's oration to the ship's crew as they falter, in the bitter cold, in their resolve:

> Are you then so easily turned from your design? Did you not call this a glorious expedition? And wherefore was it glorious? Not because the way was smooth and placid as a southern sea, but because, at every new incident, your fortitude was to be called forth, and your courage exhibited; because danger and death surrounded it, and these you were to brave and overcome. . . . Oh! be men, or be more than men. . . . This ice is not made of such stuff as your hearts may be; it is mutable, and cannot withstand you, if you say that it shall not.

"He spoke this," reports the ship's captain, even as he cedes to Frankenstein his authority over his own men, "with a voice so modulated to the different feelings expressed in his speech, with an eye so full of lofty design, and heroism, that can you wonder that these men were moved?" Melville was soon to write such a scene himself in "The Quarter-Deck" chapter of *Moby-Dick,* in which an irresistible orator exhorts his crew ("What say ye men . . . I think ye do look brave") to prove themselves in their hour of peril. He was to name this man Ahab, after the Israelite king (I Kings 16:29–33) cursed for worshipping the pagan sun god Baal.

3.

With his head brimming with these and many other instigating readings—Virgil and Milton; Goethe's musings on the "Titanic, gigantic, heaven-storming" Prometheus; William Beckford's Arabian romance, *Vathek;* Carlyle's portrait of Cromwell in *Heroes and Hero-Worship;* Shelley's mad scientist; a slew of whaling books—the idea of Captain Ahab began to take form. At first, Ahab was a composite of the questers and avengers Melville had met in Beckford's and Shelley's novels, in *Paradise Lost* (in which Satan, banished to hell by God, vows "revenge, immortal hate, / And courage never to submit or yield"), and, more variously, in the plays of Shakespeare. Until recently, he had read only scantily in Shakespeare's plays, since "every copy that was come-atable to me," as he explained to Duyckinck, "happened to be in a vile small print unendurable to my eyes." Stage performances had left him unmoved. After seeing *Othello* in London, he had merely noted in his journal that the famous William Macready (the object of the crowd's contempt at the Astor Place riot) was "painted hideously" in the role of the Moor, and that the actress playing Desdemona was "very pretty." To absorb Shakespeare's meanings, he needed the silent encounter with words on the page.

After finally acquiring a readable edition early in 1849, he discovered a Shakespeare far beyond the melodramatist (nineteenth-century productions of his plays were often grossly unfaithful to the text) who put on stage "Richard-the-third-humps and Macbeth daggers." Inspired and astonished ("if another Messiah ever comes twill be in Shakespere's person"), Melville reported to Duyckinck with almost childish delight as he read through his newly bought edition that "I now exult over it, page after page." In the

Hawthorne review, he explained more particularly what enthralled him: through such "dark characters" as "Hamlet, Timon, Lear, and Iago," Shakespeare "insinuates the things, which we feel to be so terrifically true, that it were all but madness for any good man, in his own proper character, to utter, or even hint of them." Melville had begun to see the outlines of a character through whom he could speak such things himself.

But this figure—a maimed and raging ship captain "with a crucifixion in his face"—was not yet in the book, or even distinctly in his mind. The central figure in the draft that Duyckinck read or heard described in early August was a young adventurer named Ishmael—after the son of Abraham by the slavewoman Haggar, whose story is told in Genesis 16—who leaves his onshore self behind, goes down, or up, or out (his trajectory is unclear) from New York, to New Bedford, to Nantucket, to the open sea aboard the whaleship *Pequod.* The question of what or whom he will find there is left in suspension, because while the ship is in port, the captain keeps himself hidden belowdecks and is known to the crew only by rumor.

The first fifth or so of Melville's book, probably written while he was still in New York, was devoted to this vagabond boy's journey away from himself, with Ahab out of sight and, perhaps, out of mind. Ishmael checks into an inn at New Bedford whose entry is ominously adorned with that Turneresque painting of "a long, limber, portentous, black mass of something hovering in the centre." Inside the inn, the clientele consists of "chief mates, and second mates, and third mates, and sea carpenters, and sea coopers, and sea blacksmiths, and harpooneers, and ship keepers; a brown and brawny company, with bosky beards," and Ishmael learns that by studying their skin he can tell how long they have been ashore:

> This young fellow's healthy cheek is like a sun-toasted pear in hue, and would seem to smell almost as musky; he cannot have been three days landed from his Indian voyage. That man next him looks a few shades lighter; you might say a touch of satin wood is in him. In the complexion of a third still lingers a tropic tawn, but slightly bleached withal; *he* doubtless has tarried whole weeks ashore.

But none "could show a cheek like Queequeg," the cannibal harpooneer from "an island far away to the West and South," whose skin is so densely tattooed that it looks like parchment scratched over with hieroglyphs. The amused proprietor of the Spouter Inn assigns the nervous boy to share a room, and therefore a bed, with this frightful guest. When Ishmael asks if he "is a dangerous man," the landlord replies that "he pays reg'lar"—not quite the reassurance Ishmael is looking for—and tells him that the man was last seen going off to sell the embalmed heads that he carries around with him dangling from a string like a bunch of onions. The story of Ishmael's anticipatory anxiety about meeting Queequeg is the ultimate "meet your roommate" story, told with retrospective embarrassment at how worried he had been in advance of meeting the man who is about to become his "bosom friend."

Thrown in with such company, the narrator of *Moby-Dick* starts out as a prig and a prude. When Queequeg rolls in around midnight, Ishmael has already been in bed for a while and is shocked by the stranger's appearance, then by the ritual genuflections he performs in front of a little wooden idol "the color of a three-days' old Congo baby" before getting into bed himself. Next morning, Ishmael watches with dismay as the stranger, shameless in his nakedness, dresses from top to bottom, donning first his hat, then his shirt, before putting an end to the indecency by pulling on his trousers. But as befits his name, Ishmael wanders away from his initial prudery until he is more amused by his own proprieties than shocked by Queequeg's behavior. The whole episode is a case in point of the sort of worldly education that another New York writer (a minor "Knickerbocker" named William Cox) recommended:

> The departure from home and old usages is any thing but pleasant, especially at the outset. It is a sort of secondary "weaning" which the juvenile has to undergo; but like the first process, he is all the healthier and hardier when it is over. In this way, it is a wholesome thing to be tossed about the world. To form odd acquaintance in ships, on the decks of steam boats and tops of coaches; to pick up temporary companions on turnpikes or by hedge-sides; to see humanity in the rough, and learn what stuff life is made of in different places; to mark the shades, and other important matters as you stroll along. What a universal toleration it begets!

Through his enlarging encounter with Queequeg, Ishmael, who has a capacity for humor at his own expense, learns to laugh at everything he has been taught to consider true and civilized and safe.

In an extraordinary chapter entitled "The Counterpane," Melville pushed further this theme of self-discovery, reviewing, in effect, the construction of Ishmael's self in early childhood and its deconstruction through his awakening experience of sleeping, on the verge of adulthood, with another man. The scene is half fraternal, half erotic. In their shared bed, Queequeg's tattooed arm, "thrown over me in the most loving and affectionate manner," lies across the quilted counterpane that covers Ishmael's chest; and in the first waking moments of morning, when the line between consciousness and unconsciousness remains indeterminate, Ishmael feels himself dissolve into the flesh and fabric spread out on top of him. "You had almost thought I had been his wife," he says about the cannibal's unconscious embrace, and he cannot distinguish between Queequeg's arm and the quilt, or even quite tell where his own body ends and the coverings begin.

It is a liberating confusion. It enables Ishmael to relive a "similar circumstance that befell" him when, as a child, he had incurred the wrath of his stepmother, that fairy-tale figure of cruelty, for having tried to crawl up the chimney. He had been punished by being packed off to bed early in the afternoon of a sun-drenched "21st of June, the longest day in the year"—the kind of day when it is torture for a boy to stay indoors. Now, in bed many years later with a stranger, he remembers the shock of opening his eyes that long-ago night and dimly making out his own hand as if it were disconnected from his body (we would say it had "fallen asleep"), hanging off the bed, inert, seemingly clasped in the hand of some threatening phantom. Whether the stranger was predator or protector he cannot say:

> Instantly I felt a shock running through all my frame; nothing was to be seen, and nothing was to be heard; but a supernatural hand seemed placed in mine. My hand hung over the counterpane, and the nameless, unimaginable, silent form or phantom, to which the hand belonged, seemed closely seated by my bedside. For what seemed ages piled on ages, I lay there, frozen with the most awful fears, not daring to drag away my hand; yet ever thinking that if I could but stir it one single inch, the horrid spell would be broken.*

This is the recollected childhood moment when Ishmael first discovered the proscribed otherness of his own body, as if some monitor had come into the room to prevent his hand from touching some forbidden part of himself. It was his first encounter with what Freud calls the discontents of civilization. He had been punished for behaving the way boys behave before they learn to control themselves (the sexual character of the transgression is patent in the image of penetrating the chimney), and his stepmother, after following him into the room in the form of the phantom monitor, takes up residence in his own psyche.

Having relived this formative moment ("whether it was a reality or a

---

*This recollected experience is strikingly similar to William James's famous account in *The Varieties of Religious Experience,* written some fifty years later, of the dreadful night when he "*felt* something come into the room and stay close to my bed," filling him with a "consciousness of a presence" that induced in him "not *pain* so much as *abhorrence*" (his italics).

dream, I never could entirely settle") in bed at the Spouter Inn, Ishmael begins to re-form himself through intimacy with Queequeg. In a sexually redolent phrase, he remarks "how elastic our stiff prejudices grow when love once comes to bend them," as if a prolonged erection has been relieved by another man's touch—the sort of intimacy of which he had been taught to be afraid. He has been freed, above all, from the appetite for retribution that accompanies guilt: "No more my splintered heart and maddened hand were turned against the wolfish world." The punitive grasp of the stranger has turned into a loving hug. Echoing Genesis 16:12 ("his hand will be against every man, and every man's hand against him"), Melville writes all these words in Ishmael's voice; but he writes them so feelingly that he seems to be speaking of himself.

4.

In that summer and fall of 1850, he carried forward this story of a young man's rebirth with the same jubilation with which he had reported the actual birth of his first child, Malcolm, that "perfect prodigy" whose arrival the year before had reverberated as far away as China so that they had to place "props against the great wall." But in what today we would call "bipolar" mood swings, his high moods were followed closely by lows. This phenomenon of manic depression was well known to both neoclassic and Romantic writers. "Mirth and a heavy heart . . . often meet together," as the eighteenth-century physician Benjamin Rush remarked, clinching the point with a quotation from Proverbs (one of Melville's favorite books of the Bible): "In the midst of laughter the heart is sad." Or as John Keats, that great poet whose sensibility was akin to Melville's, put it in his "Ode on Melancholy": "Ay, in the very temple of Delight / Veil'd Melancholy has her sovran shrine." Such volatility of feeling seems to be one of the costs of genius, and in Melville's case, whenever he felt what Emerson called the "currents of the Universal Being" flow through him (as in "The Mast-Head" chapter of *Moby-Dick*), he suspected that the feeling was illusory—as he confessed that summer in an astonishing letter to Hawthorne:

> In reading some of Goethe's sayings, so worshipped by his votaries, I came across this, "*Live in the all.*" That is to say, your separate identity is but a wretched one,—good; but get out of yourself, spread and

expand yourself, and bring to yourself the tinglings of life that are felt in the flowers and the woods, that are felt in the planets Saturn and Venus, and the Fixed Stars. What nonsense! Here is a fellow with a raging toothache. "My dear boy," Goethe says to him, "you are sorely afflicted with that tooth; but you must *live in the all*, and then you will be happy."

Yet even as he dismissed this promise of "the tinglings of life," he wanted desperately to believe in them:

This "all" feeling, though, there is some truth in. You must often have felt it, lying on the grass on a warm summer's day. Your legs seem to send out shoots into the earth. Your hair feels like leaves upon your head.

Much of *Moby-Dick* reads like a transcription of a patient under analysis moving from bravado to depletion, a rhythm of which Sophia Hawthorne gave a revealing account in a letter to her mother not long after Melville's first meeting with her husband:

When conversing, [Mr. Melville] is full of gesture & force, & loses himself in his subject . . . [until] his animation gives place to a singularly quiet expression out of those eyes . . . an indrawn, dim look, but which at the same time makes you feel that he is at that instant taking deepest note of what is before him—It is a strange, lazy glance, but with a power in it quite unique—It does not seem to penetrate through you, but to take you into himself.

Few people were able to see with this kind of clarity into Melville, who concealed himself by taking refuge in theatrics. Only in the presence of a soulmate did the actor's mask come off. In Hawthorne, whom Cornelius Mathews shrewdly called "Mr. Noble Melancholy," he had found such a person, and Sophia was the closest witness to the unveilings. "The freshness of primeval nature is in that man," she wrote to Duyckinck in August 1850, and, two years later, in a letter to her mother, Elizabeth, she surmised that his "ocean-experience has given sea-room to his intellect, & he is in the mere boyhood of his possibilities."

Between bouts of writing, the visits to Hawthorne became more frequent, and Sophia was pleased to report that whenever Melville stayed overnight he "was very careful not to interrupt Mr. Hawthorne's mornings," since the forenoon was her husband's inviolate working time. Their conversations, which Melville referred to as "ontological heroics," "lasted pretty deep into the night; and if the truth must be told," Hawthorne wrote in his

LEFT: Sophia Peabody Hawthorne, *etching by A. Schoff*
RIGHT: Nathaniel Hawthorne, *oil painting by Cephas Thompson, 1850*

journal, "we smoked cigars even within the sacred precincts of the sitting-room." In his relations with others, Melville continued to be, as the critic Martin Green has written, "evasive and enigmatic . . . to all who pierced the jovial surface," and "none of his friends felt they really knew him." But Hawthorne was different; he seemed to know that Melville's public jesting rose and fell in proportion to his private brooding—a division between seeming and being that Melville wrote into *Moby-Dick* in the form of Ish-mael's detachment from his own anxiety, which the young man describes as if he were trying to make a joke out of his suicidal thoughts:

> Whenever . . . it is a damp, drizzly November in my soul; whenever I find myself involuntarily pausing before coffin warehouses, and bring-ing up the rear of every funeral I meet . . . I account it high time to get to sea as soon as I can. This is my substitute for pistol and ball. With a philosophical flourish Cato throws himself upon his sword; I quietly take to the ship.

While rethinking the story told by this version of himself, Melville fur-nished clues in his essay about Hawthorne to what was driving him to rewrite. In his review (written by "the first person," Sophia thought, "who has ever in *print* apprehended Mr. Hawthorne"), he portrayed the older author as a prophetic mirror of himself—not only by crediting him with being the American who, "up to the present day" (a telling qualification), had "evinced, in Literature, the largest brain with the largest heart," but also by stressing the dark underside of a writer regarded in his own time as a spinner of bedtime tales set in the picturesque past. Compared to Poe, who was obsessed with such sinister themes as incest and cannibalism, Hawthorne seemed to most contemporary critics a writer of antiquarian entertainments who brought to life the "by-gone days" of Indians and Pilgrims. But Melville, immediately upon reading *Mosses,* recognized the darker, haunted Hawthorne, of whom he said that "spite of all the Indian-summer sunlight on the hither side of Hawthorne's soul, the other side—like the dark half of the physical sphere—is shrouded in a blackness, ten times black. . . . You may be witched by his sunlight,—transported by the bright gildings in the skies he builds over you;—but there is the blackness of darkness beyond; and even his bright gildings but fringe, and play upon the edges of thunder-clouds."

We shall never know the details of their talks, the jokes they swapped, the judgments they discussed late into the night while pondering (this is from Hawthorne's journal) "time and eternity, things of this world and of the next, and books, and publishers, and all possible and impossible matters." But the glow of their friendship still warms the pages in which they wrote to or about each other, as when Melville proposed, nearly a year after their first meeting, that they "dig a deep hole and bury all the Blue Devils" (their term for their despondencies) "there to abide till the Last Day." Sometimes the friendship reached white heat, as when, a few months later, Melville wrote in a mood of valediction, having learned that Hawthorne had given up the place in Lenox and was about to move back east:

> Whence come you, Hawthorne? By what right do you drink from my flagon of life? And when I put it to my lips—lo, they are yours and not mine. I feel that the Godhead is broken up like the bread at the Supper, and that we are the pieces. Hence this infinite fraternity of feeling.

Evoked here in the mystical language of the Eucharist, this feeling of inseparability was much more than collegial; to Melville, it was as if their minds and hearts were linked by a common network of nerves and veins. "Your heart beat in my ribs, and mine in yours," he wrote to his dear friend, "and both in God's."

Melville was drawn to the mysteries and contradictions in Hawthorne as if to plumb their depths would be to solve the riddle of existence itself. Ever alert to the proximity of death in the midst of life, he had never reconciled himself to the sudden losses of his father and brother ("let no man," he had written in *White-Jacket*, "though his live heart beat in him like a cannon—let him not hug his life to himself; for, in the predestinated necessities of things, that bounding life of his is not a whit more secure than the life of a man on his deathbed"), and he recognized in Hawthorne a kindred spirit whose "great power of blackness . . . derives its force from its appeals to that Calvinistic sense of Innate Depravity and Original Sin, from whose visitations, in some shape or other, no deeply thinking mind is always and wholly free." Yet Hawthorne seemed somehow to live equably with the fatedness of life, and Melville wrote about him as if he were a prodigy of nature—a chiaroscuro composition of bright and dark tones, each heightening the other, of the sort he found in the Berkshire forest itself. "You should see the maples," Melville wrote to Duyckinck on a Sunday evening early in October 1850, after spending the day "*Jacquesizing* in the woods" (talking to himself about how quickly one traverses the stages of life), "you should see the young perennial pines—the red blazings of the one contrasting with the painted green of the others, and the wide flushings of the autumn air harmonizing both. I tell you that sunrises & sunsets grow side by side in these woods, & momentarily moult in the falling leaves."

5.

Under these manifold influences—Shakespeare, Virgil, Shelley, and a host of other writers, as well as his colloquies with Hawthorne amid the morbid beauty of the Berkshire woods—the "enjoyable" book that Melville had promised to Duyckinck a year before changed fundamentally. In his fever of creation, Melville became Emerson's proverbial poet, whose "imperial muse tosses the creation like a bauble from hand to hand, and uses it to embody any caprice of thought that is uppermost in his mind." His book opened out into the panorama of history and myth to which he had been exposed in his reading, from the Western scriptures to Eastern tales of dervishes and devil worshippers. In *Moby-Dick*, "the remotest spaces of nature are visited," as Emerson had said of poets possessed, "and the farthest sundered things are brought together, by a subtile spiritual connection."

As he rushed about what sometimes seems the whole history of human culture, embracing "all the generations of whales, and men, and mastodons, past, present, and to come, with all the revolving panoramas of empire on earth, and throughout the whole universe, not excluding its suburbs,"

Melville took bits of Scripture and wove them into the fabric of his book—into irreverent passages as well as solemn ones, as when, having described a sailor who uses the outer skin of the whale's penis for a cloak as a good "candidate for an archbishoprick," he surrounds the pun with a cluster of sexual associations organized around Queen Maacah (mentioned in I Kings as a worshipper of phallic idols). The Leviathan of Isaiah, Psalms, and the Book of Job, so fierce that it makes the ocean heave and boil, comes alive as a symbol of inscrutable strength, and Melville conscripts a whole army of mythic warriors—"Perseus, St. George, Hercules, Jonah, and Vishnoo"—into the family of gallant whalemen who defy and pursue it. "Towards thee I roll," cries Ahab in his last outburst of half-sacred, half-demonic rage, "thou all-destroying but unconquering whale; to the last I grapple with thee; from hell's heart I stab at thee; for hate's sake I spit my last breath at thee." The whole of humankind seems to pass through these pages, as if *Moby-Dick* were an encyclopedia of "heroes, saints, demigods, and prophets" to whom lesser men turn for guidance and grace when facing the terrors of the deep.

Yet the hunt is an act of worship as well as of vengeance. The white whale, as the critic Richard Slotkin has said, is "at once masculine and feminine, a phallus and an odalisque, enticing and overwhelmingly erotic"—a creature both exquisite and appalling, in which the whole originating force of creation seems concentrated:

> A gentle joyousness—a mighty mildness of repose in swiftness, invested the gliding whale. Not the white bull Jupiter swimming away with ravished Europa clinging to his graceful horns; his lovely, leering eyes sideways intent upon the maid; with smooth bewitching fleetness, rippling straight for the nuptial bower in Crete; not Jove, not that great majesty Supreme! did surpass the glorified White Whale as he so divinely swam.

The pursuit of this "grand hooded phantom, like a snow hill in the air," becomes an allegorical chase as Melville pulls us into the action, obliterating the apparent distance between the frightful lives of whalemen and the seeming security of our life ashore:

> All men live enveloped in whale-lines. All are born with halters round their necks; but it is only when caught in the swift, sudden turn of death, that mortals realize the silent, subtle, ever-present perils of life. And if you be a philosopher, though seated in the whale-boat, you would not at heart feel one whit more of terror, than though seated before your evening fire with a poker, and not a harpoon, by your side.

As he carried forward his all-comprehending book—or was carried by it—toward its apocalyptic conclusion, he was angered by the smallest interruptions. His mother, having packed up and left after a testy visit in March 1851, complained, "Herman, I hope returned home safe after dumping me & my trunks out so unceremoniously at the Depot—Altho we were there more than an hour before the time, he hurried off as if his life had depended upon his speed. . . ." (Maria should have been used to this sort of send-off, since just the summer before, her nephew Robert had been in such a rush to put her on the train that he almost forgot her luggage.) And while those around him savored the renewed warmth and light as "spring begins to open upon Pittsfield," Melville, unused to the sun and habituated to daytime reclusiveness, wrote to Duyckinck that "like an owl I steal about by twilight, owing to the twilight of my eyes." During the days, he sat alone, as Hawthorne wrote of him, "shaping out the gigantic conception of his white whale, while the gigantic shape of [Mount] Greylock looms upon him from his study window." Arrowhead—a low-ceilinged house of modest proportions inhabited by wife, baby, and, often, by mother and sisters—felt crowded and noisy; the second-floor study was Melville's sanctuary, a bright corner room filled with morning light streaming through its eastern window and affording a view of Mount Greylock framed in a second window that looked north over an expanse of fields. Despite her best efforts, Lizzie later recalled, he sometimes worked on the book "at his desk all day not eating any thing till four or five o clock," and then, according to his own account, retired for the evening "in a sort of mesmeric state."

His furnace intensity was coupled to anxiety—a mixture so unstable as to be explosive. There are hints that for the first time (but not the last), his family feared him, or at least that they learned to cut him a wide berth so as to avoid collisions when he was hell-bent on his work. To ensure that he would keep himself fed, he arranged with Lizzie that she should come upstairs in the midafternoon and knock on his study door for however long it took till he was roused from his desk, but that she should never enter unbidden. In the country, he said, he had "a sort of sea-feeling"—an exhilarating vertigo that left him feeling on the verge of new discoveries, but also exposed, and sometimes desolate. "I look out of my window in the morning when I rise," he wrote to Duyckinck, "as I would out of a port-hole of a ship in the Atlantic. My room seems a ship's cabin; & at nights when I wake up & hear the wind shrieking, I almost fancy there is too much sail on the house, & I had better go on the roof & rig in the chimney." The sea for Melville was always a place of both freedom and terror—an "everlasting terra incognita" on which he could travel anywhere, though he had no idea of where he was or when he might drown.

Yet during these crucial months from late summer of 1850 into the summer of 1851, Melville continued to write cheerleading letters to his literary patrons. In August 1850, soon after the Monument Mountain picnic, he chided Duyckinck, with a torrent of variations on the theme of stone and mortar, for imprisoning himself in the city ("those dreary regions which are *Trans-Taconic* to me") from which he himself had escaped:

> What are you doing there, My Beloved, among the bricks and cobble-stone *boulders?* . . . I have a horrible presentiment that you are even now hanging round the City-Hall, trying to get a contract from the Corporation to pave Broadway between Clinton Place & Union-Square. For heaven's sake, come out from among those Hittites & Hodites—give up mortar forever.—There is one thing certain, that, chemically speaking, mortar was *the precipitate* of the Fall; & with a brickbat, or a cobble-stone *boulder,* Cain killed Abel.—Do you drink Lime-water in the morning by way of a stomachic? Do you use brick-bats for paper-weights in the office? Do you and Mathews pitch paving-stones, & play ball that way in the cool of the evening, opposite the Astor-house?—How do they sell mortar, by the quart now? Cheaper than ice-cream, I suppose.—A horrible something in me tells me that you are about dipping your head in plaster at Fowler's for your bust.—But enough—the visions come too thick for me to master them.

There is manic pleasure in this writing, but even as his work on *Moby-Dick* reached fever pitch, Melville was a failing author who became increasingly aware of it. After the cool reception of *Mardi* ("driven forth" by the critics, he wrote, "like a wild, mystic Mormon into shelterless exile"), he had written gamely to his father-in-law that bad reviews were "matters of course" and "essential to the building up of any permanent reputation." But *Redburn* and *White-Jacket* had only partially recouped his reputation; and to make matters worse, his responsibilities grew as his resources shrank, forcing him, as he wrote to a prospective publisher, "to regard my literary affairs in a strong pecuniary light." In March 1850, Lizzie had become pregnant again, and a second son, Stanwix, named for the site of his Gansevoort grandfather's heroics, was born that October. Melville was carrying a $1,500 mortgage and owed his father-in-law $5,000. In the spring of 1851, after the Harpers denied his request for an advance (he owed them nearly $700), he felt compelled to borrow $2,000 more, at 9 percent for five years, from his Lansingburgh friend Tertullus D. Stewart in order to cover the cost of home improvements—extravagances, according to his more frugal neighbors and friends.

With his obligations mounting, the gap between his artistic achievement and his public standing was more and more galling. "Though I wrote the

Gospels in this century," he wrote to Hawthorne in June 1851, "I should die in the gutter." He apologized for pitying himself ("I talk all about myself, and this is selfishness and egotism"), but quickly returned to the tone he had just forsworn: "Granted. But how help it? I am writing to you; I know little about you, but something about myself." The same letter rises—or sinks—into full-voiced lamentation: "The calm, the coolness, the silent grass-growing mood in which a man *ought* always to compose,—that, I fear, can seldom be mine. Dollars damn me; and the malicious Devil"—the "printer's devil," that is, the boy sent by the compositor to pick up the overdue manuscript—"is forever grinning in upon me, holding the door ajar." A few weeks later, his mood was still sour as he complained to Richard Bentley about the old sore subject of international copyright—or rather, the lack thereof: "This country is at present engaged in furnishing material for future authors; not in encouraging its living ones." To Duyckinck, as winter (and publication day) approached, he reported that he was working hard to keep "in full blast our great dining-room fire-place, which swallows down cords of wood as a whale does boats."

It may have been as late as the spring of 1851 that Melville added to his work-in-progress the chapters about Father Mapple, the thundering minister who, at New Bedford, speaks to young sailors and old salts in the language of their own experience—and they listen! These chapters were in part an allegory of his declining hopes for his own literary fortunes. Before Ishmael enters the seamen's chapel, "each silent worshipper," contemplating the memorial stones for drowned sailors on the chapel walls, has been "purposely sitting apart from the other, as if each silent grief were insular and incommunicable"; but once Mapple begins to preach, his voice fuses them into a community of linked sympathies. When Mapple has ceased, he "drooped and fell away from himself" as if in postcoital exhaustion, his listeners having been gratefully violated by his words—an act Melville no longer felt confident of achieving in his own relation to the public.* Yet even as he was scaling back his hopes for his public career, Melville was experiencing the private "happiness," as Walker Percy has memorably put it, "of

*Mapple was an invention, but also an amalgam of preachers whom Melville had actually heard, including the wonderfully named Enoch Mudge, to whom he had listened in New Bedford before sailing on his first ocean voyage, to Liverpool, in 1839, and the better-known Edward Taylor, who was enough of a cultural celebrity that when Dickens came to the United States early in 1842, he made a point of attending one of his sermons. Stirred by Taylor's "rude eloquence," Dickens believed that he studied with his "keen eye" the "sympathies and understandings" of his congregation not to impress them with "the display of his own powers" but in order to touch their hearts. Like Taylor, Father Mapple had been, Melville tells us, "a sailor and harpooneer in his youth." Charles Foster, "Something in Emblems: A Reinterpretation of *Moby-Dick*," *New England Quarterly* 34 (March 1961): 3–35, suggests that the Mapple chapters were "late insertions" in the manuscript.

the artist discovering, breaking through into the freedom of his art"—a joy one feels in every paragraph of *Moby-Dick*. "With the *Pequod* under full sail through the night with its try-pots blazing," Percy imagines Melville's hair flying in the wind of his imagination, his face aglow from the fire to which he consigned his doubts. Like one of his own characters in *Mardi*, Melville "did not build himself in with plans; he wrote right on; and so doing, got deeper and deeper into himself."

6.

A later American writer of Melvillean ambition, Norman Mailer, offers a salient comment that describes very well what happened to Melville during the writing of *Moby-Dick:* "A good half of writing consists of being sufficiently sensitive to the moment to reach for the next promise which is usually hidden in some word or phrase just a shift to the side of one's conscious intent." Here is a passage, from the early chapter entitled "Nantucket," in which Melville reaches repeatedly for the next promise, releasing a tumbling plethora of images like those in his plea to Duyckinck to forsake New York:

> Nantucket! Take out your map and look at it! . . . Look at it—a mere hillock, and elbow of sand: all beach, without a background. There is more sand there than you would use in twenty years as a substitute for blotting paper. Some gamesome wights will tell you that they have to plant weeds there, they don't grow naturally; that they import Canada thistles; that they have to send beyond seas for a spile to stop a leak in an oil cask; that pieces of wood in Nantucket are carried about like bits of the true cross in Rome; that people there plant toadstools before their houses, to get under the shade in summer time; that one blade of grass makes an oasis, three blades in a day's walk a prairie; that they wear quicksand shoes, something like Laplander snow-shoes; that they are so shut up, belted about, every way inclosed, surrounded, and made an utter island of by the ocean, that to their very chairs and tables small clams will sometimes be found adhering, as to the backs of sea turtles. But these extravaganzas only show that Nantucket is no Illinois.

What we have here is a writer scavenging in his own mind for images afloat in his memory—snowshoes, sunshades, the Cross—and seizing them for use in

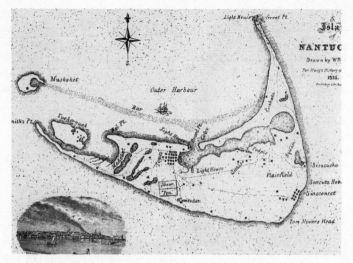

"*Nantucket! Take out your map and look at it . . . all beach, without a background.*"
Moby-Dick, *chapter 14*
Map of Nantucket by William Coffin, 1835

the purely fanciful picture he is drawing. There is no empirical observation, as Melville did not lay eyes on Nantucket until 1852. It is an ecstatic cadenza, a riff—showy, boisterous, yet somehow intimate and honest—whose real subject is not Nantucket at all but his own associative imagination. Then, in a concluding sentence that is almost contrite, he stops the adventure as abruptly as a parent puts an end to the high jinks of an out-of-control child— knowing, of course, that after resting a bit, the child will throw another tantrum.

This stylistic breakthrough had been intimated in the works of the New York years, but it came to full force in *Moby-Dick* and took off after the encounter with Hawthorne. There was something almost competitive now about Melville's writing ("Give me a condor's quill! Give me Vesuvius' crater for an inkstand!"), and one feels in this friendship, as in that later literary friendship between Ernest Hemingway and Scott Fitzgerald, the energy of rivalry as well as affection. Hawthorne had once confessed in his journal that what trickled through his own writing seemed finally a "shallow and scanty . . . stream of thought" compared to "the broad tide of dim emotions, ideas, associations, which were flowing through the haunted regions of [my] imagination, intellect, and sentiment, sometimes excited by what was around me, sometimes with no perceptible connection with them." The problem of transferring mind to page ("taking a book off the brain," Melville wrote to Duyckinck, "is akin to the ticklish & dangerous business of taking an old painting off a panel—you have to scrape off the whole brain in order to get at it with due safety") must surely have been among the subjects the two men touched upon during their late night talks about all "possible and impossible matters." To Melville, Hawthorne sometimes seemed on the verge of giving up the effort. "When we see how little we can express," the older writer had written in his journal, "it is a wonder that any man ever takes up a pen a second time"; and toward the end of his life, in a chapter of *The Marble Faun* entitled "Fragmentary Sentences," he was to compare writing to the hopeless task of "gathering up and piecing together the fragments of a letter which has been torn and scattered to the winds."

Melville relished the challenge. In December 1850, he appealed to Duyckinck to "send me about fifty fast-writing youths" so that he might dictate the thoughts that were flooding into his mind faster than he could write them down. With his powers of invention surging, he filled his book with a dazzling array of human types, each embodying some attitude or temperament captured in a revelatory phrase—from the serene and selfless Queequeg, whom he likened to "George Washington cannibalistically developed," to the lean and greedy Bildad, whose bony body is "the exact embodiment of his utilitarian character," to the blasphemously jolly third mate Flask, "so utterly lost . . . to all sense of reverence" that for him "the wondrous whale was but a species of magnified mouse, or . . . water-rat."

As his book hurtled along, Melville had trouble keeping track of its characters, saying repeatedly that the *Pequod*'s crew numbered thirty (the whaleship standard), even though the number of distinguishable persons grew to forty-four—not to mention the profusion of unnamed sailors who function in the background as a kind of chorus. Characters who seem destined for significant roles are suddenly dropped, such as Peleg, who, as his name suggests, was probably originally intended to be the *Pequod*'s peglegged captain (he is identified as her former first mate), or Bulkington, the sailor "with a chest like a coffer-dam," whom Melville introduces with fanfare and then, twenty chapters later, summarily dismisses, never to mention him again.

Most striking was what happened to Ishmael. Around the twenty-fifth chapter he fractures into multiple voices contending with one another as if taking turns in a stage play, and soon the "I" of the book is telling us things he cannot possibly know: all over the ship sailors mutter to themselves while standing in the howling wind, yet Ishmael, wherever he is, somehow hears every word. The captain sits with his three mates over dinner in his cabin, yet Ishmael—a common sailor who would never be permitted to join the offi-

cers' mess—tells us how they cut and chew their meat and who says what to
whom. He becomes a sort of mobile consciousness, extracted from his own
singular identity, then multiplied and redistributed into the mind of every
man aboard.

Looking back at his labors on *Moby-Dick,* Melville saw "two
books . . . being writ . . . the larger book, and the infinitely better, is for
[his] own private shelf. That it is, whose unfathomable cravings drink his
blood; the other only demands his ink." *Moby-Dick* was Melville's vampire
book. It sapped him—but not before he had invented a new kind of writing
that, we can now see, anticipated the kind of modernist prose that expresses
the author's stream of consciousness without conscious self-censorship.
Melville was aware of this ideal in its incipient Romantic form, having marked
approvingly a passage in an essay by William Hazlitt that declares true writing to be an "ebullition of mind," a "flow of expression" that, by analogy
with frescoes, must be executed with fast and free strokes before the wet
plaster dries—a burst of inspiration whose "execution is momentary and
irrevocable." Melville was the first American to write with such outrageous
freedom. He was the first to understand that if a literary work is to register
the improvisational nature of experience, it must be as spontaneous and self-
surprising as the human mind itself. Aware, as Freud later puts it, that "in
mental life nothing which has once been formed can perish," Melville also
knew that by concealing the existence of earlier versions of his work, he ran
the risk of falsifying himself.* In this sense, *Moby-Dick* was like an active
archeological site in which the layers of its own history are left deliberately
exposed.

7.

Consider, for instance, what happens to Bulkington, that man of "noble
shoulders" whom Ishmael glimpses at the Spouter Inn. As his name implies,

*As the art historian Meyer Schapiro has said of expressionist and post-expressionist painting,
"the subjective becomes tangible," by which he means that on a canvas by, say, Monet or Cézanne,
we see in "the mark, the stroke, the brush, the drip"—none of which is effaced or concealed—"the
drama of decision in the ongoing process of art." Melville's creative process in *Moby-Dick* was
the verbal equivalent of the "tangible subjectivity" that he had seen in the canvases of Turner. As
the English critic Henry Chorley wrote astutely in 1850, "Mr. Melville stands as far apart from any
past or present marine painter in pen and ink as Turner does" from lesser painters.

Bulkington is a natural aristocrat—an almost cartoonish paragon of manly virtue, complete with deep tan and "white teeth dazzling by contrast," and a serious contender for the position held in *White-Jacket* by Jack Chase, the democratic leader who commands respect out of trust and comradely love. When we first meet Bulkington at the Spouter Inn, he seems destined to play a major role in the book. He has about him every mark of importance: dignity, bearing, refinement. He is Melville's first candidate to resist the tyrannical Ahab once the *Pequod* is under way (a miniature version of this story survives in the chapter entitled "The Town Ho's Story"), but just as "there is but one planet to one orbit," he was later to write in *The Confidence-Man*, "so can there be but one such original character to one work of invention. Two would conflict to chaos." And so Melville replaced Bulkington with a lesser man who recognizes Ahab's madness but who cannot muster the strength to challenge him—namely, Starbuck, the first mate:

> Brave as he might be, it was that sort of bravery . . . which, while generally abiding firm in the conflict with seas, or winds, or whales, or any of the ordinary irrational horrors of the world, yet cannot withstand those more terrific, because more spiritual terrors, which sometimes menace you from the concentrating brow of an enraged and mighty man.

Detailed reconstruction of Melville's revisions of *Moby-Dick* is impossible since no manuscript or notes survive. But that he changed his ideas about who should lead and who should resist aboard the *Pequod* can hardly be doubted. Twenty chapters after introducing him, Melville says farewell to Bulkington as he stands at the helm on the bitter Christmas night when the *Pequod* heads for the open sea:

> Some chapters back, one Bulkington was spoken of, a tall, new-landed mariner, encountered in New Bedford at the inn.
>
> When on that shivering winter's night, the Pequod thrust her vindictive bows into the cold malicious waves, who should I see standing at her helm but Bulkington! I looked with sympathetic awe and fearfulness upon the man, who in midwinter just landed from a four years' dangerous voyage, could so unrestingly push off again for still another tempestuous term. The land seemed scorching to his feet. Wonderfullest things are ever the unmentionable; deep memories yield no epitaphs; this six-inch chapter is the stoneless grave of Bulkington.

This is the last we see of Bulkington as he falls back into the faceless crew that sails the ship to her doom—but not before Melville honors him with a eulogy:

"Take heart, take heart, O Bulkington! Bear thee grimly, demigod! Up from the spray of thy ocean-perishing—straight up, leaps thy apotheosis!"

But why leave him in the book at all? Why not excise the sentence in which, as one scholar puts it, Melville "introduces a character and says that there is no use in introducing him"? This decision to retain a short-lived character as what Freud calls a "memory-trace" is one of the telltale marks of Melville's method in *Moby-Dick,* and a clue to why the book, rejected in its own day, was so warmly embraced in the twentieth century as a protomodernist work. To nineteenth-century readers with a taste for unified narrative ("the idea of a connected and collected story has obviously visited and abandoned its writer again and again," complained one reviewer), these kinds of decisions made no sense. They made for a messy and lumpy book—a kind of "intellectual chowder," as Duyckinck called it when he read the published version. But "there are some enterprises," says Ishmael, "in which a careful disorderliness is the true method," and to twentieth-century readers Melville's book fit the mode of Joyce or Woolf, in which superseded stages of development express the author's evolving state of mind. With wonderful insolence, he went back to Ishmael's original description of Bulkington and simply inserted a parenthetical update: "This man interested me at once; and since the sea-gods had ordained that he should soon become my shipmate (though but a sleeping-partner one, so far as this narrative is concerned), I will here venture upon a little description of him." And when, many pages later, he devoted an entire chapter—albeit a short, "six-inch chapter"—to saying goodbye to Bulkington, he confirmed that he was writing less about the world he imagined than about the self-revising process by which he continuously reimagined it.

In 1926, when Joyce's *Ulysses* had already established itself as that oxymoron, an avant-garde classic, the English critic John Freeman recognized Melville as a prophetic writer who had anticipated the sort of modernist writing in which rationality retreats before "the unconscious mind, stealing silently between the eyes and pen . . . as it suggests, offers, presses and overwhelms the conscious mind, and makes it less an equal than a servant." The great book that carried Melville away between the spring of 1850 and the summer of 1851 was a young man's coming-of-age story, an encyclopedic inventory of facts and myths about whales, a concatenation, as Duyckinck described it with fond bewilderment, "of romance, philosophy, natural history, fine writing, good feeling, [and] bad sayings." It was all these things, but it was also an audacious attempt, long before Freud and his modernist followers, to represent in words the unconscious as well as conscious processes of the human mind itself.

CHAPTER 6
CAPTAIN AMERICA

1.

During his surge of creativity in 1850–51, Melville sometimes seemed to shut out the world and to live virtually alone in the universe of his imagination. But he did not escape the outer world entirely, and when political events broke through to him, they did so with more force and effect than at the time of the Mexican War. In that spring of 1850, the United States was facing the question of how to organize the vast territories it had won in the war. Comprising all of present-day California, Nevada, and Utah, and parts of New Mexico, Arizona, Colorado, and Wyoming, the Mexican cession, formally ratified in the Treaty of Guadalupe-Hidalgo on February 2, 1848, quickened westward migration; and when gold deposits were discovered in California later that year ("It seems a golden Hell!" Melville wrote in *Mardi*, where he described men starving in the mines and killing one another for an ounce of yellow dust), the march of settlement became a stampede.

The defeat of Mexico at first seemed another step toward the glorious fulfillment of America's manifest destiny, but it turned out to be one of those instances with which history is replete, in which military victory sets off a political crisis in the land of the victor. "The United States will conquer Mexico," Emerson declared in 1846, "but it will be as the man who swallows the arsenic which brings him down in turn. Mexico will poison us." Privately, Melville was thinking along similar lines. In his copy of the works of William D'Avenant, purchased on his London trip in 1849, he checked the following passage: "for God ordain'd not huge Empire as proportionable to the Bodies, but to the Mindes of Men; and the Mindes of Men are more monstrous and require more space for agitation and the hunting of others, than the Bodies of Whales."

Thirty years earlier, a fragile equilibrium had been established between slave states and free states when Congress agreed, in what was known as the Missouri Compromise, to partition the country along the 36°30′ parallel, permitting slavery to the south and forbidding it to the north. Although talk of southern secession had revived during a tariff dispute in 1832, the dividing line of 1820 held for three decades of relatively little political turbulence. It was in these years that Melville came of age, a member of a generation that lulled itself into thinking the slavery problem would somehow be resolved. "Let slavery take care of itself," Evert Duyckinck wrote to his brother George in 1848, and added, for good measure, "it will." But as one historian puts it, slavery remained "the unacknowledged ghost" in American politics—and everyone knew at heart that it had not been put to rest.

In the early months of 1850, the ghost began to stir. California had petitioned for admission to the Union as a free state, raising the prospect— indeed, the certainty—of another addition to the growing northern majority in Congress. On March 4, a skeletal John C. Calhoun, senior senator from South Carolina, came to the Senate chamber, his skin sallow and loose, but still with fire in his eyes. In assembling a portrait from contemporary descriptions of Calhoun, one could do worse than apply to him Melville's description of Captain Ahab: "He looked like a man cut away from the stake, when the fire has overrunningly wasted all the limbs without consuming them." Too ill to deliver his remarks himself, Calhoun asked a colleague from Virginia to read what was to be his final appeal to the North that it use its "exclusive power of controlling the Government" to guarantee the rights of the South once and for all or else face secession.

With the preponderance of power shifting northward, Calhoun insisted that the South must be protected from those who would seal off new territories from slave labor, on which the southern economy depended. It was the eleventh hour for anyone who would save the nation, which

> cannot . . . be saved by eulogies on the Union, however splendid or numerous. The cry of "Union, Union, the glorious Union!" can no more prevent disunion than the cry of "Health, health, glorious health!" on the part of the physician can save a patient lying dangerously ill.

Calhoun knew of what he spoke. Four weeks later, he would be dead.

On March 7, Massachusetts senator Daniel Webster, dressed in the brass-buttoned suit that he always wore on significant occasions, rose to speak in response. Mindful of Calhoun's warning that the time was past for windy speeches about the glories of the Union, he followed his own pledge of allegiance ("I wish to speak today, not as a Massachusetts man, nor as a Northern man, but as an American") with a pragmatic endorsement of the

John C. Calhoun,
c. 1850

proposed Fugitive Slave Law, which he regarded as a necessary concession to the South:

> Every member of every Northern legislature is bound by oath, like every other officer in the country, to support the Constitution of the United States; and the article of the Constitution [Article IV, sect. 2, para. 2] which says to these States that they shall deliver up fugitives from service is as binding in honor and conscience as any other article. No man fulfills his duty in any legislature who sets himself to find excuses, evasions, escapes from this constitutional obligation.

Historians call the outcome of this congressional session the Compromise of 1850. At stake was the future of the slaves and of their unborn children, or so we tend to think today. In fact, the primary issue on the minds of Calhoun, Webster, and almost all of their colleagues was the question of whether the United States would continue as a viable nation or was about to break in two. And since virtually no one could imagine a way of eradicating slavery (Webster had "nothing to propose" to effect its "extinguishment") while leaving the nation intact, the problem seemed as intractable as conflict in the Middle East or AIDS in Africa seems today. Men as prudent as Tocqueville and Jefferson had predicted that sooner or later the United States would collapse into a war between the races or a war over race. "We have the wolf by the ears," Jefferson had written about slavery in 1820, "and we can neither hold him, nor safely let him go."

In hopes of taming the beast, some reformers proposed gradual emancipation, with compensation to slaveowners for their property losses. But how could such a plan be financed? How could a whole region of the country be reconstructed on a new relationship between capital and labor? And what would be done with a large population of former slaves in a society where only a few crackpot dreamers took the idea of racial equality seriously? There was talk of sending them to Liberia; but, as a Whig politician named Abraham Lincoln pointed out, "if they were all landed there in a day, they would all perish in the next ten days; and there are not surplus shipping and surplus money enough in the world to carry them there in many times ten days." Lincoln, who wanted slavery banned from all federal territories that had not yet been organized into states, remarked that "if all earthly power were given me, I should not know what to do" about slavery in states where, by tradition and statute, it already existed.

These were old problems. Their intractability had led to many evasions and deferrals by which the solution had been left to the future. But in 1850 something fundamental changed, and a chronic problem became an acute one. Under the terms of the proposed compromise, California would be admitted as a free state, the Utah and New Mexico territories were to submit the question of slavery at some future date to popular vote, the slave trade in Washington, D.C., would be ended, and existing laws would be toughened to require local authorities in every state of the Union to arrest and return runaway slaves to their aggrieved masters. The effect of this omnibus bill, which passed piecemeal through Congress under the stewardship of Illinois senator Stephen A. Douglas, was to answer the question, as Bronson Alcott phrased it in April 1851, "What has the North to do with slavery?" The answer was now clear: A great deal.

For years, northerners had managed to convince themselves that slavery was somebody else's problem. Yet everyone knew that northern banks invested heavily in cotton, and that in some northern ports the slave trade itself continued as an illegal, but tacitly permitted, smuggling business. In 1846, with war against Mexico looming, Theodore Parker had remarked that "Northern Representatives . . . are no better than Southern Representatives; scarcely less in favor of slavery, and not half so open." When confronted with such charges, most northerners looked the other way.

What the Fugitive Slave Law did for blacks was to rob them of hope. What it did for whites was to deny them mental refuge in willful insouciance. As Alcott put it, the new law "visibly answered" the question of the North's relation to slavery, in the form of fugitives running for their lives without hope of finding sanctuary even in New England, where the long arm of the slavemaster could now legally reach them. In May 1851, Emerson made the matter more visible than even Alcott had done:

> If our resistance to this law is not right, there is no right. . . . This is not going crusading into Virginia and Georgia after slaves, who, it is alleged, are very comfortable where they are . . . but this is befriending in our own state, on our own farms, a man who has taken the risk of being shot, or burned alive, or cast into the sea, or starved to death, or suffocated in a wooden box, to get away from his driver; and this man, who has run the gauntlet of a thousand miles for his freedom, the statute says, you men of Massachusetts shall hunt, and catch, and send back again to the dog-hutch he fled from.

2.

In the summer of 1850, Melville was living far from where this drama was playing out, but he kept abreast of events through the local Democratic paper, the *Pittsfield Sun,* which took an acquiescent line on the new Fugitive Slave Law. His local literary friends were similarly conciliatory. Dr. Holmes, who signed a public circular in Boston praising Webster for showing statesmanship, was known to speak with nostalgia about the old days of "slavery in its best and mildest form." Among those who signed a similar resolution in Pittsfield supporting every provision of the compromise was John C. Hoadley— a young widower and friend of the new owners of Broadhall, the Morewoods, who was to marry Kate Melville in 1853. As for Melville's new friend Nathaniel Hawthorne, he was soon to write in his campaign biography of his Bowdoin classmate Franklin Pierce that in America, master and slave "dwelt together in greater peace and affection . . . than had ever elsewhere existed between the taskmaster and the serf." But if Melville's friends and family generally supported the new law, to support it was not necessarily to like it. As Lincoln later wrote, "I hate to see the poor creatures hunted down, and caught, and carried back to their stripes, but I bite my lip and keep quiet." In Boston, the chief lip-biter was Judge Lemuel Shaw.

Beginning in the fall of 1850, a rash of fugitive slave cases turned Boston into a battleground. In October, slave hunters appeared in the city looking for a pair of fugitives, William Craft and his wife, Ellen, who had escaped from bondage in Georgia. They had fled with the light-skinned Ellen disguised as an invalid white man in scarf and goggles, and her husband posing as her black attendant. With the help of Theodore Parker, whose actions on their behalf constituted a felony under the new law, the Crafts eventually escaped to England before they could be arraigned in the court where Judge Shaw would have ruled on their case. (Harriet Beecher Stowe had the Crafts in mind when she wrote some of the scenes in *Uncle Tom's Cabin* of slaves fleeing bounty hunters.) A few months later, in early February 1851, a fugitive named Shadrach, also known as Frederick Minkins, was taken into custody in the federal courthouse where Shaw presided. Shortly afterwards, a mostly Negro mob invaded the building and, "like a black squall," according to Richard Henry Dana, carried off the prisoner before he could be sent back south. In April, when another young black man, Thomas Sims, was arrested, the city marshal encircled the courthouse in heavy chains in order to prevent a repeat of the Shadrach rescue. Lawyers and judges had to stoop below the chain to enter. When Shaw delivered the order to return Sims to Georgia (where he later nearly died from a public flogging), Emerson wrote in his journal: "What a moment was lost when Judge Shaw declined to affirm the unconstitutionality of the Fugitive Slave Law!"

One effect of these events was to place Melville's father-in-law at the center of the storm and turn him into the embattled leader of New England conservatism. Having once been praised by the fervently anti-slavery Charles Sumner as "pure, fearless, and upright," Shaw now found himself regularly denounced as a truckler to what abolitionists called "the Slave Power." In fact, he saw himself as a servant of the law much as his friend Webster did. Personally, he found slavery abhorrent. When the law permitted him to act against it, he did so, as he had done in an 1836 case involving a slave transported by her mistress to New England. Shaw had ruled that "an owner of a slave in another State where slavery is warranted by law, voluntarily bringing such slave into this State, had no authority to detain him against his will"— a judgment that later furnished the basis for Justice Benjamin Curtis's dissent in the 1857 U.S. Supreme Court *Dred Scott* decision denying Negroes their citizenship rights.

But after 1850, Shaw felt obliged to enforce the Fugitive Slave Law even if it required him to issue orders for remanding fugitives to their owners. What had changed was not Shaw's position but that of the law he served, and to many of Shaw's friends and peers it seemed that the world had turned upside down. "It is strange," wrote Thomas Wentworth Higginson in 1851,

Lemuel Shaw,
1851

"to find one's self outside of established institutions . . . to see law and order, police and military, on the wrong side, and find good citizenship a sin and bad citizenship a duty." A decent man might once have lived comfortably with himself as long as he "abstains from doing downright ill," Melville was soon to write in *Pierre,* and "is perfectly tolerant to all other men's opinions, whatever they may be." But with slavecatchers and anti-slavery vigilantes prowling the streets, abstention and toleration were already fond memories and, according to some, outright crimes. Not long before, when the abolitionist William Lloyd Garrison proclaimed "NO UNION WITH SLAVEHOLDERS!," his voice had seemed a howl from the fringe. Now he seemed to speak for the center.

3.

As Melville's rather puerile sketches in *Yankee Doodle* and the political chapters of *Mardi* had made clear, he was, at best, a halfhearted political satirist. Politics never engaged him deeply. Passage of the Fugitive Slave Law did not incite him to loud outrage as it did contemporaries such as Emerson, who declared that "I wake in the morning with a painful sensation" at the smell of "infamy in the air," or Harriet Beecher Stowe, who wrote *Uncle Tom's Cabin* in hot fury at what she regarded as Webster's perfidy. But Melville found himself full of foreboding on behalf of his country, and this apprehension was reflected in his new book. The ghost of slavery had made fleeting appearances in his earlier work—showing up in *Mardi* in the form of a hand-bill promising bounty for the capture of runaway slaves posted in the "Temple of Freedom" (the U.S. Capitol). In *Redburn,* the ghost had appeared in Liverpool when Melville's young American narrator looks upon a statue of Lord Nelson standing astride four "woe-begone figures of captives emblematic of Nelson's principal victories" and finds himself thinking instead of "four African slaves in the marketplace." In *White-Jacket,* upon witnessing a black sailor being flogged, the narrator is prompted by the slavery ghost to blurt out his relief—"Thank God! I am a white"—before recanting in a spasm of shame: "There is something in us, somehow that, in the most degraded condition, we snatch at a chance to deceive ourselves into a fancied superiority to others, whom we suppose lower in the scale than ourselves."

Melville knew that in America the dignity of whites depended on the degradation of blacks, and he was, at least sporadically, ashamed to be a beneficiary of the symmetry. But like virtually everyone in his time, including most abolitionists, he took for granted that some sort of racial hierarchy had always existed and always would. Even the belligerently egalitarian Whitman, whose panoptic poems tend to blur all human subjects into a monochrome crowd ("each answering all, each sharing the earth with all"), was not above speaking of black people as a "superstitious, ignorant, and thievish race." If Emerson spoke compassionately about fugitive slaves, he also wrote in his journal that "so inferior a race must perish shortly like the Indians," while Samuel F. B. Morse, inventor of the telegraph, put the Negro just above the baboon in the great chain of being. These attitudes were so widespread that in 1842, while touring the United States, the English naturalist Charles Lyell was amazed at "the extent to which the Americans carry their repugnance to all association with the coloured race on equal terms."

On this question of race, Melville was a dissenter. "Seamen have strong prejudices," he wrote in 1855, "particularly in the matter of race," though aboard a whaleship (about the closest thing in antebellum America to an integrated society) there was, according to one black sailor writing in 1857, "no distinction as to color"—and it was on a whaleship that Melville's adult consciousness had been formed. One of his former shipmates on the *United States,* the purser's slave, Robert Lucas, had petitioned successfully to Judge Shaw for his freedom after the ship docked at Boston. And like Ishmael, Melville believed that "a man can be honest in any sort of skin." Having served with black men of all qualities, he dismissed the various theories (blacks were said to have small cranial cavities and simian brows) with which some apologists for slavery argued that they were suited by nature for servitude. As for black women, Melville had probably read the Scottish explorer Mungo Park's *Travels in the Interior Districts of Africa* (1799), or was at least favorably aware of Park's account of the kindness, refinement, and modesty of African mothers.

One consequence of Melville's years at sea was a certain cosmopolitan amusement at how human beings organize themselves into ranks, and at how those doing the organizing always reserve a place for themselves at the top. The many passages in *Moby-Dick* in which whales are listed, sorted, described, defined ("to be short, then, a whale is a *spouting fish with a horizontal tail*"), assigned a formal name ("Narwhale") or nickname ("Nostril whale"), categorized by girth or physiognomy or even character ("the Fin-Back is not gregarious"), aesthetically assessed (the mealy-mouthed porpoise has "sentimental Indian eyes of a hazel hue. But his mealy-mouth spoils all") amount to what one critic calls "a zestful-skeptical running commentary on the age's passion for comparative anatomy." These cetological chapters retard the pace of the narrative, and many readers prefer to skip them in order to get on with the great chase; but it is here that Melville makes his case, with tongue in cheek, against all forms of classification—including the racial form. "It is in vain," he writes, with more than whales in mind, "to attempt a clear classification of the Leviathan," yet

> some pretend to see a difference between the Greenland whale of the English and the right whale of the Americans. But they precisely agree in all their grand features; nor has there yet been presented a single determinate fact upon which to ground a radical distinction. It is by endless subdivisions based upon the most inconclusive differences, that some departments of natural history become so repellingly intricate.

A few years after writing *Moby-Dick,* he was to place at the center of his great novella *Benito Cereno* a white New Englander too stupid to realize that he is being manipulated by an African slave of brilliance and wit.

Melville regarded slavery, in other words, as a crime not only against one subjugated race but against humanity (a "sin it is, no less;—a blot, foul as the crater-pool of hell," he wrote in *Mardi*), yet he was not sure where to place responsibility for it or how to begin to redress it. For one thing, he doubted that northerners were morally superior merely because the slave system had never established itself in their part of the country. Naval officers "from the

Southern States," he wrote in *White-Jacket*, "are much less severe, and much more gentle and gentlemanly . . . than the Northern officers"— a judgment with which Ahab concurs when he warns the *Pequod*'s black cabin boy that there are "no hearts above the snow-line." In *Mardi*, Melville wrote that "humanity cries out against this vast enormity," but "not one man knows a prudent remedy." In *Redburn*, Melville touched the slavery theme again when the narrator complains that he has been treated "like a slave, and set to work like an ass!" with "vulgar and brutal men lording it over me, as if I were an African in Alabama."

When *Moby-Dick* began to take shape in Melville's mind, the dispute between (and within) North and South over race and slavery was coming to crisis. Political orators of all stripes warned that the ship of state was "about to be dashed to pieces amidst the breakers with which she was visibly almost in contact," yet most poets and fiction writers dealt with the crisis warily if at all. Longfellow addressed it in his "The Building of the Ship" (1850), about boatwrights who construct out of "cedar of Maine and Georgia pine" a vessel "sublime in its enormous bulk" to which they wishfully give the name *Union*. Thoreau wrote obliquely in *Walden* (1854) about the Mexican War by recounting the sight of red and black ants in a woodpile gnawing at each other with "the ferocity and carnage of a human battle" that "took place in the Presidency of Polk, five years before the passage of Webster's Fugitive-Slave Bill."

It is impossible to say just when or how the political situation seized Melville's attention; but at some point between the Webster-Calhoun exchange in Washington in March 1850 and the outbreak of conflict in Boston at the end of that year, the crisis took effect on his work-in-progress. In his earlier books, he had shunted political matters into tangential comments that read like editorials patched onto the main narrative; but in *Moby-Dick*, politics became a central element in the larger constellation of themes, as if the incidental realism of *Redburn* and *White-Jacket* had been melded with the political allegory of *Mardi*. The *Pequod* becomes a replica of the American ship of state; its thirty-man crew ("isolatoes federated along one keel") matched in number the thirty states that constituted the Union in 1850. The *Pequod*'s labor system, made up of white overseers and dark underlings, replicates that of "the American army and military and merchant navies, and the engineering forces employed in the construction of the American Canals and Railroads." And in an echo of a stock image in contemporary political cartoons showing a white planter atop the shoulders of a brawny black slave, one of the mates, Mr. Flask, perches on the shoulders of the "coal-black" harpooneer Daggoo, in order to get an aerial view of their hunting ground:

*New York newspaper
cartoon, c. 1860*

The sight of little Flask mounted upon gigantic Daggoo was . . . curious; for sustaining himself with a cool, indifferent, easy, unthought of, barbaric majesty, the noble negro to every roll of the sea harmoniously rolled his fine form. On his broad back, flaxen-haired Flask seemed a snow-flake. The bearer looked nobler than the rider.

"Thy race is the undeniable dark side of mankind," a Spanish sailor later tells Daggoo, "—devilish dark at that," to which Daggoo, half menacing, half mocking, shows his teeth.

But more than Atlas-like Daggoo, it was the diminutive black cabin boy Pip (short for Pippin) whom Melville chose to bear the weight of the racial theme in *Moby-Dick.* In one of those anomalies that Melville left unrevised in his manuscript, he describes Pip as both an "Alabama boy" and a native of Connecticut, as if South and North had collaborated in creating him. At first, Pip is little more than the stock figure of the dancing darky, amusing the crew by high-stepping to the sound of his tambourine; when he cannot find the instrument, he is told to "Beat thy belly, then, and wag thy ears." Later, in "The Castaway," we ride with Pip in Stubb's whaleboat, dragged along by a harpooned whale bucking and lurching in the maritime equivalent of a bronco ride until the boy loses his nerve, leaps out, and becomes entangled in the harpoon line. Mr. Stubb reluctantly halts the chase, allows his harpooneer to sever the line in order to save the boy at the expense of freeing the whale, and warns Pip that there will be no second rescue. "Stick to the boat, Pip," Stubb says, or next time, "by the Lord, I wont pick you up. . . . We can't afford to lose whales by the likes of you; a whale would sell for thirty times what you would, Pip, in Alabama." Sure enough, when Pip jumps a second time, he is left in the sea "like a hurried traveller's trunk."

Melville was recalling here an incident from his time aboard the *Acushnet,* when a young black sailor named Backus had leapt overboard during a chase. Now he turned the event into what must surely be the most terrifying image of human loneliness conceived by an American artist until the scene in Stanley Kubrick's *2001: A Space Odyssey* (a very Melvillean film) in which the doomed astronaut clutches at his severed air hose while tumbling into the blackness of space. Alone in the open ocean, Pip watches his "ringed horizon . . . expand around him" as the whaleboats pursue their prey, leaving him to bob in the ocean's "heartless immensity." It is an image of abandonment that makes Poe's caves and dungeons seem childish contrivances, and its horror—"the intense concentration of self in the middle of such a heartless immensity, my God! Who can tell it?"—is so far beyond imagining that Melville comes at the experience obliquely, through a contrasting image that makes us feel the terror of being cut loose into the indifferent infinite. "Mark," he says, "how when sailors in a dead calm bathe in the open sea—mark how closely they hug their ship and only coast along her sides."

By the time the ship happens to sail by and pick up Pip "by merest chance," the ocean has "jeeringly kept his finite body up" but has "drowned the infinite of his soul." Pip has lost himself. He has come to feel "indifferent as his God" (Melville had been reading in Carlyle's *Sartor Resartus* about the "centre of indifference" as a stage to wisdom), and "from that hour the little negro went about the deck an idiot," or "such, at least they said he was." Pip stands before the gold doubloon that Ahab has nailed to the mast and, to the puzzlement of his shipmates ("Upon my soul, he's been studying Murray's Grammar!"), he conjugates the verb "to look": "I look, you look, he looks; we look, ye look, they look." He has been emptied of self-consciousness, and protected by his evident idiocy against his white masters—whom he calls, knowing their propensity to rage, "white squalls"—he speaks the candid truth that they all see the world as a reflection of themselves. Even to the most explosive of them, Ahab, he dares to say: "Will ye do one little errand for me? Seek out one Pip, who's now been missing long." As for Ahab, touched for the first time by the suffering of another human being, he questions Pip gently in an exchange worthy of Lear and his Fool:

"Where sayest thou Pip was, boy?"

"Astern there, sir, astern Lo! lo!"

"And who art thou, boy? I see not my reflection in the vacant pupils of thy eyes. Oh God! That man should be a thing for immortal souls to sieve through! Who art thou boy?"

In answer, Pip can only parrot the language of an advertisement for the return of a fugitive slave:

"Pip! Pip! Pip! Reward for Pip! One hundred pounds of clay—five feet high—looks cowardly—quickest known by that! Ding, dong, ding! Who's seen Pip the coward?"

It was one hundred years before the publication of Ralph Ellison's *Invisible Man* that Melville made this touching portrait of an invisible boy who, in the "strange sweetness of his lunacy, brings heavenly vouchers of all our heavenly homes." *Moby-Dick* is a book filled with hate and ugliness, but it offers glimpses as well of a beautiful alternative world in which Pip, having once been disposed of as a nuisance, comes back to sing from his heart, and softens the roughest men with his song. Echoing Lear's deference to his Fool ("In, boy; go first, You houseless poverty,— / Nay, get thee in"), Ahab says to Pip in a fatherly moment, "Come! I feel prouder leading thee by thy black hand, than though I grasped an Emperor's!"

4.

With these allusions to what was and what might have been in the America of 1850, *Moby-Dick* became in the broadest sense a political novel. Melville made of the *Pequod* a mirror of America rushing westward, poisoning itself by eating up a continent, "a cannibal of a craft . . . tricking herself forth in the chased bones of her enemies," its bulwarks lined with whale teeth in place of wooden pins. Unlike their British counterparts, American whale-ships carried the equipment needed for boiling, or "trying out," whale blubber while at sea, and in "The Try-Works" chapter, the *Pequod* becomes a floating factory, lighting up the "darkness . . . licked up by the fierce flames" from her stone furnace in which the bodies of her victims are consumed

while the "spermaceti, oil, and bone pass unscathed through the fire."*
Melville imagines the ship as a version of Blake's "dark Satanic mills" driven
on *Walpurgisnacht* by a crew of scorched devils who pitch chunks of whale
blubber into the pots and, when the fire slackens, toss pieces of fat and flesh
directly into the flames.

This burning whaleship is an image beside which the smoking lime kiln
in Hawthorne's story "Ethan Brand" or the railroad in Thoreau's *Walden* (an
"iron horse . . . breathing fire . . . from his nostrils") seem pallid and banal:

> With huge pronged poles they pitched hissing masses of blubber into
> the scalding pots, or stirred up the fires beneath, till the snaky flames
> darted, curling, out of the doors to catch them by the feet. The smoke
> rolled away in sullen heaps. To every pitch of the ship there was a pitch
> of the boiling oil, which seemed all eagerness to leap into their
> faces. . . . Their tawny features, now all begrimed with smoke and
> sweat, their matted beards, and the contrasting barbaric brilliancy of
> their teeth, all these were strangely revealed in the capricious emblazon-
> ings of the works. As they narrated to each other their unholy adven-
> tures, their tales of terror told in words of mirth; as their uncivilized
> laughter forked upwards out of them, like the flames from the furnace;
> as to and fro, in their front, the harpooneers wildly gesticulated with
> their huge pronged forks and dippers; as the wind howled on, and the
> sea leaped, and the ship groaned and dived, and yet steadfastly shot her
> red hell further and further into the blackness of the sea and the night,
> and scornfully champed the white bone in her mouth, and viciously
> spat round her on all sides; then the rushing Pequod, freighted with
> savages, and laden with fire, and burning a corpse, and plunging into
> that blackness of darkness, seemed the material counterpart of her
> monomaniac commander's soul.

But who was this "monomaniac commander"? From what dark corner of
Melville's imagination did he come, swaying and swooning to the sound of
his own eloquence as he urges on his savage crew?

In the early chapters, before Ahab makes his first appearance, Melville
dropped some hints. As the ship makes ready to sail, the docks come alive

---

*Their British competitors, having no such capacity, brought the blubber back to port raw, a prac-
tice that limited the maximum length of their voyages, since raw blubber required more storage
space and could spoil. (British whalers averaged five months at sea, while a typical cruise by an
American whaleship lasted well over a year.) See Lance E. Davis, Robert E. Gallman, and Teresa
D. Hutchins, "Call Me Ishmael—Not Domingo Floresta: The Rise and Fall of the American
Whaling Industry," *Research in Economic History,* Supplement 6 (1991): 197.

with talk about "moody stricken" Ahab—a "grand, ungodly, god-like man," Peleg tells Ishmael, who has "been in colleges, as well as 'mong the cannibals," and is "used to deeper wonders than the waves." Shortly after receiving this report, while walking on the wharf with Queequeg, Ishmael is accosted by a shuffling stranger portentously named for the Old Testament prophet Elijah, with a withered arm and a face so pitted by smallpox that it looks like the "ribbed bed of a torrent" after the water has dried up. This unnerving fellow wants to know if Ishmael and his cannibal friend have yet laid eyes on the master ("Old Thunder," he calls him) of the ship on which they are about to embark. "No, we hav'n't," Ishmael admits. "He's sick they say, but is getting better, and will be all right again before long." Ishmael's reply strikes Elijah as the funniest thing he has heard in a while: "All right again before long! When captain Ahab is all right, then this left arm of mine will be all right, not before."

In New York and on his London trip, Melville had gotten into a theater-and operagoing habit, and in preparing the stage for Ahab his method was essentially theatrical. Subsidiary actors report rumors about Ahab as, one by one, his rivals (Peleg, Bulkington) drop away, until, at last, "Old Thunder" himself climbs up from his hideaway onto the stage—peg-legged and hideously marked by a "lividly whitish" scar that runs down his face and neck and continues under his clothes down his body like a lightning wound on a tree trunk. Something in Ahab's deformity provokes both sympathy and fear; he seems seared and torn, a frightful survivor of some unsurvivable blast. And even before Ahab begins to speak, Melville conveys the crew's amazement in a three-word phrase: "Reality outran apprehension."

With his powerful intellect and wasted body, Ahab bore an evident resemblance to John C. Calhoun. Like Calhoun, he has a heart as immovable as his mind is nimble; and like "erect" and "nervous" Ahab, Calhoun was known to his enemies as a monomaniac whose brain, as Melville's friend George W. Curtis was to write during the Civil War, "was the huge reservoir of rebellion" from which the South drew its venom. When the captain of a passing ship begs for help in searching for his son, who has fallen overboard, Ahab stands unmoved "like an anvil, receiving every shock but without the least quivering of his own," and replies, "I will not do it. Even now, I lose time." The notoriously cold Calhoun could not have done better—or worse.

It was natural for Melville to have this fearsome public figure in mind as he approached the writing of *Moby-Dick*. When the great South Carolinian died on March 31, 1850, Melville was still living in New York, where the local papers ran obituaries ranging from hagiography to grudging admiration to good riddance. News of Calhoun's death gave retrospective authority to his own warning that all efforts had failed "to prevent excitement and preserve quiet" between the northern and southern wings of the Democratic Party, which was known throughout the nation as the "American Democracy." Virtually everyone in the Duyckinck circle was a Democrat (in 1848, Melville's brother Allan had run unsuccessfully for State Assembly on the Democratic ticket), and thus vexed by the question of whether Young America could reconcile itself with the American Democracy, of which Calhoun had been chief architect, exponent, and symbol. Two years earlier, open conflict had broken out between northern and southern factions of the party when a renegade group of New York Democrats called "Barnburners," to whom Melville referred in *Mardi* as a "violently agitated" and "clamorous crowd," bolted over the slavery issue, helping to give the White House to the Whigs under their war hero candidate, Zack Taylor. By the early 1850s, once fervent Democrats were referring to their party as "the so-called democratic party," which "years of ardent contest have nursed . . . into hatreds [that] partake of the virulence of the *odium Theologicum.*"

Melville was aware that the Whigs, despite their electoral victory in 1848, were also coming apart. Their longtime leader in the South, Henry Clay, known as "the Great Conciliator," was still vital and canny enough to help secure the 1850 compromise but clearly was approaching the end of his career. In the North, the party was splitting between "Cotton Whigs" friendly to the South and "Conscience Whigs" appalled at the nomination of the slaveowning Taylor and increasingly uneasy about making common cause with any defender of slavery. In short, both parties in the two-party system were disintegrating, in what many Americans feared was a preview of what was about to happen to the nation.

As the American political system went to pieces before his eyes, Melville saw in Calhoun one model for his haunted captain; but more than that, he turned the *Pequod* into a sort of Democratic Party death convention—a ship of political fools sailing headlong for disaster. To the metaphysics, formal experiments, and maritime realism of *Moby-Dick* he added a layer of political satire: when Peleg and Bildad set up a wigwam on deck for the purpose of signing up new recruits, Melville's readers would have recognized their Indian-style tent as the symbol of the Democrats' New York headquarters, Tammany Hall. When Ishmael calls Bildad "an incorrigible old hunks," he was identifying him as a member of the "Hunker" faction (the pejorative name given by Barnburners to their old-guard opponents). And when the wood of Ahab's harpoon is said to be "hickory, with the bark still investing it," Melville's New York friends would have thought of the ceremonial hickory pole held aloft by party stalwarts at political parades, the symbol of continuity from Andrew Jackson ("Old Hickory") to James K. Polk ("Young Hickory"). By deploying these freighted political symbols, Melville introduced into *Moby-Dick* a critique of the expansionist policy of the American Democracy—a party still held in the death grip of Calhoun, and still, despite its internal dissensions and Taylor's victory, the most powerful organized political force in the nation.

As they splintered along the same sectional and ideological divide, the Whigs, too, found a place in the political allegory of *Moby-Dick*. When Father Mapple praises the man who "destroys all sin though he pluck it out from under the robes of Senators and Judges," he sounded like the increasingly vociferous critics of Webster and Shaw, who, having come out in favor of the Fugitive Slave Law, were being denounced as trimmers by anti-slavery members of their own party. And when Mapple celebrates the "top-gallant delight" felt by any man "who acknowledges no law or lord, but the Lord his God, and is only a patriot to heaven," he was echoing New York's Whig senator William H. Seward, who had delivered a notorious speech in that oratorical March of 1850 urging opponents of the Fugitive Slave Law to follow the "higher law" of God and conscience and to refuse to sell out to the Slave Power.

In spite of its author's relative political aloofness, *Moby-Dick* became a book about politics—or at least a book that lent itself to political interpretation. Writing in 1856, the black abolitionist James McCune Smith thought he recognized in Mr. Stubb the "boatsteerer" of the Whig Party, Horace Greeley. A century later, one resourceful scholar reached deep into, if not to the bottom of, the political barrel and pulled out Massachusetts Whig Robert C. Winthrop as a likely model for Mr. Starbuck. Even Bulkington has earned a place in the roster of contemporary political figures that Melville may have intended to include in *Moby-Dick*, having been plausibly identified as Thomas Hart Benton, the senator from Missouri and opponent of Calhoun who, when he was voted out of office in late 1850, took with him the last chance to stave off the rupture of the Democratic Party. Since Melville left no glossary, all such alignments between actual historical figures and their fictional counterparts in *Moby-Dick* are disputable; but it is beyond dispute that as he reworked his story of the fatal hunt, he was increasingly preoccupied by the several "Senators and Judges" who were leading the nation toward civil war.

And what of the man at the helm? Ahab has proven to be a prophetic mirror in which every generation of new readers has seen reflected the political demagogues of its own times—as when, in the 1940s, Ahab seemed to predict Adolf Hitler's monomaniacal rantings against the Jews, or, more recently, he is invoked as anticipating George W. Bush's obsession with hunting down first Osama bin Laden, then Saddam Hussein. Some readers who prefer to study Melville in relation to his own times have seen in Ahab a portrait of Calhoun, while others see his opposite, William Lloyd Garrison, who had led a raucous anti-slavery convention in New York just before Melville left town. As one scholar puts it, Ahab was Melville's "distortion of the 'political Messiah' " that he had celebrated in *White-Jacket*. He was, in other words, the American dreamer gone mad.

However historically or prophetically one prefers to read him, Ahab is a brilliant personification of the very essence of fanaticism, and therefore too grand a conception to be confined to any one exemplar of it. Like the whale itself, he was "comprehensive, combining, and subtle," a composite, as Richard Chase has written, of "many myths and many men"—some drawn from the ominous present or recent past, others from fiction (Shakespeare's Lear, Milton's Satan) and painting (Melville may have seen John Singleton Copley's *Watson and the Shark*, which depicted a shark attack that left a young boy with one leg so mangled that it had to be amputated), still others from further back in history, including, notably, Napoleon, that "man of stone and iron," as Emerson described him in 1850 (in an essay that Melville likely read), "pitiless . . . not embarrassed by any scruples," who, "in the fury of assault . . . no more spared himself" and "went to the edge of his possibility."*

5.

Whoever was his instigating original, Ahab was simultaneously the most inward of Melville's "isolatoes" and a man of "out-reaching comprehensiveness." His presence transforms everyone and everything around him. Such an "original character," Melville was later to write in *The Confidence-Man,* ". . . is like a revolving Drummond light, raying away from itself all round it—everything is lit by it, everything starts up to it (mark how it is with Hamlet), so that, in certain minds, there follows upon the adequate conception of such a character, an effect, in its way, akin to that which in Genesis attends upon the beginning of things."

*Melville had first heard about Napoleon from his father, who on a trip to Paris in 1803 had seen him reviewing French troops on the eve of the planned invasion of Britain. On his own trip to France in 1849, Melville bought a medallion of Napoleon and Josephine as a gift for Lizzie, and, for himself, an engraved bust of the great man in profile complete with laurel crown. There are Napoleonic props strewn all over *Moby-Dick*: the *Pequod* flies the red French battle flag, the crew is compared to the ragtag delegation led into the National Assembly by the revolutionary fanatic Anarcharsis Clootz, and in "The Town Ho's Story," a mutinous sailor mounts "the barricade, striding up and down" like a defiant *sans-culotte*. See Larry J. Reynolds, *European Revolutions and the American Literary Renaissance* (New Haven: Yale University Press, 1988), pp. 110–17.

The new beginning that Ahab effects aboard the *Pequod* is to turn what had been scheduled as just another business trip into a voyage of personal vengeance. Before shoving off in the pilot's boat, Bildad, co-owner of the *Pequod,* had urged the mates to "be careful in the hunt" and warned the harpooneers not to "stave the boats needlessly," since "good white cedar plank is raised full three per cent, within the year." But there is nothing careful about Ahab's hunt. *His* voyage is not about bringing back whale oil, but about revenge against the great white whale "athirst for human blood" that, years before, had wrecked his boat and nearly killed him:

> His three boats stove around him, and oars and men both whirling in the eddies; [Ahab], seizing the line-knife from his broken prow, had dashed at the whale, as an Arkansas duellist at his foe, blindly seeking with a six inch blade to reach the fathom-deep life of the whale. . . . And then it was, that suddenly sweeping his sickle-shaped lower jaw beneath him, Moby Dick had reaped away Ahab's leg, as a mower a blade of grass in the field.

For this part of the story, too, Melville had in mind actual historical events. In 1820, while cruising south of the equator near the Galapagos Islands under the command of Captain George Pollard, the Nantucket whaleship *Essex* was busy killing amid a shoal of whales when a large sperm whale, with every appearance of intent, swam directly at the vessel and struck it with such force that it opened a gash in the hull. The bilge pumps could not keep up with the rising water, and while preparations were being made to abandon ship, the whale struck again. This horror story (subsequent events were even more horrible, as the starving survivors resorted to murder and cannibalism) was well known among seafaring men and, with the publication in 1821 of a narrative by the second mate of the *Essex,* Owen Chase, it became known to the general public. Melville first learned about the fate of the *Essex* while aboard the *Acushnet* in 1841. Ten years later, while writing *Moby-Dick,* he annotated his own copy of Chase's narrative, calling it a "wondrous story" that, when he first heard it "upon the landless sea & close to the very latitude of the shipwreck," had "had a surprising effect upon me."

So Ahab was not the first to attribute murderous intention to a whale. Nor was he the first to commit himself to chasing down one particular whale. In May 1839, just before nineteen-year-old Herman Melville sailed for Liverpool, J. R. Reynolds had published in the *Knickerbocker Magazine* an account of "an old bull whale, of prodigious size and strength" that, like the "Ethiopian Albino . . . *was white as wool,*" and became the object of a vengeful hunt. Named after the island of Mocha just off the Chilean coast where he was first sighted, Mocha Dick was freakish not only in appearance but also in that he had repeatedly turned to attack his human pursuers. Reynolds's article was a putatively true relation of the chase, capture, and killing of this hoary white whale, and Melville doubtless had it in mind when he invented the story of Ahab and the white monster that had mutilated him with malicious intent.

In Melville's version, the name of the whale is slightly changed, and after its pursuer is nearly killed by its counterattack, "for long months of days and weeks, Ahab and anguish lay stretched together in one hammock" and "his torn body and gashed soul bled into one another; and so interfusing, made him mad." Among Ahab's mutilations is a sexual wound: although his ivory prosthetic leg is "entire, and to all appearances lusty, yet Ahab did not deem it entirely trustworthy"; and one night ashore—after some mysterious struggle, perhaps with himself in a nightmare, or with some violent stranger—he is found writhing in pain, the "dead bone" having "stake-wise smitten and all but pierced his groin." As W. H. Auden writes of Ahab's wound, "the rare ambiguous monster . . . had maimed his sex," and Melville was moving toward the insight that when eros is obstructed, it finds outlet as rage. He shows us Ahab—or what is left of him—turning his fury into a fanatic program for striking back at the thing that has unmanned him. The incapacitating wound makes him crave his lost potency all the more, and in this sense he belongs to—indeed, initiates—that lineage of sexually mutilated figures in our literature that includes Hemingway's Jake Barnes (in *The Sun Also Rises*) and Faulkner's Popeye (in *Sanctuary*), who, lacking the ability to rape a woman using his own body, violates her with a corncob instead.

Ahab, "dismasted," becomes a monster of calculation. Alone in his cabin, he spreads out before him nautical charts on which he traces Moby Dick's movements among the reefs and shallows, noting dates and coordinates of previous sightings, planning where and when to engage the foe, like an admiral tracking the enemy fleet. The world becomes a venue for enacting his sweet dream of revenge. Imagining the feel of his blade entering the white whale's hated flesh, he rocks and moans as if he were reliving the sexual swoon of which he is no longer capable, taking immense pleasure in his immense hate.

In an astonishing chapter entitled "The Grand Armada," Ahab drives the *Pequod* into a herd of sperm whales of "so great a multitude, that it would almost seem as if numerous nations of them had sworn solemn league and covenant for mutual assistance and protection." In fact, modern oceanographers have since confirmed that sperm whales do assemble for purposes of mutual defense, and that when the herd is attacked by sharks or other predators, individual whales will expose "themselves to increased attack" by flanking wounded members of the herd and bringing them back into the protective circle. *Moby-Dick* was, among other things, a poem of lyric praise for this mysterious tenderness in whales—creatures that combine bulk and grace, power and gentleness, and that seem to have an eerie solidarity with one another.* Melville wrote about these miraculous creatures with almost devotional awe, likening them, even as he (as Ishmael) hunted them, to sweet-tempered sheep set upon by hunters or wolves. "Beheld through a blending atmosphere of bluish haze," they give themselves away by their "vapory spouts, individually curling up into the air," which, for a contemplative moment before the chase begins, seem to the men who would kill them "like the thousand cheerful chimneys of some dense metropolis, descried of a balmy autumnal morning, by some horseman on a height." In recent years, such passages have been read as precursors to what might be called the literature of environmental sensitivity. There is no "save-the-whales message" in *Moby-Dick*, as one leading "eco-critic," Lawrence Buell, concedes; yet Melville repeatedly attributes human qualities to the hunted beasts and bestial qualities to the hunters. And years before advances in whale-killing technology required an affirmative answer, he posed (in chapter 105) the endangered-species question: "Does the Whale's Magnitude Diminish—Will He Perish?"

In the "Grand Armada" chapter, he wrote about a school of nursing mother whales whose suckling infants "calmly and fixedly gaze away from the breast . . . as if . . . still spiritually feasting upon some unearthly reminiscence . . . looking up towards us, but not at us, as if we were but a bit of Gulf-weed in their new-born sight." These beautiful creatures are Melville's equivalents to the unsullied children of Rousseau or Wordsworth. As yet unsevered from their prenatal memories, they exist in this world but are not of it. They have a kind of holiness, as if each mother and nursing baby were a submarine Madonna with Child.

Ahab could not care less. With his mind fixed on the hated white whale, he is, like a later character in *Clarel*, "Lost in . . . reminiscence sore / Of private wrong outrageous," and indifferent to all beauty and benignity. Despite his vast and devastated vanity—"I'd strike the sun if it insulted me," he tells Starbuck—he knows he needs his men if he is to achieve his murderous aim: "To accomplish his object Ahab must use tools; and of all tools used in the shadow of the moon, men are most apt to get out of order"—and Ahab's tool is exactly what the crew becomes. They are ideally suited for this role, given that, as Melville makes plain in heavily sexual language, they take orgasmic

---

* Ahab would not be surprised that modern scientists have confirmed that, by virtue of their highly developed "sonar" systems, whales can communicate through miles of water.

pleasure in killing whales, as when Ishmael describes how his boat, with "the waves curling and hissing around us like the erected crests of enraged serpents," approaches the "imminent instant":

> "That's his hump. *There, there,* give it to him!" whispered Starbuck.
> A short rushing sound leaped out of the boat; it was the darted iron of Queequeg. Then all in one welded commotion came an invisible push from astern, while forward the boat seemed striking on a ledge; the sail collapsed and exploded; a gush of scalding vapor shot up near by; something rolled and tumbled like an earthquake beneath us. The whole crew were half suffocated as they were tossed helter-skelter into the white curdling cream of the squall.

On this occasion the *coitus* is *interruptus* ("squall, whale, and harpoon had all blended together; and the whale, merely grazed by the iron, escaped"); but there are many consummated killings, as when Stubb "churned his long sharp lance" into a whale that, "spasmodically dilating and contracting his spout-hole," dies from the fatal penetration. Stubb will not be denied his postcoital smoke:

> "He's dead, Mr. Stubb," said Tashtego.
> "Yes, both pipes smoked out!" and withdrawing his own from his mouth, Stubb scattered the dead ashes over the water; and, for a moment, stood thoughtfully eyeing the vast corpse he had made.

6.

About a third of the way through *Moby-Dick*, we come to an extraordinary chapter, "The Quarter-Deck," in which Melville orchestrates these themes of eros and power into one of the great set pieces in literature about the dynamics of demagoguery. Ahab reveals himself here as the sort of man that Hawthorne described the Reverend Dimmesdale to be in *The Scarlet Letter,* another powerful orator whose "vocal organ was in itself a rich endowment" capable of swaying his listeners, as a lover does, "to and fro by the mere tone and cadence." Melville was writing, as the historian Lawrence Levine reminds us, in "an oral world in which the spoken word was central," where melodrama held the stage, and gifted speakers were public heroes. Whitman reports that as a young man he entertained his fellow passengers aboard the Broadway omnibuses by "declaiming some stormy passage from *Julius Caesar*," and as a schoolboy Melville himself had had "vague thoughts of becoming a great orator like Patrick Henry." It was a time when Americans expected such masters of symphonic speaking as Webster and Calhoun to deliver waves of emotion from *piano* to *fortissimo,* with plenty of *vibrato* along the way. As one of Webster's auditors put it, he seemed a "mount that might not be touched, and that burned with fire," his voice so affecting that his audience thought their "temples would burst with the gush of blood."

It is hard today to feel the force in such descriptions. To us, there is something ridiculous about the gesticulating man with stentorian voice, pouting and preening and all but weeping (Melville describes Ahab as emitting an "animal sob, like that of a heart-stricken moose"), whom we know only through crackling old recordings of the likes of William Jennings Bryan, or in the guise of some soapbox lunatic whom we hurry to get past on the street. But in Melville's time the orator was a democratic hero, and Ahab, deploying what one critic calls his "language of the screamer," was among the best of them.

He proves it in "The Quarter-Deck." The chapter begins quietly enough, with Ahab walking one morning on deck as "country gentlemen . . . take a few turns in the garden" after breakfast. On this particular morning, he has an air of brooding intensity unusual even for him. " 'D'ye mark him, Flask?' whispered Stubb; 'the chick that's in him pecks the shell. T'will soon be out.' " But not quite yet. For the rest of the day, Ahab goes down and up, to and from his cabin, where he shuts himself up for a while, then re-emerges into the open air, some "bigotry of purpose" ever more evident in his concentrated brow if not yet revealed to his men. Finally, toward evening, he plants his ivory leg in the auger-hole—his "stand-point"—that the carpenter has drilled into the deck at his command and orders Starbuck to send the whole crew aft.

With his men eyeing him warily, he resumes pacing until, bewildered by his behavior, they wonder if they have been "summoned . . . for the purpose of witnessing a pedestrian feat." Suddenly he barks out, "What do ye do when ye see a whale, men?," and there begins a series of call-and-response exchanges through which the men revert to the condition of children excited by the mounting approval of an adult whose displeasure they fear. "From a score of clubbed voices" comes their answer: "Sing out for him!" And as Ahab grows "fiercely glad and approving," the men marvel at "how it was that they themselves became so excited at such seemingly purposeless questions":

"Good!" cried Ahab, with a wild approval in his tones. . . . "And
what do ye next, men?"

"Lower away, and after him!"

"And what tune is it ye pull to, men?"

"A dead whale or a stove boat!"

At last, he gets to the point—to his "stand-point," that is—in which, swivel-
ing like the Drummond light, he scans his men while producing a bright
gold coin that he rubs, very slowly, to high polish on the skirts of his jacket
as he hums to himself. He requests a hammer from Starbuck, nails the doubloon to the mast, and, in a clear loud voice, promises the crew that "whosoever of ye raises me . . . [the] white whale, he shall have this gold ounce, my
boys!"

First to take the bait is Stubb's harpooneer, Tashtego, who wonders
aloud if the white whale is "the same that some call Moby Dick":

"Moby Dick?" shouted Ahab. "Do ye know the white whale then,
Tash?"

"Does he fan-tail a little curious, sir, before he goes down?" said the
Gay-Header deliberately.

"And has he a curious spout, too," said Daggoo, "very bushy, even
for a parmacetty, and mighty quick, Captain Ahab?"

"And he have one, two, three—oh! good many iron in him hide, too,
Captain," cried Queequeg disjointedly, "all twiske-tee be-twisk, like
him—him—" faltering hard for a word, and screwing his hand round
and round as though uncorking a bottle—"like him—him—"

Supplying the elusive word, Ahab becomes co-author of the obstructed sentence:

"Corkscrew!" cried Ahab, "aye, Queequeg, the harpoons lie all
twisted and wrenched in him; aye, Daggoo, his spout is a big one, like a
whole shock of wheat . . . aye, Tashtego, and he fan-tails like a split jib
in a squall. Death and devils! men, it is Moby Dick ye have seen—Moby
Dick—Moby Dick!"

At first, his voice is strong, while his accompanists are tentative and halting;
but as the music builds, the men come alive to their captain's fantastic purpose, and crew and captain come together in a crescendo of fused hatred that
is the literary equivalent of Wagner's orgiastic spectacle of *Gotterdämmerung*.

But there remains one dissident voice. " 'Captain Ahab,' said Starbuck, who, with Stubb and Flask, had thus far been eyeing his superior with increasing surprise, but at last seemed struck with a thought which somewhat explained all the wonder." Starbuck, unswayed for the moment, is the sort whom Melville will describe in *The Confidence-Man* as "the moderate man," whose weakness makes him "the invaluable understrapper of the wicked man." His prudence holds him back: " 'Captain Ahab, I have heard of Moby Dick—but it was not Moby Dick that took off thy leg?' " This is the fulcrum moment on which the chapter turns. Ahab's initial response is denial: " 'Who told thee that?' cried Ahab; then pausing"—a pause during which he makes the fateful decision not to conceal himself any longer. Baring his inflamed soul, he will plead with his men to make his cause their own and thus sweep away the obstacle that Starbuck has placed in his path:

> "Aye, Starbuck; aye, my hearties all round; it was Moby Dick that dismasted me; Moby Dick that brought me to this dead stump I stand on now. Aye, aye," he shouted. . . . "Aye, aye! it was that accursed white whale that razeed me; made a poor pegging lubber of me for ever and a day!" Then tossing both arms, with measureless imprecations he shouted out: "Aye, aye! and I'll chase him round Good Hope, and round the Horn, and round the Norway Maelstrom, and round perdition's flames before I give him up. And this is what ye have shipped for, men! to chase that white whale on both sides of land, and over all sides of earth, till he spouts black blood and rolls fin out. What say ye, men, will ye splice hands on it, now? I think ye do look brave."

His flatteries and imprecations have done their work; even Starbuck confesses that "he drilled deep down, and blasted all my reason out of me! . . . Will I, nill I, the ineffable thing has tied me to him; tows me with a cable I have no knife to cut." And now Ahab has them all in his grip:

> "Aye, aye!" shouted the harpooneers and seamen, running closer to the excited old man: "A sharp eye for the White Whale; a sharp lance for Moby Dick!"

Some eighty years before it emerged as the central political fact of the twentieth century, Melville had described in *Moby-Dick* the reciprocal love between a demagogue and his adoring followers.

But Ahab's appeal goes to the inquiring mind as well as to the susceptible heart. He speaks to the human need for finding meaning in suffering, to what he calls the "lower layer" of consciousness from which arises the demand to know if the "inscrutable" whale is the agent of "some unknown but still reasoning thing" that has sent it on its mission or if it is a mindless beast driven by purposeless instinct. To Ahab, we are all prisoners of our metaphysical ignorance about the meaning of our suffering, and so he demands of the dubious Starbuck, "how can the prisoner reach outside except by thrusting through the wall?" He follows his rhetorical question with an answer that both stirs and appalls:

> "To me, the white whale is that wall, shoved near to me. Sometimes I think there's naught beyond. But 'tis enough. He tasks me; he heaps me; I see in him outrageous strength, with an inscrutable malice sinewing it. That inscrutable thing is chiefly what I hate; and be the white whale agent, or be the white whale principal, I will wreak that hate upon him. Talk not to me of blasphemy, man; I'd strike the sun if it insulted me."

This speech is delivered by a man unafraid that meaning itself may prove to be an illusion, yet who is willing to destroy himself and, indeed, his whole world in pursuit of it. As W. H. Auden has remarked, Ahab is "a representation, perhaps the greatest in literature," of defiant despair—a man willfully beyond comfort because, in the Kierkegaardean formulation that Auden aptly invokes, "comfort would be the destruction of him." In his temperate moments, Ahab understands his own nature: "All my means are sane, my motive and my object mad." Yet in his ranting he gives his men ground for believing in their own heroic significance to his campaign to purify the world. In describing Captain Ahab, Melville struck a note that would resound through modern history in ways he could never have anticipated:

> All that most maddens and torments; all that stirs up the lees of things; all truth with malice in it; all that cracks the sinews and cakes the brain; all the subtle demonisms of life and thought; all evil, to crazy Ahab, were visibly personified and made practically assailable in Moby Dick.

Writing some thirty years later in *The Genealogy of Morals,* Nietzsche remarks that "every sufferer instinctively seeks a cause for his suffering . . . a 'guilty' agent who is susceptible to pain" on whom he can vent his rage and thereby "*dull* by means of some violent emotion [his] secret, tormenting pain." In 1928, the French critic Julien Benda, having recognized that

Europe was drifting into an age of reactionary nationalism, identified the moving force as xenophobia and accurately predicted that "hatred becomes stronger by becoming more precise." Here was Melville's theme; and while there is no evidence that Benda participated even privately in the Melville revival under way in the 1920s, parts of his famous book *La Trahison des Clercs* (*The Treason of the Intellectuals*) read like a commentary on "The Quarter-Deck"—as when he describes the rise of national feeling as the formation of a "*homogeneous,* impassioned group, in which individual ways of feeling disappear and the zeal of each member more and more takes on the color of the others." But it was not until the 1930s, when the power of demagoguery transformed the world into a charnelhouse, that the prescience of Melville's creation was fully recognized. Writing after the fascists had seized most of Europe, the leading American literary scholar of his generation, F. O. Matthiessen, saw in Ahab a figure who "provided an ominous glimpse of what was to result when the Emersonian will to virtue became in less innocent natures the will to power and conquest." To Lewis Mumford, writing during the last months of World War II, Melville was a prophet "as profoundly aware of the existence of radical evil as a contemporary theologian such as Dr. Reinhold Niebuhr. No one in our time who had fathomed his demonic characters . . . could have attributed the malignancy of fascism to merely economic difficulties that might be appeased by bribes or settled by compromise."

Soon after the war, when the full horror of the death camps had become known, Henry Murray described *Moby-Dick* as a "prophecy of the essence of fascism." A little later, in 1953, the Trinidadian writer C. L. R. James, while incarcerated on Ellis Island courtesy of a xenophobic demagogue named Joe McCarthy, compared Ahab's monomania to the "intense subjectivism" with which Hitler "repeatedly over-rode the opinions of trained diplomats and the German General Staff, committing blunder after blunder" that led to disaster. As late as 1964, Leo Marx, one of Matthiessen's most distinguished students, who had come of age in the 1930s and 1940s, saw in the crew of the *Pequod* under Ahab's spell "a pliant, disciplined, committed, totalitarian unit."

What all these readers recognized is that though Melville had been born and had died in the nineteenth century, *Moby-Dick* was the work of a twentieth-century imagination. As we begin our transition into the twenty-first century, this book has lost none of its salience. In Captain Ahab, Melville had invented a suicidal charismatic who denounces as a blasphemer anyone who would deflect him from his purpose—an invention that shows no sign of becoming obsolete anytime soon.

CHAPTER 7
"HERMAN MELVILLE CRAZY"

1.

In the fall and winter of 1851–52, Melville was living at Arrowhead amid a circle of women that included his wife, his frequently visiting mother, and a rotating delegation of sisters. The other males in the house were the nearly three-year-old Malcolm and, as of October 22, 1851, the newborn Stanwix. Then, on November 14, there arrived from Harper & Brothers the first copies of *Moby-Dick*. Melville had dedicated the book to Hawthorne, "in token of my admiration for his genius," and that same day he took a copy over to Lenox and invited his friend out to dinner at the local hotel for a proper farewell just a week before the Hawthornes were scheduled to leave for Concord. Though in the midst of packing, the dedicatee wasted no time in reading the book, and two days later, he wrote a letter of appreciation to the author. Hawthorne's letter has been lost, but Melville's response survives:

> Your letter was handed me last night on the road going to Mr. More-wood's, and I read it there . . . I felt pantheistic. . . . A sense of un-speakable security is in me this moment, on account of your having understood the book. I have written a wicked book, and feel spotless as the lamb. Ineffable socialities are in me. I would sit down and dine with you and all the gods in old Rome's Pantheon. . . . I shall leave the world, I feel, with more satisfaction for having come to know you. Knowing you persuades me more than the Bible of our immortality.

Hawthorne seems to have proposed that he review *Moby-Dick;* but Melville, perhaps suspecting an element of obligatory reciprocity in the offer, asked him to keep his praise private. "Don't write a word about the book," he replied. "That would be robbing me of my miserly delight." Refer-ring to his "Hawthorne and His Mosses" of two summers ago, he added, "I am heartily sorry I ever wrote anything about you—it was paltry," and by the next breath he was bragging that his new book-in-progress would be even larger in conception than the monster work just completed: "So, now, let us add Moby Dick to our blessing, and step from that. Leviathan is not the biggest fish;—I have heard of Krakens." But feeling one of his mood swings coming on, Melville confessed that the "unspeakable" joy that had filled him when he first read Hawthorne's letter was already fading. "In me," he wrote, "divine magnanimities are spontaneous and instantaneous—catch them while you can. The world goes round, and the other side comes up. So now I can't write what I felt." Melville's letter is a transcript of one of his manic-depressive episodes.

Two months later, with the first reviews coming in, he was thoroughly deflated. His book had been published in two versions—in October, in London, under the title *The Whale,* and in November, in New York, under the title by which it has been known ever since. He had tried to control the process by conveying his manuscript directly to the Fulton Street printer Robert Craighead (typesetter for *The Literary World*) and by checking the proofs himself before creation of the plates from which the book would be printed once he reached terms with Harper & Brothers, whose offices were a few blocks east of Craighead's shop. In June 1851, he told Hawthorne, he had come down to New York "to bury myself in a third-story room, and work and slave on my 'Whale' while it is driving through the press," but he had fled the hot city and finished the work in the Berkshires in July.

Because of the greater protection afforded by British copyright law, it was customary for American books, if they could find a British market, to appear in England before publication in the United States—and so throughout the summer Melville had been corresponding with Bentley. By September, terms had been reached. Melville's brother Allan shipped a set of proofs to London even before final agreement had been achieved with the New York publishers, and a few days later, acting as Herman's legal agent, he wrote to Bentley again. His brother, he explained, had settled on a new title—*Moby-Dick*—and had added a dedication to Nathaniel Hawthorne. The new title, he said, is "legitimate," since "if I may so express myself," the whale "is the hero" of the work. At some point during the interval between Melville's proofreading in the hot days of August and late September, when Allan sent these last-minute emendations to England, Melville evidently lost patience with the process (as he wrote about the hero of his new novel) of preparing his book for the press:

> The proofs . . . were replete with errors; but preoccupied by the thronging, and undiluted, pure imaginings of things, he became impa-

tient of such minute, gnat-like torments; he randomly corrected the worst, and let the rest go; jeering with himself at the rich harvest thus furnished to the entomological critics.

Here was a prophecy—amply vindicated since—that armies of scholars would someday pore over the words of the two first editions of *Moby-Dick,* trying to sort out the author's intentions from errors introduced by this or that meddler.

Before giving up, Melville had made substantial changes in the proofs destined for England (adding a long footnote, for instance, elaborating on the word "galley"); but once he received the first printed copies from Bentley later that fall, it was clear that someone else had tampered with the text. Either Bentley himself or one of his subordinates had cleaned it up, removing passages that seemed blasphemous or obscene. Where Melville had described Ahab standing "before them with a crucifixion in his face," the pious reviser substituted "an apparently eternal anguish in his face." Where Melville had likened an old male whale to a marauding Turk who, in his youth, had left "anonymous babies all over the world" before entering "upon the impotent, repentant, admonitory stage of life," some self-appointed censor struck out the word "impotent." The proposed new title was never used for the English edition, and there were unauthorized structural changes. The Extracts, which Melville intended as a kind of overture, were printed at the end of the work, and the Epilogue, in which Ishmael explains how he survived the shipwreck, was left out altogether. And so it was hardly surprising that British reviewers objected to a story told by a first-person narrator who had, presumably, drowned with his shipmates. How could one of the "miners in a pit," wondered a critic for the London *Spectator,* tell his own tale if he is among those who have perished?

Seeing his book mutilated and mocked had the effect of angering Melville permanently against publishers and critics. In fact, *Moby-Dick* fared better than *Mardi,* since for every sniggering critic there was someone who expressed respect. But the disproportion between achievement and reception was large enough to confirm what he had written to Hawthorne ("Try to get a living by the Truth—and go to the Soup Societies"), and by early 1852 Melville was referring almost bitterly to his new work-in-progress, *Pierre, or the Ambiguities,* as if it were a concession to the public taste that *Moby-Dick* had failed to satisfy. (Total earnings from the American sales of *Moby-Dick* would ultimately come to $556.37, considerably less than Melville had realized from any previous book.) "The Fates," he wrote to Sophia Hawthorne in January 1852, "have plunged me into certain silly thoughts and wayward speculations," and he went on in a tone of injured irony to say that his next book would be a modest confection suited for the ladies: "I shall not again send you a bowl of salt water. The next chalice I shall commend, will be a rural bowl of milk."

But by spring 1852 he was flying again and believed he was back on track. Or perhaps he was censoring himself. Writing to Bentley on April 16, he promised that his next book possessed "unquestionable novelty, as regards my former ones,—treating of utterly new scenes & characters;—and, as I believe, very much more calculated for popularity than anything you have yet published of mine—being a regular romance, with a mysterious plot to it, & stirring passions at work, and withall, representing a new and elevated aspect of American life."

This prediction proved to be a poor one, and Bentley guessed better. Dismayed by the string of disappointments since *Typee* and *Omoo,* he was skeptical about Melville's prospects, no matter how "regular" and "elevated" the new work might be, and after chiding him for producing books "in too rapid succession," he proposed a contract that Melville took as an insult. As for the Harpers, the best they would offer now was a royalty of twenty cents per copy, a considerable comedown from the terms (splitting profits fifty-fifty) on which they had contracted for *Moby-Dick.* At one point in the negotiations, Melville made the pathetic suggestion that his new book might sell better if it were brought out under a pseudonym.

2.

When *Pierre* was published in July 1852, it bore its author's own name, and the critics savaged it. The *New York Day Book* reviewed it under the headline "HERMAN MELVILLE CRAZY," and the *American Whig Review* agreed, declaring that his "fancy is diseased." The respected critic Fitz-James O'Brien, playing on the pun of *Pierre* with *pierre* (the French word for stone), was more polite but still severe: "Let Mr. Melville stay his step in time. He totters on the edge of a precipice, over which all his hard-earned fame may tumble with such another weight as *Pierre* attached to it." As another critic has put it, *Pierre* was "the burning out of Melville's volcano." It was a performance at once furious and feeble, and of all Melville's works the one whose tone is hardest to get hold of—a book, as John Updike has remarked, that "runs a constant fever" and whose characters are "jerked to and fro by some unexplained rage of the author's."

Most of Melville's biographers have explained the rage as Melville's reaction to the reception of *Moby-Dick* and to the faltering of his literary career; but some fifty years ago, W. Somerset Maugham put forward a different explanation. Melville's anger, Maugham said, arose from his "disappointment with the married state." The idea that something was amiss in Melville's marriage has had many subscribers before and since. In the summer of 1919, a Columbia professor named Raymond Weaver sought out Melville's granddaughter Eleanor Metcalf, whom Weaver described, upon first meeting her, as an "English-looking woman, with flat heels [and] a rain coat." She met him on a rainy day at a suburban Boston train station with the following greeting: "This weather is enough to provoke conversation . . . but you don't want to talk about the weather. So I'll tell you at once the worst. . . . You say, in your *Nation* article, that Melville was happily married. He wasn't." This view had been transmitted to Eleanor by her mother, Frances Melville Thomas (the Melvilles' second daughter), who construed her own parents' quarrels as more than standard marital squabbling. Lewis Mumford, having interviewed Mrs. Thomas in the 1920s when he was working on his own study of her father, recalled much later that "only one condition limited that interview: on no account might I even mention her father's name!" Her silence, he felt, "reopened the dark chapter of Melville's long alienation from his family."

But neither Frances's silence nor Eleanor's cryptic brevity clarified the Melvilles' unhappiness, and the few eyewitness comments on their relation, along with the single surviving letter from Herman to Lizzie, are not much help. Early in the marriage, Lizzie herself had written with newlywed gladness to her brother Sam that, while she worried about giving up "dear old crooked Boston" for the unfamiliar novelties of New York, she was sure that "with Herman with me always, I can be happy and contented anywhere." And to her stepmother she explained that she made herself look "as bewitchingly as possible" for Herman after his long day at his desk. But who knows if he was, in fact, bewitched, or if Lizzie was working at her appearance because she sensed that her husband's interest in her was already flagging? Years later, Melville's brother-in-law John C. Hoadley described Lizzie's "tone and look of love" for Herman as the family sat together around the fireplace; but who can say if the look was warm and spousal or sisterly and chaste? "Of all chamber furniture in the world best calculated to cure a bad temper, and breed a pleasant one," Melville had written in *White-Jacket* after Malcolm's birth, "is the sight of a lovely wife." But he had never been altogether pleased when his home became a nursery. When one's wife dandles the babe or is run ragged by the toddler, she may lose her charm, and when the children "are teething, the nursery should be a good way upstairs; at sea, it ought to be in the mizzen-top."

In the winter of 1852, while she was nursing Stanwix, Lizzie developed a lingering breast abscess that left her so exhausted that the floral design of the bedside wallpaper swam before her eyes until someone took pity and hung a white sheet over the paper to cover the pattern. It was months before she felt well again. Perhaps the only thing one can say with confidence about Melville's married life is that when he took up sex as a literary theme in *Pierre,* he was experiencing sexual deprivation.

3.

What goes on between husband and wife is a sealed mystery even if one hears the couple through the bedroom wall—and so we cannot hope to know much about Melville's actual sexual life. But we do know something about the responsibilities he thought were entailed in managing the human sex drive, in whatever form it takes. This was his theme in *Pierre.* In *Moby-Dick,* he had written obliquely about sex as a moral problem, describing the quasi-erotic power that Ahab exerts over his men, and he was to take up the subject again at the end of his life in *Billy Budd* with the portrait of Mr. Claggart, whose obstructed desire ("Claggart could even have loved Billy but for fate and ban") is perverted into hatred. In these works, Melville wrote not so much about sex as about sin: about how human beings are liable to be seized, not just in their sexual frenzy, by a passion that reduces the world to a means of achieving self-satisfaction. Like many Western writers at least since Augustine, Melville suspected the body's unruly independence from the will; and in that drab winter of 1852, he took this suspicion and constructed around it a full-scale story. The result was a book, as F. O. Matthiessen described it, that may be "the most desperate in our literature."

Pierre Glendinning grows up pampered in an arcadian country villa under the loving eye of his widowed mother. In fact, she is rather too loving. Mary Glendinning dotes on her son with a "playfulness of . . . unclouded love" that seems a rehearsal for sex play, and mother and son coquettishly

call each other sister and brother. The flirting titillates Pierre, since "much
that goes to make up the deliciousness of a wife, already lies in the sister,"
and he regrets that "a sister had been omitted from the text" of his life.

But if he misses a sister, Pierre also misses the childhood friends with
whom he had once tumbled and tussled, and he preserves a particularly
"ardent sentiment" for his male cousin Glen, with whom he had explored
"the preliminary love-friendship of boys." Glen's name is a truncated version
of Pierre's surname, Glendinning—suggesting a variation on the Greek idea,
which Melville knew from Plato's *Symposium,* that sexual love manifests the
primal memory of having once been whole and the urge to complete oneself
by coupling with one's severed half. In a poem entitled "After the Pleasure
Party," which he may have drafted not long before writing *Pierre,* Melville
put forth this idea of sex as self-reunification in the voice of a woman who
has forsworn the life of the body in favor of the life of the mind:

> *Why hast thou made us but in halves—*
> *Co-relatives? This makes us slaves.*
> *If these co-relatives never meet*
> *Self-hood itself seems incomplete.*

And such the dicing of blind fate
Few matching halves here meet and mate.

In just this sense, Pierre and Glen's feelings for each other are "much more than cousinly attachment"—so much more that Melville takes the occasion to reflect, in almost baroque prose, that "the letters of Aphroditean devotees" are not "more charged with headlong vows and protestations, more cross written and crammed with discursive sentimentalities, more undeviating in their semi-weekliness, or dayliness, as the case may be, than are the love-friendship missives of boys."

This is one of several passages in which Melville seems to anticipate Freud's idea of "uncertainty in regard to the boundaries of what is to be called normal sexual life." In 1905, in his *Fragment of an Analysis of a Case of Hysteria* (better known as the *Story of Dora*), Freud was to write that as for "the sensual love of a man for a man,"

> each one of us in his own sexual life transgresses to a slight extent—now in this direction, now in that—the narrow lines imposed upon him as the standard of normality. The perversions are neither bestial nor degenerate in the emotional sense of the word. They are a development of germs all of which are contained in the undifferentiated sexual predisposition of the child. . . . When, therefore any one has become a gross and manifest pervert, it would be more correct to say that he has *remained* one, for he exhibits a certain stage of *inhibited development*.

Pierre is a novel about a boy who remains in a state of inhibited, or (as the German *Entwicklungshemmung* is more commonly translated) arrested, development. He is looking for his missing half but has no idea where to find it.

Pierre's mother wants to keep it that way. She is a model of the overbearing mother whom Freud blames for homosexual tendencies in boys, and since she has some inkling of her son's preoccupations, she wants him coaxed away from his "uncelestial" desires. So she arranges his betrothal to a "reverential, and most docile" girl, Lucy Tartan, who will keep him out of trouble. At first Pierre is dutifully pleased with his fair-haired fiancée, but he has presentiments that she is too delicate for the coming exertions of marriage. "Methinks," he muses, speaking like some vexed lord in an Elizabethan play, "one husbandly embrace would break her airy zone, and she exhale upward to that heaven whence she hath hither come, condensed to mortal sight." In this respect, Pierre shared Melville's own tastes at a time when fashionable ladies used whitening powders to simulate the pallor associated with female purity. The "stiffness, formality, and affectation" of a proper lady struck Melville as a poor substitute for the "artless vivacity and unconcealed natural graces of . . . savage maidens." He had written in *Typee* that to witness a lady and a "savage maiden" standing side by side would be to see "a milliner's doll" beside the *Venus de' Medici*. Although he may not have quite shared his friend Nathaniel Willis's "passion for fat women," Melville was put off, no less than Willis, by women whose "skinny scrawny arms" reminded him of "reptiles and crawling things."

Lucy is more than a bit reptilian. Given her resemblance to the woman Melville married (Longfellow's wife remarked about Elizabeth Shaw that after Melville's "flirtations with South Sea beauties," she was a "peculiar choice"), one wonders what Lizzie thought when she met herself in her husband's new book. The likeness was hard to miss. Lucy, like Lizzie, is the daughter of "an early and most cherished friend" of the father of her betrothed. And Mary Glendinning (in whom Maria Gansevoort Melville could have recognized herself) senses her son's hesitations about his designated bride.

Meanwhile, Pierre has been having a recurrent vision of another young woman whose face floats into his mind in moments of reverie, and Mrs. Glendinning worries that he might be susceptible to some such "dark-eyed haughtiness" if he should ever meet her in the flesh. She tries to reassure herself:

> Yes, [Lucy is] a very pretty little pint-decanter of a girl; a very pretty little Pale Sherry pint-decanter of a girl; and I—I'm a quart decanter of—of—Port—potent Port! Now, Sherry for boys, and Port for men—so I've heard men say; and Pierre is but a boy; but when his father wedded me,—why, his father was turned of five-and thirty years.

This is whistling in the dark. Mrs. Glendinning is right to worry: her son is overdue for the taste of port.

Pierre wants to travel to some sexual terra incognita, but Lucy, he is beginning to realize, is not the woman to take him there. Soon enough, he gets a better chance. Not long after the first visitation of the haunting face, he calls at the home of two charitable spinsters who employ wayward girls as seamstresses—a sanctuary that seems straight out of the pages of some didactic novel warning women of what will become of them should they fail to guard their virginity. When Pierre is introduced by name to the fallen girls bent over their needlework, a raven beauty in the back of the room lets out a muffled shriek. He stares, recognizing her as the creature of his dreams, his eyes traveling down from her face onto the "contracting and expanding" velvet collar that encircles her beautiful neck. This is the moment at which

Pierre discovers sex—discovers, that is, an object that focuses his hitherto inchoate cravings. Like a boy confused by his first wet dream, he rushes home to question his mother about what is happening to him. Who can this girl be? Why this mutual feeling of electric excitement? When Mrs. Glendinning deflects his questions, he gets the feeling that he is being lied to about something he needs to know.

It is the first in a series of blows to Pierre's fabricated world. He has been living in a household drenched in mother love and consecrated to the spotless memory of his father, but he somehow knows that it is a world of lies, and that some dangerous and delicious truth is to be found in this renegade girl who beckons and excites him. Constrained by the decency standards of his time, Melville had to write discreetly of Pierre's "all too obvious emotion." In a recent edition of the novel, the artist Maurice Sendak is more explicit, translating Pierre's "emotion" at his first encounter with Isabel into visual terms by picturing him in a pair of tights that shows off his erection.

After managing for a while to keep himself under control, the horny boy gets his next shock as he walks at dusk toward Lucy's house and notices "beneath the pendulous canopies of . . . the weeping elms of the village" a light bobbing along across the road that keeps up with him as if synchronized to his own pace. He tries to convince himself that this light belongs to some elderly townsman equipped with a lantern; but just as he reaches the cottage door, the light crosses toward him, held by a hooded man who presents him with a letter, then disappears into the night. These pages have much the same atmosphere as the eerie street scenes in which the tempted protagonist (Dr. Harford) of Stanley Kubrick's film *Eyes Wide Shut* hears the footfalls of a man following him as he is about to plunge into a sexual underworld.

Melville was groping here, as in "The Counterpane" chapter of *Moby-Dick,* toward a psychological vocabulary that he did not quite possess, in a book whose subject, as Lewis Mumford was among the first to realize, "was not the universe, but the ego." He was pushing toward the insight that the content of the portentous letter somehow already resided in the young man's mind. After receiving it, but still before reading it, Pierre steps up to Lucy's cottage. His hand recoils from the cold feel of the iron knocker (a sure sign that the girl behind the door is frigid), and without having knocked, he rushes home. So much for Lucy. When he arrives at his own house with the hot letter in hand, Pierre sees himself in a hallway mirror and feels strangely split between the self he has known and the reflected figure whose "features [are] transformed, and unfamiliar to him." Echoing Faust's discovery that "two souls, alas, dwell in my breast," he comes "distinctly to feel two antagonistic agencies within him; one of which was just struggling into his consciousness, and each of which was striving for the mastery." All this before opening the envelope.

When he finally sits down to read, the words set Pierre on fire, and with amazing alacrity and "boundless expansion" he renounces everything he has previously believed about his family, his obligations, and his place in the world. The girl, whose name is Isabel, claims that she is his illegitimate sister by his father's French mistress. Since her abandonment by their common father, she has lived bereft, subject to the charity and abuse of strangers; but now, at last, she is within reach of Pierre's redemptive love. As his eye rushes across the page, he can almost feel her hot breath:

> Dearest Pierre, my brother, my own father's child! art thou an angel, that thou canst overleap all the heartless usages and fashions of a banded world, that will call thee fool, fool, fool! and curse thee, if thou yieldest to that heavenly impulse which alone can lead thee to respond to the long tyrannizing, and now at last unquenchable yearnings of my bursting heart? Oh, my brother!

As suddenly as St. Augustine is converted by the voice in the garden, Pierre is transformed by Isabel's letter. He is appalled at what he takes to have been the treachery of his father: "Not only was the long-cherished image of his father now transfigured before him from a green foliaged tree into a blasted trunk, but every other image in his mind attested the universality of that electral light which had darted into his soul." As for his mother, she is instantly changed in his eyes into a dissembler draped in "scaly, glittering folds of pride" for having put her own respectability ahead of the girl's welfare. Pierre feels duped by everyone and everything. The trees that had once given him shade, the mossy rocks over which he had scrambled with never so much as a skinned knee, now taunt him with their indifference to the enormity of what he has learned. But there is one compensation: in Isabel he has found an object of desire that delivers a rush of pleasure in which rage and love are deliciously commingled.

4.

Melville's weird book was made up of elements borrowed from the Gothic thrillers of his time, but he mixed them into a concoction unlike anything yet served up by an American writer, and his readers did not know what to make of it. He took up standard themes, which one scholar has inventoried as "the dark-haired 'forest girl' [who] casts her shadow between the hero and his betrothed; brother and sister [who] discover each other, passionately, by ancestral tokens . . . and mysterious portraits and letters [that] unveil a hidden world of secret kinship, broken taboos, and pervasive sexual innuendo," and turned them into something overwrought and self-parodying. To read *Pierre* is to feel the discomfort one feels in the presence of a brilliant friend who, in the grip of some new passion, has gone "over the top." It is the first of Melville's books in which one feels the proximity of genius to madness. Until now, Melville had "not yet . . . dropped his angle into the well of his childhood, to find what fish might be there," and there is something embarrassingly personal about the book, as if it were an anthology of grudges against his mother, wife, sisters, publishers, and, most of all, himself. Some readers have regarded *Pierre* as "spiritual autobiography in the form of a novel," though Melville's granddaughter Eleanor Metcalf, writing some thirty years after her meeting with Raymond Weaver, issued an appropriate caution: "Here [was] a sick man writing of some matters known to be true, some entirely untrue, combined in such a way that the family feared its members and their friends might assume all to be true."

One theory that has proven especially enduring has been that Melville's father had, in fact, produced an illegitimate daughter—and, sure enough, there eventually came to light (in 1977) a letter that seemed to back up this theory with a fact. The letter had been written in 1832 to Lemuel Shaw by Allan's brother Thomas Melvill, Jr., who reported that two women, apparently mother and daughter, had recently called twice at the home of the old Major Thomas Melvill, seeking payment owed to them by his recently deceased son Allan. The senior Melvill was not at home, so Thomas Junior went after the petitioners to pay them off, perhaps to keep them from embarrassing the family further by dredging up his brother's past. It is biologically and geographically possible that the younger of these two women was, in fact, the product of Allan Melvill's youthful love or lust. Her mother (not, as it turns out, the older woman who accompanied her on the dunning expedition to Major Melvill's house) had probably been a twenty-one-year-old shop assistant in Boston in the summer of 1797 when she conceived her child. At the time, fifteen-year-old Allan Melvill had been living in the neighborhood and was possibly employed as an apprentice in the same store. "Judging from what we know of his sons," writes one scholar who is agnostic about Allan's early paternity, he "was not slow to reach physical maturity," and in taking advantage of a willing shopgirl Allan may in fact have been fast.

This is a slender thread from which to hang a claim about a shameful family secret, but whether or not Melville actually had (or thought he might have had) a half sister, he certainly brought to the writing of *Pierre* a volatile mixture of defensiveness and anger toward his father.* Ever since witnessing Allan's downfall and collapse, he had felt both allegiance and contempt toward the respectabilities to which his father had aspired, and he remained angry at him for foisting the illusion of gentility upon the family—angry, as well, at what the world had done to his father and thereby to himself. Melville was divided much as Pierre is shown to be: dissatisfied by pre-scribed family life as the standard for right living, yet frightened by the prospect of losing the stability his family provided. Sometimes he felt him-self coming apart under the pressures of this internal conflict between the drive to rebel and the need to conserve.

One effect of his dividedness was a split between sympathy and con-tempt for the quasi-autobiographical character around whom he built the novel. This kind of ambivalence is turned to effect in two works that Melville greatly admired, *King Lear* and *Don Quixote,* but he never found in *Pierre* the balance between melodrama and farce. He reached deep with this book into his own ambivalence toward the official pieties of a culture in which, as Thornton Wilder once put it, "the heroic flourished side by side with the mock-heroic, and the mock-heroic itself seemed to be a smiling tribute to the heroic." Pierre in this sense was Melville's representative American—a quixotic believer who trusts his own righteousness even as he swings wildly between allegiances (Mother vs. Father, Lucy vs. Isabel) that are incompati-ble with one another. The rest of the novel follows this fanatic-in-the-making on what he thinks is a pilgrimage to heaven but turns out to be a journey into hell. As the critic Sacvan Bercovitch has written, the story of Pierre proceeds "from ambiguity to ambiguity, until it ends in a solipsistic void," with the hero "ranting to no one about a New Revelation that remains forever unrecorded, unfulfilled, except in the mock apocalypse of his self-destruction."

First Pierre renounces Lucy. Then he rescues Isabel by pretending to the world that he has married her, and for good measure he completes his menage by taking in another fugitive girl (with the rather bovine name Delly Ulver) who has been disowned by her parents for having fallen to some sex-

---

*Some scholars still cling to an earlier theory that when the young Allan Melvill had shared a house in Paris in 1809 (this was the time when he saw Napoleon) with his brother Thomas Junior and Thomas's French wife, Françoise, he may have shared his brother's wife as well. On this the-ory, the French-born Priscilla Melvill, reputedly Herman's cousin, was actually Herman's half sis-ter conceived in adulterous union between Allan Melvill and his sister-in-law. See Jean Simon, *Herman Melville: Marin, Métaphysicien et poéte* (Paris: Boivin & Cie, 1939), pp. 28–29.

ual tempter. Meanwhile, Pierre is tempted by his own "sister," listening with rapture as Isabel tells her story, "his eyes fixed upon the girl's wonderfully beautiful ear, which chancing to peep forth from among her abundant tresses, nestled in that blackness like a transparent sea-shell of pear." In case the reader misses the vaginal characteristics of Isabel's ear, Melville has her sing the rest of her story while accompanying herself, with positively Polynesian abandon, on her exceptionally resonant guitar:

> The wild girl played on the guitar; and her long dark shower of curls fell over it, and vailed it; and still, out from the vail came the swarming sweetness, and the utter unintelligibleness, but the infinite significancies of the sounds of the guitar . . . bounding and rebounding as from multitudinous reciprocal walls; while with every syllable the hair-shrouded form of Isabel swayed to and fro with a like abandonment, and suddenness, and wantonness. . . .

The young Pierre may have felt "more than cousinly attachment" for his male cousin Glen, but the older Pierre is aroused by the sight of Isabel's nestled "ear" and craves the sensation of being enveloped by the throbbing walls of her "guitar."

5.

As Pierre commits himself to this wanton girl, Melville launches a violent attack on the provincial culture that has expelled and stigmatized her. In this respect, especially in the account of Pierre's confrontation with his family minister, Mr. Falsgrave, *Pierre* anticipated such books as *Main Street, Winesburg, Ohio,* and even, in its combination of prurience and prudishness, *Peyton Place.* Mr. Falsgrave is a personification of Main Street hypocrisy. One of the most repulsive characters in American fiction, he is nominally (falsely grave) a clergyman, but in fact he is a glorified valet to Pierre's mother—kin to the many prevaricating village parsons in the novels of Anthony Trollope (*Pierre* was published in the same year as Trollope's *The Warden*). Slender and sinuous, he is a figure whom one can imagine having been painted collaboratively by Bronzino and Beardsley, the "image," as Melville puts it with palpable disgust, "of white-browed and white-handed, and napkined immaculateness." Much of the writing in *Pierre* can be loose and blowzy, but Melville's animosity toward Falsgrave sharpens his wit and yields a marvelous description:

> Mr. Falsgrave was just hovering upon his prime of years; a period which, in such a man, is the sweetest, and, to a mature woman, by far the most attractive of manly life. Youth has not yet completely gone with its beauty, grace, and strength; nor has age at all come with its decrepitudes; though the finest undrossed parts of it—its mildness and its wisdom—have gone on before, as decorous chamberlains precede the sedan of some crutched king.

Falsgrave is a close relative of the flute-playing Reverend Runt in Thackeray's novel of 1844, *The Luck of Barry Lyndon,* and a virtuoso of ingratiation: "Heaven had given him his fine, silver-keyed person for a flute to play on in this world, and he was nearly the perfect master of it." Always studying himself, fidgeting, rearranging his personal decor, he recoils from contact with the untidy world as if touching anything outside himself would pollute him. One suspects that his favorite companion is his mirror.

After receiving Isabel's letter and learning of Delly's expulsion, Pierre, like Hamlet coming to Polonius, comes knocking late one night at this man's door. The smarmy minister leans out his bedroom window to see what the fuss is about. "In heaven's name, what is the matter, young gentleman?," he asks, to which Pierre replies: "Everything is the matter; the whole world is the matter. Will you admit me, sir?" Mr. Falsgrave, suddenly nimble, descends the stairs with candle in hand and hops to the door to let in the young zealot, desperate to stop the knocking lest the neighbors be annoyed. He asks again, "For heaven's sake, what is the matter . . . ?," and Pierre replies: "Heaven and earth is the matter, sir! shall we go up to the study?" Still with candle in hand, Falsgrave takes him upstairs, then waits in a funk of apprehension for Pierre to get to the point.

"Thou art a man of God, sir, I believe," says Pierre. In recording the clergyman's answer, which is the verbal equivalent of a squirm, Melville puns wickedly on "aye" and "I": "I? I? I? Upon my word, Mr. Glendinning!" Pierre helps him out: "Yes, sir, the world calls thee a man of God. Now, what has thou, the man of God, decided, with my mother, concerning Delly Ulver?" This question sends the minister into another stutter: "Delly Ulver! Why, why—what can this madness mean? . . . She?—Delly Ulver? She is to depart the neighborhood; why, her own parents want her not."

This man of God, confronted by a young man looking for someone to validate and salve his anger, might have been expected to seize the moment to step back from Caesar and turn, in penitence and charity, to Christ. Instead, he speaks from the depths of his calculating, trimming, prevaricating self. Pierre responds by unleashing a tirade that Melville conveys through an attack of italics: "*How* is she to depart? *Who* is to take her? Art *thou* to take her? *Where* is she to go? *Who* has the food for her? *What* is to keep her from the pollution to which such as she are every day driven to contribute, by the detestable uncharitableness and heartlessness of the world?" Pierre has discovered what Harold Bloom, in his book *The American Religion,* calls "the immense difficulty of becoming a Christian in any society ostensibly Christian."

With the savage portrait of Falsgrave, Melville turned the fractured mirror of his inward novel outward, affording us fragmentary reflections of the moral and political world in which he was living. It was a time, according to Lemuel Shaw's college friend Joseph Story (whose collected works were published in the same year as *Pierre*), of "ultraism of all sorts," and in *Pierre* Melville portrayed exactly the sort of "importunate reformer" who stormed through the world leaving, in Story's view, "desolation and ruin on every side." The sorts of questions Pierre asks were being asked everywhere at a time when, as Emerson wrote to Thomas Carlyle, Americans were "all a little wild with numberless projects of social reform." What was to be done for those excluded from the vaunted bounty and freedom of American life? Who would take up their cause? Antebellum America was alive with reformers demanding answers to such questions—feminists, temperance advocates, activists for the deaf and the blind, proponents of public education, and, most conspicuously, abolitionists—all of whom contributed elements to the portrait of Pierre. In Melville's allegory, Falsgrave is Mr. Respectability and Pierre is Mr. Rash Radical.

He sounds, for instance, more than a little like William Lloyd Garrison, who had announced in his abolitionist paper *The Liberator,* "I do not wish to think, or speak, or write, with moderation. No! no! Tell a man whose house is on fire to give a moderate alarm; tell him to moderately rescue his wife from the hands of the ravisher; tell the mother to gradually extricate her babe from the fire . . . but urge me not to use moderation in a cause like the present. I am in earnest—I will not equivocate—I will not excuse—I will not retreat a single inch—and I WILL BE HEARD." As for Falsgrave, his was the countervailing voice of prudence, in which Melville heard only empty sententiae—perhaps the best elaboration in our literature of what Emerson had called the "formalist" who usurps the pulpit, leaving the worshippers feeling "defrauded and disconsolate." And Falsgrave had his models, too. He may

Orville Dewey

have been based in part on the Shaw family minister, Orville Dewey, and he may even have incorporated aspects of Shaw himself, whose "intense and doating biasses" for "Unitarianism and Harvard College" (according to Richard Henry Dana, Jr.) held him steady during the storm over the Fugitive Slave Law that broke out not long before Melville began writing *Pierre.* Melville's granddaughter noted in her copy of *Pierre* that the "almost infantile delicacy and vivid whiteness" of Falsgrave's hands were characteristic of Judge Shaw.

Early in 1851, Dana recorded in his journal his confrontation with Shaw over the arrest and imprisonment of the fugitive slave Thomas Sims. As soon as he heard news of the arrest, Dana, whose law office was near the courthouse where Sims was being held, had gone straight to the judge with a petition for habeas corpus. The passage could be transported intact into the Delly Ulver episode in *Pierre:*

> The Ch. Justice read the petition, & said, in a most ungracious manner—"This won't do. I can't do anything on this." & laid it upon the table & turned away, to engage in something else. . . . I asked him to be so good as to tell me what the defects were, saying that I had taken pains to conform to the Statute. He seemed unwilling to notice it, & desirous of getting rid of it, in short, he attempted to *bluff me off.*

It is Falsgrave in his house, trying to get rid of the intruder.

Cymbeline, *Act 2,*
Scene 2: "A bed
chamber; Imogen
in Bed," print in
Melville's collection

6.

The foaming hatred that Pierre feels for Mr. Falsgrave is matched only by his
passion for Isabel as he rushes out of the minister's snug house into the
night. He then flees to New York with both girls in tow, as if Hamlet were
running away from Elsinore to the nunnery not with one Ophelia but with
two. En route he receives a cryptic warning in the form of a philosophical
pamphlet, in the mode of Plutarch, that falls into his hands aboard the city-
bound coach, the gist of which is that one must strive in life for a "virtuous
expediency," taking a little, giving a little, staying away from extremes. Pierre
is the wrong reader for this type of middle-of-the-roadism. After Ahab, he is
the strongest exemplar of the theme that Hannah Arendt (one of those who
saw Melville as a prophet warning against totalitarianism) considered the key
to his writing: the idea that once "the absolute [is] introduced into the political realm," righteousness becomes madness. What begins as a wish to cor-
rect some personal or historical wrong becomes fanaticism, and Pierre
embarks on the road to madness.

There were many sources—visual as well as literary—that mixed in
Melville's imagination to make a fertile seed ground for *Pierre.* For the scenes
in Books II and XI when Pierre enters Lucy's bedroom, Melville may have

Dante, Inferno,
Canto 5, *illus-
trated by John
Flaxman.
Melville bought a
set of Flaxman
illustrations in
Paris in 1849.*

had in mind a scene from Shakespeare's *Cymbeline*—a play about a thwarted marriage between a sister and stepbrother—of which he owned an engraved illustration in which Iachimo spies on the sleeping Imogen. On his European trip in 1849, Melville had purchased a set of literary illustrations, including some of Dante's *Inferno,* by the English artist John Flaxman. Pierre associates the mysterious face that comes to him in his dreams with "Francesca's mournful face" in "Flaxman's Dante," and when Melville writes of the "long dark shower" of Isabel's hair, he evidently had in mind Flaxman's depiction of Francesca's flowing locks in Canto 5, where in the most erotic passage of the poem Dante recounts her quasi-incestuous passion for Paolo, her brother-in-law. As Pierre runs off with his girls, allusions pile up to Dante's *Inferno* and to Enceladus, the mutilated Titan child of incest doomed to an eternity of "writhing from out the imprisoning earth" as he struggles heavenward while locked in dirt and stone. As befits his name, Pierre imagines himself the rock of a new church; he wants to "gospelize the world anew," to tear it down and rebuild it, cleanse it and repopulate it. But in rushing off toward his new heaven he sinks into a hell of his own making, and unlike Dante, who is guided into and out of hell by his master poet Virgil, Pierre will not emerge wiser and stronger. In fact, he will not emerge at all.

Seeking the "sublime heaven of heroism," Pierre arrives instead at the infernal city, loses himself among "frantic, diseased-looking men and women of all colors . . . all imaginable flaunting, immodest, grotesque" forms, "leaping, yelling, and cursing around him," and becomes—what else?—a writer. In this city of demons, he comes to believe his own messianic dream of hav-

Sleighing in New York, *lithograph by Thomas Benecke, 1855*

ing been called to witness and denounce sin ("I will write such things—
I will . . . show them deeper secrets than the Apocalypse!—I will write it!
I will write it!"), yet turns into a pitiable figure sitting alone in his room:

> From eight o'clock in the morning till half-past four in the evening,
> Pierre sits there in his room;—eight hours and a half!
> From throbbing neck-bands, and swinging belly-bands of gay-
> hearted horses, the sleigh-bells chimingly jingle;—but Pierre sits there
> in his room; Thanksgiving comes, with its glad thanks, and crisp
> turkeys;—but Pierre sits there in his room; soft through the snows, on
> tinted Indian moccasin, Merry-Christmas comes stealing;—but Pierre
> sits there in his room; it is New-Year's, and like a great flagon, the vast
> city overbrims at all curbstones, wharves, and piers, with bubbling
> jubilations;—but Pierre sits there in his room:—Nor jingling sleigh-
> bells at throbbing neck-band, or swinging belly-band; nor glad thanks,
> and crisp turkeys of Thanksgiving; nor tinted Indian moccasin of
> Merry Christmas softly stealing through the snows; nor New-Year's
> curb-stones, wharves, and piers, over-brimming with bubbling
> jubilations:—Nor jingling sleigh-bells, nor glad Thanksgiving, nor
> Merry Christmas, nor jubilating New Year's:—Nor Bell, Thank,
> Christ, Year;—none of these are for Pierre. In the midst of the merri-
> ments of the mutations of Time, Pierre hath ringed himself in with the
> grief of Eternity; Pierre is a peak inflexible in the heart of Time. . . .

The mockeries in this passage are multiple and merciless. It mocks the sentimental poetry of sleigh bells and Christmas cheer. It mocks the holiday rituals ("Thank, Christ, Year") from which Pierre exempts himself. It confirms that Pierre ("peak inflexible") has aroused himself to onanistic pride, spewing out, like the mountain peak that once towered over his childhood home, "unstinted fertilizations" on himself, bathing in the spurtings of his own ego. And finally, with the image of the hermit artist indifferent to a world that generously returned the indifference, Melville was bitterly mocking himself. He could not decide whom he loathed more, the blocked but stupendously pretentious writer who could squeeze out only puny productions or the publishers and promoters who were eager to have him sit for a daguerreotype. Among other things, *Pierre* was Melville's belated valedictory message to the New York literary scene—a message that might be summed up as "Up yours."

Here is Melville's visual representation of Pierre's pretension and the teeny-tiny foundation on which it rests:

THE

COMPLETE WORKS

OF

GLENDINNING

AUTHOR OF

That world-famed production, "The Tropical Summer: A Sonnet,"
"The Weather: a Thought." "Life: an Impromptu," "The
late Reverend Mark Graceman: an Obituary." "Honor:
a Stanza." "Beauty: an Acrostic." "Edgar:
an Anagram." "The Pippin: a Paragraph."
&c. &c. &c. &c.
&c. &c. &c.
&c. &c.
&c."

What we have here is a parody of the Romantic author imagining himself as high priest charged by God to bring forth Truth. It was an idea of authorship first articulated for the English-speaking world by Carlyle, who in 1827 had introduced Anglo-American readers to the ideas of the German philosopher Johann Fichte:

According to Fichte, there is a "Divine Idea" pervading the visible Universe; which visible Universe is indeed but its symbol and sensible manifestation. . . . To the mass of men this Divine Idea of the world lies hidden; yet to discern it, to seize it, and live wholly in it, is the condition of all genuine virtue, knowledge, freedom; and the end therefore of all spiritual effort in every age. Literary Men are the appointed interpreters of this Divine Idea; a perpetual priesthood, we might say, standing forth generation after generation, as the dispenser and living types of God's everlasting wisdom.

This vision of the Literary Man as the voice of God had been advanced in America by Emerson ("I look for the new Teacher that shall . . . see the world to be the mirror of the soul") and Whitman ("the priest departs, the divine literatus comes"), and Melville, too, had once imputed such power to himself, as when he boasted in *Moby-Dick* of the "out-reaching comprehensiveness of sweep" of his own imagination. Filled though *Moby-Dick* had been with bravado passages announcing in "placard capitals" the secrets of the sea, Melville had backed away from that part of himself which had sought the Divine Idea. Such, after all, was Ahab's quest—to pierce through the "pasteboard mask" of appearances—and Melville had treated Ahab's will to metaphysical knowledge as a species of insanity. In *Pierre* we find Melville contending, as Ahab had done ("Sometimes, I think there's naught beyond"), with the prospect that there *is* no Divine Idea behind Nature, and that those who pursue it are stark mad. Nature in *Pierre* is a tease and a taunt, flattering us into thinking that what we find in the landscape or seascape is the visage of God, when in fact she is nothing but a mocking reflection of ourselves: "Say what some poets will, Nature is not so much her own ever-sweet interpreter, as the mere supplier of that cunning alphabet, whereby selecting and combining as he pleases, each man reads his own peculiar lesson according to his own peculiar mind and mood." This was Melville's retort to romantic dreamers whose belief in the "all-controlling and all-permeating wonderfulness" of the world (his parodic paraphrase of Emerson) blinds them to the truth that nature is nothing but a vast blankness on which man inscribes his fantasies.

As Pierre scribbles away in romantic ecstasy at his manuscript, which one imagines is a screed in the genre of *Mein Kampf*, his menage grows to include the ever faithful Lucy, who, despite his having broken their engagement in order to run away with Isabel, shows up with her easel to pursue her painting while he works at his writing. Lucy, with her unshakable fidelity, is as unbearably virtuous as ever: "almost a nun," Pierre explains to Isabel, who "hearing of our mysterious exile" and "without knowing the cause, hath yet as mysteriously vowed herself ours—not so much mine, Isabel, as ours,

ours—to serve *us*." As for Pierre's mother, she has died embittered against her son and left her estate to his successor in suing for Lucy's affections—none other than cousin Glen, who, when Lucy flees to New York, feels jilted by Pierre for a second time.

In telling this wild story, Melville intimates that Pierre is waging a losing battle against some taboo desire that he cannot bring himself to state outright: "Never, never would he be able to embrace Isabel with the mere brotherly embrace; while the thought of any other caress . . . was entirely vacant from his uncontaminated soul, for it had never consciously intruded there." Not consciously, perhaps; but he and Isabel are fooling themselves when they assure each other that "there is no sex in our immaculateness":

> He held her tremblingly; she bent over toward him; his mouth wet her ear . . . the girl . . . leaned closer to him, with an inexpressible strangeness of an intense love, new and inexplicable. Over the face of Pierre there shot a terrible self-revelation; he imprinted repeated burning kisses upon her . . . they coiled together, and entangledly stood mute.

With "tremendous displacing and revolutionizing thoughts," Pierre begins to think about what it might mean, as Henry Murray nicely puts it, that "he 'fell' for the Face before he knew it was his sister's." Starting to doubt her, he starts to doubt himself. When Isabel moans, "I am too full without discharge," Pierre's pity is infused with lust, each feeding the other as the girl's "big drops fell on him."

The novel's pace and tone have by now become as frantic as the processes of Pierre's mind; his fervid language ("Oh, I am sick, sick, sick!") matches the agony of Beatrice Cenci, raped by her father, as recounted in Shelley's poem *The Cenci*, to which Melville repeatedly alludes:

> *O blood, which art my father's blood,*
> *Circling through these contaminated veins,*
> *If thou, poured forth on the polluted earth,*
> *Could wash away the crime, and punishment*
> *By which I suffer . . .*

Finally, Pierre loses what remains of his mental stability—the word "ambiguity," which Melville used in his subtitle, referred in his day to mental disorder—and murders Glen in a rage. At the revelation that Isabel is Pierre's sister, Lucy dies, apparently of shock. Pierre and Isabel, together in prison, succumb to self-administered poison as the book stumbles toward a corpse-strewn conclusion in which the prison guards stand around making scatological jokes.

7.

One way to make sense of *Pierre* is to think of it as a nineteenth-century preview of the camp sensibility that became pervasive more than a hundred years later in late twentieth-century culture. At the beginning of the novel, when Pierre is skipping through the vernal hills crooning nature hymns—"Oh, praised be the beauty of this earth, the beauty, and the bloom, and the mirthfulness thereof"—he seems a nineteenth-century Tiny Tim doing his eyeball-rolling rendition of "Tiptoe Through the Tulips." One never knows in this book whether Melville is being straight or arch, which is just the sticking point: there is something stirring about Pierre's outrage, but there is also something utterly ludicrous about his sense of having been appointed to set the world right.

Pierre is a botched book. While its hero may be kin to Captain Ahab ("Lo!," Pierre shrieks after reading Isabel's letter, "I strike through thy helm, and will see thy face, be it Gorgon! . . . From all idols I tear all veils; henceforth I will see the hidden things. . . ."), there is an absurd disproportion between his vaulting emotion and the occasions that set it off. Pierre is Ahab gone camp. Melville never brings into focus the casus belli that drives Pierre to declare war on the world, and so *Pierre* remains a work, as T. S. Eliot famously said of *Hamlet,* whose "emotion is in excess of the facts as they appear"—and here is the reason why so many readers have tried to identify some secret emotion that might explain it.

When Maugham identified the emotion as "disappointment with the married state," he was not talking about post-honeymoon cooling between husband and wife. What he meant, and intimated elsewhere in his essay, was that Melville had "married in order to combat inclinations that dismayed him"—inclinations, that is, toward his own sex. Since Melville lived and died before the word "homosexual" came into wide use, there is something plausible about Maugham's suspicion that Melville may have been perplexedly aware—in himself as well as in others—of impulses for which there was no established language, and that *Pierre* was his attempt to write about them. Pierre, after all, feels "much more than cousinly attachment" for Glen, who in turn feels scorned by Pierre. By Melville's time, there had long been legal penalties for specific homosexual acts (grouped under the general rubric of "sodomy"), but the idea that some men felt a confirmed sexual preference for other men was only beginning to be voiced—or, rather, whispered.

In the 1850s, a few literary figures, Whitman being the most prominent, celebrated male-male eroticism as requisite for the comradely spirit of democracy, and new terms were entering the language by which same-sex love could be given a name. Whitman liked the term "adhesiveness," which he borrowed from what Melville called (in *Moby-Dick*) the "semi-science" of phrenology, a technique for identifying the particular lobe or sector where this or that emotion or aptitude was located within the human brain. By midcentury it had become fashionable for gentlemen and ladies to submit to examination by a phrenologist, who was trained to feel the swells and valleys of the skull (the cranial equivalent of fingerprints) and thereby supply a profile of one's character by assessing the relative size of, say, the "cautiousness" bump. There was something slightly daring about going to a phrenologist, whose trade, like that of psychoanalysts in the early years of the twentieth century, occupied the border between science and quackery.

In the vocabulary of phrenology, "amativeness" was the term for love between a man and a woman. "Adhesiveness" was the term for what today we might call male bonding. And by 1850, a few phrenologists were speaking of "excessive adhesiveness" as a pathological condition. Though it is hard now to take seriously this method for matching inner mental qualities to the outer contours of scalp and bone, phrenology was an attempt, however primitive, to explore the mysterious relation between brain and mind—and one of its implications was that human sexuality varied in intensity and in its objects of desire.*

As far as we know, Melville never submitted to a phrenological examination, but it would be prudish to doubt that during his nearly four years at sea he had found himself aroused in the company of other men. In the maritime world of his youth, the pairing up of older with younger men in a relation known as "chickenship" was evidently common. When one young sailor, Philip Van Buskirk, asked a veteran seaman in 1853, "Well, White, what's your opinion of those men who have to do with boys? If you were King, wouldn't you kill every one of 'em?" he got a nuanced answer:

---

*Without identifying himself, Mark Twain once submitted to a phrenological examination, only to be told that his "Organ of Humor" was unusually small.

White: "Yes; Every feller that lives ashore and does *that,* I'd shoot Him—yaas, by—, I'd shoot him."

Van Buskirk: "And if you had a navy, wouldn't you kill every man in it found guilty of *that*?"

White: "*No;*—what can a feller do?—three years at sea—and hardly any chance to have a woman. I tell you . . . a feller *must do so.* Biles and pimples and corruption will come out all over his body if he don't."

Whether Melville availed himself of male partners, or relieved himself in as much privacy as he could find aboard ship, or waited for the next contact with island women, no one can say. But it is certainly true, as Maugham writes, that he had an "eye for masculine beauty." In his vagabond days in the Pacific, he had admired the "matchless symmetry of form" of Polynesian boys and relished the services of one in particular, Kory-Kory, who "never for one moment left my side," having been assigned the task of "adjusting everything to secure my personal comfort," including "tenderly" bathing his limbs. Even in the evenings when the girls chased away Melville's personal attendant during their anointing of his "whole body," Kory-Kory "nevertheless retired only to a little distance and watched their proceedings with the most jealous attention."

Consider as well this description in *Redburn* of Carlo, "a rich-cheeked, chestnut-haired Italian boy," who makes his living walking the streets of Liverpool, playing on his hand-organ:

> The head was if any thing small; and heaped with thick clusters of tendril curls, half overhanging the brows and delicate ears, it somehow reminded you of a classic vase, piled up with Falernian foliage.
>
> From the knee downward, the naked leg was beautiful to behold as any lady's arm; so soft and rounded, with infantile ease and grace. His whole figure was free, fine, and indolent; he was such a boy as might have ripened into life in a Neapolitan vineyard; such a boy as gipsies steal in infancy; such a boy as Murillo often painted, when he went among the poor and outcast, for subjects wherewith to captivate the eyes of rank and wealth; such a boy, as only Andalusian beggars are, full of poetry, gushing from every rent.

The narrator of *Redburn* is transported "in dreams Elysian" by this boy, who, "pulling and twitching the ivory knobs at one end of his instrument," is able to "make, unmake me; build me up; to pieces take me; and join me limb to limb."

One avowedly gay critic, writing early in the age of AIDS, goes so far as to claim that "every positive depiction of sexuality in Melville is a depiction of male masturbation, frequently mutual." This was a practice—distinguished in Melville's day from sodomy, a term generally reserved for anal or oral penetration—to which he seems to allude in the ecstatic "A Squeeze of the Hand" chapter in *Moby-Dick,* in which the men of the *Pequod* gather around tubs of spermaceti, squeezing the congealed lumps until they melt into a sort of warm whale soup. One recent critic calls it a "circle jerk":

> Squeeze! squeeze! squeeze! all the morning long; I squeezed that sperm till I myself almost melted into it; I squeezed that sperm till a strange sort of insanity came over me; and I found myself unwittingly squeezing my co-laborers' hands in it, mistaking their hands for the gentle globules. Such an abounding, affectionate, friendly, loving feeling did this avocation beget; that at last I was continually squeezing their hands, and looking up into their eyes sentimentally; as much as to say,—Oh! my dear fellow beings, why should we longer cherish any social acerbities, or know the slightest ill-humor or envy! Come; let us squeeze hands all round; nay, let us all squeeze ourselves into each other; let us squeeze ourselves universally into the very milk and sperm of kindness.

What can one conclude from such passages about Melville's sexual life? He may have felt constrained in his marriage to his "milliner's doll" wife, and he may have longed for some dark-eyed Isabel. He may have been an "androgynic personality," or bisexual, as Henry Murray believed. These inferences can reasonably be drawn not from this passage alone—which was less freighted with sexual meaning in its nineteenth-century idiom than it might seem today—but from the whole range of Melville's writings about the sensory life.

Maugham surmised that Melville had discovered early in his marriage that "the expectation of sexual intercourse is more exciting than the realization." If this was so, *Pierre* may indeed have been his attempt to write about the constraints of conventional sexual life. Others have gone further and suggested that Melville was consciously struggling to come to terms with inclinations considered wayward in his time. To follow this theme through the history of Melville criticism is to watch the critics register one of the significant developments of modern life—the growing acceptance of same-sex desire—and, not surprisingly, it was in the second half of the twentieth century that *Pierre* came to be recognized as a work of deep psychosexual insight. When Henry Murray proposed, in 1949, that "Isabel is the personi-fication of Pierre's unconscious," he meant that she is Pierre's "anima," or the archetypal image of the female within himself:

> One reason for the anima's attracting power is that she embodies the repressed and as-yet unformulated components of the man's personal-ity: the child in him who felt unloved, the passivity and the death wishes which were forsworn, the grief and the self-pity which have been bottled up, the feminine dispositions which have been denied, and, in addition, scores of nameless intuitions and impulses, the open expression of which has been barred by culture.

Melville was extending in *Pierre* the symbolic expression of uncon-scious mental processes that he had begun to develop in *Moby-Dick,* where he had described Fedallah (the atavistic harpooner whom Ahab secretly brings aboard the *Pequod*) as "such a creature as civilized, domestic people in the temperate zone only see in their dreams," one of those "odds and ends of strange nations come up from the unknown nooks and ash-holes of the earth." In effect, he retold in *Pierre* the story of Ahab—this time as the tale of a self-deluded boy who declares his independence from the wicked world and withdraws his allegiance from false gods, bestowing it instead upon himself. This boy-man turns himself into a "self-reciprocally efficient hermaphrodite" and, with slowly dawning horror, begins to sus-pect that he has merely found a rationale for following his own unholy desires.

Until relatively recently, the norms of critical discourse required that such matters be discussed elliptically. When the secretly gay critic Newton Arvin observed in 1950 that Melville "felt himself emotionally trapped between his mother and his wife," he could only venture the prolix hint that Melville's "fantasies took the form of imagining an escape from them both through a relationship that would be as tabu in quality as brother-sister incest, even if it were not literally that." Some forty years later, as the veil was lifting on homosexual life, an openly gay critic could state outright that the incest theme in *Pierre* was Melville's way of "transferring his guilt for homo-sexual desire to a sexual transgression of which he was innocent." Other gay critics have suggested that Melville felt no guilt at all, pointing to "the wink of homosexuality" in his work, by which they mean that he planted welcoming clues that only members of the perforcedly secret gay society would recog-nize—as when, in *Redburn,* he marks Harry Bolton's pleasure den with a purple light rather than the red light by which sailors find their way to conventional brothels.*

Whether hinting at it or saying it loud and clear, these critics are saying the same thing: that Melville was homosexual. Yet it remains difficult to know whether this attribution of homosexual feeling is an overdue acknowledgment of something of which Melville was aware or a projection on the part of gay readers who find themselves drawn to him—or, perhaps, both. The quest for the private Melville has usually led to a dead end, and we are not likely to fare better by speculating about his tastes in bed or bunk. He never reduced the complexity of experience to adage or aphorism or any other simplifying summary. On the one hand, *Pierre* can be interpreted as a covert gay text about a confused young man unable to reveal himself: "for the deeper that some men feel a secret and poignant feeling; the higher they pile the belying surfaces." As the book proceeds, Melville describes Pierre more and more in androgynous terms until in a burst of self-hatred the "woman-soft" boy destroys both himself and all who love him. "For Pierre is neuter now!" and can consort with neither man nor woman.

On the other hand, as befits a novel whose subtitle is *the Ambiguities*, *Pierre* can be read as a satire of a spoiled man-child who fails to stand or walk as an adult must learn to do:

> Watch yon toddler, how long it is learning to stand by itself! First it shrieks and implores, and will not try to stand at all, unless both father and mother uphold it. . . . But, by-and-by, grown up to man's estate, it shall leave the very mother that bore it, and the father that begot it. . . . There now, do you see the soul.

Pierre never advances very far into this process of maturation, ending his days soulless, mired in infantile self-pity, a "toddler . . . toddling entirely alone, and not without shrieks."

---

*Older critics tended to be too reticent about sexual themes in Melville, but recent critics can be overzealous in finding the gay "code." In an article on *Redburn* ("Melville's Secret Sex Text," *Village Voice Literary Supplement* [April 1982]), for example, Jonathan Ned Katz seizes on Melville's reference in his description of a London bordello to "such pictures as Martial and Suetonius mention as being found in the private cabinet of the Emperor Tiberius," implying that this allusion somehow identifies Melville's own sexual preferences as certainly gay. In fact, when Melville notes homosexual behavior as a fact of maritime life, the context is by no means always favorable—as when, in *White-Jacket,* he mentions a midshipman who is "apt to indulge at times in undignified familiarities with some of the men," and has them flogged when they resist his advances (*WJ*, ch. 52, p. 216). As for Tiberius, he was notorious for his wide range of depraved sexual appetites (he liked to use unweaned infants to suck his penis). Suetonius does mention a pornographic picture that Tiberius kept in his bedroom, but the picture depicted the woman warrior Atalanta performing oral sex on her male lover, Meleager.

Among Melville's contemporaries who found themselves dismayed by *Pierre* was Evert Duyckinck, to whom Melville had once complained "that an author can never—under no conceivable circumstances—be at all frank with his readers," and for whom Melville had written, in his review of Hawthorne's *Mosses*, that "in this world of lies, Truth is forced to fly like a scared white doe in the woodlands; and only by cunning glimpses will she reveal herself." As for Melville's latest novel, Duyckinck found its "cunning glimpses" altogether too revealing:

> we cannot pass without remark, the supersensuousness with which the holy relations of the family are described. Mother and son, brother and sister are sacred facts not to be disturbed by any sacrilegious specula-tions. Mrs. Glendinning and Pierre, mother and son, call each other brother and sister, and are described with all the coquetry of a lover and mistress. And again, in what we have termed the supersensuous-ness of description, the horrors of an incestuous relation between Pierre and Isabel seem to be vaguely hinted at.

Pierre may not have been, as one recent critic has called it, "the finest psychological novel anyone had yet written in English," but it was a work, as Melville had said about the plays of Shakespeare, that made "short, quick probings at the very axis of reality." It amounts to an argument that the socialized self is hopelessly divided between proscribed inner longings and compulsory outward performance. It is a book that goes beyond satire, in which Melville curses sentimental culture for refusing to recognize that its standards and practices are arbitrary and its collective memory as entranced by myth as that of distant savages—but a book in which he finds no salvation in the release from culture.

Among American writers, only Hawthorne had come close to match-ing its psychological penetration, in such stories as "The Birthmark" and "Rappaccini's Daughter," about men obsessed with cleansing the world—especially the bodies of their wives and daughters—of blemish and imper-fection. In *Pierre*, Melville somehow managed to produce both a serious anatomy of the radical imagination that anticipates Dostoevsky's *The Pos-sessed* and a manic burlesque that looks toward Gore Vidal's *Myra Breck-inridge*. After Lizzie finished reading it, she must have turned to the wall, losing herself gratefully in the whirling patterns of the wallpaper.

CHAPTER 8
SEEING TOO MUCH

1.

Toward the end of August 1852, a cousin of Hawthorne's wrote to a friend that "the Harpers think Melville is a little crazy." *Pierre* had appeared in New York on August 6 under the Harper & Brothers imprint, and with every new review, public judgment seemed to merge more completely with private opinion. According to the *Boston Post*, Melville's latest book, which sold fewer than two thousand copies, "might be supposed to emanate from a lunatic hospital," and William Gilmore Simms, never one to mince words (he had described Melville's portrait of Calhoun in *Mardi* as "loathsome"), declared in the *Southern Quarterly Review* that Melville had "gone 'clean daft.'" Lest he be misunderstood, Simms added that "the sooner this author is put in ward the better."

Earlier that summer, Melville had accepted an invitation to accompany his father-in-law on a trip to what in Massachusetts are still known as "the islands"—Nantucket, Martha's Vineyard, and, as Melville called it then, "the solitary Crusoeish island of Naushon." Their destination was the most distant island, which the author of that rollicking fantasy tour in *Moby-Dick* ("Nantucket! Take out your map and look at it!") had yet to see with his own eyes. En route, they stopped in New Bedford, where a friend of Judge Shaw's, Massachusetts attorney general John Clifford, joined them for the boat trip across the Sound. At dinner one night, Mr. Clifford, thinking that a novelist might find the case intriguing, talked at length about an inheritance dispute that had once crossed his desk. Melville must have shown some interest, since a few weeks later Clifford sent him the court clerk's copy of his notes on the case.

It was a simple story. A shipwrecked sailor named Robertson, who had been accustomed to finding "a wife (for a night) in every port," married the woman who had rescued him, but after making her pregnant, he deserted her. Seventeen years later, he returned with some tokens for his wife and the child whom he had never seen. Then he left again. After another interval he came back to bring a bridal gift to his daughter, only to set off once more. Upon his death, it became known that Robertson had married two other women during his absences; but his first wife, Agatha Hatch, remained faithful to him in fact and feeling, and in order not to disturb their daughter's goodwill toward her father, she refrained from ever speaking ill of him.

Melville found Clifford's story a nice illustration of "the peculiarly latitudinarian notions, which most sailors have of all tender obligations" toward their wives, and of "the great patience, & endurance, & resignedness of the women" while their husbands are away. Drawn to Agatha, perhaps, as a validation of his portrait of the ever faithful Lucy in *Pierre,* he toyed with the idea of writing something based on her story. But after thinking of Hawthorne's eerie tale "Wakefield," about a man who abandons his wife in the city and then spies on her from a hideaway around the block, he enclosed the clerk's notes with a letter to Hawthorne saying that "in this matter you would make a better hand at it than I would."

His deference, however, went only so far. In the same letter, which reads like the episode in Scott Fitzgerald's *The Last Tycoon* where the Hollywood mogul explains to a novice how to make a movie, Melville coached his friend on how the story should be written:

Supposing the story to open with the wreck—then there must be a storm; & it were well if some faint shadow of the preceding *calm* were thrown forth to lead the whole.—Now imagine a high cliff overhanging the sea & crowned with a pasture for sheep; a little way off—higher up,—a light-house, where resides the father of the future Mrs. Robinson [*sic*] the First. The afternoon is mild & warm. The sea with an air of solemn deliberation, with an elaborate deliberation, ceremoniously rolls upon the beach. The air is suppressedly charged with the sound of long lines of surf. There is no land over against this cliff short of Europe & the West Indies. Young Agatha (but you must give her some other name) comes wandering along the cliff. She marks how the continual assaults of the sea have undermined it; so that the fences fall over, & have need of many shiftings inland. The sea has encroached also upon that part where their dwelling-house stands near the light-house.— Filled with meditations, she reclines along the edge of the cliff & gazes out seaward. She marks a handful of cloud on the horizon, presaging a storm thro' all this quietude. (Of a maratime family & always dwelling on the coast, she is learned in these matters) This again gives food for thought. Suddenly she catches the long shadow of the cliff cast upon the beach 100 feet beneath her; and now she notes a shadow moving

along the shadow. It is cast by a sheep from the pasture. It has advanced
to the very edge of the cliff, & is sending a mild innocent glance far out
upon the water. There, in strange & beautiful contrast, we have the
innocence of the land placidly eyeing the malignity of the sea.

When Hawthorne replied, in effect, thanks but no thanks, Melville
decided after all to take a crack at the story himself. The result was a novel-
length manuscript, now lost, submitted the following spring to Harpers
under the title *The Isle of the Cross* and promptly rejected, possibly because
the Harpers anticipated a legal dispute involving descendants of Agatha and
her bigamous husband. Melville later made cryptic reference to having been
"prevented from printing" it.

2.

Perhaps to soften the blow, the Harpers asked if he had anything else suitable
for their three-year-old monthly magazine, and in response Melville sent
three stories that were slight and slightly frantic. Two were about coming to
terms with failure ("The Fiddler" and "The Happy Failure") and the third
(published in *Harper's New Monthly Magazine* in December 1853) was
"Cock-A-Doodle-Doo!," an extended dirty joke about a country gentleman
awakened every morning by a "glorious" and "noble cock" whose lusty
crowing makes him feel, by comparison, dried up and slack. He is unable to
rise to its invitation to romp in a landscape that "looked underdone, its raw
juices squirting all around," and the answer to his lassitude seems to be to get
hold of an irrepressible cock for himself. Seeking it far and wide, he comes
upon a woodsawyer and asks if he knows "any gentleman hereabouts who
owns an extraordinary cock" and might want to sell it. It turns out that the
prodigious desideratum belongs to the sawyer, who, not surprisingly, has no
intention of giving it up.

The mood revealed in these stories was a mix of grimness and hilarity at
his own expense, and Melville's family was getting worried. In a letter to her
brother in April 1853, Maria wrote that "the constant in-door confinement
with little intermission to which Hermans occupation as author compels
him does not agree with him," and she expressed fear that "this constant
working of the brain, & excitement of the imagination, is wearing Herman
out." A month later, Lizzie gave birth to their third child and first daughter,

Elizabeth. Meanwhile, Herman was unable to make the interest payments on the loan from Stewart, and the Harper brothers, having sold less than half the first printing of *Pierre,* were in no mood to advance him more money. He was drifting away from Duyckinck, who had given *Moby-Dick* a mixed review in *The Literary World,* and even his friendship with Hawthorne was cooling.

In the first months of their acquaintance, Melville already had objected to a certain chilly reserve in Hawthorne. "There is something lacking— a good deal lacking—to the plump sphericity of the man. What is that?" he had written with confidential cattiness to Duyckinck early in 1851, then answered his own question: "He does'nt patronise the butcher—he needs roast-beef, done rare." Even in his lavishly praising review of *Mosses,* Melville had raised the question of whether "Hawthorne has simply availed himself of this mystical blackness as a means to the wondrous effects he makes it to produce in his lights and shades; or whether there really lurks in him, per- haps unknown to himself, a touch of Puritanic doom," and he had answered his own question equivocally: "This, I cannot altogether tell." These words amounted to a preliminary version of what Henry James was to say a quarter century later: that the sense of sin is not native to Hawthorne's mind but "exclusively *imported*" from the curiosity shop of history, that sin for him "seems to exist . . . merely for an artistic or literary purpose," that it was "only, as one may say, intellectual . . . not moral and theological," not some- thing that "discomposed, disturbed, haunted" him "in the manner of its usual victims," but something by which he was amused in the manner of an artist at play. This was the charge that Melville intimated in his essay "Hawthorne and His Mosses." Was Hawthorne, he wondered, finally a voyeur rather than a sympathetic participant in life?

Writing to Hawthorne after returning to Pittsfield from the trip to the islands, with his own career in decline and Hawthorne's soaring, Melville filled his letter with a cascade of half-sincere congratulations:*

> This name of "*Hawthorne*" seems to be ubiquitous. I have been on
> something of a tour lately, and it has saluted me vocally & typographi-
> cally in all sorts of places & in all sorts of ways. . . . On a stately piazza,
> I saw it gilded on the back of a very new book [*Twice-Told Tales*], and in

---

***The Scarlet Letter* (published in March 1850), having sold as many copies in ten days as *Moby- Dick* sold in three years, had already achieved such prestige that its author was the subject of col- lege commencement orations. On August 15, 1851, Hawthorne noted in his journal ("I should have been curious to hear it") that Mr. Edwin Holsey Cole, a Wesleyan student from Cromwell, Connecticut, spoke about him at that spring's Wesleyan commencement.

the hands of a clergyman.—I went to visit a gentleman in Brooklyne, and as we were sitting at our wine, in came the lady of the house, holding a beaming volume in her hand, from the city—"My Dear," to her husband, "I have brought you *Hawthorne's* new book." I entered the cars at Boston for this place. In came a lively boy "*Hawthorne's* new book!"—In good time I arrived home. Said my lady-wife "there is Mr. *Hawthorne's* new book, come by mail." . . . Well, the Hawthorne is a sweet flower; may it flourish in every hedge.

When, in an earlier letter, Melville declared their everlasting solidarity ("The divine magnet is in you, and my magnet responds. Which is the biggest? A foolish question—they are *One*"), he was protesting too much that the comparative size of their "magnets" did not concern him.

But the trouble between them was more than rivalry. Hawthorne was a man who reserved his self-revelations for his wife, for whom his passion was frank and abundant. "My breast is full of thee; thou art throbbing throughout all my veins," he wrote to Sophia two years into their courtship; and later, after a few weeks' absence, one feels insatiate desire in his lament that "it is an age since thou hast been in my arms." But if his love for his wife was brimming and boundless, to others he seemed inward and stingy, "self-centered, self-reproductive, & soliloquial," according to one ungenerous acquaintance, who described him as a "hermaphroditical sort of thinker and artist," puffed up with the arrogance of his self-sufficiency. To those whom he did not allow close to him—everyone, it seemed, except Sophia—he appeared to be the kind of man who registers everything but reveals nothing, a man of "unsearchable eyes." His truest confidante put the matter more appreciatively, contrasting Melville's eager volubility with Hawthorne's receptive quiet. "Nothing pleases me more," Sophia wrote to her sister Elizabeth, "than to sit & hear this growing man [Melville] dash his tumultuous waves of thought against Mr. Hawthorne's great, genial, comprehending silences . . . without doing anything on his own except merely being, it is astonishing how people make him their innermost Father Confessor."

Hawthorne was an instance of what Henry James (who saw in him his only true predecessor in America) called "that queer monster, the artist": a vampiric monster, that is, who sucks up for his own sustenance the loves and sorrows of his human subjects. As if to brace himself for disappointment, Melville had written in "Hawthorne and His Mosses" that "on a personal interview no great author has ever come up to the idea of his reader." Years later, in *Clarel*, he was to model on Hawthorne a character named Vine, of whom he wrote that "Under cheer / Of opulent softness, reigned austere / Control of self," and he may have had the same person in mind in

The Confidence-Man when one character says of another that "there appears to be a certain—what shall I call it?—hidden sun, say, about him, at once enlightening and mystifying."

One senses Hawthorne's resistant presence in the many scenes of confrontation that recur in Melville's fiction between men of ardor and men of reserve: Ahab and Starbuck, Pierre and Falsgrave, even the needy man of "Cock-A-Doodle-Doo!" and the well-equipped woodsawyer. If Melville was not passing judgment, he almost certainly had been bruised by the collision with his unyielding friend, who, as he was to write of Vine, "could lure / Despite reserve which overture / Withstood." By the end of 1852, there was in his letters to Hawthorne, as Newton Arvin has remarked, a certain "dryness and tiredness"; perhaps the temperamental differences between the two men were proving to be unbridgeable, and so, finally, was their intellectual and spiritual divide. Hawthorne was a great psychological detective, adept at exposing covert motives behind overt convictions—sexual hunger in those who claim to be devoted to purity, lust for power in those who profess love of equality. Yet he was also, as James was to call him, an apparently "unperplexed" man who hid his contradictions and, like the aptly named Coverdale in his own novel *The Blithedale Romance*, peeped at the world from a hiding place of his own making. Vine's heart, Melville wrote in *Clarel*, was "a fountain sealed."

At some point between completing *Moby-Dick* and undertaking *Pierre*, Melville may have gotten close to some explosive secret in his friend's private life, and Hawthorne may have pushed him away. We do not know, and are unlikely ever to find out. Some scholars speculate that the theme of incest in *Pierre* cut too near to sensitivities that "hiddenly reside" (Melville's phrase from his essay on *Mosses*) in a man whose feelings for his darkly beautiful sister Elizabeth may have verged on the erotic. But whatever precipitated the estrangement, it seems clear that Melville, like Ahab, was driven by a burning need to get at the *why* of things, while Hawthorne, like Starbuck, found something puerile and reckless in his friend's Faustian urge to know the unknowable. A blurter-outer confronting a man of circumspection, Melville was a seeker whereas Hawthorne was endowed with what Keats had called "negative capability"—the ability, that is, to live among "uncertainties, mysteries, doubts, without any irritable reaching after fact and reason." Perhaps his equanimity was the real object of Melville's envy.

Whatever were the disturbances between them, by 1853 the two men had subsided into a more formal friendship. After Franklin Pierce was elected president in November 1852, Allan Melville, knowing that Hawthorne had gained the lucrative consulship at Liverpool for himself, wrote him to ask for help in securing a diplomatic post for Herman. Hawthorne agreed, and it was the beginning of a lobbying campaign that, as it turned out, reprised the futile hunt for a patronage job that Melville had made back in 1847 when newly married. This time, however, he stayed on the sidelines and let friends and family do the begging. Uncle Peter weighed in with Edwin Croswell, editor of the *Albany Argus,* who in turn wrote to the new U.S. attorney general, Caleb Cushing, that for Mr. Melville "constant brain labor seems to render some change of climate & position if not indispensable" at least "very desirable." Everyone who contributed to the campaign agreed that Honolulu would be best, though a posting in England would be fine and even Antwerp would do—anywhere distant from the scene of his failures. It is uncertain whether Lizzie and the children would have accompanied Herman if something had worked out, but nothing did.

Even the harshest critics of *Pierre* conceded that Melville had talent left to squander. In a review that called the book "perhaps the craziest fiction extant," the *Boston Post* lamented that "it is too bad for Mr. Melville to abuse his really fine talents." By the spring of 1853, friends and family were wondering if he was spent. Then, late that summer, after the rejection of *The Isle of the Cross,* the failed lobbying effort, the last salvos in the critical bombardment of *Pierre,* and the troubles with Hawthorne, he somehow summoned the discipline to compose a story that is among the great achievements of world literature.

3.

"Bartleby, the Scrivener" was published in *Putnam's Monthly Magazine* in two installments, in November and December 1853. Though the first issue of *Putnam's* had appeared less than a year earlier, it had already emerged as the nation's leading literary monthly, and, by 1855, was declared by William Makepeace Thackeray to be "much the best Mag. in the world." Edited by Melville's old New York acquaintance Charles Frederick Briggs, *Putnam's* was broadly anti-slavery and Whiggish; it drew writers from Horace Greeley's stable at the *Tribune,* and had obtained the subscription list of the *American Whig Review* in order to build circulation. The fact that he fit in well in the *Putnam's* circle suggests how far Melville had moved from the Democratic allegiances of his New York literary mentors and his brothers— one reason, perhaps, why his bid for a political appointment had failed. "Herman has always been a firm Democrat," Uncle Peter claimed in his letter of recommendation to Croswell, who felt obliged to transmit the appeal to Cushing with the emendation that Melville was a Democrat only to the extent that "a literary devotee can be supposed to enter the political arena," which was, of course, hardly at all.

For the setting of his new story, Melville returned to the world he had first known as a visitor to Gansevoort and Allan's law firm, and which he had always shunned for himself. "Bartleby" was in this respect an elaboration of that passage in *Moby-Dick* where crowds along the Battery gaze out to sea, seeking respite from their lives "pent up in lath and plaster—tied to counters, nailed to benches, clinched to desks." The support staff in Melville's fictional law office consists of two copyists, nicknamed Turkey and Nippers, and a gofer who answers to Ginger Nut in honor of the waferlike spice cake that his officemates require him to fetch from vendors in the street. Turkey tends to be hungover in the morning, bleary-eyed yet focused; but as the day goes on, he turns florid from his "afternoon devotions," spattering ink and bearing down so hard that his quill pens are liable to split. Nippers's rhythm is just the opposite: vague and distracted in the morning, he expends his energy by shifting his desk back and forth, sliding it sideways, slipping bits of wood or flakes of blotting paper under its legs to try to level it at the perfect working height. By afternoon he has given up his quest for the right relation between his desk and himself. These two men—one dull in the morning and wild in the afternoon, the other "twitching in his chair with a dyspeptic nervousness" before settling down—amount between them to one full-time employee.

In contrast, their nameless boss is level and tolerant, "an eminently *safe* man," as he says of himself—someone, that is, to whom one can entrust both secrets and money as if to a vault. Only once, when Turkey wets a wafer in his afternoon delirium with his own saliva and tries to press it onto the document in place of sealing wax, does the lawyer even think of firing him. He is a version of Poe's phlegmatic narrator in his 1840 story "The Business Man" ("I am a business man. I am a methodical man. Method is *the* thing, after all"), whom one meets as well in magazine sketches by Washington Irving or George W. Curtis (a *Putnam's* editor): a spongy gentleman who absorbs an incident in the morning and saves it for a vignette to be told in the evening over cigars and brandy at the club. He fills his speech with buffering words like "quite" and "rather," and on those rare occasions when permitting himself a boast, he muffles it in double negatives, as when speaking of the approval he had once enjoyed from the Donald Trump of his day, John Jacob Astor: "I was not unemployed in my profession by the late John Jacob Astor . . . I was not insensible to the late John Jacob Astor's good opinion."

If Melville had met versions of this lawyer in literature and life, he also had models in mind for the scriveners. One of the minor figures in *Bleak House,* which had been serialized in *Harper's* in the months just before Melville wrote "Bartleby," is a gaunt and sickly copyist to whom Dickens gives the telltale Latin name Nemo (No one) to signify his dispensability, since a hundred men are lined up to take his place. In Charles Briggs's New York novel, *The Adventures of Harry Franco,* the first job Harry lands upon coming to town is in the "dull business" of legal copying, which he "strove hard to do . . . well . . . and . . . quick" in a town where, as in Dickens's London, the supply of labor was outstripping demand. So many young men were looking for advantage in the brisk New York market for scriveners that in 1852 one enterprising penmanship teacher came up with the gimmick of placing on his desk a bronze cast of his own arm and hand in the act of writing so his pupils might emulate his form.

Like the whaleships Melville had once written about, the law office in "Bartleby" is a workplace on whose products (deeds, contracts, wills) many readers depended but whose inner workings they barely knew. In this sense "Bartleby," like *Moby-Dick,* disclosed a world usually kept out of sight, and it has always been uncomfortable reading for believers in the American Dream. It was a story about a commercial society that depended increasingly on multiple copies of many kinds of documents, but in which no technology for copying yet existed beyond the handheld pen. A few years after Melville's story appeared, Abraham Lincoln, in one of his frequent professions of faith in the promise of upward mobility, proclaimed America to be the nation where "the prudent, penniless beginner in the world labors for wages awhile, saves a surplus . . . then labors on his own account another while, and at length hires another beginner to help him." But the law office at "No.— Wall-street" is no place for dreamers. The glut in the Manhattan labor supply was destroying the old apprentice system whereby merchants took on apprentices from their own social class, who then rose in the hierarchy to join or succeed their masters. By the 1850s, apprenticeship in a law office was more likely to be a dead-end job than a stepping stone to a legal career, and so the law office in "Bartleby" is a dungeon where broken men grow old, fidgeting away their vitality until the last sparks of life go out. Its windows command "an unobstructed view of a lofty brick wall, black by age and everlasting shade." As for its interior arrangements, it is divided by opaque glass doors into separate spaces for employer and employees, who, immured in what Karl Marx (who contributed articles to Greeley's *Tribune* in the 1840s) called alienated labor, scratch away at papers that document the extent of other men's property. They are, in effect, human Xerox machines—and, for the sake of efficiency, the less human, the better.

Into this lifeless place, in response to an advertisement for a new scrivener, there walks one morning a pale and quiet young man. He is "incurably forlorn," like Dickens's Nemo, who, when he is found dead in his freezing room, is not immediately recognized as having died, since his appearance while alive was barely distinguishable from that of the corpse he has become. In his "cadaverous" gloom, Bartleby seems a similarly ideal candidate for this kind of work—polite, uncomplaining, barely breathing. But on his third day of employment (Melville refers to his arrival as his "advent," and with caustic irony conforms the story to the schedule of Christ's resurrection), the new man comes strangely to life. In response to a request that he help compare the copy of a document with its original, he declines, not with a blunt "No" or "I don't want to," but with a gentle deflection: "I would prefer not to." Bartleby has been presented with an utterly ordinary request, like ordering dinner from a waiter or asking a cabdriver to drive to your destination. But since there is not "the least uneasiness, anger, impatience or impertinence" in the clerk's refusal, the lawyer feels more dismayed than angry and lets the matter pass. The "I would prefer not to"— a phrase that echoes the lawyer's own gentility of phrasing—is a brilliant stroke: it leaves him disoriented and uncertain just what to say or do.

A few days later, the circumstance repeats itself when Bartleby again declines, but this time the lawyer presses him:

> "*Why* do you refuse?"
> "I would prefer not to."
> With any other man I should have flown outright into a dreadful passion, scorned all further words, and thrust him ignominiously from my presence. But there was something about Bartleby that not only strangely disarmed me, but in a wonderful manner touched and disconcerted me. I began to reason with him.
> "These are your own copies we are about to examine. It is labor saving to you, because one examination will answer for your four papers. It is common usage. Every copyist is bound to help examine his copy. Is it not so? Will you not speak? Answer!"

But no matter how much the lawyer prods ("I burned," he says, "to be rebelled against again"), he cannot provoke Bartleby to an outburst that would authorize one of his own. Trying to get a response out of Bartleby is like trying to "strike fire with my knuckles against a bit of Windsor soap":

> "Bartleby," said I, "Ginger Nut is away; just step round to the Post Office, won't you? (it was but a three minutes walk,) and see if there is any thing for me."

"I would prefer not to."

"You *will* not?"

"I *prefer* not."

"Prefer" is neither a street word nor an office word; it belongs in a formal dining room, with the ring of silver tinkling against crystal. It is a word that gently mocks the lawyer's circumlocutions, and its anachronistic sound spreads around the office, infecting everyone, as on this occasion when "Nippers's ugly mood was on duty, and Turkey's off":

> "Say now you will help to examine papers to-morrow, or next day: in short, say now that in a day or two you will begin to be a little reasonable:—say so, Bartleby."
>
> "At present I would prefer not to be a little reasonable," was his mildly cadaverous reply. . . .
>
> "*Prefer not,* eh?" gritted Nippers—"I'd *prefer* him, if I were you, sir," addressing me—"I'd *prefer* him; I'd give him preferences, the stubborn mule! What is it, sir, pray, that he *prefers* not to do now?"

For Nippers, the word "prefer" has become a sanitized substitute for "kick his ass" or "tell him to stuff it" or some such practical recommendation. Still,

> Bartleby moved not a limb.
>
> "Mr. Nippers," said I. "I'd prefer that you would withdraw for the present." . . .
>
> As Nippers, looking very sour and sulky, was departing, Turkey blandly and deferentially approached.
>
> "With submission, sir," said he, "yesterday I was thinking about Bartleby here, and I think that if he would but prefer to take a quart of good ale every day, it would do much towards mending him, and enabling him to assist in examining his papers."
>
> "So you have got the word too," said I, slightly excited.
>
> "With submission, what word, sir?" asked Turkey. . . .
>
> "I would prefer to be left alone here," said Bartleby, as if offended at being mobbed in his privacy.
>
> "*That's* the word, Turkey," said I—"*that's* it."
>
> "Oh, *prefer?* Oh yes—queer word. I never use it myself. But, sir, as I was saying, if he would but prefer—"
>
> "Turkey," interrupted I, "you will please withdraw."
>
> "Oh, certainly sir, if you prefer that I should."

Bartleby's little curtsy of a phrase conveys the bitter deference of someone who knows that his only recourse against his master is to compel him to give up the pretense of softheartedness and to acknowledge the hard fact of his mastery.

But rather than back down or think about what he is asking, Bartleby's master insists that he is being perfectly reasonable. "Every copyist," he points out, "is bound to help examine his copy. Is it not so?" Yet the more he explains the grounds of his requests, the less grounded they come to seem, even to himself. The more he speaks, the more he feels like the child who repeats some vowely word like "owl" or "banana" until, after a few repetitions, it comes to sound like nonsense to the speaker himself. The word "prefer" has an amazing effect. Once confident that he was living the Right and Good Way, the lawyer starts to lose his focus on things he has previously seen clearly: "It is not seldom the case that when a man is browbeaten in some unprecedented and violently unreasonable way, he begins to stagger in his own plainest faith. He begins, as it were, vaguely to surmise that, wonderful as it may be, all the justice and all the reason is on the other side." What "Bartleby" brings into view is the fact that all boundary lines between power and submission, mine and yours, right and wrong, too little and too much are finally nothing more than conventions to which we cling lest we lose our grip and tumble away into the infinity of unforeseen possibilities.

As these alternative worlds open up and threaten to swallow him, the lawyer tries to stick to his routines. Stopping by his office one Sunday morning to catch up on work, he finds his key obstructed by something inserted from the inside of the door. To his amazement, he is admitted by Bartleby, who has evidently been living in the office, day and night, on ginger nuts and bits of cheese, "sole spectator of [his own] solitude." At the sight of the young man in all his "miserable friendlessness and loneliness," the lawyer is flooded by an unaccustomed despondency:

> For the first time in my life a feeling of overpowering stinging melancholy seized me. Before, I had never experienced aught but a not-unpleasing sadness. The bond of a common humanity now drew me irresistibly to gloom. A fraternal melancholy! For both I and Bartleby were sons of Adam. I remembered the bright silks and sparkling faces I had seen that day, in gala trim, swan-like sailing down Broadway; and I contrasted them with the pallid copyist, and thought to myself, Ah, happiness courts the light, so we deem the world is gay; but misery hides aloof, so we deem that misery there is none. These sad fancyings—chimeras, doubtless, of a sick and silly brain—led on to other and more special thoughts, concerning the eccentricities of Bartleby. Pre-

sentiments of strange discoveries hovered round me. The scrivener's pale form appeared to me laid out, among uncaring strangers, in its shivering winding sheet.

Until this moment, this man's awareness of human deprivation has been limited to "not-unpleasing" representations in sentimental stories and poems. Until now, he has been a representative city citizen: affable and blasé, walking through the world with blinders on so as not to be distracted or disturbed, equipped with an inventory of gestures adequate to get him through the fleeting encounters that fill an urban day, without getting entangled in any real human exchange. But now, at the sight of Bartleby in all his terrible aloneness, he feels for the first time what Redburn felt at the sight of the dying mother in the Liverpool gutter—that all his life he has been "making merry in the house of the dead." He feels himself spinning away from all things fixed and stable until he becomes one of those, as Marx famously put it, for whom "all that is solid melts into air" and who "are forced to face . . . the real conditions of their lives and their relations with their fellow men."

The lawyer is a decent man. He redoubles his efforts to pull Bartleby back into the world of civility and order; but each time he is met with "I would prefer not to," until one evening, having had enough, he tries to cut loose by giving Bartleby polite and proper notice, leaving him his wages and a little severance pay. But this expedient fails to put an end to the matter. Walking home that night amid the mingled voices of Broadway, he cannot get the young man out of his mind. He overhears fragments of speech (" 'I'll take odds he doesn't,' said a voice as I passed") and answers as if talking to himself, " 'Doesn't go?—done!' said I, 'put up your money,' " reaching instinctively into his pocket to place his bet that, yes, Bartleby will go, until he realizes it is Election Day and that these men are talking about which candidate is likely to win the vote.

Next morning, of course, Bartleby has gone nowhere, and things start to get nasty. How about a clerkship in a dry-goods store? the lawyer wants to know. Or perhaps some position for which your charm and loquacity will serve you well—bartender, bill collector, or a chaperone for a young man traveling in Europe, whom you could "entertain . . . with your conversation?" Bartleby responds to these barbed invitations as usual—he prefers not to—until the lawyer, pushed past the point of exasperation, declares his intention to move out of the office himself, hoping that his "motionless" vagrant will continue to exhibit his gift of inertia and stay put. He gets his wish. But when his successor finds Bartleby still squatting there, immovable as a rooted stump, he comes around to the lawyer to complain. "You are responsible," he says, "for the man you left there."

4.

With this accusation, we approach the sad end of a sad story. "Bartleby" touches a nerve with every reader who has ever tried to manage an unmanageable relationship with a parent, child, lover, spouse—anyone who compels our better self to try and try again but pushes us toward cruelty and a final "Enough!" It is the story of one of those Melvillean characters like Pip (and, in works yet to be written, Hunilla in *The Encantadas* and Colonel Moredock in *The Confidence-Man*), who has been shocked by some incommunicable experience that has left him scarred and less than whole. It is a city story about one of those innumerable urban casualties who makes us feel both sympathy and disgust, as well as fear, given that he might be a preview of what could happen to us upon some comparable reversal of fortune. But Melville's aim is far from a pitch for pity or charity. As we follow Bartleby's descent into the New York City jail (known even then as "the Tombs") where he is sent to die alone, the story becomes ineffably sad but also bitterly funny, blending, as Richard Henry Dana, Sr., recognized, "the pathetic and the ludicrous,"* as the half-crazy Turkey and Nippers, like a couple of tramps in a Beckett play, climb up to ride tandem on their high horse in order to show Bartleby who's boss.

Perhaps some precipitating event in Melville's life might explain the half-despondent, half-delirious mood of this remarkable story. Perhaps it was a story about Melville's own fall into obscurity or an allegory of Hawthorne's emotional recalcitrance (Melville describes Vine, in *Clarel,* as "opulent in withheld replies"). Searching for some explanation for the despair he had seen in Bartleby's eyes, the lawyer reports in a brief Epilogue a rumor that the young man had once worked in the Dead Letter Office, where the clerks take piles of undeliverable mail and file them away into storage, where they will gather dust for eternity. It may be that the seed of "Bartleby" had been planted in Melville's mind by an article, "The Lawyer's Story," about an odd clerk that was published in February 1853 in the *New York Times,* or by one that had run in September 1852 in the *Albany Register* about the Dead Letter Office, where "great sacks, locked and sealed . . . [are] piled in the halls, containing undelivered love notes, locks of hair . . .

---

*This mix of pathos and farce is captured well in Jonathan Parker's expressionistic 2002 film adaptation of "Bartleby."

Daguerreotype portraits . . . lottery tickets and tickets for rail or ship passage, household keys, diamond ornaments," all tokens of thwarted human
dreams. Perhaps Bartleby had had such an encounter with the dead-
endedness of life and had thereby, as we would say today, "gone postal"—no
longer capable of sorting through his fingers the paper traces of a million
ruined lives.

Melville's treatment of the lawyer's confusion over how to respond to
this mutilated soul is a finely wrought portrait of a morally vexed man. But it
is also a meditation on a large moral issue under dispute in antebellum
America: how to define collective responsibility at a time when the old ad
hoc welfare system of churches and charities could no longer cope with the
growing number of workers and families left destitute by the boom-and-bust
cycle of the industrial economy. As casualties mounted, the scope of corporate responsibility was being narrowed in the courts by business-friendly
judges who routinely ruled against plaintiffs in cases of workplace injury and
property loss. (One suit, brought against the Boston & Worcester Railroad
in 1842 by an employee who had been injured in a derailment caused by
another employee's negligence, had been dismissed in a precedent-setting
case by none other than Judge Lemuel Shaw.) In the 1850s, the United States
was fast becoming a laissez-faire society with no articulated system for pro-
tecting individuals against impersonal power. In this respect, Bartleby—
homeless, friendless, the urban equivalent of "a bit of wreck in the mid
Atlantic"—was a figure more representative than eccentric.

Yet there was an opposite thrust in midcentury America that Melville
also registered in "Bartleby." This was the fundamentally religious impulse,
expressed chiefly in the abolitionist movement but also in the whole array of
reform movements from temperance to public education, to *expand* the
scope of responsibility—to insist, that is, that the sufferings of some people
must be the business of all people. This groping toward a widened sense of
accountability was driven by multiple forces, among them the force of technology (railroads, canals, steamboats, and, especially, the telegraph) that
enabled news to be circulated more broadly and rapidly than ever before, as
well as by the evangelical movements that were springing up everywhere
from the seaboard cities to the frontier. When the lawyer in "Bartleby" finds
himself indisposed to taking his usual seat in his pew at Trinity Church ("the
things I had seen disqualified me for a time from church-going"), he looks
back, with a penitent sense of his own insufficiency, into the writings of the
great evangelical theologian Jonathan Edwards, for whom religion is "not
only . . . the business of Sabbath days, or . . . the business of a month, or a
year, or of seven years . . . but the business of life." The lawyer knows that he
cannot rise to this impossible standard, which amounts to a call to put away

"the old Adam of resentment" and to embrace the new Adam of selfless love in a lifelong act of *imitatio Christi*. But Melville does not write about the lawyer in a prosecutorial spirit. He writes about him as a witness to a good man trying to become a better man in the face of another man's suffering.

What Melville achieved in "Bartleby, the Scrivener" was the integration of the radical insight that the standing social order is morally outrageous and must be rejected with the conservative insight that custom and precedent are precious and fragile and must be defended. "Bartleby" registers the truth of both views. It integrates the moral truth that we owe our fellow human beings our faith and love with the psychological and social truth that sympathy and benevolence have their limits—that, as the historian Thomas Haskell has put it, "the limits of moral responsibility have to be drawn somewhere and . . . the 'somewhere' will always fall far short of much pain and suffering that we could do something to alleviate." The radical voice in Melville says, "Save him, succor him, embrace him as a child of God," while the conservative voice says, "What more can I do for him? And if I turn my whole life over to him, what will become of the others who depend on me?" In "Bartleby," these two voices speak as they do in life: they speak, that is, simultaneously.

CHAPTER 9
THE MAGAZINIST

1.

In its themes, "Bartleby" was continuous with Melville's previous work, but in its style it was a departure. It marked the moment that Melville left behind the "ejaculatory prose" (F. O. Matthiessen's phrase) of his novels, in which spoken words seem "never to have belonged to the speaker, to have been at best a ventriloquist's trick." If the characters in Melville's novels sometimes hold forth as if to an audience outside the action, in "Bartleby" the dialogue has the feel of people actually talking with one another. Melville had found a new capacity, as Richard Henry Dana, Sr., put it, to play upon "the nicer strings of our complicated nature"—and was thereby making, after the sound and fury of *Pierre,* one of the notable artistic recoveries in our literary history.

But for an artist of vaulting ambition, the effort to keep down the volume can be trying, and by the fall of 1853 Melville was again showing signs of enervation. He was occupied that fall with what he described in a letter to the Harpers as his "Tortoise Hunting Adventure," a series of sketches about the Galapagos Islands, where he had stopped on his first whaling cruise ten years earlier. Serialized in *Putnam's* in the spring of 1854 under the title *The Encantadas,* these sketches were set in the same volcanic isles that Charles Darwin had explored aboard HMS *Beagle* in 1836, when the idea of natural selection had begun to form in his mind. Melville had read Darwin's journal (published in 1839) and he drew upon it now in his own reminiscence of the Galapagos, which was less akin to Darwin's vision of wondrous plenitude than it was a preview of what T. S. Eliot calls, in *The Waste Land,* a "heap of broken images where the sun beats." The setting was once again the wide Pacific, but the author was not exactly in a tropical mood:

Take five-and-twenty heaps of cinders dumped here and there in an outside city lot; imagine some of them magnified into mountains, and the vacant lot the sea; and you will have a fit idea of the general aspect of the Encantadas, or Enchanted Isles. A group rather of extinct volcanoes than of isles, looking much as the world at large might, after a penal conflagration. . . .

In this charred version of the enchanted isles that he had described in *Typee* and *Omoo*, "bandit birds with long bills cruel as daggers" fly above the "prostrate trunks of blasted pines."

By the end of 1853, Melville had a new reason to have cinders on his mind. On December 10, the Harper & Brothers warehouse on Cliff Street in Manhattan went up in flames, burning to the ground till nothing was left, according to the *Herald,* but a "mass of rubbish, comprising six houses on Cliff Street, running through to Pearl." Since Harpers stored its stereotype plates in fireproof vaults, the plates were saved, but the whole inventory of Melville's unsold books, including those still in unbound sheets, was lost. Years later he explained to his father-in-law that the fire reduced his already meager income, since upon receiving orders for his books, the Harpers now assessed a reprinting charge for which they debited his account.

In the eighth of the ten *Encantadas* sketches, probably written before the loss of his books, Melville played a variation on the story of Agatha Hatch that Harper & Brothers had refused to publish the previous summer. This time the fated woman is not a Nantucket bride but an Indian woman, Hunilla, dropped off by a whaleship with her husband and brother on an expedition to gather Galapagos tortoises, prized for the sweetness of their meat. While awaiting the ship's return, the two men are caught in a squall that capsizes their catamaran:

> Before Hunilla's eyes they sank. The real woe of this event passed before her sight as some sham tragedy on the stage. She was seated in a rude bower among the withered thickets, crowning a lofty cliff, a little back from the beach. The thickets were so disposed, that in looking upon the sea at large she peered out from among the branches as from the lattice of a high balcony. But upon the day we speak of here, the better to watch the adventure of those two hearts she loved, Hunilla had withdrawn the branches to one side, and held them so. They formed an oval frame, through which the bluely boundless sea rolled like a painted one. And there, the invisible painter painted to her view the wave-tossed and disjointed raft, its once level logs slantingly upheaved, as raking masts, and the four struggling arms undistinguishable among them; and then all subsided into smooth-flowing creamy waters, slowly drifting the splintered wreck; while first and last, no sound of any sort

was heard. Death in a silent picture; a dream of the eye; such vanishing shapes as the mirage shows.

With this harrowing passage, Melville joined a number of nineteenth-century writers who were drawn to the theme of what Shakespeare had called, in *The Rape of Lucrece,* "double death" ("'Tis double death to drown in ken of shore"). In *David Copperfield,* which he and Lizzie had read aloud in the winter of 1850–51, Dickens describes a schooner foundering just off shore while helpless spectators watch until the last man clinging to the mast goes down in a shower of splinters and spray. Melville now followed his own version of "double death" with a portrait of the surviving witness eviscerated by what she has seen: year after year, Hunilla "trod the cindery beach" with "her spell-bound eye bent upon the incessant waves," hoping without hope for the sight of a sail.*

There were other passages of emotional power in *The Encantadas,* but the linkages between them were weak, and the other stories that occupied Melville during this period were even weaker. He turned to a new form: diptychs, or pairs of contrasting scenes that illustrate this or that social pathology (rural poverty vs. urban snobbery, sham piety vs. Christian charity) by which his indignation had been aroused. He had read about the diptych tradition in a book by Charles Eastlake, *Materials for a History of Oil Painting,* that had been borrowed from the Athenaeum Library by Judge Shaw while Melville was visiting in Boston in the summer of 1848; and on his trip to London the following year, Melville had seen at the National Gallery dual saint portraits attributed to Taddeo Gaddi, as well as, in Paris, carved ivory diptychs at the Hôtel de Cluny.† Now, in the first panel of "Poor Man's Pudding and Rich Man's Crumbs" (published in *Harper's Monthly Magazine* in June 1854), we meet an impoverished rural couple struggling to survive; in the second, we see dissolute aristocrats throwing banquet scraps to the poor. In "The Two Temples," Melville juxtaposed the "fat-paunched, beadle-faced" sexton of New York's Grace Church, whose job is to prevent loiterers from coming inside to beg or sleep, with a London theater usher who takes pity on a man whom he assumes to be a beggar and offers him free beer.

*In her novel *The Pearl of Orr's Island* (1862), Harriet Beecher Stowe wrote a similar scene of closely witnessed shipwreck; a variant of the theme occurs in one of Emily Dickinson's poems, probably composed in the early 1860s, in which the promise of salvation is described as God's cruel lie to man: "To lead Him to the Well / And let Him hear it drip / Remind Him, would it not, somewhat / Of His condemned lip?" The greatest nineteenth-century work on the theme of shipwreck close to shore was Gerard Manley Hopkins's poem *The Wreck of the Deutschland* (1876).

†Melville mentions the Cluny ivories in his journal entry for December 5, 1849, and the Gaddi portraits at the National Gallery on December 17.

Putnam's rejected "The Two Temples," as Charles Briggs explained, because its "pungent" satire risked "offending the religious sensibilities of the public" and, more particularly, of the powerful "congregation of Grace Church," so the story was never published in Melville's lifetime. In "The Paradise of Bachelors and the Tartarus of Maids," published in *Harper's* in April 1855 (the magazine had bought the story in May 1854), the first sketch describes the camaraderie of a London gentleman's club, while the second describes an unheated New England paper mill where shivering girls operate machines that turn rags into pulp and pulp into paper. This was the most interesting of the diptychs, but its allegory was heavy-handed (the paper mill is located in a hollow known as "Devil's Dungeon," where a gnarled hemlock tree grows "undulatory as an anaconda"), and Melville simply could not overcome the limitation to which allegorical fiction is always subject: making unearned generalizations about big truths.

In all these stories, setting and incident seem chosen in order to illustrate this or that dinner-table point about, say, the differences between England and America or the degrading effects of factory labor. Melville was writing now about experiences tangential to his life—an excursion to an old-boys' club on his London trip, a winter's day tour of a papermaking factory. He was no longer writing fiction. He was writing commentaries in the form of fiction.

2.

In August 1853, Melville turned thirty-four years old—roughly the halfway point toward death for a nineteenth-century man who expected still to live a generous number of years—and his powers of invention were patently declining. In the past, he had poached incidents or descriptions from other writers, but he had never looked to others for subject or theme. Now he did so. At some point in the late 1840s he had acquired a copy of *The Life and Remarkable Adventures of Israel R. Potter,* a ghost-written memoir by a Revolutionary War veteran who had been taken prisoner by the British and, after nearly a half century of exile in England, returned to his native land to peddle his story in hopes of obtaining a government pension. Melville had been thinking about basing a book on Potter's story when, in London in 1849, he bought an eighteenth-century map of the city that he thought might be useful "in case I serve up the Revolutionary narrative of the beggar."

In the winter of 1853–54, with map at hand, he reread Potter's book, along with other books that took him back to the world of his grandfathers: *The Life and Correspondence of John Paul Jones*, Ethan Allen's *Narrative of Captivity*, and James Fenimore Cooper's *History of the Navy*. Potter's memoir was the story of a Rhode Island boy who fought at Bunker Hill (where he obeyed the famous order not to shoot till he could see the whites of the enemy's eyes), was taken prisoner during the British blockade of Boston, and shipped off to England. Beginning with Israel's boyhood flight from his parents in order to seek his fortune, the story moves through his exploits as a soldier, his imprisonment behind stout and bolted doors in a foreign land, his escape and years of wandering, till he returns home as an old man. An *Odyssey* that failed to culminate in reunion or renown, it was also a truncated retelling of the Cincinnatus myth, in which the gentleman-farmer, called to public service, brings his pastoral virtue to his country's cause but spends the rest of the tale trying in vain to get back to the fields whence he came. When, after a lifetime of being "harassed by night and day . . . and driven from place to place," Israel finally returns to his native land, he is an unsung hero without garland or even greeting.

This story of a life that starts out gloriously but leads nowhere suited Melville's mood. It was a report from the dark underside of the world he had heard extolled as a child, and in the spring and early summer of 1854, he rewrote it as *Israel Potter: His Fifty Years of Exile*. Published in *Putnam's* in nine installments that ran from July 1854 through March 1855, this work (published as a book immediately after the last installment) vacillated between imitation and invention, and was pervaded by what Alfred Kazin has called the feeling of "exile as a lifetime experience, exile as a feeling about life unexplained by the circumstances of exile."

The tone of *Israel Potter*, which Melville wrote partly in a breathless present tense, is mock-heroic. Israel starts out as a kind of eighteenth-century Forrest Gump ("before hastening to one duty, he would not leave a prior one undone") who, when called to arms, finishes plowing his half-plowed field before tearing off to fight the British at Boston. A "sturdy farmer" (as Melville had called Cincinnatus in *Redburn*), Israel reserves his deepest feelings for hearth and home. But if he is not of keen mind, he fights with resourcefulness; during his captivity he learns to feign sleep or injury until his captors relax their vigilance. At the first chance at escape, he springs into action, and once at large he wins the confidence of anyone inclined to help or harbor him.

Sized up by a pro-Yankee cabal of English gentlemen as a reliable courier, Israel is dispatched with a secret message to Benjamin Franklin, who is in Paris trying to coax the French to join the war on the rebel side.

Melville portrays Franklin as a sententious windbag—salacious and stingy, a randy old man with a touch of "primeval orientalness," who, though he takes an interest in his young visitor, saves the best cognac and prettiest chambermaids for himself, thus teaching the boy a useful lesson about the world. Israel's next mentor is the brazen and brutal John Paul Jones, that "jaunty barbarian in broadcloth," who conscripts Israel as his sidekick in raiding British ports, where they land by night in order to spike the cannon and torch the town, a team of marauders delighted to bring the colonial war to the colonialists' homeland.

Some of the strongest writing in *Israel Potter* came in Melville's account of the sea battle between Jones's *Bonhomme Richard* and the British warship *Serapis*—a battle that had found its way, by Melville's day, into American myth as the occasion of Jones's famous reply to the British commander's demand for surrender: "I have not yet begun to fight." Melville heard in that story an echo of his Gansevoort grandfather's reply ("it is my determined resolution . . . to defend this fort . . . to the last extremity") when the British commander demanded that he give up Fort Stanwix.

But *Israel Potter* recounted a war that had neither dignity nor decorum, and in this sense the whole book was a kind of extended anti-myth. In one grim scene, Jones's men wriggle out onto the yardarm to toss grenades as if they were dropping apples from a tree overhanging a neighbor's field, blowing the enemy to bits with their "sour fruit." The two ships, at close quarters, pour fire into one another, no longer belligerents "in the ordinary sense" but "a co-partnership and joint-stock combustion-company . . . two houses through whose party-wall doors have been cut" so that death can flow freely between them. This kind of writing was not exactly consonant with the national myth of America born in blood and glory; there was plenty of blood in *Israel Potter,* but precious little glory, and Melville concluded his account of Jones's naval exploits by remarking, "in view of this battle one may well ask—What separates the enlightened man from the savage? Is civilization a thing distinct, or is it an advanced stage of barbarism?"

After the war, Israel leads a life of hard labor in the "Egypt" of England. "Desperate with want," he joins a work gang of "spavined-looking old men" among smoking brick kilns under a "ridged and mottled sky," where they ladle into wooden trays the heavy dough that hardens into the building blocks of industrial Britain. Later, he turns to caning chairs, then works with shovel and spade in a fence-enclosed London park where, amid the greenery, he dreams "himself home into the mists of the Housatonic mountains." (By the time Israel gets back, factories of the sort that Melville had written about in "The Paradise of Bachelors and the Tartarus of Maids" could be found in those mountains.) After a half century of exile, he sails into Boston

Harbor on the Fourth of July, 1826, the date on which both John Adams and Thomas Jefferson died, and is almost trampled by a holiday mob before heading west to the Berkshires "to get a glimpse of his father's homestead," only to discover that "it had been burnt down long ago." Having petitioned for support as a veteran, he is denied because of "certain caprices of law," and with his "scars . . . his only medals," Israel Potter "died the same day that the oldest oak on his native hills was blown down."

Beneath its picaresque surface, a weariness of tone kept *Israel Potter* from rising above the level of minor work as Melville worked at it into the summer of 1854. It was probably then that he also wrote "The Lightning-Rod Man," an acerbic sketch of a country con man who peddles such advice as avoiding tall men during thunderstorms, as well as two short stories that Melville referred to, in a letter to *Harper's* on September 18, as a "brace of fowl—wild fowl." These unruly birds were "Jimmy Rose," about a New York bankrupt reminiscent of Allan Melvill, a tale about failure told in the voice of a superannuated gentleman who lives in a leaky house that is half museum, half mausoleum, and "The 'Gees," a sketch of the mixed race of Portuguese and Cape Verde islanders whose preference for biscuits over wages makes them popular with whaleship captains. Each of these stories had touches of tart wit but was otherwise undistinguished.

In May or June, Lizzie had become pregnant with the child who would be the Melvilles' last, Frances, born on March 2, 1855. There is little direct evidence of what life was like in the Melville household, though there survives a speculative account in a letter to Herman from his sister Helen, who was living in Brookline with her husband, George Griggs, and who, in May, chided her brother with a mix of affection and exasperation for ignoring her letters:

> I should have sent one of my numerous epistles to your particular address ere now, if I had not been so well acquainted with your usual mode of treating such documents—"Any letters? Herman?" cries Gus [Herman's sister Augusta], or Lizzie, or Fanny [Herman's sister Frances], as you are reining up old Charlie in gallant style at the pump-room door. "Y-e-s-s—one from Helen I guess—for some of you—here 'tis." "Why Herman, it's directed to you!"—"Is it? Let me see—why so it is! Well, take it along, I'll be in presently, and then some of you can read it to me."

In May, Melville missed the annual interest payment on T. D. Stewart's loan for the third year in a row, and knowing that the full amount was due the following year, his distractions now included financial obligations that he feared he could not meet. The previous winter, while he was working on a long story about an American merchant ship captain who encounters a mysterious slaveship in the South Atlantic, an attack of back pain—"so bad that he was helpless," Lizzie later wrote—had come on and lingered for months. Eventually, he sought treatment from his neighbor Dr. Holmes, whose son, the great jurist Oliver Wendell Holmes, Jr., remembered his father's patient seventy years later as a "rather gruff taciturn man." Melville's mother worried about "dear Herman's" physical and financial health, both of which, she advised her daughter-in-law, could be improved by the purchase of "half a (½) dozen lb of Halibut once a week it is much cheaper than meat, & is delicious when cold dressed like Lobster."

3.

By the spring of 1855, George W. Curtis had concluded that Melville "does everything too hurriedly now," and he advised Joshua A. Dix, one of the new owners of *Putnam's,* to "decline any novel from Melville that is not extremely good." Some of the stories that Melville composed during this period, such as "The Bell Tower" and "The Apple-Tree Table," probably written between spring and fall of 1855, merited the caution. Their prose, if not quite "arthritically clumsy," as one critic has judged it, strains to express their themes in allegorical form. "The Bell Tower" is an elaborately concocted tale of hubris punished, and "The Apple-Tree Table" retells a piece of New England lore about an insect that, with an eerie ticking noise, eats its way out of an applewood table in which it has been imprisoned for years. Thoreau alludes to the same story in the conclusion to *Walden* and draws spiritual refreshment from it: "Who does not feel his faith in a resurrection and immortality strengthened by hearing this?" But Melville turned the tale into a joke at the expense of his narrator who, until the "small shining beetle or bug" makes its appearance, is half convinced by the ticking noises that his house is inhabited by a ghost.*

These works were a cut above hackwork, yet Curtis retained enough interest in Melville to be "anxious to see" the longer story that he had been

---

*Melville makes reference in "The Apple-Tree Table" to the Fox sisters, who had recently become famous for the putative ghosts in their upstate New York house, which made themselves known by "spirit rappings."

working on while the final installments of *Israel Potter* were appearing. For this work, Melville had turned again to another writer for "a skeleton of actual reality" on which "to build about with fulness & veins & beauty." It was set once again in the past, but this time the theme—slavery—was utterly current. When Curtis read *Benito Cereno* in April 1855, he found it "a little spun out,—but . . . very striking & well done," and he urged that it be accepted. *Benito Cereno* appeared in installments in the last three months of the year.

It was a story well suited for *Putnam's,* which was becoming increasingly belligerent on the slavery issue. Within a year of Franklin Pierce's election in 1852, *Putnam's* had run a piece by Parke Godwin, a refugee from the Democratic Party, attacking the new Democratic president for trying "to dance upon . . . cross wires" over the political abyss rather than defend the principle of "the equality and brotherhood of the human race." By the mid-1850s, the magazine was being denounced by the virulently pro-slavery *DeBow's Review* as "the leading review of the Black Republican party," and it is easy to see why. Among the articles in the same October 1855 issue that ran the first installment of *Benito Cereno* was a long piece on "the suicide of slavery," by which the *Putnam's* editors meant to prophesy not the death of the peculiar institution but the death of the republic itself. "We sit with dull eyes and heavy spirit," they wrote about the widening sectional divide, as we "listen to the tick of a death-watch as armed marauders of Missouri" carry their slaves into Kansas under protection of Congress, which had recently annulled the Missouri Compromise by declaring the Kansas Territory open to slaveholders. Readers today tend to encounter *Benito Cereno* in the neutralizing context of some "Great Short Works" anthology, but its original appearance was in a partisan magazine committed to the anti-slavery cause.

Melville's source for his new story was a memoir by a Massachusetts merchant sea captain named Amasa Delano, whose ship, the *Perseverance,* had been anchored off the island of Santa Maria in February 1805 when it encountered a Spanish slaveship in foggy weather and evident distress. Delano devoted one chapter to this incident, which Melville developed into an extended retelling that took its title from the name (Bonito Sereno, as Delano spelled it) of the Spanish captain. The result has provoked more critical contention than anything else Melville wrote—a work that has been increasingly recognized as among his greatest achievements.

Delano's original was not much to work with, recounting the incidents matter-of-factly: having been rowed over to the slaveship, the *Tryal* (Melville, by altering the name to *San Dominick,* alluded to the island of St. Domingo, where slaves had revolted in bloody rage against their French masters in 1799), Delano discovered its officers, crew, and slaves dying of hunger and thirst. He summoned relief supplies from the *Perseverance* and, while awaiting their arrival, witnessed behavior aboard that he could not explain: a black boy assaults a white sailor as if they are equals in a street fight, while the Spanish captain watches with apparent indifference, looking nervously toward one particular Negro, "who kept constantly at the elbows of Don Bonito and myself." When Delano asked to speak privately with the Spaniard about the state of affairs on his ship, he declined, explaining that he always kept by his side "his confidant and companion." Delano could not put his finger on what was amiss until, having shoved off in his boat to return to the *Perseverance,* Don Bonito leapt from the gunwale into the departing boat and poured out his story: the slaves, led by Bonito's slave attendant, had commandeered his ship, killed a score of his men, and demanded to be sailed to Senegal. The rest of the narrative recounts the attack by the *Perseverance* on the *Tryal,* the capture and execution of the mutinous slaves, and what Delano regarded as the surly ingratitude of the Spaniard, who refused to reward the man who had saved him.

On this bare foundation Melville constructed a work that, in the view of Lewis Mumford (writing in 1929), made the rebellious slaves into symbols of "human treachery." But others, including the notable black writers Sterling Brown and Ralph Ellison, have found in *Benito Cereno* a sympathetic portrayal of brutalized people driven to violence in order to regain their freedom. In our own time of terror and torture, *Benito Cereno* has emerged as the most salient of Melville's works: a tale of desperate men in the grip of a vengeful fury that those whom they hate cannot begin to understand. It is the story of an American, Amasa Delano, caught in a whirlwind of mutual cruelty, a man, as Benjamin Barber has recently written, whose "blindness to evil" leaves him incapable of recognizing "the moral debacle of slavery itself." Russell Banks, author of a historically informed novel about that avenging terrorist John Brown, describes *Benito Cereno* as one of the few works of American literature to confront unflinchingly "the African Diaspora and the violent history of race in America."

Benito Cereno is also our best evidence that during his years of personal withdrawal from the intellectual circle to which he had once belonged, Melville had kept his eye on the gathering storm. He turned to the subject of slavery at a time when Americans on both sides of the divide feared that slave rebellion was imminent. By the 1850s, pro- and anti-slavery polemics had become fierce and frequent; apologists who had once described slavery as a benign paternalism toward a childlike race now described blacks as beasts requiring strict oversight, while opponents of slavery declared that years of white cruelty would soon incite—and justify—black reprisal. After years of self-suppression, writers on both sides of the question brought slavery into the mainstream of American literature, culminating with the publication in 1852 of *Uncle Tom's Cabin*. The escaped slave Frederick Douglass, in his widely read *Narrative of the Life of an American Slave* (published in 1845 and reprinted eight times within three years), described how he had seen his master "tie up a lame young woman, and whip her with a heavy cowskin upon her naked shoulders, causing the warm red blood to drip" while he quoted from the Gospel of Luke: " 'He that knoweth his master's will, and doeth it not, shall be beaten with many stripes.' " In 1854, with this kind of outrage in mind and referring to an infamous slave uprising against the French on the island of Hispaniola, Theodore Parker warned that "to mutilate . . . Africans whom outrage has stung to crime . . . is only to light the torches of San Domingo." The South, he added, "sits on a powder magazine" that sooner or later was bound to ignite.

But if people on both sides of the debate agreed that the explosion was coming, they disagreed about how or even whether it might be forestalled. With one side calling for suppression of the black "domestic enemy" and the other calling for abolition, *Putnam's* readers were likely to be found between these two positions—sympathetic to the slaves, but frightened of what would happen if they should break their chains. The historical Amasa Delano, too, had inhabited this borderland, and in *Benito Cereno*, Melville made him into a representative type in whom his readers could see themselves: a basically decent man trying to reconcile the unwritten natural law of charity with the written law requiring him to defend a slaveowner's rights.

In the mid-1850s, a tale of slave revolt at sea was not a far-fetched fiction. In 1839, the Spanish schooner *Amistad* was sailing between the Cuban ports of Havana and Guanja, carrying some fifty slaves illegally purchased in Africa (Spain was a signatory to an 1817 treaty banning the international slave trade), when the slaves rebelled, killed two crew members, and demanded to be returned home. Having wandered off course, the ship was seized by an American naval vessel off the coast of Long Island, and the legal battle that ensued went all the way to the U.S. Supreme Court, where the venerable John Quincy Adams argued successfully in favor of the slaves' freedom.

Two years after the *Amistad* incident, a similar event at sea led to a similar result in court. The American ship *Creole* was transporting legally purchased slaves from Virginia to New Orleans when, in the fall of 1841, nineteen slaves seized control and, after killing a white sailor, forced the crew to sail to the British Bahamas. Despite demands for restitution by Secretary of State Daniel Webster, the mutineers were freed under the British Act of Emancipation, which in 1833 had eliminated slavery throughout the empire.

More than a decade after the *Creole* uprising, Frederick Douglass made the leader of the revolt, Madison Washington, the hero of his short novel *The Heroic Slave*, published in Douglass's newspaper, *The North Star*, in March 1853.

Years before undertaking his one sustained work about slavery, Melville had written a sentence in *White-Jacket* that furnishes a clue to what he now set out to do with these and other precedents in mind: "Depravity in the oppressed is no apology for the oppressor; but rather an additional stigma to him, as being, in a large degree, the effect, and not the cause and justification of oppression." Here was the theme of *Benito Cereno:* the mirroring relation between oppressor and oppressed.

4.

The story begins with Captain Delano being awakened at dawn in his cabin by his first mate, who brings news that a "strange sail" has been sighted entering the bay where the *Perseverance* lies at anchor. Sleepy and sluggish, he ascends to the deck and, trying to discern the approaching vessel, finds himself staring into an impenetrable fog through which he can barely distinguish the wings of gulls from the enveloping grays of sea, cloud, and sky. Against this background, the phantom ship "showed no colors" by which its origin or intent might be known.

As he had done in *The Encantadas,* Melville organized *Benito Cereno* pictorially. With "shreds of fog here and there raggedly furring her," the ship appears to Delano "like a white-washed monastery after a thunder-storm, seen perched upon some dun cliff among the Pyrenees"—an impression intensified by dark figures in "dark cowls" moving about the deck like "Friars pacing the cloisters." These images are supplied by an apparently omniscient narrator who stands outside the action and tells the tale in the third person ("Delano continued to watch . . ."), but whose perspective is so close to Delano's that the two seem to merge.

Having "ordered his whale-boat to be dropped," Delano is rowed over to the slaveship *San Dominick,* a sort of Gothic death-ship complete with "shield-like stern-piece" in which is carved the image of a masked satyr stepping on the writhing body of a defeated enemy, also masked. Once aboard, Delano is struck by the scarcity of whites amid the blacks. In the historical Delano's account, this scene occupies one phrase ("captain, mate, people and slaves, crowded around me to relate their stories"), but Melville expands it to a full paragraph as the human cargo pours out its tale:

> Climbing the side, the visitor was at once surrounded by a clamorous throng of whites and blacks, but the latter outnumbering the former more than could have been expected, negro transportation-ship as the stranger in port was. But, in one language, and as with one voice, all poured out a common tale of suffering; in which the negresses, of whom there were not a few, exceeded the others in their dolorous vehemence. The scurvy, together with a fever, had swept off a great part of their number, more especially the Spaniards. Off Cape Horn, they had narrowly escaped ship-wreck; then, for days together, they had lain tranced without wind; their provisions were low; their water next to none; their lips that moment were baked.

The slippage here from narration by the omniscient narrator ("all poured out a common tale") into indirect discourse by the slaves ("The scurvy . . . had swept off a great part of their number. . . .") moves us so close to Delano's perspective that we witness the scene as if over his shoulder and hear the "clamorous" crowd as if through his ears.

As the crowd tells its tale of woe, Delano is made "the mark of all eager tongues," and "his one eager glance took in all the faces, with every other object about him." But who is taking in whom? Delano is an easy "mark" (already, by 1850, a colloquial term for the victim of a confidence trick), and when the crowd disperses like the chorus in an opera making way for the lead performers—the Spanish captain and his personal slave, Babo—the slave plays his part especially well. Setting his face in the guise of "a shepherd's dog . . . mutely turned up into the Spaniard's," Babo strikes the gullible Delano as a portrait of "sorrow and affection . . . equally blended." With "master and man . . . before him, the black upholding the white, Captain Delano could not but bethink him of the beauty of that relationship which could present such a spectacle of fidelity on the one hand and confidence on the other."

Yet Delano has a vague sense that something is wrong in this interracial pas de deux, as if the two men, "for some unknown purpose, were acting out . . . some juggling play" for his benefit. The fawning little black man seems part valet, yet also part manager, subordinate yet somehow superior. When Cereno's voice goes hoarse, Babo speaks for him; when Cereno falls silent, Babo prompts him. When the captain swoons against him, the black man half naked in skirtlike trousers cut from the topsail, the two conjoin in a kind of grotesque simulacrum of coitus.

Robert Lowell's 1964 stage adaptation of Benito Cereno,
*with Frank Langella as Benito, Roscoe Lee Browne as Babo,
and Lester Rawlins as Amasa Delano*

Captain Delano's resources for understanding this performance are far from sufficient. A man of "singularly undistrustful . . . nature," he carries in his head a parcel of platitudes that the historian George Fredrickson has called "romantic racialism"—the prevailing view among antebellum northerners that blacks are by nature "childlike, affectionate, docile, and patient." This particular string of adjectives was strung together in 1844 by the New York Unitarian minister Orville Dewey, who may have been Melville's model for that simpering minister Mr. Falsgrave in *Pierre,* and such a view was by no means eccentric. In fact, it was so prevalent and, to Delano, so obviously true that Melville chose the archaic verb form "bethink" ("Delano could not but bethink him of the beauty of that relationship") to suggest that he does not so much think his thoughts as they think him.

Still, Delano feels uneasy, and the more questions he asks about what is going on, the fewer answers he gets. When he asks Don Benito for the "whole story," the Spaniard can only blanch and flinch. "He is like one flayed alive, thought Captain Delano; where may one touch him without causing a shrink?" Now and then it seems that something—a silent hand signal or a hissing whisper from one of the whites—might cut through Delano's haze and awaken him to the true situation, but he always reverts to "tranquilizing" thoughts about the black man's natural servility and the white man's natural strength. Something below the level of his consciousness seems to hold him back from pressing his inquiries—as when he feels "an apprehensive twitch in his calves" at the sound of blacks polishing a pile of hatchets.

The world of the *San Dominick* is a world turned upside down: a regal black slave stands unbowed before a white captain who trembles with fear. These anomalies drive Delano to reach deep into his store of complacencies, and each time he feels momentarily relieved (at one point he persuades himself that the so-called Benito Cereno must be some "low-born" impostor), but the cumulative effect drives him to distraction:

> he leaned against the carved balustrade, again looking off toward his boat; but found his eye falling upon the ribbon grass, trailing along the ship's water-line, straight as a border of green box; and parterres of seaweed, broad ovals and crescents, floating nigh and far, with what seemed long formal alleys between, crossing the terraces of swells, and sweeping round as if leading to the grottoes below. And overhanging all was the balustrade by his arm, which, partly stained with pitch and partly embossed with moss, seemed the charred ruin of some summer-house in a grand garden long running to waste.
>
> Trying to break one charm, he was but becharmed anew. Though upon the wide sea, he seemed in some far inland country; prisoner in some deserted chateau, left to stare at empty grounds, and peer out at vague roads, where never wagon or wayfarer passed.

This is the same psychological impasse at which the lawyer in "Bartleby" had arrived, and the same that Pierre had experienced on his journey to New York when he first reads the mysterious pamphlet:

> If a man be told a thing wholly new, then—during the time of its first announcement to him—it is entirely impossible for him to comprehend it. For—absurd as it may seem—men are only made to comprehend things which they comprehended before (though but in the embryo, as it were). Things new it is impossible to make them comprehend; in their own hearts they really believe they do comprehend; outwardly look as though they *did* comprehend; wag their bushy tails comprehendingly; but for all that, they do not comprehend.

Captain Delano has lost his bearings because "it is entirely impossible for him to comprehend" the new thing with which he is confronted. That new thing is a world in which blacks are in charge and whites are in subjection.

5.

Reading *Benito Cereno* is something like being teased with a promise of sexual relief but having it continually deferred. About halfway along comes a scene in which the teasing reaches a point of intensity that is almost cruel. It begins with an authoritative-sounding statement of how well suited blacks are to such personal services as manicuring, hair-dressing, and barbering (these were, in fact, among the few trades open to free blacks in antebellum America):

> There is something in the negro which, in a peculiar way, fits him for avocations about one's person. Most negroes are natural valets and hair-dressers; taking to the comb and brush congenially as to the castinets, and flourishing them apparently with almost equal satisfaction. There is, too, a smooth tact about them in this employment, with a marvelous, noiseless, gliding briskness, not ungraceful in its way, singularly pleasing to behold, and still more so to be the manipulated subject of.

With these thoughts in mind, Delano follows Cereno and Babo into the captain's cabin, where the slave prepares his master for a shave. Warming to his work, Babo fetches a piece of bright-colored bunting from the flag-locker and wraps it, with elaborate obsequiousness, around his master's neck as a bib. He sets up a basin under Cereno's chin, fills it with salt water, then dips in a cake of soap, lathering the Spaniard on the upper lip and "low down under the throat." Then comes the master stroke:

> Setting down his basin, the negro searched among the razors, as for the sharpest, and having found it, gave it an additional edge by expertly strapping it on the firm, smooth, oily skin of his open palm; he then made a gesture as if to begin, but midway stood suspended for an instant, one hand elevating the razor, the other professionally dabbling among the bubbling suds on the Spaniard's lank neck.

Melville develops this scene, which has no source in the historical Delano's memoir, into a meditation on subjectivity itself. Of course, thinks

Delano, a good Negro will do *anything* to serve his master—even use his own skin as a razor strop. But while the American savors this "tranquilizing" thought, his Spanish counterpart is trembling with terror. There is something almost comic here—like a vaudeville act in which some clueless fool is pickpocketed or cuckolded in full view of the audience while he himself has no idea of what is going on. When Babo drags the blade across his palm, Delano hears the sound of a black man abasing himself. What Cereno hears is the black man warning him: if you make one move toward candor, I will cut your throat.*

In his agitation, Cereno has loosened the bright-colored cloth around his neck, which Delano now recognizes as the Spanish flag with a "castle in a blood-red field diagonal with a lion rampant in a white." What, he wonders, can this indignity signify? For an instant, the "antic conceit" enters his mind that the black is a "headsman" and the white "a man at the block." But he shakes off the thought and reminds himself that, like children, blacks love all things brightly colored, so there is nothing amiss about Cereno sitting with his nation's flag wrapped around his neck and Babo standing over him with blade drawn. Delano's capacity for self-deception is limitless.

Still, Babo takes no chances. He improvises a new scene: with a flick of the razor, he draws a spot of blood "which stained the creamy lather under the throat" and, pulling "back his steel, and remaining in his professional attitude," rebukes the man in the chair: "See, master,—you shook so—here's Babo's first blood." For Delano's benefit, he concludes Cereno's toilette "with comb, scissors and brush; going round and round, smoothing a curl here, clipping an unruly whisker-hair there, giving a graceful sweep to the temple-lock, with other impromptu touches evincing the hand of a master," as if he were "a Nubian sculptor finishing off a white statue-head."

But Babo is not quite finished. With Cereno in tow, and out of sight of Delano, who has preceded them out of the cabin, he cuts his own face. Once emerged onto the deck, he holds his hand to his cheek till he sees that Delano is watching, then lifts the hand away to reveal the bleeding. "Ah, ah, ah," Babo mutters, in a little soliloquy, "cutting Babo with the razor, because, only by accident, Babo had given master one little scratch. . . ." Shocked at

*Three years after the publication of *Benito Cereno,* Thomas Wentworth Higginson told the American Anti-Slavery Society: "I have wondered in times past, when I have been so weak-minded as to submit my chin to the razor of a coloured brother, as his sharp steel grazed my skin, at the patience of the negro shaving the white man for many years, yet [keeping] the razor outside the throat." See Eric Sundquist, "*Benito Cereno* and New World Slavery," in Sacvan Bercovitch, ed., *Reconstructing American Literary History* (Cambridge, MA: Harvard University Press, 1986), p. 112.

first by this instance of hot Spanish petulance, Delano is soon relieved to see that the spat ("but a sort of love-quarrel, after all") has passed and that Don Benito once again leans "on his servant as if nothing had happened." This pattern of tension followed by release gives *Benito Cereno* its teasing rhythm of flow-and-ebb, which, since the release is never complete, has the incremental effect of building pressure toward the bursting point.

The burst finally comes as Delano prepares to return to his own ship. Loath to let him go, the Spaniard clutches his hand—"Adieu, my dear, dear Don Amasa. Go—go! . . . go, and God guard you better than me, my best friend"—and just as Delano shoves off in his boat, the Spaniard snaps. The masquerade is over. The masks come off. There is no more pretense of order, only chaos: "Don Benito sprang over the bulwarks, falling at the feet of Captain Delano; at the same time, calling toward his ship, but in tones so frenzied, that none in the boat could understand him." Several whites leap after him and swim for their lives—yet Delano, in his amazing obtuseness, still fails to grasp what is happening and somehow persuades himself that they are coming to rescue their captain from what they think is an abduction by the Americans. When Babo then leaps after Cereno with dagger in hand, Delano thinks the slave, too, is defending his master out of "desperate fidelity." After wrestling the black man down to the bottom of the boat, Delano keeps him supine by standing in triumph astride him.

Up to this point, Melville has composed *Benito Cereno* with the eye of a painter. But now he works as if he were sculpting, arranging his figures in poses reminiscent of objects he had seen on his travels. On his European trip in 1849, he had marveled at the "most unique collection" of medieval artifacts in the Hôtel de Cluny, a Gothic structure built on the ruins of Emperor Julian's Roman baths, which had recently opened as a museum in Paris. In this fifteenth-century building, whose ancient foundations Melville used in *Moby-Dick* as a metaphor for the "larger, darker, deeper part" of Ahab's soul (an "antique buried beneath antiquities"), he would have seen objects and images which he now used to construct an iconography that his scripturally literate readers would recognize.

Among the carvings at Cluny was a medieval Judas whispering in the ear of Christ (as Babo does to Benito) and a delicately carved ivory mirror case depicting King Solomon and his queen stepping upon the lion and adder as prophesied in Psalm 91. Especially striking were several alabaster carvings of the resurrected Christ emerging from his boatlike tomb, his left hand grasping the Cross while stepping with his right foot upon the prostrate body of a Roman soldier.

For centuries, Christian commentators had interpreted the image of the

The Resurrection of
Christ, *fifteenth
century, Musée
du Moyen Age
(Cluny), Paris*

monster underfoot (Luke 10:19: "Behold, I give you power to tread on serpents") as Christ empowering the faithful to defeat and demean the devil by
stamping upon him in insult as well as exultation. Throughout *Benito
Cereno*, Melville plays variations on this image. The carved medallion on the
stern of the *San Dominick* presents a reversal or dark twin of the traditional
Christian tableau: a "dark satyr in a mask" (Babo) holds "his foot on the
prostrate neck of a writhing figure" (Benito Cereno) "likewise masked."
But in the climactic scene, the traditional Christian scene of virtue triumphant is apparently restored: Delano becomes the savior subduing the fiend-
ish African, grinding down the "prostrate Negro" with his right foot while
holding up the swooning Spaniard with his left hand.

   Amasa Delano is a visual echo of the Savior bringing truth and light—
but Melville deliberately misuses his religious materials and leaves this
"savior" utterly in the dark. He is an image of Christ rendered ironically.
Despite all the hints and clues that have been strewn in his path, he still mis-
reads the dance of death between Babo and Cereno as a lovers' duet. His
moment of highest triumph is also his moment of deepest ignorance, as he
continues to believe that the slave has leapt into the boat in order to rescue
his master. In Amasa Delano, Melville represented the American colossus as
a colossal fool.

6.

At last, with enemies subdued, the fool's eyes snap open. The masks are shed. This moment, too, Melville delivers in scriptural language: "Captain Delano, now with the scales dropped from his eyes, saw the negroes, not in misrule, not in tumult, not as if frantically concerned for Don Benito, but with mask torn away, flourishing hatchets and knives, in ferocious piratical revolt."* The revelation comes to Delano while he looks down and sees that Babo has concealed a second dagger "in his wool" and, "snakishly writhing" like the serpent of Luke 10:19, is aiming it "from the boat's bottom" at the heart of his master, "his countenance lividly vindictive, expressing the centered purpose of his soul":

> That moment, across the long-benighted mind of Captain Delano, a flash of revelation swept, illuminating in unanticipated clearness his host's whole mysterious demeanor, with every enigmatic event of the day, as well as the entire past voyage of the San Dominick. He smote Babo's hand down, but his own heart smote him harder. With infinite pity he withdrew his hold from Don Benito.

Here, at last, is the release for which we have been waiting: "Not Captain Delano, but Don Benito, the black, in leaping into the boat, had intended to stab." The doltish Delano has finally gotten the "whole story."

Or has he? This extraordinary sentence ("Not Captain Delano, but Don Benito, the black, in leaping into the boat, had intended to stab") is among the most contorted sentences in all of Melville's writing: gnarled, syntactically disordered, a stretch of twisted prose in which subject, verb, and object seem to want to merge with one another, separated by a string of commas that barely keeps the sentence from collapsing into itself. So tortuous a sentence requires exertion if we are to make sense of it; and once we have managed to parse it, we feel the kind of relief that Delano has been seeking since the moment he ascended from his bunk into the morning fog.

The trouble is that he is still in the fog—and so are we. There is much more yet to tell. The blacks, taunting the whites from afar "with upthrown

---

*Acts 9:18: "And immediately the scales fell from his eyes, and his sight was restored."

gestures hailing the now dusky moors of the ocean—cawing crows escaped
from the hand of the fowler," are now pursued, attacked, and subdued. The
prisoners are brought to trial in Lima. En route, during "the long, mild voyage" on which Delano accompanies his Spanish friend, the American reverts
to type and closes his mind to what he has seen. As for Cereno, he has seen
stabbings and drownings and bleedings to death, yet Delano wonders why
he seems disturbed. Cereno has seen his friend Don Alexandro Aranda,
owner of both ship and slaves, tortured and dismembered, his flesh offered
as carrion to the gulls and his picked bones strapped as a memento mori fig-
urehead to the bow (the blacks had wrapped it in a sail to conceal it from
their American visitor). But " 'you are saved,' cried Captain Delano . . . 'you
are saved; what has cast such a shadow upon you?' " " 'The negro,' " is
Cereno's only answer. Delano's stupidity is staggering.

    In Amasa Delano, Melville created a character whom we recognize as an
ancestor of those callow Americans who walk through the novels of Henry
James mistaking malice for charm, botching uncomprehended situations
with the unintended consequences of their good intentions. Melville placed
this representative American at the center of a thrice-told tale. It is told first
as a mystery (who is in charge, who is in thrall?); then from the Spaniard's
point of view in a long legal deposition as a story of black treachery and
white courage—the sort of courtroom transcript, as the legal scholar Robert
Ferguson has written, that reveals only "the story that a community is willing
to tell itself." Finally, in Babo's silence, the story is told yet again—or, rather,
eloquently untold. This last (un)telling is the unheard tale that begins not
with a revolt aboard a slaveship but long before, in Senegal, where a black
boy is stolen, branded, and shipped into slavery for the use of some white
buyer in the New World. It is a tale that most Americans could not—and still
cannot—bear to hear.

    Today, one recognizes in *Benito Cereno* a prophetic vision of what Ben-
jamin Barber calls "American innocence so opaque in the face of evil that it
seems equally insensible to slavery and the rebellion against slavery"—the
kind of moral opacity that seems still to afflict America as it lumbers through
the world creating enemies whose enmity it does not begin to understand.
Melville was able to write with such savage irony because he had mastered in
Benito Cereno the art of magazine fiction, producing a story whose moral
depth is rivaled among his short works only by "Bartleby, the Scrivener." To
the casual reader, *Benito Cereno* is a story with the pace and intrigue of good
suspense writing in the genre of Poe's "The Purloined Letter" (1845), about
a mystery hidden in plain sight (Lewis Mumford declined to "spoil *Benito
Cereno* for those who have not read it by revealing its mystery"), but like
"Bartleby" it has immense reach and resonance. As the distinguished Melvil-

lean Merton Sealts has concluded (quoting Melville's own phrases from his 1850 essay on Hawthorne), he "had managed" in *Benito Cereno*, "to work on more than one level, not alternately but simultaneously, so as to reach not only the 'superficial skimmer of pages' but also the 'eagle-eyed reader.' "

Among the "eagle-eyed" readers who dove deep into *Benito Cereno* was Ralph Ellison, who borrowed this passage for an epigraph to his great novel *Invisible Man:*

> "You are saved," cried Captain Delano, more and more astonished and pained; "you are saved; what has cast such a shadow upon you?" "The negro."

Benito Cereno, Ellison knew, plumbs the depths of a white man's infinite ignorance and, by leaving the black man "voiceless" to the end, acknowledges that the "whole story" of New World slavery is truly unspeakable. Alone among our classic American writers, Melville had thereby made a start toward telling it.

CHAPTER 10
ADRIFT

1.

Newton Arvin calls them the "black years," the years in which, having given up his Vesuvian ambitions, Melville was in retreat like a painter who had once done palace frescoes but was now reduced to doing pencil sketches. Sensitive to the diminution, one English reviewer of *Israel Potter* remarked that the novel made him "feel that the author is capable of something better, but . . . is resolved to curb his fancy and adhere to the dustier routine." Though the print run (3,700 copies) had been relatively large, and sales (around 2,500 copies) respectable, proceeds were small. After deductions for advances, royalties due to Melville in the fall of 1855 amounted to $48.31. As for *The Piazza Tales,* published by Dix & Edwards (the successors to Putnam) in May 1856, in which Melville included "Bartleby" and *Benito Cereno,* the *New York Times* found them not without merit, but offered Melville the unwelcome advice that he "should do something higher and better than Magazine articles."

These were black years, too, in the sense that they have proven impenetrable to even the most determined scholars, who have been unable to illuminate the state of Melville's marriage or the fate of his children, much less the secrets of his soul—though there has been no shortage of pronouncements about all these matters. D. H. Lawrence was sure that "after an ecstasy of a courtship," Melville endured "fifty years of disillusion" with a woman who (in Arvin's phrase) "proved no fulfillment of his deepest needs." Ever loyal to the floral Fayaway, Bernard De Voto made the same point more anatomically: "if [Lizzie] had breasts . . . no one crushed flowers between them."

Maybe not. But in a dedicatory preface to a group of poems left unpublished at his death, Melville recalled how he had saved Lizzie's roses at Arrowhead from an early snow ("winter's folic skirmisher in advance") and taken them indoors to her so they could sit together and watch the melting of "the fleecy flakes into dew-drops rolling off from the ruddiness." Looking back in the spring of what was to be his last year upon their long shared life, he begged her to remember that she had called the tiny drops "Tears of the Happy" and to accept his poems, written in "that terminating season on which the offerer verges," as love offerings like those "dissolved snow-flakes on the ruddy oblation of old."

But not all—or even most—of Lizzie's tears had been tears of happiness, and there is reason to suspect that the mid-1850s were a trying time in her life with Herman. In a story called "I and My Chimney," published in *Putnam's* in March 1856 and probably composed in the spring of 1855 after the completion of *Benito Cereno*, Melville wrote about the great chimney that, running straight through the center of their house and opening on the ground floor into a wide-mouthed hearth, gets in the way of his wife's desire for a spacious central foyer. Poking out above the roof, the chimney looks oddly squat and foreshortened, the result of its having been chopped down in a "surgical operation" with a masonry saw—circumcised, in effect—after the roofline had been lowered, thereby exposing to "the open air a part of the chimney previously under cover." The narrator of "I and My Chimney" gives this phallic chimney a good deal of tender loving care, "humbly bowing over it with shovel and tongs, I much minister to it," while his harpy-wife, whose "maxim is, Whatever is, is wrong," wants nothing to do with it ("her eggs, too—can't keep them near the chimney, on account of hatching") and "is desirous that . . . I should retire into some sort of monastery." Melville was in his mid-thirties when he wrote these passages about a man whose wife regrets that her husband's chimney requires constant care. "My wife," the narrator adds for good measure, "cares not a fig for my philosophical jabber." Years later, Lizzie wrote in the margin of her copy of the story the self-exonerating comment that "all this about the wife applied to his mother."

In the summer of 1856, Lizzie's half brother Sam wrote to his parents that Herman suffered from "ugly attacks," and Judge Shaw heard from Lizzie herself that she felt "great anxiety" on behalf of her husband. She worried about his physical health, as his back pain became chronic and he suffered more and more from eye strain; and she worried as well about his mental condition. Melville had always been fascinated by madness (in his copy of the *Final Memorials of Charles Lamb* he marked the passage about Lamb's unwavering love for his sister "even when she was a prisoner in the Asylum after the fatal attack of lunacy"), and the renditions of madness in his own writing were alarmingly convincing. As early as 1851, the Melvilles' Berkshire neighbor Sarah Morewood had half-jocularly written that "the recluse life he was leading made his city friends think he was slightly insane." Two years earlier, when his friend Charles Fenno Hoffman was committed to an asylum, Melville had described him to Duyckinck in terms that could have been self-referential ("imaginative, voluptuously inclined, poor, unemployed, in the race of life distanced by his inferiors") and remarked that "this going mad of a friend or acquaintance comes straight home to every man who feels his soul in him. . . . For in all of us lodges the same fuel to light the same fire."

Having touched upon the theme of madness in "Bartleby" and *Benito Cereno,* Melville now expressed his own state of mind, as he had done in brief in "I and My Chimney," in a half-deranged book that turned out to be the last of his novels to be published in his lifetime. In the spring of 1855, there was widespread press coverage of a New York swindler who fleeced his victims by passing himself off as an honest soul in need of an emergency loan. Melville had always been interested in dupes and duping, and in October, when he began writing *The Confidence-Man,* he had before him, in addition to these newspaper accounts that classic novel of gullibility and illusion, *Don Quixote,* which he had acquired in the Jarvis translation from an Albany bookstore.

The work he now devoted to these themes, possibly with the intention of magazine serialization before publication in book form, was, as Arvin has put it, "a series of conversations rather than an action." It was set on a Mississippi steamboat ironically named the *Fidèle,* where a con man in multiple guises preys on potential buyers who range in their responses from eager greed to misanthropic skepticism to naive credulity. Like a storefront clairvoyant who senses the wants and fears of each client, he customizes his prophecies until they fit each victim as perfectly as a bespoke suit.

Whether he is selling counterfeit stock, extorting money for some spurious charity, or "borrowing" an item of value with a promise to return it with interest, the confidence man offers his customers what they most want: hope, hope for themselves, hope for the world. *The Confidence-Man* was an extended answer to a question that Melville had asked in *White-Jacket:* "Who can forever resist the very Devil himself, when he comes in the guise of a gentleman, free, fine, and frank?" One by one, the passengers of the *Fidèle* step forward to be fleeced, introduced by a narrator whose tone is that of a mellow movie voice-over commenting on the fools and follies that pass before our eyes. And with his frequent costume changes, the confidence man leaves us "at a loss to determine where exactly the fictitious character had been dropped, and the real one, if any, resumed."

This dizzying story was set on a riverboat of the type on which Melville had traveled down the Mississippi twenty years earlier with his friend Eli Fly. But it also borrows from the world he had known more recently in New York, where merchants mixed sand with their salt and tavernkeepers watered their ale before serving it up as pure brew. *The Confidence-Man* included thinly veiled caricatures of such New York con men as P. T. Barnum. In an 1852 issue of *Hunt's Merchants' Magazine,* a writer, one "Martin Takemthrough," observed that "there are but two classes in the world—the *Skinner* and the *Skinned,*" and offered some sound New York advice: "if you do not skin, you must assuredly *be* skinned—so you can make your own choice."

But Melville's book was more than a retrospective catalogue of con artists he had known or known about. It belonged to the same genre as Joseph Baldwin's *The Flush Times of Alabama and Mississippi* (1853), a collection of sketches whose narrator seems somehow in collusion with the crooked bankers and lawyers whom he exposes as swindlers and fakes. *The Confidence-Man* was about a time of hectic expansion when, in Baldwin's phrases, "swindling was raised to the dignity of the fine arts" and Americans were continually inventing new forms of "elaborate machinery of ingenious chicane." It was a time when paper money was promiscuously printed ("let the public believe that a smutted rag is money," as Baldwin put it, and "it is money"), when every borrower was ready to cheat every lender by putting up as collateral arid land, or infirm slaves, or worthless stock, and when lenders cheerfully loaned money that they did not have. Confidence, it seemed, was always misplaced.

When Melville's highly topical book first appeared, on April Fool's Day, 1857, the critics were baffled. Public reviews were vicious. (One reviewer, declaring *Typee* the best of Melville's works and *The Confidence-Man* "decidedly the worst," concluded that "Mr. M.'s authorship is toward the nadir rather than the zenith, and he has been progressing in the form of an inverted climax.") The critic for the London *Illustrated Times* reported with contempt:

> We began the book at the beginning, and, after reading ten or twelve chapters . . . found . . . that we had not yet obtained the slightest clue to the meaning (in case there should happen to be any). . . . After reading the work forwards for twelve chapters and backwards for five, we attacked it in the middle, gnawing at it like Rabelais's dog at the bone, in the hope of extracting something from it at last. . . . As a last resource, we read the work from beginning to end; and the result was that we liked it even less than before.

Private responses were almost as harsh, as when Lem Shaw, Lizzie's half brother, complained that there were "pages of crude theory & speculation to every line of narritive—& interspersed with strained & ineffectual attempts to be humorous."

But in our own time *The Confidence-Man* has been rehabilitated as a

work that "holds up a mirror to the American people," as Walter McDougall
puts it in his comprehensive history of the United States—a key book of our
culture that risked "telling the truth . . . about the tricks Americans played
on themselves in their effort to worship both God and Mammon." And if
The Confidence-Man is being reclaimed today for its broad insights into the
American psyche, recent critics have also construed it more narrowly as a
series of satirical portraits of Melville's contemporaries. The amiable Mark
Winsome, who believes in what another character (Charlie Noble, possibly a
representation of Hawthorne) calls the "latent benignity" of rattlesnakes, has
been identified as a portrait of Emerson. Winsome's "practical disciple"
Egbert appears to have been a portrait of Thoreau, and there is a rhapsodic
beggar who, with his dissolute babble, seems a stand-in for that ranting alco-
holic Edgar Allan Poe—author, as Melville may have recalled, of an article
published in 1845 in the *Broadway Journal,* "Diddling Considered as One
of the Exact Sciences." One scholar has recently asserted that the busybody
merchant Henry Roberts "embodies Melville's accumulated resentment
toward his sometime literary friend and benefactor" Evert Duyckinck. The
pompous "Man in Gold Buttons" may have been Melville's version of the
philanthropic industrialist Abbott Lawrence, and the (seemingly) passionate
do-gooder, the "Man in Gray," a portrait of the unappeasable Theodore
Parker. For Goneril, an unfaithful wife with a nasty Shakespearean name who
is as embraceable as a cactus, Melville seems to have had in mind the actress
Fanny Kemble Butler, about whom he had once written (to Duyckinck) that
"had she not, on unimpeachable authority, borne children, I should be curious to learn the result of a surgical examination of her person in private."

This most time-bound of Melville's works has been well described by
another historian, Jean-Christophe Agnew, as having an "allusiveness that
only adds to the elusiveness of the narrative as a whole." And perhaps for just
that reason it was rediscovered in the 1950s and '60s as a precursor of
the labyrinthine fictions then being written by such writers as Vladimir
Nabokov (*Pale Fire*) and John Barth (*Lost in the Funhouse*) that induce the
same feeling of trying to navigate an amusement park hall of mirrors, where
every step leads into a wall of glass. Melville's book now seems a prophetically postmodern work in which swindler cannot be distinguished from
swindled and the confidence man tells truth and lies simultaneously:

> I do not jumble them; they are coordinates. For misanthropy,
> springing from the same root with disbelief of religion, is twin with
> that. It springs from the same root, I say; for, set aside materialism, and
> what is an atheist, but one who does not, or will not, see in the universe

a ruling principle of love; and what a misanthrope, but one who does not, or will not, see in man a ruling principle of kindness? Don't you see? In either case the vice consists in a want of confidence.

There is something right and wise about this pronouncement that love can save us from despair, but the speech is also designed to win over a doubter who might have the wit to resist the con man's next sting.

In this book of sensible nonsense, humor is both a saving quality and the last resort of the nihilist. Nature is a fountainhead of health ("poets send out the sick spirit to green pastures, like lame horses turned out unshod to the turf to renew their hoofs") but also the source of suffering ("who froze to death my teamster on the prairie?"), and only machines can be trusted:

> Machines for me. My cider-mill—does that ever steal my cider? My mowing-machine—does that ever lay a-bed mornings? My corn-husker—does that ever give me insolence? No: cider-mill, mowing-machine, corn-husker—all faithfully attend to their business. Disinterested, too; no board, no wages; yet doing good all their lives long; shining examples that virtue is its own reward—the only practical Christians I know.

Convinced that "the mystery of human subjectivity" is impenetrable, Melville devoted the better part of one chapter to a debate between two "convivialists" over whether the letters "P.W." on the label of a wine bottle signify port wine, pure wine, or poison wine. Since a taste test might be fatal, the question is left hanging.

But *The Confidence-Man* is not only about illusion and masquerade. It is also about hatred as a form of authenticity, on the premise that all great "haters have at bottom loving hearts." Ever since his memorable portrait of a misanthropic sailor, Jackson, in *Redburn*—a "Cain afloat" who "seldom spoke, but to contradict, deride, or curse"—Melville had been fascinated by soul-dead characters who stand apart from life and laugh at the living. Now, in a chapter entitled "The Metaphysics of Indian-Hating," he introduced a "backwoodsman" who, when he was a boy, had learned that his mother and siblings had been slaughtered by Indians:

> He was just entering upon manhood, when thus left in nature sole sur-vivor of his race. Other youngsters might have turned mourner; he turned avenger. His nerves were electric wires—sensitive, but steel. He was one who, from self-possession, could be made neither to flush nor

pale. It is said that when the tidings were brought him, he was ashore sitting beneath a hemlock eating his dinner of venison—and as the tidings were told him, after the first start he kept on eating, but slowly and deliberately, chewing the wild news with the wild meat, as if both together, turned to chyle, together would sinew him to his intent. From that meal he rose an Indian-hater.

As "straggling thoughts of other outrages troop to the nucleus thought, assimilate with it, and swell it," this man "commits himself . . . to act upon a calm, cloistered scheme of strategical, implacable, and lonesome vengeance." In its dark eloquence, this passage pointed back to Captain Ahab in *Moby-Dick* and forward to Mr. Claggart in *Billy Budd.* Melville had always recognized in such characters something of himself, and one deep purpose of his writing was to save himself from becoming too much like them.

2.

As he was working on this bilious book in the spring of 1856, T. D. Stewart was pressing him for repayment of the loan he had made to him five years before, on which Melville had fallen behind. With full settlement of principal and interest due on May 1, Melville started selling off portions of his land in order to raise cash and also wrote to his publishers to inquire if he might expect any income any time soon. Lem noted that his brother-in-law was feeling "dispirited and ill," and Judge Shaw, who regarded his subsidies as advances on his daughter's inheritance, agreed to finance a trip for Herman through Europe to the Middle East, in the hope that travel might restore his spirits. It was fashionable at the time for cultivated Americans to tour Arabia and Judea (also called the Holy Land, or the Levant), and Melville had long been curious to see Greece and Italy as well. The prospect of a journey bolstered him, though he might have recognized himself with chagrin in Emerson's comment that America was full of over-the-hill "authors . . . who have written out their vein, and who, moved by a commendable prudence, sail for Greece or Palestine."

Early in October 1856, having dispatched Lizzie and the children to his in-laws in Boston, he came down to New York, according to Duyckinck, "fresh from his mountain, charged to the muzzle with his sailor metaphysics and jargon of things unknowable." Melville in these years swung sharply between sociability and withdrawal, between talk and silence; one visitor who saw him in Pittsfield, probably in late summer 1855, described him as "the most silent man of my acquaintance," and reported that he would walk his land alone, "patting" the trees "upon the back" as if they were his best companions. But the same visitor, a New York acquaintance named Maunsell Field, also attended a raucous dinner at the home of Dr. Oliver Holmes, where Melville discoursed "with the most amazing skill and brilliancy" on the topic of "East India religions and mythologies."

With his old New York friends, he was in the latter mood. After delivering the manuscript of *The Confidence-Man* to his publisher, Dix & Edwards, a day or two before leaving for points east, he had a long and lubricated dinner with the Duyckincks, highlighted by his telling, as Evert described it, that "good story from the Decameron of the *Enchantment* of the husband in the tree." This was Boccaccio's tale about a young wife who persuades her much older husband that the pear tree in their garden has the power to make jealous forebodings seem real. Having convinced him that he should test the truth of what she says by climbing the magical tree, she has eager intercourse with a servant before her husband's eyes, humping away as if in perfect seclusion, while the husband blames his jealousy rather than his wife. Melville made this story the centerpiece of what Duyckinck called an "orgy of indecency and blasphemy" that went on into the night a few days before he left, on October 11, bound by steamer for Scotland.

He kept no journal en route, but began to make notations once he reached Glasgow, where the banks of the River Clyde reminded him of the towpath along the Erie Canal, and the cathedral, looming over sod and thatch houses, called to his mind a "picture of one of the old masters smoked by Time." Now and then, a flash of color broke through the Scottish gloom, as when soldiers in red coats scattered among the coastal rocks caught his eye "like flamingoes among the cliffs," but even the fleeces of grazing sheep seemed gray with chimney soot. Melville's journal was written in the mood of *Benito Cereno,* in which the world is shrouded in fog and shadow.

Upon arriving in England, he sought out Hawthorne in a Liverpool suburb where the writer-turned-diplomat had lived with his family when they first arrived in 1853. Finding that the Hawthornes had since moved, Melville caught up with his old friend in his office at the consulate. Decades later, Julian Hawthorne, who had been a boy of ten in 1856, remembered his father's visitor as "depressed and aimless." The reunion received spare comment in Melville's journal—"An agreeable day. Took a long walk by the sea. Sands & grass. Wild & desolate. A strong wind. Good talk"—but Haw-

thorne was more expansive, entering in his own journal a striking account of
a friendship that had not only survived but deepened:

November 20th, Thursday. A week ago last Monday, Herman Melville
came to see me at the Consulate, looking much as he used to (a little
paler, and perhaps a little sadder), in a rough outside coat, and with his
characteristic gravity and reserve of manner. He had crossed from New
York to Glasgow in a screw steamer, about a fortnight before, and had
since been seeing Edinburgh and other interesting places. I felt rather
awkward at first; because this is the first time I have met him since my
ineffectual attempt to get him a consular appointment from General
Pierce. However, I failed only from real lack of power to serve him; so
there was no reason to be ashamed, and we soon found ourselves on
pretty much our former terms of sociability and confidence. Melville
has not been well, of late; he has been affected with neuralgic complaints in his head and limbs, and no doubt has suffered from too constant literary occupation, pursued without much success, latterly; and
his writings, for a long while past, have indicated a morbid state of
mind. So he left his place at Pittsfield, and has established his wife and
family, I believe, with his father-in-law in Boston, and is thus far on his
way to Constantinople. I do not wonder that he found it necessary to
take an airing through the world, after so many years of toilsome pen-
labor and domestic life, following up so wild and adventurous a youth
as his was. I invited him to come and stay with us at Southport, as long
as he might remain in the vicinity; and, accordingly, he did come, the
next day, taking with him, by way of baggage, the least little bit of a bun-
dle, which, he told me, contained a night shirt and a tooth-brush. He is
a person of very gentlemanly instincts in every respect, save that he is a
little heterodox in the matter of clean linen.

Melville remained with the Hawthornes for three days, on the second of
which he and Nathaniel took their walk along the sea at the coastal resort of
Southport, where they

sat down in a hollow among the sand hills (sheltering ourselves from
the high, cool wind) and smoked a cigar. Melville, as he always does,
began to reason of Providence and futurity, and of everything that lies
beyond human ken, and informed me that he had "pretty much made
up his mind to be annihilated"; but still he does not seem to rest in that
anticipation; and, I think, will never rest until he gets hold of a definite
belief. It is strange how he persists—and has persisted ever since I

knew him, and probably long before—in wandering to-and-fro over these deserts, as dismal and monotonous as the sand hills amid which we were sitting. He can neither believe, nor be comfortable in his unbelief; and he is too honest and courageous not to try to do one or the other. If he were a religious man, he would be one of the most truly religious and reverential; he has a very high and noble nature, and better worth immortality than the rest of us.

Hawthorne threw his usual dash of irony into these remarks about Melville's metaphysical preoccupations—arguably the most incisive account of his temperament ever written. In trying to imagine what he said to Melville on that windy day, it is tempting to hear Hawthorne's voice in this rebuke spoken by Vine in *Clarel:*

> *Art thou the first soul tried by doubt?*
> *Shalt prove the last? Go, live it out.*

But the tone of Hawthorne's journal entry is mostly gentle and leavened by pity, and he captures perfectly Melville's uneasy suspension between faith and skepticism, a yearning that gave him the air of distractedness that some found trying.

Over the weekend, the two men took an excursion to the cathedral town of Chester, where they saw the Roman wall, an old stone bridge, and bits of a castle whose turret was said to have been built by Julius Caesar—just the sort of picturesque ruin that had eluded Redburn in his search for traces of Olde England. Having returned to Liverpool and parted "at a street-corner . . . in the rainy evening," they saw each other again the day before Melville left for the Mediterranean aboard the screw-steamer *Egyptian.* Hawthorne found his friend "much overshadowed since I saw him last," and sensed that he "did not anticipate much pleasure in his rambles, for that spirit of adventure is gone out of him." A day or two before departing, Melville left his trunk at the consulate, retaining only a carpetbag, which prompted Hawthorne to muse that traveling light

is the next best thing to going naked; and as he wears his beard and moustache, and so needs no dressing-case—nothing but a toothbrush—I do not know a more independent personage. He learned his travelling habits by drifting about, all over the South Sea, with no other clothes or equipage than a red flannel shirt and a pair of duck trowsers. Yet we seldom see men of less criticizable manners than he.

3.

As the *Egyptian* steamed through the Straits of Gibraltar along the African coast ("peeps of villages, wild looking"), there came into view a scattering of houses amid lush gardens, and Melville found himself thinking of the story in *Don Quixote* of the Moorish traveler and his beautiful bride. But as the ship coasted past the whitewashed houses of Algiers, they became a blotchy blur of light spots on a dark background that made him think of a large "sloping rock, covered with bird lime." This was to be his recurring pattern of response: at first, some pleasurable association arises in his mind as he glimpses some sight with anticipation, but expectancy soon gives way to disgust. At the Greek port of Syra, he disembarked (December 2) for a tour of the "warren of stone houses or rather huts," which may have reminded him of the slums of New York and seemed a "terrible nest for the plague." There he recorded scenes that delivered stabs of sadness, such as the sight of a "man ploughing with a peice [*sic*] of old root."

As the ship approached Constantinople, Melville beheld the Church of Hagia Sophia from the deck through fog so thick that he was able to make out its base and walls only dimly and could not see the dome at all. "It was a coy disclosure, a kind of coquetting, leaving room for imagination & heigthing [*sic*]the scene." But his imagination was no longer up to the task. Once ashore, he filled his journal with images of breakage, occlusion, and "nature feeding on man." In the city he witnessed a woman fling herself across "a new grave—no grass on it yet," howling in grief. "This woman and her cries," he wrote, "haunt me horribly." He remarked about one mosque that it "would make a noble ball room" and, about the dome of St. Sophia, that it had "a kind of dented appearance, like crown of old hat. Must inevitably cave in one of these days." Inside the great church, he was followed by "rascally priests" trying to sell handfuls of mosaic tile that had fallen from the ceiling. Outside in the streets, he felt menaced.

As the trip wore on, Melville sometimes retrieved what the biographer Hershel Parker calls his "old . . . intense, verbally inventive badinage," as when, at Smyrna, he described a camel:

> From his long curved and crain-like neck, (which he carries stiffly like a
> clergyman in a stiff cravat) his feathery-looking forelegs, & his long
> lank hind ones, he seems a cross between an ostrich and a gigantic

grasshopper. His hoof is spongey, & covered with hair to the ground, so that walking through these muddy lanes, he seems stalking along on four mops.

More common were images of decay and obstruction, reported in a flat tone of the sort one associates with Camus' description of the North African heat. At Cairo, Melville saw blind men with "flies on the eyes at noon" staring into the unseen sun. Climbing the pyramid at Cheops, he struggled for breath and suspected treachery from his Arab guides. Watching an old man stagger and faint, he felt himself reeling too, fearful of being beaten and robbed in one of the inlets that here and there broke up the "dead calm of masonry."

When he finally arrived in Palestine, Melville surveyed the "stony moun-tains & stony plains; stony torrents & stony roads; stony walls & stony feilds [*sic*], stony houses & stony tombs" and ventured the "theory . . . that long ago, some whimsical King of the country took it into his head to pave all Judea, and entered into contracts to that effect; but the contractor becoming bankrupt mid-way in his business, the stones were only dumped on the ground, & there they lie to this day."* In this wretched landscape, he tried to jolly himself ("no wonder that stones should so largely figure in the Bible") but, standing by the water's edge at the Dead Sea, found that the "foam on beach & pebbles" reminded him of "slaver of mad dog" and noted the

> smarting bitter of the water,—carried the bitter in my mouth all day—
> bitterness of life—thought of all bitter things—Bitter is it to be poor &
> bitter, to be reviled, & Oh bitter are these waters of Death.

Even the wind felt hot. In the dead of night, he would rise from damp sheets and cut himself tobacco for a calming smoke, which he hoped might help to disperse the fleas.

---

*Melville later drew extensively on his journal for the writing of *Clarel*, as in this rhymed and metered version of the riff on stones (pt. II, 10, ll. 1–22), by which he rediscovers his old delight in wordplay:

> In divers ways which vary it
> Stones mention find in hallowed Writ:
> Stones rolled from well-mouths, altar stones,
> Idols of stone, memorial ones,
> Sling-stones, stone tables . . .
> . . . .
> By stones died Naboth; stoned to death
> Was Stephen meek; and Scripture saith,
> Against even Christ they took up stones.

On January 6, 1857, the day he first laid eyes on the "blank, blank towers" of Jerusalem (as he was later to describe them), Melville was greeted
inside the Jaffa Gate by the choral whine of lepers begging. In *Clarel*, published nearly twenty years later, he was to recall the explanations of the
guides as they led tourists along the Via Dolorosa, retracing the route on
which Christ had borne the Cross:

> . . . *'tis here*
> *They scourged Him; soldiers yonder nailed*
> *The Victim to the tree; in jeer*
> *There stood the Jews; there Mary paled;*
> *The vesture was divided here.*

In the journal he kept during his visit, Melville reports this scene as a
mixture of phony solemnity and vulgar hawking: "*Talk of the guides,* 'Here is
the stone Christ leaned against & here is the English Hotel.' Yonder is the
arch where Christ was shown to the people, & just by that open window is
sold the best coffee in Jerusalem, &c&c&c." At the Church of the Holy
Sepulchre, Jews were forbidden to enter by Turkish policemen, who sat
"cross-legged & smoking, scornfully observing the continuous troops of pilgrims entering & prostrating themselves before the anointing-stone of
Christ," and the "reputed Calvary" was dimly lit by "the smoky light of old
pawnbrokers lamps." The anointing stone itself was "veined with streaks of a
mouldy red" that made it look, to Melville's eye, "like a butcher's slab."

His writing had always been rich in images of holy places gone to ruin or
lost in mist or fog, as in *The Encantadas*, where he compared the sight
of seagulls perched on coastal rocks to "the eaves of [an] . . . old . . .
abbey . . . alive with swallows," or in *Benito Cereno*, where he described the
looming slaveship's first impression on Delano's dim mind as akin to a
"white-washed monastery" in the Pyrenees. Now, at the sacred heart of the
Christian world, he watched veiled Muslim women hurry home from market
and old Jews shuffle toward their own holy places, indifferent to the putative
power of the Christian sites that left him, too, unmoved. It was a wonder to
him that anyone could hear God's voice in this land. He later wrote in *Clarel*
about the sight of Jews at the Wailing Wall, that "the Turk permits the tribes
to creep / Abject in rear of those dumb stones."

From January till April, he continued to write almost daily journal entries
as he made his way back to England via Lebanon, Cyprus, Greece, Italy, and
Switzerland. In February, passing the isle of Patmos on an Austrian steamer,
he was "again afflicted with the great curse of modern travel—skepticism.
Could no more realize that St. John had ever had revelations here, than when

off Juan Fernandez, could believe in Robinson Crusoe according to DeFoe." One effect of the trip was to confirm Melville's sense that the Bible was a collection of improbable fictions, and he cursed the secular scholars who had lately exposed it as an unreliable book compiled over time by fallible men rather than written by God. "When my eye rested on arid heigth [*sic*], spirit partook of the barreness.—Heartily wish [Barthold Georg] Niebuhr and [David Friedrich] Strauss to the dogs.—The deuce take their penetration & acumen. They have robbed us of the bloom."

Melville's journal is a document of spiritual exhaustion. It registered not only his sense of deflation in the presence of religious monuments from which he had hoped to get some hint of sublimity but also his loss of pleasure in making the sort of stretched associations that had once been the glory of his prose. He was no longer the writer (to use a phrase from *The Confidence-Man*) of "bravadoing mischievousness" who had compared the splintered wreck of a whaleboat to "grated nutmeg in a swiftly stirred bowl of punch," or who had recalled winters at sea so cold that a "man could have undergone amputation with great ease, and helped to take up the arteries himself." Now and then, he still had salivary moments, as when he savored his meals and snacks in Florence and in the charming village of Fiesole, especially when he felt he had gotten good value. But mostly he felt dull and aimless, as when, experiencing pain in his chest and back, he wrote in Rome, on March 15, "This day saw nothing, learned nothing, enjoyed nothing, but suffered something." Heading north in mid-April out of the Italian sun, he stopped at Berne and Strasbourg, then made a quick trip across the Channel to two English landmarks, Madame Tussaud's and Oxford, where he felt at last an "amity of art & nature" in the college gardens. On May 4, he returned to Liverpool to pick up his trunk and bid farewell to Hawthorne, for what turned out to be the last time. On May 5, he sailed for home.

4.

Back at Arrowhead, Melville was uncertain whether he would ever write again. Lem Shaw wrote to his brother Sam that Herman had decided he was "not going to write any more," though Lem qualified the statement by adding the phrase "at present." In the summer of 1857, Melville responded to a request from *The Atlantic*, saying, yes, he would like to write for them but could not "name the day when I shall have any article ready." He had come home to four children: eight-year-old Malcolm and six-year-old Stan-wix, along with their sisters Bessie, now four, and Frances (or Fanny), age two. The family, according to Melville's granddaughter, "had begun to suffer not only from insufficient funds for daily needs, but far more from his bursts of nervous anger and attacks of morose conscience." He complained now to everyone about everything: to his publishers for their failure to pay or pro-mote him, to the cook about the preparation of his coffee, which, like Pierre, he wanted roasted and ground "instantaneously previous to the final boiling and serving." To a Williams College student who called on him in the spring of 1859, he seemed, though he was not quite forty, "a disappointed man, soured by criticism, and disgusted with the Civilized world and with our christendom in general and in particular."

Among his worries, as usual, was money. And so he had begun to think—at his mother's urging—about putting his gift of gab and what was left of his celebrity to use in public lecturing. With her usual combination of coaxing and coercion, Maria Melville expressed high hopes for this plan, which she had had in mind for Herman for a long time: "My dear darling Herman," she had written him back in 1854, "all your friends, relatives & admirers, say that you are the very man to carry an audience, to create a sen-sation, to do wonders . . . to do that thing, which at once, and by the same agreeable act, will bring us fame & fortune." In *Pierre,* when the unappreci-ated boy complains of a "low purse," one of his friends advises him to "Stump the State on the Kantian Philosophy! A dollar a head, my boy! Pass around your beaver, and you'll get it." Melville hoped that this advice would now prove pertinent, and profitable, to himself.

In antebellum America, public speaking (as distinguished from preach-ing or political speechmaking) was indeed a form of beggary, or, as Dr. Holmes said at dinner one night with Melville at the table, just a notch above whoring. "A lecturer," Holmes declared, is "a literary strumpet subject for a greater than whore's fee to prostitute himself." There was a certain indignity in depending on a paying audience to turn out, a prospect that depended in turn on the willingness of local newspapers to publicize the event in advance. And there was the opposite risk that the papers would scoop the speaker by printing what he had said in some nearby town the week before. Emerson, who had been on the circuit for years, once exploded at the editor of the *Salem Commonwealth* for printing a detailed account of the talk he was about to deliver: "My lectures are written to be read as lectures in different places, & then to be reported by myself," and "your reporter [has done] all he can to kill the thing to every hearer, by putting him in possession beforehand of the words." Aware of these risks, Melville was not optimistic about his chances of success. As if to explain his failure in advance, he wrote with sour irony in the fall of 1857 to George W. Curtis, who had advised him to stick to elevated themes, that he was inclined to speak on the "daily progress of man towards a state of intellectual and moral perfection, as evidenced in history of 5th Avenue & 5 Points."

Since none of the lectures was published, they can only be very roughly reconstructed from contemporary newspaper accounts. Melville began his speaking career in Lawrence, Massachusetts, in November 1857, with a talk on the "Statues of Rome," and concluded it in February 1860, in Cambridgeport, where (as a last-minute substitute after Emerson canceled) he addressed the general theme of traveling. In the intervening years, he spoke at Boston, Albany, Montreal, New Haven, Milwaukee, Chicago, Yonkers, and a score of other towns, with decidedly mixed results. He earned praise for his "justness of vision" but met with complaints that his words were "articulated so feebly that they died long before they reached a twelfth part of his audience." One reviewer, having heard him speak about the South Seas, accurately concluded that lecturing was "not his forte, his style as well as the subject matter being intensely 'Polynesian' and calculated to 'Taboo' him from the lecture field in the future," while another, after hearing him speak on Roman statuary, noticed that "some nervous people . . . left the hall; some read books and newspapers; some sought refuge in sleep, and some, to their praise be it spoken, seemed determined to use it as an appropriate occasion for self-discipline in the blessed virtue of patience." Though he evidently never managed to replicate for the public in the lecture hall the energy and charm he had brought to family and friends by the fireside, his cousin Henry Gansevoort, who attended one of his public talks in a favorable seat, was reminded of the "vivid stories" Herman used to tell at home "under the inspiration of Madeira."

As for his themes, they were utterly, even perversely, out of touch with the issues of the day. In the spring of 1856, a vicious, if local, civil war had broken out in Kansas between slaveowners and Free-Soilers. In May, South Carolina representative Preston Brooks attacked Massachusetts senator Charles Sumner with a cane and left him half dead at his desk in the Senate chamber. In March 1857, in the *Dred Scott* decision, the Supreme Court effectively revoked the citizenship of black Americans. And in October 1859, John Brown led a raid on the federal arsenal at Harpers Ferry in the hope of fomenting slave insurrection. He failed, and was executed six weeks later.

These and many other shocks made clear that the nation was hurtling toward disunion, and even among intellectuals of relatively proximate views there were deepening rifts over how to respond to what was happening. Emerson's reaction to Brown's capture and execution was to praise him as a martyr who would "make the gallows as glorious as the cross," while Hawthorne, enraged by Brown's vigilantism, declared that "never was a man so justly hanged." Meanwhile, Melville went on talking amiably and, according to many who heard him, aimlessly about "Traveling: Its Pleasures, Pains, and Profits."

To yammer on about Polynesian girls and ancient statues was to fiddle while Rome burned. Melville never had his heart in his words, which all but died on his lips, coming "through his moustache," as one of his auditors complained, "about as loud and with as much force as the creaking of a field mouse through a thick hedge." Much of what he said was lost in his mumbling, but among the recoverable themes are his skepticism at the cant of progress and his sense of the elusiveness of knowledge: he spoke, for instance, of how people tend to confuse their partial perspectives with universal truths, as when Magellan named the ocean "Pacific" because the sea happened to be calm on the day he came through the straits.

As he traveled about the country (he got as far south as Clarksville, Tennessee, and Louisville, Kentucky), Melville's performances continued to be weak and the returns paltry. If he had spoken with anything like the zest with which that "lion of the platform" Bayard Taylor recounted his own exotic travels, he might have made a place for himself as an escapist entertainer in anxious times. But he was unwilling or unable. According to one visitor who came to see him in 1859, he was still an imposing man, with keen eyes and abundant dark hair, but his "countenance [was] slightly flushed with whisky drinking." In three seasons, he earned roughly $1,200 (about a third less than Emerson was paid in a single season, and less than a quarter of what Taylor took in over a few months), not nearly enough to make a material improvement in his circumstances. In the spring of 1860, he transferred ownership of Arrowhead to Judge Shaw, who deeded it, in turn, to Lizzie, in exchange for forgiveness of Herman's debts to him. Melville was now, as one scholar puts it, "in the unmanning position of being a guest in Lizzie's home."

5.

By May 1860, he had decided to set off once more on what he hoped would be a restorative journey, and it is unclear whether Lizzie felt more relief or regret that he was leaving her again. Their marriage was now, at the least, troubled; in notes taken after an interview with Lizzie Melville's niece,

Josephine Shaw, Raymond Weaver recorded the niece's memories of what her aunt had told her:

> Mrs. Melville planned to leave Herman twice. The first time his trip to Holy Land a tentative separation. He wrote nothing home—for a time. She in Boston. 2nd time she came to Boston with girls . . . some crisis possible but not known. But the Melville women settled down in persuasion—and Herman appeared heartbroken—and Lizzie went back home. . . . Herman violent—Lizzie's life not always safe. . . . Herman kinder to daughters—hated sons. Malcolm—affectionate—moody—loved mother—hated father for violence.

At the end of the month, Herman embarked on a trip around Cape Horn aboard the clipper ship *Meteor,* under the command of his seafaring brother, Tom. The *Meteor* was bound for that place of "solar optimism," California, which he hoped (as he had put it in *The Confidence-Man*) would "restore me the power of being something else to others than a burdensome care, and to myself a droning grief."

The trip did not revive him. Susceptible to seasickness now, he could not read much, though he managed to play a game or two of chess at night with his brother, on a set made for them by the ship's carpenter. A couple of days after the *Meteor* had passed within sight of the coast of Tierra del Fuego ("Horrible snowy mountains—black, thundercloud woods—gorges—hell-landscape"), a young Nantucket seaman lost his grip in the rigging and fell to his death on deck, his body oozing blood for hours as the crew waited for the squalls to subside long enough to allow a brief burial ceremony. "I . . . read & think, & walk & eat & talk, as if nothing had happened," Melville reproached himself in his journal, "—as if I did not know that death is indeed the King of Terrors—when thus happening; when thus heartbreaking to a fond mother—the King of Terrors, not to the dying or the dead, but to the mourner—the mother.—Not so easily will his fate be washed out of her heart, as his blood from the deck." He made no further journal entries, at sea or ashore.

He did write to his children. In a letter to eleven-year-old Malcolm, he described how the young man's body was laid out upon a plank while Uncle Tom prayed over the corpse, and then, "at a given word, the sailors who held the plank tipped it up, and immediately the body slipped into the stormy ocean, and we saw it no more. . . . Such is the way a poor sailor is buried at sea." There is an instructional severity in this letter, as if it were past time for the boy to show manly fortitude in facing life's terrors. Even in his tender moments, Melville stressed to his son that life does not permit much peace or pleasure—"I think of you, and Stanwix & Bessie and Fanny very often; and often long to be with you. But it can not be, at present. The picture which I have of you & the rest, I look at sometimes, till the faces almost seem real"—and then he concluded with a fatherly injunction:

> I hope that you have called to mind what I said to you about your behavior previous to my going away. I hope that you have been obedient to your mother, and helped her all you could, & saved her trouble. Now is the time to show what you are—whether you are a good, honorable boy, or a good-for-nothing one.

To seven-year-old Bessie he wrote, more gently, about the speckled seabirds, "big as chickens," that followed the ship and burst into "mighty cackling" when he threw them bread crumbs. It was, perhaps, with a sense of affinity that he explained, "These birds have no home, unless it is some wild rocks in the middle of the ocean."

Melville was still enough of a figure that upon his arrival in San Francisco, the *Daily Evening Bulletin* ran a small announcement that, traveling "in pursuit of health," he was seeking "new experiences to turn to account in a literary way." This statement was somewhere between a warranted inference and an editorial flourish. He ended up staying in San Francisco barely a week. All that is known about Melville's time there is that he was hosted one evening in her house overlooking Golden Gate by Jessie Benton Frémont, wife of General John C. Frémont, and daughter of Senator Thomas Hart Benton, on whom Melville may have modeled Bulkington a decade earlier in *Moby-Dick*.

On October 20, the *Evening Bulletin* reported his departure, this time identifying him, with stinging out-of-dateness, as "Herman Melville, the author of 'Omoo' and 'Typee,' who arrived here but a few days since from around Cape Horn." He left aboard the steamship *Cortes* bound for Panama, where he crossed the isthmus by rail and then, on the Caribbean side, boarded the steamship *North Star* for New York. Upon disembarking in his native city on November 13, 1860, he learned that the Republican candidate for president, Abraham Lincoln, had won the election a week earlier with a plurality of votes in a field of four candidates, and that there was talk of secession by slaveholding states. During what he later called this "gloomy lull" preceding the outbreak of war, he stayed briefly with Allan in New York before rejoining Lizzie and the children in Boston, then returned to Pittsfield to prepare the house for winter.

It was—for all Americans—a winter of nervous waiting. By the end of

RIGHT: *Stanwix, Frances, Malcolm, and Elizabeth Melville, c. 1860. "The picture which I have of you & the rest, I look at sometimes, till the faces almost seem real.— Now, my Dear Boy, good bye, & God bless you." Letter from Melville to his son Malcolm, written at sea aboard the* Meteor, *September 1860*

BELOW: *Melville's letter to his daughter Bessie, written aboard the* Meteor, *September 1860*

Pacific Ocean
Sep. 2ᵈ 1860

My Dear Bessie: I thought I would send you a letter, that you could read yourself— at least a part of it. But here and there I purpose to write in the usual manner, as I find the printing style comes rather awkward in a rolling ship. Mamma will read these part to you. We have seen a good many sea-birds. Many have follow-wed the ship day after day. I used to feed them with crumbs. But now it has got to be warm weather, the birds have left us. They were about as big as chickens— They were all over speckled— and they would

Melville's letter to his wife, Washington, DC, March 1861

January 1861, seven slaveholding states, outraged by Lincoln's campaign promise to ban slavery in the federal territories, had seceded from the Union while the lame-duck president, James Buchanan, disapproved and dithered. Amid rumors that Lincoln would be assassinated en route, the president-elect was forced to travel incognito to his own inauguration, switching from the official train to an unmarked train that arrived at Union Station after dark. Toby Greene, who had once seen and heard Lincoln, wrote to Melville that he was a courageous man who, despite all the assassination talk, would bravely "take the oath on the Capitol steps." So he did on March 4, speaking firmly but magnanimously to the South.

For the ensuing months, there is only the usual spotty record of Melville's movements and activities, but we do know that he was being encouraged once again to pursue a government appointment. His circle of friends was made up now of moderate Democrats and a few Republicans who, while opposed to slavery, were equally opposed to any radical action to end it. He also knew men of more strident opinions, such as the New York merchant Richard Lathers, a Democrat and passionate Calhounite related by marriage to Herman's brother Allan, and Kate's husband, John Hoadley, a fervent Republican and close friend of Sumner's.

Shortly after Lincoln took office on March 4, Hoadley asked Sumner to lobby for his brother-in-law, who he claimed was particularly well suited for the consulship at Florence. By the twenty-second of March, Melville was in Washington attending a public reception at the White House. After standing among the office seekers in the reception line, he described the new president as "working hard" at shaking hands "like a man sawing wood at so much per cord." Waiting for results, he wandered one morning into Lafayette Park across from the White House, "sunning myself on a seat," where he might have been mistaken for a bum with nowhere else to go. "The grass is bright & beautiful," he wrote to Lizzie, "& the shrubbery beginning to bud. It is just cool enough to make an overcoat comfortable sitting out of doors. The wind is high however, & except in the parks, all is dust." This sole surviving letter from Melville to his wife has a softness—"Kisses to the children. Hope to get a letter from you today"—that suggests even amidst their troubles an enduring love between them. Above his signature he wrote: "Thine, My Dearest Lizzie."

Melville's case for employment could not have been helped by the fact that his recommenders described him as a man in frail health in need of a change of scene. At the end of March, Melville received news of his father-in-law's deteriorating health, and was forced to leave Washington without a job. Several days later, he was back in Pittsfield, where he learned upon his arrival (Lizzie had just received the news by telegram) that his father-in-law was dying. The family rushed to Boston by train, but arrived too late to see the judge alive. Among the papers found in Shaw's wallet were two letters from his first love, Herman Melville's aunt Nancy, which he had carried on his person for the forty-eight years since her death. "Yes, my dear friend," she had written to him not long before she died, "that heart which you have formed shall be yours, you have taught it the endearments of the purest friendship, and for you alone ought it glow. . . ." Shaw's half century of devotion to Nancy's memory may help explain his tolerance of his difficult Melville son-in-law, who now went back to Pittsfield alone.

CHAPTER 11
SEASON OF DEATH

1.

About a year before his California trip, Melville had written a letter to a New York friend on whose name he punned in a faux-pastoral invitation to come up to Arrowhead for a binge. The friend's name was Daniel Shepherd, and the letter was written entirely in verse:

> *Come, Shepherd, come and visit me:*
> *Come, we'll make it Arcady*
>
> . . . .
>
> *—Of Bourbon that is rather new*
> *I brag a fat black bottle or two,—*
> *Shepherd, is this such Mountain-Dew*
> *As one might fitly offer you?*

To judge Melville's poetic gift by this bit of drinking doggerel would be about as fair as judging Picasso's draftsmanship on the basis of a sketch dashed off on a napkin in some Montmartre café. Beginning in the late 1850s, however, many of the poems he wrote with the hope of publication were not much stronger. Here is the very sober "Greek Architecture," probably composed around the same time:

> *Not magnitude, nor lavishness,*
> *But Form—the Site;*
> *Not innovating wilfulness,*
> *But reverence for the Archetype.*

Exactly when Melville started writing verse is unknown, but by the spring of 1860 he had accumulated enough poems to fill a small manuscript;

and while in New York waiting to board the *Meteor*, he asked his brother Allan to place it with a publisher. Here is the companion piece to "Greek Architecture," entitled "Greek Masonry":

> *Joints were none that mortar sealed:*
> *Together, scarce with line revealed,*
> *The blocks in symmetry congealed.*

The proposed book never reached print. A few of its contents survive because they were among several poems Melville gathered many years later under the rubric "Fruit of Travel Long Ago" in a privately printed volume, *Timoleon, etc.,* that appeared in an edition of twenty-five copies just before his death. Reading these poems is like overhearing a musician who no longer expects to play public recitals but who still practices in private in order to keep his fingers limber. "If we are completely to understand Melville's poetry," as Robert Penn Warren has written, "we must see it against the backdrop of his defeat as a writer."

2.

Warren used the word "writer" to mean prose writer, because he knew that for Melville the turn to poetry amounted to an attempt to start his life anew amid a sense of failure. Years later, while working on his long narrative poem about a pilgrim to the Holy Land, *Clarel,* he still wanted the full extent of his conversion from prose to verse kept secret. "Pray do not mention to *any* one," Lizzie wrote her stepmother in 1875, that Herman "is writing poetry— you know how such things spread and he would be very angry if he knew I had spoken of it—and of course I have not, except in confidence to you and the family."

His first sustained poetic theme was the Civil War. On April 13, 1861, a few days after Judge Shaw's funeral,* he was probably in the crowd in Pittsfield that gathered at the town bulletin board (" 'No seeing here,' " cries one— 'don't crowd'— / You tall man, pray you, read aloud"), straining to see the posted telegraph dispatches reporting the night attack on Fort Sumter in Charleston, South Carolina. In a poem ("Bridegroom Dick") composed years later, Melville tried to capture the shock of that day in nautical metaphors:

*Presided over by Orville Dewey.

> *But ah, how to speak of the hurricane unchained—*
> *The Union's strands parted in the hawser over-strained;*
> *Our flag blown to shreds, anchors gone altogether—*
> *The cashed fleet o' States in Secession's foul weather.*

"How to speak" about the war was a question he never satisfactorily answered. "Obscure as the wood, the entangled rhyme / But hints at the maze of war," he wrote in his poem about the ferocious battles that took place over many months in the Virginia backwoods known as "the Wilderness." In 1866, after the war had ended, he published five poems in *Harper's* that, lightly revised, became part of a book entitled *Battle-Pieces and Other Aspects of the War,* to which he appended a prose "supplement" calling for reconciliation between North and South. He arranged the book as a roughly chronological narrative, from the hanging of John Brown through the assassination of President Lincoln and the postwar testimony of Robert E. Lee before Congress. Yet one reads these poems without getting much sense of the cocky indignation with which the North greeted the war or the shock that shortly followed when Union troops were routed at Bull Run and, "baffled, humiliated, panic-struck" (Whitman's words), fled back to Washington amid talk of the government surrendering the city. Nor do they convey the grinding horror of the months and years that ensued. He had always written best about things of which he had close knowledge, but *Battle-Pieces* was a secondhand "chronicle," as Edmund Wilson once put it, "of the patriotic feelings of an anxious middle-aged non-combatant as, day by day, he reads the bulletins from the front."

This war, like so many before and since, outstripped the worst anticipations of how much death it would bring. By the time Melville began writing in the spring of 1865 ("with few exceptions," he explained in a prefatory note to his Civil War book, "the Pieces in this volume originated in an impulse imparted by the fall of Richmond"), more than half a million men and boys had died in what remains today by far the deadliest conflict in American history. Melville read about the carnage in black-bordered newspaper articles and "saw" it in photographs; but his closest contact with the war itself came in April 1864, when he visited his cousin Henry Gansevoort, who held the rank of lieutenant colonel, at the Virginia front, where, according to Lizzie, he "saw various battlefields and called on Gen. Grant."

The best poems in *Battle-Pieces* were about things that Melville did witness. In August 1863, he saw survivors of the Forty-ninth Massachusetts Volunteers parading in Pittsfield with the twice-wounded Colonel William Francis Bartlett on horseback at their head. In "The College Colonel,"

Bartlett leads the procession with "Indian aloofness" and the aspect of a weary mariner:

> He brings his regiment home—
> Not as they filed two years before,
> But a remnant half-tattered, and battered, and worn,
> Like castaway sailors, who—stunned
> By the surf's loud roar,
> Their mates dragged back and seen no more—
> Again and again breast the surge,
> And at last crawl, spent, to shore.

At the time of the Mexican War, Melville had written to Gansevoort that the day was not far off "when we will be able to talk of our killed & wounded like some of the old Eastern conquerors reckoning them up by thousands," and in *Moby-Dick* he had favorably compared the "disordered . . . decks of a whaleship" slippery with whale guts to "the unspeakable carrion of those battle-fields from which so many soldiers return to drink all ladies' plaudits." The Civil War made maimed veterans a common sight in many cities and towns, and seeing them in Pittsfield, Melville thought back to the early days before the dying had begun:

> How should they dream that Death in a rosy clime
> Would come to thin their shining throng?
> Youth feels immortal, like the gods sublime.

He retrospectively imagined (he had had no window in the town) the sight of boys strutting toward the killing fields:

> One noonday, at my window in the town,
> I saw a sight—saddest that eyes can see—
> Young soldiers marching lustily
>   Unto the wars,
> With fifes, and flags in mottoed pageantry;
> While all the porches, walks, and doors
> Were rich with ladies cheering royally.

There is a sad inevitability in these friezelike images of boys marching toward death; yet the poem, like all of *Battle-Pieces*, has a certain hampered carefulness. It feels constructed, with none of the adventurous freedom of Melville's stories and novels, in which, as Robert Penn Warren puts it, he absorbed "thousands of vivid images and rhythms . . . into the texture of the prose." In his prose, even when the glut of imagery impedes the narrative flow, the excess gives the writing a singular richness and density; but in his poems, the images ("rosy clime," "starry heights," "gladsome air") tend to be formal and inert, as if they have been dusted off after long storage in some Depository of Poetical Tropes.

But if *Battle-Pieces* looked to the past for its diction and forms, its themes belonged to the future. It was full of allusions to iron and fire and the new machinery by which the art of killing was being advanced. "War shall yet be, but warriors / Are now but operatives," he wrote of the clash of iron-clad warships that took place in March 1862. In *The Confidence-Man,* he had enumerated an industrial inventory worthy of Charlie Chaplin's *Modern Times* ("carding machines, horse-shoe machines, tunnel-boring machines, reaping machines, apple-paring machines, boot-blacking machines, sewing machines, shaving machines, run-of-errand machines, dumb-waiter machines, and the Lord-only-know-what machines"), to which it was now necessary to add the arsenal of military inventions, from armored ships to repeating rifles, that made the Civil War the first large-scale demonstration of mechanized warfare—a rehearsal, as it turned out, for World War I.

Though Melville was fully a Union man and dedicated *Battle-Pieces* "to the memory of the three hundred thousand who in the war for the maintenance of the Union fell devotedly under the flag of their fathers," he sympathized with the enemy who resisted the mechanic power ("Perish their Cause! But mark the men—") and whose loneliness in defeat he evokes in these lines about a rebel soldier released after the war into the festive streets of New York:

> *He hears the drum; he sees our boys*
> *From his wasted fields return;*
> *Ladies feast them on strawberries,*
> *And even to kiss them yearn.*

It is typical of Melville's poetry that he wrenches the syntax in order to complete the rhyme, acknowledging at the same time that "rhyme's barbaric cymbal" clashes with his theme.

Battle-Pieces, like *Pierre,* was a book about the futility of heroic gestures in the face of massive force. Where Whitman saw the people "bearing the brunt of the labor of death . . . of their own choice, fighting, dying for their own idea," Melville saw a people led to slaughter by a fate over which they had no control. In "The Conflict of Convictions," he expressed his fear that the nation was losing its democratic ideals in the very struggle to save them:

Power unanointed may come—
Dominion (unsought by the free)
And the Iron Dome,
Stronger for stress and strain,
Fling her huge shadow athwart the main;
But the Founders' dream shall flee.

One reason that *Battle-Pieces* did not sell well is that it sounded a disso-
nant note at a time of high nationalist feeling. The South was fighting for
independence as a slaveholding republic. Many people in the North, though
Lincoln did not articulate this aim till late in the war, wanted a Union purged
of slavery. Toward the end of that bloodbath year of 1863, Emerson declared,
"We are coming—thanks to the war,—to a nationality," and even the usually
wary Hawthorne had become a flag-waver: "Strange to say," he wrote in 1861,
this war "has had a benevolent effect upon my spirits . . . it was delightful to
share in the heroic sentiment of the time, and to feel that I had a country—
a consciousness which seemed to make me young again." (Hawthorne
acknowledged that he could revel in this sentiment only because "I am too
old to shoulder a musket and . . . Julian is too young.") But Melville
demurred. He modulated the patriotic emotion of *Battle-Pieces* with his
sense of war as wasting tragedy. Perhaps his most representative poem was
"The Apparition," prompted by the news, in July 1864, that Union troops
had dug a tunnel in which they set off a huge explosion under the Confederate entrenchments at Petersburg. Evil, disguised in pastoral green costume,
spreads its poison at the moment of release:

Convulsions came; and when the field
Long slept in pastoral green
A goblin-mountain was upheaved

. . . .

But ere the eye could take it in,
or mind could comprehension win,
It sunk!—and at our feet.

So, then, Solidity's a crust—
The core of fire below;
All may go well for many a year,
But who can think without a fear
Of horrors that happen so?

The rhyme is forced ("take it in . . . comprehension win"), and the theme cheapened by the didacticism of the last two lines. And "at our feet" is a false note, as Melville was not there to hear the screams and see the body parts fly.

In "Gettysburg," he resorted again to maritime metaphors in an effort to describe a place and event he had not seen:

> Before our lines it seemed a beach
>   Which wild September gales have strown
> With havoc on wreck, and dashed therewith
>   Pale crews unknown—

And in "The House-Top," he imagined himself (he was in Pittsfield) on a roof during the New York City draft riots of July 1863, as white mobs, enraged at the new conscription laws, hunted down blacks and hanged them from lampposts. Having seen none of this with his own eyes, he depended on newspaper accounts, which he filtered through his memory of Aeneas standing on a roof in Troy as the Greeks advance upon the city with (in Dryden's rendering of Virgil's Latin) "frightful Sounds" as if "a Flood of Fire by Wind is born, / Crackling it rowls, and mows the standing Corn." Here, in his mind's eye, Melville looks down over the New York mob:

> Beneath the stars the roofy desert spreads
> Vacant as Libya. All is hushed near by.
> Yet fitfully from far breaks a mixed surf
> Of muffled sound, the Atheist roar of riot.
>
> .   .   .   .
>
> The Town is taken by its rats—ship-rats
> And rats of the wharves. All civil charms
> And priestly spells which late held hearts in awe—
> Fear-bound, subjected to a better sway
> Than sway of self; these like a dream dissolve,
> And man rebounds whole aeons back in nature.

Melville wrote only one poem, "Formerly a Slave," that touched directly on what Lincoln called "the cause of the war," and this poem was provoked not by an encounter with an actual person but by an oil portrait of a freed slavewoman that he had seen on exhibit in a New York gallery.

Reviewing *Battle-Pieces* for *The Atlantic* in 1867, the young William Dean Howells asked the right questions:

Is it possible—you ask yourself, after running over all these celebrative, inscriptive, and memorial verses—that there has really been a great war, with battles fought by men and bewailed by women? Or is it only that Mr. Melville's inner consciousness has been perturbed, and filled with the phantasms of enlistments, marches, fights in the air, parenthetic bulletin-boards, and tortured humanity shedding, not words and blood, but words alone?

3.

Having passed forty before the war began, Melville faced no requirement or expectation that he enlist. Like most Americans of means (the draft riots were, in part, a poor man's protest against the policy that allowed rich men to purchase "substitutes" to fight in their place), he and his family were spared the worst. But if he spent the war in distant safety, every mail delivery made him fearful of receiving bad news about his brother Tom or his cousins Henry and Guert, who were serving in the Union forces. All survived, though Guert, suspected of drunkenness, was court-martialed for running his ship aground and damaging it so badly that it had to be scuttled. Among friends and family outside the fighting ranks, death was busy. Judge Shaw had died just before the shooting began. By the end of 1863, George Duyckinck and Sarah Morewood were gone, both at age thirty-nine. In May 1864, Melville received news that Hawthorne had died while traveling in New Hampshire to take the mountain air in an attempt to revive his failing health. Herman "was much attached to him," Maria wrote to Uncle Peter, "& will mourn his loss." Lizzie confirmed that he was very "much shocked."

Early in 1863, the Melvilles had reached a decision they had been coming to in stages: to close up their country life and return to the city. After having spent the winter of 1862 in New York, they had returned to Arrowhead. But, finding the farm harder than ever to maintain, they moved in October 1862 into a rented house on South Street in the town of Pittsfield. On one of the trips back to the farm in November to collect belongings in what was a prolonged and piecemeal move, Melville's horse bucked in panic when the carriage hit a bump and the ironwork ripped away from the wooden frame. Melville, thrown into a ditch, sustained painful if not serious injuries— a bruised or broken shoulder and a shock to the ribs, which remained tender for months. The brush with death was close enough that it left him, more than a month later, with mortality still on his mind. "This recovery," he wrote to his brother-in-law Sam Shaw,

> is flattering to my vanity. I begin to indulge in the pleasing idea that my life must needs be of some value. Probably I consume a certain amount of oxygen, which unconsumed might create some subtle disturbance in Nature. . . . I once, like other spoonies, cherished a loose sort of notion that I did not care to live very long. But I will frankly own that I have now no serious, no insuperable objections to a respectable longevity. I don't like the idea of being left out night after night in a cold church-yard.—In warm and genial countries, death is much less of a bugbear than in our frozen latitudes. A native of Hindostan takes easily and kindly to his latter end. It is but a stepping round the corner to him. He knows he will sleep warm.

Even in this self-denigrating little note, Melville was mocking the kind of cosmic egotism that his Romantic contemporaries were wont to express. Here, for example, is Poe, writing in 1848: "If I venture to displace, by even the billionth part of an inch, the microscopical speck of dust which lies now upon the point of my finger . . . I have done a deed which shakes the Moon in her path, which causes the Sun to be no longer the Sun, and which alters forever the destiny of the multitudinous myriads of stars that roll and glow in the majestic presence of their Creator." In his youth, Melville's voice had sometimes risen into that high register, as when, in *White-Jacket,* he declared that "I have a voice that helps to shape eternity; and my volitions stir the orbits of the furthest suns." But the author of the letter to Sam is a writer who jokes at his own expense when asserting that if he were to stop breathing, "Nature" would be disturbed. Nature, he knew, would not care a bit about his extinction. This is the same self-satirizing writer who had writ-ten of pantheism as delusion in "The Mast-Head" chapter of *Moby-Dick,* and who expressed impatience at Emerson's "insinuation, that had he lived in those days when the world was made, he might have offered some valu-able suggestions." One reason for Melville's dissonance in his own time is that he felt so acutely the fact of human insignificance—a fact of which he was apparently reminded by being tossed unceremoniously into the ditch.

Since the mid-1850s, he had from time to time put parcels of his land on the market in order to raise cash. Now, in February 1863, having recovered from the driving accident, and finding himself restless in what young Stan-wix called their "square, old-fashioned" rental house in Pittsfield after sev-eral failed attempts to sell the whole Arrowhead property, he approached his brother Allan, who had moved with his second wife (Sophia had died five years before) into a new Manhattan residence, with the offer to hand over Arrowhead in partial exchange for Allan's house on East Twenty-sixth Street. A deal was struck, and he and Lizzie, who had inherited part of her father's real estate holdings, agreed to take over what remained of Allan's mortgage in the city.

When Melville returned to New York City for good on November 3 or 4, 1863, it was with no intention of resuming the active literary life he once had led there. On the last day of 1863, he thanked Duyckinck for sending him a book but declined to review it. "As for scribbling anything about it," he wrote, "tho' I would like to please you, I have not spirit enough." Three years later, with *Battle-Pieces* in print, the search for a government job finally paid off; but instead of a foreign posting in some sunny port, it was a four-dollar-a-day, six-day-a-week job across town on the Hudson River piers. In December 1866, Melville reported for work as Deputy Inspector No. 75 of the United States Custom Service.

And then the darkness closed in. He had long been one of those "bards," in Emerson's phrase, who "love wine, mead, narcotics, coffee, tea, opium, the fumes of sandalwood and tobacco, or whatever other procurers of animal exhilaration" they can lay their hands on. In this respect, he was among the most ardent of lovers. At the height of his friendship with Hawthorne, he had gleefully protested that "I won't believe in a Temperance Heaven," and proposed that when the two men meet in paradise, they must "smuggle a basket of champagne there" to mark the occasion. Looking forward to seeing Hawthorne before the next life, Melville urged him to "keep some Champagne or Gin for me" in this one, and to "have ready a bottle of brandy because I always feel like drinking that heroic drink when we talk ontological heroics together." For his part, he promised to provide a "most potent Port" to share as they "crack jokes & bottles from morning till night." In *Pierre,* he expressed contempt for "lean ones" who subsist on Graham crackers and cold water, recommending instead that they "attach the screw of your hose-pipe to some fine old butt of Madeira! Pump us some sparkling wine into the world!" Cyrus the Great was also, in Melville's view, Cyrus the Wise, since he ordered this epitaph to be engraved on his tombstone: "I could drink a great deal of wine, and it did me a great deal of good."

But as Melville's drinking increased, the joking subsided. It is likely, as Charles Olson once speculated, that he became "periodically violent to his wife." "His moods he had," as he was to write about a character in *Clarel,* "mad fitful ones, / Prolonged or brief outbursts or moans," and sometime after the return to New York, things between him and Lizzie evidently turned desperate. In a letter of May 1867 to Henry Whitney Bellows, minister of the

New York Unitarian church where the Melvilles rented a pew, Sam Shaw alluded to the minister's proposal that since Lizzie was (in Sam's words) "convinced that her husband is insane," her brothers must find a way to rescue her. Bellows was sufficiently alarmed by Melville's behavior that he believed Lizzie should leave him and retreat to the care of her brothers. But in the end, she did not leave. How, or whether, the matter was resolved remains unknown, since all that survives is a brief note in which she thanked her pastor for counseling her in the face of "whatever further trial may be before me."

As the Melvilles' marriage touched bottom, so did their firstborn, Malcolm. An eighteen-year-old of "purity . . . gentleness [and] truthfulness," according to his uncle Hoadley, Malcolm had joined a regiment of volunteers who, having been spared by age and social standing from army service, met in the afterglow of war for drills and calisthenics. They were boys playing at being military men. At home, Malcolm proudly sported his uniform, complete with working pistol; and to his parents' dismay, he often stayed out late with his comrades.

On the night of September 10, 1867, he did not come home till three o'clock in the morning. His mother, unable to sleep, had stayed up waiting for him. The next morning, Malcolm did not appear downstairs or report to his job in Richard Lathers's law office. According to Sam Shaw's account of the events, Malcolm answered yes when one of his sisters called to him through his bedroom door. Before leaving for work, Herman advised Lizzie to let him sleep and take whatever reprimand or penalty Lathers thought fit. Over the course of the day, Malcolm failed to respond to his mother's periodic calling. When Herman came home that evening, the door was broken down, and the parents found their boy dead in his bed from a pistol shot to the head. Here is how, many years later, Melville's great-grandson (grandchild of Frances) described the children's fate:

> And there were the children:
> Mackey,
> Stanny,
> Bessie,
> & Fanny,
> hovering at the edge of the storm, the vortex, and
> killed, crippled or withered, according to the order of birth, to how
> near in time (the father's Space) they came
> to the eye of it.

At first, the coroner ruled Malcolm's death a suicide. But a few days later, perhaps under pressure from the family, the jurors of the inquest reversed the ruling on the grounds that "no motive having appeared," it was more plausible that Malcolm's "boyish whim" of "sleeping with his pistol under his pillow" had led to an accident in "disturbed or somnambulistic sleep."* After the funeral, in which Malcolm lay in an open coffin, his father wrote to Hoadley: "I wish you could have seen him as he lay in his last attitude, the ease of a gentle nature. Mackie never gave me a disrespectful word in his life, nor in any way ever failed in filialness."

Between the high-spirited letter that Melville wrote to Allan four days after Malcolm's birth ("He's a perfect prodigy . . . I think of calling him Barbarossa—Adolphus—Ferdinand . . . Grandissimo—Hercules—Sampson—Bonaparte") and these remarks written five or six days after Malcolm's death eighteen years later, there is next to nothing in the record by which to take the measure of Herman Melville's feeling toward his son. There is a poem, "Monody," that some scholars believe (on little evidence) is about Melville's estrangement from Hawthorne, but that seems more likely to have been a meditation on his son, who was buried on the rolling grounds of Woodlawn Cemetery in the Bronx:

> *To have known him, to have loved him*
> *After loneness long;*
> *And then to be estranged in life,*
> *And neither in the wrong;*
> *And now for death to set his seal—*
> *Ease me, a little ease, my song!*

> *By wintry hills his hermit-mound*
> *The sheeted snow-drifts drape,*
> *And houseless there the snow-bird flits*
> *Beneath the fir-trees' crape:*
> *Glazed now with ice the cloistral vine*
> *That hid the shyest grape.*

---

*In 1973, the psychologist Edwin S. Shneidman organized a dubious experiment at a Los Angeles hospital in which the staff of the L.A. Suicide Prevention Center was asked to provide a "psychological autopsy" of a fictitious teenager who, they were told, had recently died of a self-inflicted gunshot. Charged with the task of determining whether the death was accidental or intentional, the staff was provided with information drawn from letters written more than a hundred years earlier by relatives and friends about Malcolm Melville. On the basis of these materials, the staff reached the "near-unanimous" conclusion that the case was a suicide, and that the boy had kept a pistol by his bed in order to protect himself from his abusive father. "On the morning of his death, the choice for Malcolm was between the memory of his mother's kiss a few hours before and the terror of (and the need to protect himself against) his father's rage to come." Shneidman, "Some Psychological Reflections on the Death of Malcolm Melville," *Suicide and Life-Threatening Behavior* 6, no. 4 (Winter 1976): 231–42.

Whether or not this poem was a too-late expression of love for his lost Malcolm, we do know that Melville was capable of taking joy in the presence of children. On New Year's Eve, 1850, while baby Malcolm was away from Pittsfield with his mother in Boston, Augusta Melville predicted in a note to their sister Helen that Herman, who sorely missed his wife and child, would "fairly devour" his baby son upon their return. And a sweet letter survives from ten-year-old Stanwix to his Boston grandmother reporting that Papa had taken him in 1861 to see the soldiers drilling at the Pittsfield parade ground; after the parade was canceled (the men were needed to put out a factory fire), he took Stanny for a happy ride in the country, during which they stopped to play a game of catch and to make "little round curls of the dandelion stems."

In the journal that Nathaniel Hawthorne kept during his Berkshire years, there is a similar glimpse of avuncular Melville putting the beaming little Julian beside him in the carriage during a moonlit ride and, on another occasion, dismounting from his horse and hoisting him into the saddle, then walking beside the animal while the boy rode proudly with the "fearlessness of an old equestrian." Melville was capable, as not all adult men are, of showing children that combination of solicitude and respect that lights up their child's eyes with the knowledge of being taken seriously; and five-year-old Julian assured his father that he "loved Mr. Melville as well as me, and as mamma, and as Una." In a charming letter to Julian after the Hawthornes had moved to Newton, Melville expressed his gratitude: "I am very happy that I have a place in the heart of so fine a little fellow as you."

There is no reason to believe that Melville withheld these kinds of tenderness from his own firstborn son, who was still an infant when Julian was five—though one may wonder whether he had the patience required of the father of an adolescent, especially one who tended toward laziness and posturing. Immediately after Malcolm's death, shocked to his core and worried about his wife, Melville received permission to take a week off from work and accepted Allan's suggestion that he and Lizzie go by themselves to their old home at Arrowhead. Although their time there went unrecorded, it is known that a neighbor presented the grieving parents with a book of hymns into which Lizzie inscribed the words that had been carved into Malcolm's gravestone: "So good, so young, / So gentle, so sincere, / So loved, so early lost, / May claim a tear." In a letter to Allan's daughter Maria (named for the family matriarch), Herman wrote that he and his wife were having photographs made from two tintypes of Malcolm, "one representing him in his ordinary dress, and the other in the regimental one." He thanked her for her concern, adding that he was "touched at the way in which you speak of Mackie." There is no trace of a further eulogy to his son until, some twenty

LEFT: *Malcolm Melville*
RIGHT: *Malcolm Melville in military dress*

years later, he poured his heart into *Billy Budd,* the story of a beautiful boy whose last act is to bless the severe yet tender man who has ordered that he be put to death.

4.

In the months following, and for most of the next ten years, Melville devoted himself to a long narrative poem, *Clarel,* about an American student who journeys to the "barrenness of Judea" in search of his lost faith. In "Bartleby" he had written about the "innate and incurable disorder" of the human mind, and in *The Confidence-Man* he had noted that "the mind is ductile . . . but images, ductilely received into it, need a certain time to harden and bake in their impressions." By the time he began working on *Clarel* in the late 1860s, it had been a "certain time" since his trip to the Holy Land, and now, out of his memories, and with Malcolm's death in constant view, he constructed a work that was, in part, a work of mourning.

As he was later to explain to an English correspondent, *Clarel* was "a metrical affair, a pilgrimage or what not, of several thousand lines, eminently adapted for unpopularity." It did indeed prove unpopular with the public, as well as with Lizzie, who referred to it as a "dreadful *incubus* of a book (I call it so because it has undermined all our happiness)." *Clarel* ran to 18,000 verses divided into 150 cantos, a vast "philosophical verse-novel" whose structure provided Melville with a sort of template that spared him from having to invent, as he had once done in prose, his own forms. After a day on the piers, the quiet hours in his study producing his daily complement of rhymed octosyllabic lines (over ten years, he averaged roughly five lines per day) served as a salutary discipline for a writer whose well of invention was depleted if not dried up.

There is an apposite comment by Seamus Heaney about Robert Frost that applies to Melville's mood and motive in the years he worked on *Clarel:* "Frost believed," Heaney says, ". . . that individual venture and vision arose as a creative defense against emptiness, and that it was therefore always possible that a relapse into emptiness would be the ultimate destiny of consciousness." Such a relapse—or fear of it—was Melville's subject in *Clarel,* and the labor of composing the poem was his stay against emptiness. He set the poem in a place, as he had described it a decade earlier in the fractured prose of his travel journal, of "whitish mildew pervading whole tracts of landscape—bleached—leprosy—encrustation of curses—old cheese—bones of rocks,—crunched, knawed & mumbled—mere refuse & rubbish of creation." Into this place of death comes an American student seeking some seed of faith amid the holy sites of Jerusalem, that city of "blind arches . . . sealed windows," with "portals masoned fast" against the encroaching desert:

> *The student mused: The desert, see,*
> *It parts not here, but silently,*
> *Even like a leopard by our side,*
> *It seems to enter in with us—*

Clarel was set in a world of heat and sand, but its deeper locale was the spiritual desert of the mind. Shadowed by the death of his son, Melville was writing as well in the shadow of Darwin, whose theory of evolution had destroyed the idea of superintending providence and replaced it with blind chance as the primary force at work in nature and, by implication, in history. "How," he asks in *Clarel,* can faith "be derived from things / Subject to change and vanishings?" The chief doctrines of Christianity—the Fall, Original Sin, the Atonement, the Resurrection and Redemption—were incompatible with the new truths of science, and though Melville had never exactly been a believer, religious ideas had always exerted power over his imagination. But by the late 1860s, no educated person could think blithely of nature as the work of divine consciousness, or of the human creature as created in the image of God and endowed with an immortal soul. As Melville's contemporary Emily Dickinson put the matter in a poem that registered the Civil War carnage in which faith itself was among the casualties, God's "Hand is amputated now / And God cannot be found."

Melville lived when "the great curse . . . of skepticism" (as he called it in his Mediterranean travel journal) was pushing back in time the age when God had communicated directly to human beings as if they were impressionable children. The rational Protestantism that Melville imbibed from his father's side of the family had little use for claims of religious inspiration, which it regarded as the foolish and dangerous delusions of gullible people. The age of miracles, when God had instructed human beings with gaudy demonstrations of his power through plagues or miracles, was long past ("Men have come to speak of the revelation," Emerson wrote in 1838, "as somewhat long ago given and done, as if God were dead"), and had been supplanted by an age of reason in which man must seek God in the impersonal processes of nature or the fitful progress of history. This kind of deracinated Protestantism, as Orestes Brownson wrote in 1844, condemned those who hungered for some manifestation of divine spirit in their lives "to feed only on inspirations made in the past."

Melville, craving more, still looked with longing into the natural world for signs of divine immanence, hoping to immerse himself in what Emerson called "the divine *aura* which breathes through forms." He sometimes did feel, as Emerson had written in *Nature*, the "floods of life stream around and through us," as when, exhilarated by his discovery of a kindred spirit in Hawthorne, he declared the world (in 1850) "as young today as when it was created; and this Vermont morning dew . . . as wet to my feet as Eden's dew to Adam's," or when, the previous year, he recalled in *Redburn* his youthful feeling at sea of being enveloped in the lap of God:

> Every happy little wave seemed gamboling about like a thoughtless little kid in a pasture; and seemed to look up in your face as it passed, as if it wanted to be patted and caressed. They seemed all live things with hearts in them that could feel; and I almost felt grieved, as we sailed in among them; scattering them under our broad bows in sunflakes, and riding over them like a great elephant among lambs.

But Melville could never escape the melancholy suspicion that his feelings of divine immanence were illusory—and at the next moment, the luminous world fades away and he finds himself in chill and darkness:

> I could not see [from high in the rigging] far out upon the ocean, owing to the darkness of the night; and from my lofty perch, the sea looked like a great, black gulf, hemmed in, all round, by beetling black cliffs. I seemed all alone; treading the midnight clouds; and every second, expected to find myself falling—falling—falling, as I have felt when the nightmare has been upon me.

He tried to hold on to his glimpses of transcendence for the flashes of consolation they delivered. Without them, he knew, the vein of bitterness within might burst and bleed into his soul, leaving him, like Ahab, to experience the world as a wasteland.

By the time he wrote *Clarel*, Melville was losing the struggle, and in his defeat he was representative. By the 1870s, as Frank Kermode has written, there had "departed the last hope of a science which could regard natural history as a phenomenal representation of the operations of divine providence." Science, so full of promise for its insights into the processes of nature, could do nothing to satisfy what William James was soon to call "the craving of the heart to believe that behind nature there is a spirit whose expression nature is," and *Clarel* was Melville's reproach of science for its failure to slake his craving:

> *Shall Science then*
> *Which solely dealeth with this thing*
> *Named Nature, shall she ever bring*
> *One solitary hope to men?*

The anguish here is expressed in the form of a question, but it was a question that Melville had answered earlier in the poem:

> *The abbot and the palmer rest*
> *The legends follow them and die—*
> *Those legends which, be it confessed,*
> *Did nearer bring them the sky—*
> *Did nearer woo it to their hope*
> *Of all that seers and saints avow—*
> *Than Galileo's telescope*
> *Can bid it unto prosing Science now.*

What Melville did in *Clarel* was to distribute himself among a range of characters—seekers, cynics, pilgrims looking for respite, proselytizers looking for converts, men broken by grief—and by personifying his own shifting moods in these characters perform a kind of exorcism on himself. There is Celio, a lapsed believer who feels nothing when he pauses at the arch where Pilate, crying "*Ecce Homo!*" presented Christ to the mocking mob:

> *Won men to look for solace there;*
> *But, crying out in death's eclipse,*
> *When rainbow none his eyes might see,*
> *Enlarged the margin for despair—*

There is the bitter ex-revolutionary Mortmain (death is in his name), who "roved the gray places of the earth," and who, like a version of Pierre returned from the dead, renounces the callow belief in human virtue that he once had held. When Mortmain considers the crucifixion, he sees in it no uplifting example of selfless sacrifice, but only measureless human cruelty, as Christ's tormentors insure that his "hands, nailed down, / Might not avail to screen the face / From each head-wagging mocking one." There is a scientific materialist, Margoth, who believes only in telegraphs and railroads, and spits out the water of the Jordan as if it were wine turned to vinegar. There is an affable Anglican named Derwent, a spiritual descendant of Falsgrave, who welcomes the "last adopted style" and "abreast kept with the age, the year." And there is Rolfe, Melville's fullest self-portrait, who understands the human craving for belief ("Yea, long as children feel affright / In darkness, men shall fear a God; / And long as daisies yield delight / Shall see His footprints in the sod"), but who cannot begin to answer the need for himself.

The landscape through which these people travel is littered with taunting hints of a vanished God. A guide identifies an indentation in a rock as Christ's footprint, but according to one of the literary sources that Melville used in composing his poem, it was "nothing but a simple cavity in the rock, with no more resemblance to a human foot than to anything else. . . ." As for the local human landscape, it is a gallery of grotesques; peddlers sell putative relics to gullible pilgrims, while lepers with "faces, yet defacements too" pester tourists for alms.

One of the pilgrims is a frontier American of Puritan stock named Nathan. In early manhood, he was haunted by the sight of Indian mounds that "Dim showed across the prairie green / Like dwarfed and blunted mimic shapes / Of Pyramids at distance seen," and began to drift away from the cold ancestral creed that had never satisfied his need for a vital faith. Now looking for it, he moves serially through deism to pantheism, then briefly joins a local sect; but at every stage the promise proves false and leaves him

"Alone, and at Doubt's freezing pole" as "He wrestled with the pristine forms / Like the first man."

When Nathan at last finds peace, it comes from "a source that well might claim / Surprise": he falls in love with a Jewish woman. In his earlier works, Melville had expressed conventional nineteenth-century ideas about Jews— that their "bigoted Hebrew nationality" keeps them self-lovingly tribal and that they bear the shame of "looking for [the Messiah] in a chariot, who was already among them on an ass." But in *Clarel,* though he still speaks of "the mind infertile of the Jew," he makes this patient and kindly Jewish woman, Agar, into a sort of maternal sibyl. Nathan converts, marries her, and— mistaking her laments over her people's exile for a desire actually to return to Palestine—becomes a Zionist. With a convert's zeal, and to Agar's consterna- tion, Nathan wants to *act* on the Passover pledge of "next year in Jerusalem" rather than merely to repeat it every year at the family seder as part of the annual holiday ritual. He misses the whole point of Diaspora Judaism—its rootedness in the very condition of exile—and soon enough he demands that his wife and children leave America and move with him to the holy city of his adopted faith:

> *The Hebrew seers announce in time*
> *The return of Judah to her prime;*
> *Some Christians deemed it then at hand.*
> *Here was an object: Up and do!*
> *With seed and tillage help renew—*
> *Help reinstate the Holy Land.*

The family scene, in which one imagines Agar rolling her eyes at her gentile husband's zeal to be a better Jew than the Jews, is as close to humor as *Clarel* gets. The poem is often a lugubrious work in which, as one critic puts it, Melville "deliberately hobbled his muse" by keeping himself within its highly confining structure of rhythm and rhyme. There are bursts of power, too, especially in the evocations of desert landscape and descriptions of Jerusalem built atop "dark quarries" into which the holy city seems poised for imminent collapse. And there are passages of concentrated emo- tion, as when Melville describes how the innocent believer Nehemiah sleep- walks to his death in the Dead Sea, and how his comrades find his body at dawn lying on the sand wrapped in morning mist:

> *Slant on the shore, ground-curls of mist*
> *Enfold it, as in amethyst*
> *Subdued, small flames in dead of night*
> *Lick the dumb back-log ashy white.*

"He's gone," says Margoth, the "Hegelized" Jew who believes only in the material world described by science and regards the corpse as nothing more than a lump of dead tissue: "czars, stars must go / Or change! All's chemistry. Aye so"—to which Derwent replies feebly, "*Resurget*," and Vine can only add, "*In pace*." Having said these reticent blessings, the survivors bury their comrade in a protected spot on the beach, using the ribs of a camel's skeleton to dig a trench in the sand. But *Clarel* is finally a hopelessly talky poem, its intertwined stories over-earnest in the style of *Mardi,* yet without the madcap energy that made Melville's early failures seem rehearsals for something grand.

Still, he continued to reach for large themes. In the story of Nathan, he wrote about a futile effort to find changeless truth in this changeable world (the restless questing that Hawthorne had noted in Melville himself), and to Nathan's story he added a sort of genealogical sequel that furnished the poem with its main plot. Clarel falls in love with Nathan and Agar's daughter, Ruth, a mixture of Yillah in *Mardi* and Lucy in *Pierre* who stuns Clarel with her purity:

> *One he perceived, as it befell,*
> *Whose air expressed such truth unfeigned,*
> *And harmonies inlinked which dwell*
> *In pledges born of record pure—*
> *She looked a legate to insure*
> *That Paradise is possible*
> *Now as hereafter. 'Twas the grace*
> *Of Nature's dawn: an Eve-like face*
> *And Nereid eyes with virgin spell*
> *Candid as day, yet baffling quite*
> *Like day, through unreserve of light.*

The story Clarel and Ruth share is one of unconsummated love (she dies before he can marry her) through which Melville tried to suggest the exquisite mixture of pain and pleasure that comes of seeking the unattainable.

Melville wrote *Clarel* by snatching a few night hours after his day's work at the docks, and there is weariness throughout. His daughter Frances, who became a proficient musician later in life, recalled how as a teenager she would listen, disapproving the monotony of the rhythm, as her father recited "while pacing the floor, certain verses he had written, looking for approbation, she thought, from his wife and daughters." One can only wonder what this New York girl (if these were among the verses she heard her father recite) made of his melded memories of the ocean he had known in his youth and the desert he had visited in middle age:

*Last known
photograph of
Maria Gansevoort
Melville, c. 1872*

> *Sands immense
> Impart the oceanic sense:
> The flying grit like scud is made:
> Pillars of sand which whirl about
> Or arc along in colonnade,
> True kin be to the water-spout.
> Yonder on the horizon, red
> With storm, see there the caravan
> Straggling long-drawn, dispirited;
> Mark how it labors like a fleet
> Dismasted, which the cross-winds fan
> In crippled disaster of retreat
> From battle—*

During the years he worked on *Clarel*, Melville saw his family—young as well as old—raided by death. He had begun work on his immense poem not long after the death of his firstborn child in 1867, and completed it four years after the death of his mother in the spring of 1872. While he was checking page proofs in January 1876, Lizzie wrote to his cousin Kate Lansing, who was contemplating a visit, that "Herman . . . is in such a frightfully nervous state & particularly now with such an added strain on his mind, that I am actually *afraid* to have any one here for fear that he will be upset entirely, &

not be able to go on with the printing." *Clarel* did not rise to the level of the great effort Melville put into it. Yet of all his works, it is the one in which he best expressed the craving for belief that Hawthorne had detected in him as they walked together on the Southport dunes, talking of "Providence and futurity and of everything that lies beyond human ken." Some of its best lines are wrenchingly beautiful, as when Derwent speaks:

> *There's none so far astray,*
> *Detached, abandoned, as might seem,*
> *As to exclude the hope, the dream*
> *Of fair redemption. One fine day*
> *I saw at sea, by bit of deck—*
> *Weedy—adrift from far away—*
> *The dolphin in his gambol light*
> *Through showery spray, arch into sight:*
> *He flung a rainbow o'er that wreck.*

As Melville brought *Clarel* to completion in the winter of 1876, he proposed, for the second time in his life, that his work be published anonymously. His uncle Peter Gansevoort paid the costs, and, in the end, the publisher, Putnam's, prevailed on Melville to let his name appear on the title page, though he authorized no mention of his earlier works. Probably in the early 1870s, while midway through the poem, he had marked in his copy of Matthew Arnold's *Essays* a passage dismissing the value of a public literary career in favor of the "well-kept secret of one's self and one's thoughts." In June 1876, *Clarel* appeared in an edition of 350 copies, of which about a third were sold and the rest, three years later, pulped. When Lewis Mumford, in 1925, came to read one of the surviving copies in the New York Public Library, he found its pages uncut.

CHAPTER 12
THE QUIET END

1.

In a comment that has since become a commonplace, F. Scott Fitzgerald, declining into drink and depression while still in his forties, looked back at his early success and remarked that "there are no second acts in American lives." Melville is often cited as the exemplary literary case of this putative truth. Having scaled the heights with *Moby-Dick,* he slipped back (or so goes the standard account) and, after several failed attempts to regain his footing, fell into a long silence.* This version of his career has become so well known that when John Updike's fictional author Henry Bech wins the "Melville Medal, awarded every five years to that American author who has maintained the most meaningful silence," Updike had no reason to doubt that readers would get the joke.

None of it, of course, is exactly true. After *The Confidence-Man,* Melville did stop writing fiction. But whatever else they were, *Battle-Pieces, Clarel,* and the poems of his later years were not silence. Then, in the late 1880s, almost seventy and suffering from recurrent skin and lung infections, he returned to prose for what would be his last sustained literary effort: the story of a handsome young sailor unjustly accused of mutiny aboard a British warship. "My vigor sensibly declines," Melville replied in December 1889 to a young Canadian who had written to him in admiration of his earlier work, and "what little of it is left I husband for certain matters yet incomplete, and which, indeed, may never be completed." Among these "matters" was a short novel called *Billy Budd.* It had begun as the headnote to a ballad recited in the accused sailor's voice, but Melville found himself repeatedly returning to the headnote, expanding it until the prose outgrew the verse. In

*This narrative was initiated by D. H. Lawrence's friend John Middleton Murry in "Herman Melville's Silence," a review of *Billy Budd* for the *Times Literary Supplement* (July 10, 1924). Two years later, the fine English critic John Freeman could refer to Melville's "nearly forty years' supineness" as an uncontested fact.

the course of revision, he shifted the poem here and there within the enlarged story until finally placing it at the end as a sort of coda to what had become a full-scale prose narrative.

The much-written-over manuscript of *Billy Budd* is preserved today in the Houghton Library at Harvard, a gift from Melville's granddaughter. With its many excisions, insertions, and addenda in Melville's cryptic hand on interleaved sheets and on pinned or pasted scraps, it was difficult even for its own author to decipher. "More than once," according to the best scholarly authorities, "believing his work to be essentially complete, he undertook to put his manuscript into fair-copy form, but each time was led into further revision and elaboration." Lizzie helped him with the copying. While she worked at her writing table, Herman rose periodically from his reading or resting to take a leaf from her, on which he changed a word here and there, then returned it to its place in the growing stack—a partnership between husband and wife that is touchingly revealed in their mingled handwritings.

Since there survives only one letter from Melville to his wife (written from Washington during his quest for a government job in that ominous spring of 1861), and since he never wrote at length about marriage except in the fervid pages of *Pierre*, there is little on which to draw for an inner history of the life they shared for more than forty years. Sometime in the 1870s, Melville marked in an essay by Hazlitt a passage advising that "whoever . . . dost seek happiness [should] seek it . . . in books, pictures, and the face of nature, for these alone we may count upon as friends for life." We cannot know if some deficiency of companionship in his own life occurred to him when he read that passage, or if it provoked him to think of intimacies—with his father, his older brother, his son—that had been broken off by early death. As for his marriage, especially without any letters to compare to the passionate correspondence between Nathaniel and Sophia Hawthorne, the Melvilles' marriage has come to seem a more or less contractual affair: a quasi-arranged match between two venerable families, one sound and the other faltering, suited for fruitful alliance.

Yet in their later years, a settled tenderness took hold between Herman and Lizzie, as expressed in "L'Envoi," his poem about homecoming that he probably wrote while working on *Billy Budd,* and placed at the end of the self-financed edition of *Timoleon* published only four months before he died:

> *My towers at last! These rovings end.*
> *Their thirst is slaked in larger dearth:*
> *The yearning infinite recoils.*
>   *For terrible is earth!*

. . . .

*Elizabeth Shaw
Melville, 1885*

*But thou, my stay, thy lasting love
One lonely good, let this but be!
Weary to view the wide world's swarm
But blest to fold but thee.*

Some thirty years after Melville's death, Raymond Weaver, having obtained access to the manuscript of *Billy Budd* from Melville's granddaughter Eleanor, transcribed it at the request of an English editor who had arranged for Melville's works to be published in a uniform edition. And so, in 1924, his last work, which had been stored for years in a tin bread box, became available to the public just as Melville was achieving posthumous fame as the author of *Moby-Dick*. The difference in scale and tone between the two works was so large that even Weaver, the first scholar to examine *Billy Budd*, did not know what to make of the change; indeed, he missed "the sparkle, the verve" of Melville's earlier writing. But in the eighty years since, it has been recognized as a supreme example of what the Germans call *Spätstil*—an end-of-life style of great complexity, yet filled, as has been said of the late quartets of Beethoven, with "songful passages of extreme simplicity."

Billy Budd, as E. M. Forster was among the first to recognize, "reaches straight back into the universal, to a blackness and sadness so transcending our own that they are undistinguishable from glory." With its almost ethereal combination of sorrow and serenity, it was the cherished work of Melville's old age, to which he brought his deepest feelings of love and loss. As a young man, he wrote in gusts and rarely went back to revise; now he wrote slowly, meticulously reworking what he had done, as if he could not bear to let it go.

2.

When Melville began writing *Billy Budd,* he had been working for nearly two decades for the U.S. Custom Service, "clinging like a weary but tenacious barnacle to the N.Y. Custom House," according to Hawthorne's son-in-law, "& very much averse to publicity." Many years later, W. H. Auden imagined his days and nights:

> *Towards the end he sailed into an extraordinary mildness,*
> *And anchored in his home and reached his wife*
> *And rode within the harbour of her hand,*
> *And went across each morning to an office*
> *As though his occupation were another island.*

For the better part of twenty years, beginning in 1866, he took the horse car down Broadway six times a week, then headed west, where he walked the docks along the Hudson down to the Battery. (Later, he was assigned to an East River pier uptown at Seventy-ninth Street and traveled to work on the new Third Avenue El.) On West Street, wearing a brass-buttoned woolen coat modeled on a naval officer's uniform, he shared an office with other inspectors in what was little more than a dockside shack, where he prepared and filed his paperwork. His job was to ensure that the required duties were paid on unloaded cargo. He may have occasionally inspected the personal baggage of disembarking passengers, but his main tasks were to confirm the accuracy of cargo lists from newly docked ships, secure the mail, collect fees, and dispatch runners off to merchants awaiting delivery. It was not savory work. According to John Hoadley, who wrote on his brother-in-law's behalf supporting a request for promotion, he was "surrounded" in his job "by low venality" in the face of which he put "all quietly aside,—quietly declining offers of money for special services,—quietly returning money which has been thrust into his pockets behind his back, avoiding offence alike to the corrupting merchants and their clerks and runners, who think that all men can be bought."

Melville may have refused bribes that were offered, but he had to pay those that were demanded. That is, he paid 2 percent of his annual salary to the New York Republican State Committee and, for a time in the 1880s, an equal amount to the national Republican Party. This was, in effect, a tax for political protection—a small price, perhaps, for job security, but a bribe nevertheless. It was one element in a system by which the party in office extorted money from civil servants, thereby encouraging them to pass on the cost to merchants whose goods they had the power to detain or impound. According to the authors of an investigative report issued in 1881, men of Melville's rank were left "unprotected against arbitrary exactions from their salaries—which they saw used by scheming politicians without audit or responsibility." Many of his fellow inspectors "retaliated in neglect of duty through which vast amounts of revenue were lost, and in extortions from merchants through which Custom-House morals were debauched."

Melville's tone in *Billy Budd* toward the cheats and sneaks among its minor characters suggests that his mood toward his colleagues at the Custom House was more weary than incensed. There was something grim about holding a job in which graft was a matter of course, since to acquiesce was demeaning while to hold oneself aloof was self-punitive. In January 1886, after he had retired on the strength of his wife's inheritance from her aunt Martha Marett, who died in 1878, and her half brother Lemuel Shaw, Jr., who died in 1884, Lizzie wrote, "For a year or so past he has found the duties too onerous for a man of his years, and at times of exhaustion, both mental and physical, he has been on the point of giving it up, but recovering a little, has held on, very naturally anxious to do so, for many reasons." Melville himself marked a passage, possibly during his last illness, in his copy of Schopenhauer's *Studies in Pessimism:* a "man of genius . . . will occasionally feel like some noble prisoner of state, condemned to work in the galleys."

He had arrived, as Frederick Busch imagines him in his novel *The Night Inspector,* "within a very short distance of depletion." As early as the spring of 1877, we find him making a revealing comment in a letter to Hoadley. At fifty-nine, Hoadley was a year older, yet Melville thought of himself as Hoadley's senior: "You are young but I am verging upon threescore and at times a certain lassitude steals over one—in fact, a disinclination for doing anything except the indispensable. At such moments the problem of the universe seems a humbug, and . . . well nepenthe seems all-in-all." In a postscript, he repeated himself, but more bluntly: "You are young (as I said before) but I aint; and at my years, and with my disposition, or rather, constitution, one gets to care less and less for everything except downright good feeling. Life is so short, and so ridiculous and irrational (from a certain point of view) that one knows not what to make of it, unless—well, finish the sentence for yourself." Then he added a second P.S.: "*I aint crazy.*"

Later that year, Melville's behavior became a source of shame to his daughters, especially when a friend or suitor was present. Still a man of what he had once called (in *Pierre*) "uncelestial appetite," he was known to shovel potatoes into his mouth while talking long and loudly, and to attack a plate of crabs with a hammer as if he were outdoors trying to break a rock.

If his daughters were embarrassed, his wife was alarmed. Early in 1877, Lizzie wrote to a cousin that her husband was becoming "*morbidly* sensitive" and pleaded with her not to fail to "mention Herman's name in your letters" lest he think (Lizzie and Herman apparently read each other's mail) that he was regarded as superseded or beside the point. In his copy of Edward FitzGerald's translation of the *Rubáiyát of Omar Khayyám,* Melville marked many passages of regretful retrospect ("Yet Ah, that Spring should vanish with the Rose! / That Youth's sweet-scented manuscript should close!"), and in his own poems, which he continued to write till the end, he turned again and again to memories of dead friends:

> *Like tides that enter creek or stream,*
> *Ye come, ye visit me, or seem*
> *Swimming out from seas of faces,*
> *Alien myriads memory traces,*
> *To enfold me in a dream!*

In his best poems, such as "The Maldive Shark"—"that pale ravener of horrible meat"—he retrieved images from his mariner past that evoked the eerie serenity of the cruel sea. In "The Berg," a ship sinks slowly in white mist after colliding with a mountain of ice ("The impact made huge ice-cubes fall / Sullen, in tons that crashed the deck")—an almost mute event that disturbs neither the massive berg nor the "seals, dozing sleek on [its] sliddery edges," nor the "slimy slug that sprawls / Along thy dead indifference of walls," but drowns a host of human lives.* In the last section of *Clarel,* probably composed in the early 1870s, Melville likened the swelling and ebbing tones of a church organ to the sound of drowning mariners whose "cries decrease— / The voices in their ferment cease: / One wave rolls over all and whelms to peace."

*Robert Penn Warren points out (Introduction to *Selected Poems of Herman Melville,* p. 53) the startling similarity between Melville's sea-slug and the worm in Thomas Hardy's great poem on the sinking of the *Titanic,* "The Convergence of the Twain": "Over the mirrors meant / To glass the opulent / The sea-worm crawls—grotesque, slimed, dumb indifferent."

Lizzie had reason to fear that her husband was sinking. Chronic pain in his hands made writing difficult, and even when the pain eased, he was dogged by the old problem of poor handwriting. Late in 1881, he wrote to a friend that "I have been recently improving my penmanship by lessons from a High Dutch professor who teaches all the stylish flourishes imaginable," with the goal of passing the promotion exam (12 percent of the grade was awarded for penmanship) and thus increasing his salary. As Melville's biographer Hershel Parker points out, the so-called Dutch professor was probably himself.

There were some mitigations. His works were enjoying a small revival in England, championed by writers who today are footnotes in histories of the Fabian and Pre-Raphaelite movements. In August 1885, the British magazine *Academy* published a bit of verse by one Robert Buchanan, who praised Melville as "my sea-magician" at the expense of such "haberdashers" as Howells:

> *Melville, whose magic drew Typee*
> *Radiant as Venus, from the sea,*
> *Sits all forgotten or ignored,*
> *While haberdashers are adored!*

Upon the publication in 1888 of his small book of poems *John Marr and Other Sailors,* Melville received a favorable squib in the *New York Mail and Express* noting his "vein of true poetical feeling," and the following year he got a letter from his Canadian admirer, Archibald MacMechan (later to be instrumental in reviving Melville's reputation), praising the "unique merits" of *Moby-Dick* and regretting that they "have never received due recognition." MacMechan was more accurate than he knew. On March 4, 1887, Melville received his final royalty statement from Harper & Brothers, which had not reprinted any of his books since 1876.

He had become so thoroughly obscure that Henry James, despite the immense scope of his literary awareness, mentions him only once in all his critical writing, as part of the "Putnam's group" that included George W. Curtis and "Ik Marvel" (Donald G. Mitchell), author of such light diversions as *Reveries of a Bachelor,* all of whom James recalled in 1898 as minor writers of "prose, as mild and easy as an Indian summer in the woods." That other literary representative of fin de siècle New York, Edith Wharton, a woman of not quite thirty when Melville died, wrote in her memoir that "as for Herman Melville," he was "a cousin of the Van Rensselaers, and qualified by birth to figure in the best society," but was "doubtless excluded by his deplorable Bohemianism." By the 1930s, she had become aware of him, yet in the 1880s—a bookish young woman, living in the same city—Wharton "never heard his name mentioned, or saw one of his books."

With the legacies from Lizzie's aunt and brother, Melville was able to bear at least the financial cost of his failure. A few years earlier, Lizzie had written anxiously ("it is hard enough to get along at all") to her stepmother that she and Herman lived in fear that his "pay should be reduced, as so many others have." But now they were free from this worry for the first time since the start of their marriage. She gave him a monthly allowance so he could browse the curio shops, build up his collection of maritime prints, and even frame those he had bought—recklessly, some thought—in the years when money was scarce.

He took pleasure as well in visits from his granddaughters. Eleanor (born in 1882) recalled much later that her grandfather's study, with its high bookcases "topped by strange plaster heads that peered along the ceiling level, or bent down, searching blindly with sightless balls," had seemed menacing; but once she dared to enter, she was rewarded with one of the sticky sweet figs he kept on his desk. Eleanor's younger sister, Frances (the girl whom Melville, in his absentmindedness, may once have left behind in Madison Square), was less daunted. "I could play with anything on those days when I was invited into the study," she recalled much later. "Sometimes I piled books into houses on the floor." Since they were "not too heavy to handle and of a nice palish blue color," her favorite building blocks were the volumes of Schopenhauer.

Without children to break the quiet (the Melvilles' last resident daughter, Bessie, was thirty-three in 1885, and afflicted with arthritis), the household was susceptible to gloom. There was a back porch on which Herman liked to smoke, but the house itself was short on daylight, since the front, where the larger windows were situated, faced north. On a visit in 1883, Julian Hawthorne found his late father's friend "pale, sombre, nervous," obsessively getting in and out of his chair in order to open or close the parlor window.[*]

Death was circling, and with increasing frequency it swooped in for a kill. Allan Melville had died suddenly and long ago, in 1872. By the spring of 1884, Herman and Lizzie had lost as well their brothers Tom and Lemuel Junior. The following year, Allan Melville's daughter Lucy, not yet thirty years old, fell ill and slipped quickly away; that July, Melville's sister Fanny died, having been tormented by bone tumors. Then, in February 1886, death

---

[*]Julian, whom Melville had hoisted onto his horse some thirty years before, had by the 1880s become something of a literary posturer, and later would be sent to prison for taking part in a stock swindle.

Stanwix Melville

struck far away but close to home: Stanwix, who had failed at everything
from the wholesale business to mining and dentistry, died alone in a San
Francisco hotel. Since the death of his older brother nearly twenty years earlier, Stanny had been the focus of his parents' hopes. A sensitive boy, he was,
according to his mother, susceptible to "bowel trouble," and, ever eager not
to disappoint, always promised more than he could deliver, leaving his parents in a state of chronic worry about his future.

Through a heartbreaking series of letters that begins in his early twen-
ties, one may follow Stanny's fluctuating plans—as a sheep farmer ("the most
profitable business in California," his mother wrote to his grandmother, "if
Stanny will only persevere . . ."), in the iron and steel business, finally as a
dentist—only to discover some disinclination or disability that dashed his
hopes and left him each time with less reserve on which to draw for trying
again. Having discovered in 1873, when he was twenty-two, that his near-
sightedness posed a "serious obstacle" to his dream of becoming a "number
one dentist," he wrote to his kindhearted grandmother Hope Savage Shaw
that "fate is against me in most of my undertakings."

Months after Stanny's miserable end thirteen years later at age thirty-
five, Melville's sister Helen found Lizzie "unable to find solace for her grief—
it was *so* hard,—the sickness and death so far away!" And there was, of
course, the merciless presence of the ghost of Malcolm, who had died so
long ago in his room upstairs. As Melville wrote in the headnote to his poem
"John Marr," "while the acuter sense of his bereavement becomes mollified
by time, the void at heart abides."

That same headnote contains another touch of self-portraiture:

As the growing sense of his environment threw him more and more upon retrospective musings, these phantoms . . . became spiritual companions, losing something of their first indistinctness and putting on at last a dim semblance of mute life; and they were lit by that aureola circling over any object of the affections in the past for reunion with which an imaginative heart passionately yearns.

3.

Around the time that Melville wrote those words, most likely in 1886, he had begun composing another sailor's reminiscence in verse, possibly intended for inclusion in *John Marr and Other Sailors*. It was called "Billy in the Darbies" ("darbies" was nautical slang for handcuffs), expressing a sailor's thoughts on the night before he is to be executed for plotting mutiny:

> Good of the chaplain to enter Lone Bay
> And down on his marrowbones here and pray
> For the likes just o' me, Billy Budd.—But, look:
> Through the port comes the moonshine astray!
> It tips the guard's cutlass and silvers this nook;
> But 'twill die in the dawning of Billy's last day.
> A jewel-block they'll make of me tomorrow,
> Pendant pearl from the yardarm-end
> Like the eardrop I gave to Bristol Molly—
> O, 'tis me, not the sentence they'll suspend.
> Ay, ay, all is up; and I must up too,
> Early in the morning, aloft from alow.
> On an empty stomach now never it would do.
> They'll give me a nibble—bit o' biscuit ere I go.
> Sure, a messmate will reach me the last parting cup;
> But, turning heads away from the hoist and the belay,
> Heaven knows who will have the running of me up!
> No pipe to those halyards.—But aren't it all sham?
> A blur's in my eyes; it is dreaming that I am.
> A hatchet to my hawser? All adrift to go?

The drum roll to grog, and Billy never know?
But Donald he has promised to stand by the plank;
So I'll shake a friendly hand ere I sink.
But—no! It is dead then I'll be, come to think.
I remember Taff the Welshman when he sank.
And his cheek it was like the budding pink.
But me they'll lash in hammock, drop me deep.
Fathoms down, fathoms down, how I'll dream fast asleep.
I feel it stealing now. Sentry, are you there?
Just ease these darbies at the wrist,
And roll me over fair!
I am sleepy, and the oozy weeds about me twist.

The subject of mutiny had strong personal bearing for Melville. In the 1840s, his cousin Guert Gansevoort had been a junior officer aboard the U.S. brig-of-war *Somers* while Melville was whaling in the Pacific, and when suspicions of a mutinous plot arose aboard the *Somers* during a peacetime cruise, a shipboard court of inquiry, of which Guert Gansevoort was a member, found insufficient evidence to convict. But under pressure from the captain, the court reconvened and ultimately returned guilty verdicts for three men, who were subsequently hanged. Although young Guert stoutly claimed that "the consciousness of having done my duty shall ever sustain me," he returned from his tour of duty aboard the *Somers* so shaken that, though he was barely thirty, he struck his family as "an infirm man of seventy." The burden of the decision in which he had participated stayed with him all his life.

At some point after the completion of the poem, Melville's mind moved outward—perhaps propelled by memories of his cousin, to whom he had alluded in his poem "Bridegroom Dick"—from the interior consciousness of the condemned man to the officers who have brought him to the brink of execution. A prose work began to grow out of the poem and soon surpassed it. In its earlier drafts, the poem is sung by a "tarry hand" who wants to memorialize his shipmate, a man of the world who over the years has given out more than his share of trinkets to buy favors in port. But as the work developed, the poem fell out of tune with the prose, and the seasoned Billy of the ballad became an ingenuous boy—one of those whom Melville had called (in *John Marr*) "unworldly servers of the world."

More child than man, this beautiful child was an amalgam of Melville's lost sons. While continuing to revise and tinker, Melville noted in the manuscript on April 19, 1891, that the ballad spoken in the voice of the original Billy should be moved to the end of the story. It survives in the published version of *Billy Budd* as one of those "ragged edges" that he never trimmed, a trace of what had once been a story about a salty old sailor caught scheming but that became the story of a boy defamed.

We first meet the new Billy aboard a merchant ship, tellingly named *Rights-of-Man,* on which he is adored by officers and crew alike, including the rough and tough among them. He is a boy of radiant beauty, "and despite his all but fully developed frame, in aspect looked even younger than he really was, owing to a lingering adolescent expression in the as yet smooth face all but feminine in purity of natural complexion." When the *Rights* is boarded by a naval lieutenant on a mission of impressment from a nearby warship (Melville had originally called the ship *Indomitable,* but changed the name to *Bellipotent,* a Latin compound meaning warpower), the predatory officer immediately spots Billy and orders him to go below to pack his belongings for the trip to his new home. While waiting for his prize conscript, the officer invites himself down to the captain's cabin to take some grog. With "rueful reproach," the disconcerted host says, "Lieutenant, you are going to take my best man from me." Drawing back the tumbler "preliminary to a replenishing," the unwelcome visitor gives a dismissive response: "Yes, I know, Yes, I know. Sorry."

With this legal kidnapping, Melville lifts the story out of history into allegory. Although he fixes the date in the summer of 1797, the action seems to take place in a murky long-ago, "in the time before steamships," when the idea of the rights of man was only just stirring. And though we hear of the recent death of Admiral Nelson at Trafalgar in the war against Napoleon (a passage that Melville omitted, then restored) and of actual uprisings in the British fleet, Melville showed little interest in achieving period-piece fidelity. *Billy Budd* was less a work of historical fiction than a kind of parable or fable.

It had become the story of a boy doomed by his physical and moral beauty. When the bluff officer breaks into the dreamworld where Billy has been living on borrowed time, he takes him by force. And though the fatherly captain of the *Rights-of-Man* is powerless to save him, he cannot suppress a protest: "A virtue went out of him," he says of Billy, "sugaring the sour ones. . . . Ay, Lieutenant, you are going to take away the jewel of 'em; you are going to take away my peacemaker!" To this cry of parental emotion, the lieutenant replies with a sneer, in the form of a blasphemous paraphrase of the Sermon on the Mount:

> "Well," said the lieutenant, who had listened with amused interest to all this and now was waxing merry with his tipple; "well, blessed are the peacemakers, especially the fighting peacemakers. And such are the

seventy-four beauties some of which you see poking their noses out of the portholes of yonder warship lying to for me," pointing through the cabin window at the *Bellipotent*.

These words, meant to be jocular, are an ominous forecast of the world that Billy is about to enter. As he is rowed across to the waiting warship, we get a preview of where he is going when, "in a terrible breach of naval decorum . . . the new recruit jumped up from the bow where the coxswain had directed him to sit, and waving hat to his silent shipmates sorrowfully looking over at him from the taffrail, bade the lads a genial good-bye." Then Billy sang out, "And good-bye to you too, old *Rights-of-Man*." The conscripting lieutenant is outraged, having detected in the boy's words "a covert sally . . . a sly slur at impressment in general, and that of himself in especial." With a roar, he orders him: "Down, sir!"

But Billy intends no coded defiance. Irony is beyond him. "The will to it and the sinister dexterity were alike wanting," and he is equally incapable of recognizing irony when he encounters it from others. "A novice in the complexities of factitious life," he says exactly what he feels, like a child bidding goodbye to a parent with emotion laid bare. He is a man of integrity in the root sense of being whole, undivided: "to deal in double meanings and insinuations of any sort was quite foreign to his nature."

What we have here is a pure instantiation of Melville's erstwhile faith that at sea men free themselves from the layers of pretense with which they conceal themselves ashore. Billy exemplifies what Melville had written long before in *Mardi*—that on the ocean, "the contact of one man with another is too near and constant to favor deceit. . . . Vain all endeavors to assume qualities not yours, or to conceal those you possess. Incognitos, however desirable, are out of the question." Billy is not a character whom one would expect to meet in the incidental fiction of Melville's younger contemporaries Howells or James; his portrait is not assembled out of distinctive features of speech or gesture or telltale preferences in what he eats or wears or wants. He has no sense of himself as a social being ("of self-consciousness he seemed to have little or none") and no strategy for getting along in the world. In his transparent simplicity, he is like one of those speechless angels imagined by religious ecstatics—a creature who does not need the gross and cumbersome instrument of language to mediate between himself and the human world.* With Billy, surface and interior are one. His inner self moves out-

---

*Jonathan Edwards, for instance, writes that in heaven "the glorious saints . . . will have ways of expressing the concord of their minds by some other emanations than sounds." Edward Hickman, ed., *The Works of Jonathan Edwards,* 2 vols. (Boston, 1834), II, 619.

ward not through spoken words calibrated to the expectations of others but in the uncalculated form of spontaneous music: "He was illiterate; he could not read, but he could sing, and like the illiterate nightingale was sometimes the composer of his own song."

Like Adam before the fall, Billy is sensuously alive without having arrived at a defined masculinity or femininity; his body tends toward androgyny—combining the repose "which the Greek sculptor . . . gave to his heroic strong man, Hercules" with a delicacy suggested by his "ear, small and shapely, the arch of the foot, the curve in mouth and nostril . . . but, above all, something in the mobile expression, and every chance attitude and movement, something suggestive of a mother eminently favored by Love and the Graces." A literary descendant of Adonis, he is also a forebear of the beautiful boy Tadzio in Thomas Mann's *Death in Venice,* whose "expression of sweet and divine gravity . . . recalled Greek sculpture of the noblest period." Billy is Melville's version of the sacred idea of *beforeness:* what man had been before he acquired the sense of boundary between himself and others (between what Emerson called the "Me" and the "Not-Me"), or the urge toward sex, with its concomitant strife and guilt, or the consciousness of death as dissolution and extinction rather than transition into some higher form of life. Billy is the Romantic dream personified—the dream of man restored to the integrity he had possessed before (again in Emerson's phrase) man "became . . . disunited with himself."

Having dropped into the world from "a period prior to Cain's city and citified man," this child has no history, at least none of which he is aware. To the mustering officer's question, "Who was your father?," he can only answer, "God knows, sir"—explaining that he is a foundling, having been discovered in a "silk-lined basket [left] hanging one morning from the knocker of a good man's door." With this portrait of Billy as a visitor from the prelapsarian world, Melville was revisiting for the last time the heartfelt theme to which he had given voice in *Moby-Dick:*

Men may seem detestable as joint stock-companies and nations; knaves, fools, and murderers there may be; men may have mean and meagre faces; but man, in the ideal, is so noble and so sparkling, such a grand and glowing creature, that over any ignominious blemish in him all his fellows should run to throw their costliest robes.

Yet if Billy Budd is Melville's reprise of "man, in the ideal," he does have a defect: he stammers. "Under sudden provocation of strong heart-feeling," he is afflicted by an "organic hesitancy" that will turn out to be his fatal flaw.

He may be an emissary from Eden, but like Adam he is vulnerable to the mischief of Satan—and his story will be nothing less than the story of the fall of man.

4.

Once Billy has crossed over from the *Rights-of-Man* to the *Bellipotent*, the story properly begins. Satan is aboard, and his name is John Claggart. He is the "master-at-arms," an office that bears the name of its original function of training men in the use of sword and cutlass, but that in the age of gunpowder has evolved into the job of doling out punishment for minor infractions and reporting to superior officers any sign of trouble in the crew. Darkhaired, with skin the amber "hue of time-tinted marbles," Claggart seems once to have occupied a place of ease and leisure in the world ashore. Men below him construe his haughtiness as contempt, while those above him must endure his sycophancy. He is regarded by his inferiors with fear and hatred and by his superiors with suspicion and distaste, but he is very good at his job, to which he brings a "peculiar ferreting genius" for sniffing out sedition.

Like Billy's, Claggart's history is obscure. "The two men," as Hannah Arendt has written, "come, socially speaking, from nowhere." And like Billy's, Claggart's physical delicacy suggests some past life in which he had not worked much with his hands. "He looked like a man of high quality . . . who for reasons of his own was keeping incog," and so he is the subject of gossip. Perhaps he is a foreign-born nobleman, a "*chevalier* who had volunteered into the King's navy by way of compounding for some mysterious swindle whereof he had been arraigned at the King's Bench." But all attempts to discover Claggart's true identity are futile. "About as much was really known . . . of the master-at-arms' career before entering the service as an astronomer knows about a comet's travels prior to its first observable appearance in the sky."

In Claggart, we meet Billy's dark twin. He is the demon to Billy's angel, and a terrible collision between them feels as inevitable as the working out of a Greek tragedy. When an old Danish sailor, using Claggart's nickname, warns the boy that "Jemmy Legs is down on you," Billy is bewildered. Claggart, after all, has been all smiles and compliments: " '*Jemmy Legs!*,' ejaculated Billy, his welkin eyes expanding. 'What for? Why, he calls me "the sweet and pleasant young fellow," they tell me.' " " 'Does he so?,' grinned the grizzled one; then said, 'Ay, Baby lad, a sweet voice has Jemmy Legs.' " When Billy persists in disbelieving ("I seldom pass him but there comes a pleasant word"), the old sailor makes a point that is beyond the boy's comprehension: " 'And that's because he's down upon you, Baby Budd.' " In Melville's allegory, Claggart's appointed role is to play the part of irony—or, to put it more broadly, to be the voice of the fallen world. The more he seems to fawn on Billy, the more his hatred grows; the more he witnesses Billy's purity, the more he wants to corrupt it. He is Satan redivivus, intent on bringing down God's favorite until the child crawls beside him in the dust.

Although Melville had created in Claggart one of the most chilling representations of evil in literature, he could not explain his own creation: "His portrait I essay, but shall never hit it." Claggart has been scarred by some irretrievable experience, but unlike Ahab or the Indian-hater of *The Confidence-Man,* he cannot be accounted for by some past trauma or wound. Melville puts the insoluble problem in interrogative form: "What was the matter with the master-at-arms?" It is a question, he says, that ought to lead us back to what St. Paul in II Thessalonians calls "the mystery of iniquity," but since religion has lost its explanatory power ("the doctrine of man's Fall . . . now popularly ignored"), Claggart seems nothing more than a brute fact without metaphysical significance. He is a version of what Coleridge, describing Iago, the satanic figure in Shakespeare's *Othello,* called "motiveless malignity"—a monster of indeterminate origin, without a part to play in any larger design.

In *Billy Budd,* Melville was dramatizing in advance Wallace Stevens's insight that "the death of Satan was a tragedy for the imagination." Having lost the means to explain "elemental evil" (Melville's phrase for Claggart), we can only stand before it, like Billy, bewildered and dumb.

5·

However timeless its theme, *Billy Budd* is set at a particular historical moment: at the height of the Napoleonic Wars, when the aftershocks of the French Revolution were still being felt, and England was regarded by some as the last bulwark against anarchy, by others as the bastion of reaction. The *Bellipotent* is a floating outpost of the British Empire, a weapon deployed to defend the old order at a time when (these are, once again, Emerson's words) "the opinion of the million" was coming to a boil; and to keep it from spilling over required a "layer of soldiers; over that, a layer of lords; and a king on the top; with clamps and hoops of castles, garrisons, and police."

Aboard the *Bellipotent*, Claggart is "chief of police." As such, he is the man on whom the captain relies to snuff out any spark of the rebellion that has been threatening to ignite the fleet. There have lately been uprisings put down and followed by executions, some in far-flung places, off Cadiz and in the West Indies, others just a few miles from Britain's home shore, at Spithead (a small landmass between Portsmouth and the Isle of Wight) and at Nore (a sandbank at the mouth of the Thames). "To the British empire," Melville explains with a vividly persuasive analogy, "the Nore Mutiny was what a strike in the fire brigade would be to London threatened by general arson." Things have reached the point where officers "stand with drawn swords behind the men working the guns."

In this respect, *Billy Budd,* though set at sea in the distant past, was also a book about the time and place in which Melville was living when he wrote it. America, too, in the 1880s stood on the verge of war with itself—a nation, as one contemporary observer put it, where "workmen are denied the right of organization for self-protection," and where, when they try to organize, "a hireling army . . . is established to shoot them down." This was not a sensationalist claim. After Federal troops had been withdrawn in 1877 from the former Confederate states, soldiers were redeployed—sometimes as state militiamen, sometimes as mercenaries—to keep order among restive workers in the North. Private armies of "security" guards patrolled America's railroad yards and factories, while one New York newspaper editorialized that what was needed was a New World Napoleon—someone who knew that "the one way to deal with a mob is to exterminate it."

With wages suppressed and prices inflated by the trusts that controlled the nation's commodities (oil, grain, steel) and services (railroads, shipping, urban transit), the vast majority of agricultural and industrial laborers possessed no rights at all. Tension between owners and workers broke out periodically into violence. Twelve people were killed by the Maryland militia during a wildcat strike in 1877 against the Baltimore & Ohio Railroad. Soon thereafter, nearly sixty died as strikers against the Pennsylvania Railroad were attacked in Pittsburgh by hired thugs. In March 1886, in a violent strike that took place not far from the Melvilles' home, thousands of Manhattan streetcar workers demanded relief from seventeen-hour workdays, supported by crowds that blocked the tracks, which the transport company tried to keep open by using scab labor. In May of that same year, a rally in Chicago protesting the killing of a picket at a McCormick harvester plant ended with several police officers dead from a dynamite bomb, and with many more in the crowd shot by the police in reaction. Eighteen months later, four self-avowed anarchists, whose connection to the bombing was never established, were hanged.

Melville left no letters, journal entries, or reported remarks by which we might know directly his response to these events. But in comparing Billy Budd to "a young horse fresh from the pasture suddenly inhaling a vile whiff from some chemical factory," he left a clue. *Billy Budd* was his eulogy for the hopes of his youth, when he had written (in *Redburn* and *White-Jacket*) about poverty and fear as if these were rare European imports and aberrant in America. *Billy Budd* is about the loss of the democratic ideal. It is about a society where the "people" (the naval term for ordinary seamen) have turned sullen and the officers tense. Mutiny feels imminent. By the time Melville wrote *Billy Budd,* he had seen his country go from being the vanguard nation of what he had once called "divine equality" to a nation deeply divided between poverty and wealth. He had seen the party of abolition become the party of big business. He had witnessed the principle of inalienable rights perverted into a legal rationale by which giant corporations secured inviolable rights for themselves. In Melville's youth, suspicion of government had been institutionalized in government itself; but, as Howells remarked with sharp irony about the Haymarket hangings, Americans were living now in a "free Republic [that] killed five men for their opinions." Included in Howells's body count was a fifth defendant who committed suicide in prison.

Melville had seen the country he had once celebrated as democracy's New Jerusalem ("the seed is sown," he had written in *Redburn,* "and the harvest must come; and our children's children, on the world's jubilee morning, shall all go with their sickles to the reaping") descend into what one contemporary called "European conditions" of misery for the many and luxury for the few. The city of his childhood had become the headquarters of oligarchic capitalism, where uptown millionaires ("Mammonite freebooters," he called them in *Clarel*) hosted treasure hunts at their country estates, burying diamonds in the lawn and furnishing their friends with golden trowels. Downtown, immigrants lived in windowless rooms that doubled as sweatshops and had to go outside to relieve themselves into holes in the ground covered (sometimes) by a few boards. At Park Row, near where Melville had worked some fifty years earlier at a spare desk in his brothers' law office, the newspaper magnate Joseph Pulitzer erected a building that soared higher than the spire of Trinity Church, topped off with a gilded dome.

Forty years before he wrote *Billy Budd,* Melville had written in *White-Jacket* that, for Americans, the

Past is dead, and has no resurrection; but the Future is endowed with
such a life, that it lives to us even in anticipation. The Past is, in many
things, the foe of mankind; the Future is, in all things, our friend. In the
Past is no hope; the Future is both hope and fruition. The Past is the
text-book of tyrants; the Future the Bible of the Free. Those who are
solely governed by the Past stand like Lot's wife, crystallized in the act
of looking backward, and forever incapable of looking before.

But in *Clarel,* in the voice of Mortmain, he had warned himself, "Come, thou
who makest such hot haste / To forge the future—weigh the past." Aboard
the *Rights-of-Man,* Billy Budd is a citizen of Melville's "old imagined America"; but once he boards the *Bellipotent,* he becomes, like Melville himself, a
stranger in a strange land.

6.

So the *Bellipotent,* no less than the *Pequod,* was a floating symbol of
Melville's America—but the captain who rules over it is nothing like Ahab.
Captain the Honourable Edward Fairfax Vere is a Burkean conservative, a
learned man with that "bias toward those books to which every serious mind
of superior order occupying any active post of authority in the world naturally inclines." He understands the fragility of the standing order to whose
defense he has pledged himself. He is a bulwark against the revolutionary
furies that, "like live cinders blown across the Channel from France,"
threaten to ignite fortress England, and "a dike against those invading waters
of novel opinion social, political, and otherwise, which carried away as in a
torrent" the minds of democratic dreamers.

Much of the power of *Billy Budd* stems from the way Melville writes
about this man, as if Vere were that part of himself that has given up the
dreams of youth and given itself over to prudence. Melville takes seriously
Vere's conviction that society is held together by a delicate web of codes and
constraints, and that even a small shock to the structure can send it tumbling
into chaos. "With mankind," Vere believes, "forms, measured forms, are
everything." Claggart, too, takes this view seriously, and thereby finds his
opening. In his capacity as "chief of police," he is obliged to report to Vere
any hint of restiveness in the crew, and like many in his trade before and
since, he resorts to entrapment in order to have something to report. To infil-

trate and tempt the hired men, he employs an agent, a "tool for laying little traps" aptly nicknamed Squeak, a diminutive squealer who pokes and prods at this crewman or that with a promise of money or liberty and then runs back to Claggart with the news when anyone takes the bait.

Claggart's prime target is Billy. So Squeak arranges one warm night for one of his own minions to wake Billy with a whispered temptation. Bending close to the ear of the boy while he is still in the haze of half-sleep, Squeak's man murmurs that some of the impressed sailors have hatched a plan to free themselves from involuntary service—and wouldn't Billy care to join them? Billy, roused, shooes the man away with a stuttering no: "D—d—damme, I don't know what you are d—d—driving at, or what you mean, but you had better g—g—go where you belong!" But, since "it never entered [Billy's] mind that here was a matter which . . . it was his duty . . . to report," he has given Claggart what he needs to accuse him of fomenting mutiny.

The scene in which Claggart calls on Vere to make the accusation is a masterpiece of stagecraft. Having taken himself to the customary spot where petty officers are permitted to beg the captain for a moment's audience, Claggart stands there "deferentially . . . with the air of a subordinate grieved at the necessity of being a messenger of ill tidings." Vere, pacing the deck, notices him and is flooded with the "repellent distaste" one feels at some petitioner whose deference means that he is about to make a demand. Claggart does not disappoint him. To Captain Vere's "Well? What is it, Master-at-arms?" he performs a *danse macabre* around his point, insinuating that he suspects at least one dangerous man among those "who had entered his Majesty's service under another form than enlistment." Vere barks back, "Be direct, man; say *impressed men,*" and with "a gesture of subservience," Claggart gets to the point. Alluding to the Nore Mutiny, he reports "something clandestine" among the men and declares that the ringleader is "William Budd, a foretopman, your honor."

Vere is astonished. Claggart parries his doubt by pointing out that Billy's charm is precisely what makes him dangerous. "You have but noted his fair cheek," he tells the captain; Billy is the "mantrap . . . under the ruddy-tipped daisies." But the charge strikes Vere as a calumny, and he minces no words in reply—"Stay . . . heed what you speak . . . in a case like this, there is a yardarm-end for the false witness"—and then follows up with a plan "practically [to] test the accuser" by compelling Claggart to repeat the charge face-to-face with Billy in the captain's quarters.

A man of "exceptional moral quality," who strives to uphold both law and justice, Vere knows that Claggart is a liar and that Billy is incapable of lying. As the scene shifts to the cabin, the stage is set for the confrontation between them:

With the measured step and calm collected air of an asylum physician approaching in the public hall some patient beginning to show indications of a coming paroxysm, Claggart deliberately advanced within short range of Billy and, mesmerically looking him in the eye, briefly recapitulated the accusation.

Not at first did Billy take it in. When he did, the rose-tan of his cheek looked struck as by white leprosy. He stood like one impaled and gagged. Meanwhile, the accuser's eyes, removing not as yet from the blue dilated ones, underwent a phenomenal change, their wonted rich violet color blurring into a muddy purple. Those lights of human intelligence, losing human expression, were gelidly protruding like the alien eyes of certain uncatalogued creatures of the deep. The first mesmeristic glance was one of serpent fascination; the last was as the paralyzing lurch of the torpedo fish.

Billy stands stunned and mute, with "an expression like that of a condemned vestal priestess in the moment of being buried alive," while the captain, in a tone somewhere between commanding and beseeching, urges him to "Speak, man! . . . Defend yourself!" Then, recognizing the blockage in the boy's speech, Vere tries to calm him: "There is no hurry, my boy. Take your time, take your time." But these "words so fatherly in tone, . . . touching Billy's heart," only stymie the boy further until his obstructed passion bursts forth in the concentrated fury of a single blow to Claggart's forehead and the master-at-arms falls dead.

" 'Fated boy,' breathed Captain Vere in tone so low as to be almost a whisper, 'what have you done!' " With Billy's help, and with the feeling of revulsion one has in "handling a dead snake," he props the corpse into a sitting position. And then, in a brilliantly rendered scene of metamorphosis, Melville describes Vere's transformation from father to lawgiver:

> Regaining erectness, Captain Vere with one hand covering his face stood to all appearance as impassive as the object at his feet. . . . Slowly he uncovered his face; and the effect was as if the moon emerging from eclipse should reappear with quite another aspect than that which had gone into hiding. The father in him, manifested towards Billy thus far in the scene, was replaced by the military disciplinarian. In his official tone, he bade the foretopman retire to a stateroom aft (pointing it out), and there remain till thence summoned.

When, at Vere's behest, the ship's surgeon enters to confirm the death, he finds the captain agitated in a way that no one aboard has ever seen him.

"Catching the surgeon's arm convulsively," Vere exclaims, making reference to the biblical story of Ananias, who having "lied . . . unto God" (Acts 5:3–5), suffers miraculous death: "It is the divine judgment on Ananias! Look! . . . Struck dead by an angel of God! Yet the angel must hang!"*

7.

Every reader of *Billy Budd* asks, Why? Why must Billy die? Why does Melville seem to side with Vere, who insists that the prescribed penalty be applied to the slandered boy? And why does Vere rush to punishment, since he sees Billy as God's unconscious agent in ridding the world of the beast? The answers lie in the crystal clarity of the Royal Navy's Articles of War: "If any officer, mariner, soldier, or other person in the fleet, shall strike any of his superior officers, or draw, or offer to draw, or lift any weapon against him, being in the execution of his office, *on any pretence whatsoever,* every such person being convicted of such offence, by the sentence of a court martial, shall suffer death. . . ."

The march toward Billy's execution is unbearable to watch. Yet that is what Melville now compels us to do. He takes us step by step through the convening of the drumhead court (against the preference of the junior officers that the "matter should be referred to the admiral"), through Billy's testimony as defendant and Vere's as sole witness, then finally to the verdict and the hanging:

> In the jugglery of circumstances preceding and attending the event on board the *Bellipotent,* and in the light of that martial code whereby it was formally to be judged, innocence and guilt personified in Claggart and Budd in effect changed places. In a legal view the apparent victim of the tragedy was he who had sought to victimize a man blameless; and the indisputable deed of the latter, navally regarded, constituted the most heinous of military crimes. Yet more. The essential right and wrong involved in the matter, the clearer that might be, so much the

---

*Melville had seen Raphael's cartoon of *The Death of Ananias* at Hampton Court in 1849, and, since 1871, he had owned a copy of Hazlitt's *Criticism on Art,* which devotes four pages of discussion to that work. See Robert K. Wallace, "Melville's Prints: David Metcalf's Prints and Tile," *Harvard Library Bulletin* 8, no. 4 (Winter 1997): 19.

worse for the responsibility of a loyal sea commander, inasmuch as he
was not authorized to determine the matter on that primitive basis.

This contradiction between a "legal" and "essential" view of events is
the key to *Billy Budd.* All our instincts incline us toward the latter and
toward horrified awareness of its incompatibility with the former, and no one
grasps the discrepancy better than Vere, who, standing before the judges of
the court, articulates what we all feel: "How can we adjudge to summary and
shameful death a fellow creature innocent before God, and whom we feel to
be so?—Does that state it aright?"

One of the judges, groping for some reason to defer judgment, wonders
aloud if there is anyone in "the ship's company . . . who might shed lateral
light . . . upon what remains mysterious in this matter."

"That is thoughtfully put," said Captain Vere; "I see your drift. Ay,
there is a mystery; but, to use a scriptural phrase, it is a 'mystery of iniquity,' a matter for psychologic theologians to discuss. But what has a
military court to do with it? Not to add that for us any possible investigation of it is cut off by the lasting tongue-tie of—him—in yonder,"
again designating the mortuary stateroom. "The prisoner's deed—with
that alone we have to do."

Insisting that the transcendent question of good and evil be kept strictly
apart from the business of enforcing the military rules, Vere choreographs
the scene by placing himself before the porthole, his back to the officers of
the court as he stands gazing out upon "the monotonous blank of the twilight sea." He knows that the "critical ocean" (Melville's phrase from *Moby-
Dick*) dissolves all norms, and so he insists that his officers avert their eyes
from the sea and keep them fixed on the cramped little world of naval codes
and precedents in which they have agreed to expend their lives. This is the
profoundest sense in which *Billy Budd* was, as Melville described it in its
subtitle, an "inside narrative." In a speech that plays a variation on St. Paul's
promise (Acts 17:28) that God is the medium in which "we live, and move,
and have our being," Vere concedes that "it is Nature" to feel sorrow and pity
for the man they are about to convict:

But do these buttons that we wear attest that our allegiance is to
Nature? No, to the King. Though the ocean, which is inviolate Nature
primeval, though this be the element where we move and have our
being as sailors, yet as the King's officers . . . [our] vowed responsibil-

ity is in this: That however pitilessly that law may operate in any instances, we nevertheless adhere to it and administer it.

Vere does not deny—indeed, he insists—that a vast gulf divides natural from human law, and that good men will want to convert their outrage into some effectual action that might close it. With every moment the court hesitates, the men of the *Bellipotent* are building toward irrepressible anger. To keep Billy aboard while postponing trial, as some officers have proposed, would be (to use an anachronistic analogy) like keeping Nelson Mandela in prison, allowing the legend of the prisoner to grow into a revolutionary myth. To mitigate the sentence would be worse: "*Why?* they will ruminate," says Vere. "You know what sailors are. Will they not revert to the recent outbreak at the Nore? Ay. They know the well-founded alarm—the panic it struck throughout England. Your clement sentence they would account pusillanimous. They would think that we flinch."

As if some mischievous philosopher has dropped by to divert us with an epistemological riddle, Melville opens the debate over Billy's fate with a pair of rhetorical questions: "Who in the rainbow can draw the line where the violet tint ends and the orange tint begins? Distinctly we see the difference of the colors, but where exactly does the one first blendingly enter into the other?"* The answers are implicit in these questions: no one, and nowhere. No one, that is, can make out a demarcation line between the vibrating colors of the rainbow. Even the tough-minded empiricist, having measured the light with his spectrometer, must rely on established norms to say this is violet whereas that is orange. The rainbow was Melville's metaphor for culture. He was writing at just the time when, in William James's phrase, the last vestiges of "tender-minded" faith in "the great universe of God" were fading away, and the metaphor of the rainbow amounts to Melville's corollary of James's remark that "we carve out groups of stars in the heavens, and call them constellations, and the stars patiently suffer us to do so,—though, if they knew what we were doing, some of them might feel much surprised at the partners we had given them." The stars know nothing. All knowing is the work of man. And so, for Melville, as for Vere, our fate as human beings is to live by norms that have no basis in divine truth, but that have functional truth for the conduct of life. These norms are the grammar of culture, and the culture that

*Hershel Parker points out, in his biography (Vol. 2, pp. 15–16), that Melville had likely read a similar passage in an essay by Francis Palgrave: "In considering the actions of the mind, it should never be forgotten that its affections pass into each other like the tints of the rainbow: though we can easily distinguish them when they have assumed a decided colour, yet we can never determine where each hue begins."

Vere has sworn to defend is that of the Royal Navy in time of war. Billy killed an officer. Billy must hang.

As a young man, Melville had pushed against the norms in order to expose them as provincial and suppressive contingencies. If in one culture he found cannibals and polygamists, while in another he found faithful vegetarians, so much the better for an insolent young writer full of skepticism toward all authorities. But in the works of his maturity—*Moby-Dick, Pierre,* "Bartleby," *Benito Cereno*—Melville wrote more and more about the cost of overturning the norms, however contingent they might be. By 1850 he already had become a reformed, if not repentant, romantic, who saw the fragility as well as the deformity of culture; the young Melville had written in outrage about poverty in *Redburn,* and about flogging in *White-Jacket,* but by the time he composed *Billy Budd,* he was not so much outraged as resigned to the disjunction between law and justice. *Billy Budd* was his farewell to what he had called, in *Pierre,* the "beautiful illusions of youth."

Since it was never published in its own day, we cannot know if contemporary readers would have recognized its pertinence to their own times. But to read *Billy Budd* today with some awareness of its contemporary context is to see that it arose from the same historical circumstances that produced such ephemeral books as Ignatius Donnelly's *Caesar's Column* (1891) or Edward Bellamy's *Looking Backward* (1888)—books that described the world as a battleground between the powerful and the powerless, a world on the verge of some radical transformation. In the former case, we get a dystopian vision in which rich and poor are locked in a death struggle leading toward apocalypse; in the latter we get a utopian vision in which the conflict between wealth and poverty has been resolved in a paradise of social equality. In *Billy Budd,* Melville imagined a future of neither public doom nor deliverance. Instead, he wrote about two human beings who, just as they are being swept apart by the forces of history, experience a private moment of redemptive love.

Billy Budd was a story, as Melville put it in a penciled note near the end of the manuscript, about "what sometimes happens in this incomprehensible world of ours," where innocence is doomed by its own infirmity and evil earns "fair repute"—as Claggart does posthumously in the authorized naval account that, like the deposition in *Benito Cereno,* whitewashes what had actually taken place. In the official version of events that is disseminated throughout the fleet, Claggart becomes a man of "strong patriotic impulse" "vindictively stabbed to death by the suddenly drawn sheath knife of Budd," ringleader of a mutinous plot.

In this respect, *Billy Budd* was a book about politics—or at least about the manipulation of truth for political purposes. And ever since it became part of our literary heritage in the 1920s, it often has been cited in debates over the perennial question of what makes authority legitimate and what justifies resistance. Like Conrad's *Heart of Darkness,* it is one of those texts that has generated a body of critical responses (from E. M. Forster, W. H. Auden, Albert Camus, Thornton Wilder, Eugenio Montale, Hannah Arendt, Lionel Trilling, Yvor Winters, Roger Shattuck, and many others) so rich and varied that they may be read as a chronicle of modern intellectual life. In fact, charting the attitudes pro and con toward Captain Vere is one way to follow the contours of twentieth-century political thought. At times of high regard for constituted authority, Vere tends to come off as a heroic figure who, with tragic awareness of his responsibilities, sacrifices an innocent for the sake of the state. At times of public suspicion toward established power, Vere tends to be condemned as a despot whose callous commitment to the letter of the law, "however pitilessly" it grinds the innocent, is ultimately no different from Ahab's doctrinaire will.

In 1947, when many American liberals were still enraptured by the dream of utopia in its Marxian form, Lionel Trilling—in his only novel, *The Middle of the Journey*—invented a fictional character, loosely based on Whittaker Chambers, who is desperate to express his reasons for having left the Communist Party. He does so in the form of an essay on *Billy Budd,* arguing that Melville's great work could no longer be understood by the modern progressive mind, blinded as it is to the "tragedy of Spirit in the world of Necessity." Some forty years later, two prominent legal intellectuals—a left-leaning professor sympathetic to the "critical legal studies" movement that was attacking the law (even within America's leading law schools) as an instrument of class oppression, and a right-leaning judge who saw the law as our bulwark against chaos—fought out their differences over *Billy Budd.* For the former, Vere is a man driven by half-articulated resentments to prosecute a defenseless victim; for the latter, Vere bears the "awesome responsibility" of "sole command of a major warship in a major war" and has no choice but to pursue capital punishment for a defendant who, "in the eyes of the law . . . was guilty of a capital crime."

Whatever we make of Vere, Melville had too much tact to take us into the cabin to witness his informing Billy of the court's decision. Vere enters the cabin not as a father confessor but as a confessing father seeking absolution from his son. To intrude would be to violate a private moment that Melville feels as intensely as if he were bidding farewell to his own child—and so we are required to wait outside.

After Vere steps out, the first to encounter him is the ship's surgeon, who surmises from the agony legible in his captain's face that "the condemned one suffered less than he who mainly had effected the condemnation."

Scholars who have studied the manuscript of *Billy Budd* have shown that Melville repeatedly revised the sections dealing with Vere in order to keep in view the excruciating difficulty of his decision and the good faith with which he makes it.

Faith is the heart of the matter:

> There is no telling the sacrament, seldom if in any case revealed to the gadding world, wherever under circumstances at all akin to those here attempted to be set forth two of great Nature's nobler order embrace. There is privacy at the time, inviolable to the survivor; and holy oblivion, the sequel to each diviner magnanimity, providentially covers all at last.

It is hard to read these words without feeling that Melville had Mackie and Stanny in mind as he wrote them.

When the sentence is carried out next morning at dawn, Billy Budd dies as the Son of Man had died, ascending into the eastern sky "shot through with a soft glory as of the fleece of the Lamb of God," and the last act of his *imitatio Christi* is a variant of Christ's plea for forgiveness on behalf of his tormentors. "God Bless Captain Vere," he sings out in a voice miraculously "unobstructed in the utterance . . . delivered in the clear melody of a singing bird on the point of launching from the twig," and then, as if some "current electric" ran from his heart to the hearts of the men summoned to witness his execution, they shout out a "resonant sympathetic echo: 'God Bless Captain Vere!' "

These words tell us what had happened in the cabin between the "fated boy" and the agonized man who sends him out of the world. But if Billy has reenacted the death of Christ in this tale of sacrifice and redemption, Vere is no Pilate. He is Abraham performing the sacrifice of Isaac, torn to the depths of his soul by the conflict between love and duty—except that in Melville's reprise of the father-and-son story from Genesis, there is no intervention by a merciful God. There is no God at all.

8.

The prose in which Melville wrote this heartrending tale was an altogether different expressive instrument from that of his earlier books. He had made what he had called, in *Pierre,* "that strange transition from the generous impulsiveness of youth to the provident circumspectness of age," and his prose in *Billy Budd* is no longer lush and fleshy. It has become skeletal, more akin to a linear sketch than to the full-palette paintings of forty years before. Yet it is still very intricate. It has not been boiled down to the minimalism of certain modernist writers (Hemingway published his first stories a few years before the first publication of *Billy Budd*), but the layered richness of the early works is gone, leaving the junctures and linkages exposed. The young Melville had worked accretively, piling on variants and synonyms as if repeated iteration (as in such phrases as "umbrageous shade" or "outreaching comprehensiveness") could capture in glutinous language the plenitude of creation. But the words in *Billy Budd* jostle and push against each other, as in the euphemisms for impressment ("arbitrary enlistment," "enforced enlistment"), where the ideas of compulsion and freedom are held tensely together, or in the definition of irony ("sinister dexterity"), in which there is open conflict between the Latin words for left (*sinister*) and right (*dexter*).

Like Vere's conscience, the writing in *Billy Budd* is divided against itself. It is retrospective. It "holds the action at a remove," as one of Melville's finest critics, Warner Berthoff, has put it, and "works by a kind of filtered and distilled recollection"—a mood established even before the tale begins, with the dedication to Melville's old friend Jack Chase:

Dedicated to
JACK CHASE
ENGLISHMAN
Wherever that great heart may now be
Here on Earth or harbored in Paradise
Captain of the Maintop
in the year 1843
in the U.S. Frigate
United States

Melville wrote this work of remembrance while living in a city of faded and fractured memories to which he had returned to live for the second time since his father's disgrace long before. New York was by now a place much like the city we know, a place of skyscrapers and cavernous streets, electrified, increasingly international, crisscrossed by mechanized trains and trolleys with the beginnings of a subway system below, linked to the neighboring municipality of Brooklyn by a traffic-laden suspension bridge that was among the technological marvels of the world. Melville watched this city demolish and rebuild itself, burying a little more each day of what was left of his personal past.

He had found as early as 1870 that not even the proprietor of the Gansevoort Hotel on Little West Twelfth Street, near his "office" at the Hudson piers, had any idea why the establishment bore the Gansevoort name. To Melville's inquiry at the reception desk, "Can you tell me who was this Gansevoort?," he got a blank stare, until a guest who had overheard him spoke up to say that the Gansevoorts were a once rich family formerly with property holdings "hereabouts." Nothing was said, because nothing was known, about the hero of Fort Stanwix. Afterwards, in a letter to his mother, Melville mused "upon the instability of human glory and the evanescence" of all things. By the time he wrote *Billy Budd*, Melville had become a version of one of those characters in the late stories of Henry James, who "seemed to wander through the old years with his hand in the arm of a companion who was, in the most extraordinary manner, his other, his younger self," walking through a half-familiar New York from which "the old people had mostly gone, the old names were unknown," where "here and there an old association seemed to stray, all vaguely, like some very aged person, out too late, whom you might meet and feel the impulse to watch or follow, in kindness, for safe restoration to shelter."

While working on his last masterpiece, Melville was also reworking some of his old unpublished poems; and if we credit the few surviving reports from people who visited him, he spent his waning months wrapped more and more tightly in his memories. The writer who had once declared that "no great and enduring volume can ever be written on the flea" now tinkered with a poem about a chipmunk:

> Heart of autumn!
> Weather meet,
> Like to sherbert
> Cool and sweet.
>
> *Stock-still I stand,*
> *And* him *I see*
> *Prying, peeping*
> *From Beech Tree,*
> *Crickling, crackling*
> *Gleefully!*
> *But, affrighted*
> *By wee sound,*
> *Presto! vanish—*
> *Whither bound?*

> *So did Baby;*
> *Crowing mirth,*
> *E'en as startled*
> *By some inkling*
> *Touching Earth,*
> *Flit (and whither?)*
> *From our hearth!*

In the final line, Melville changed "the hearth" to "our hearth," thereby bringing into focus the personal bearing of the poem on the unbearable brevity of Baby Malcolm's—Mackie's—"peeping" vanished life. "Whither bound?" was his constant question now, as his sons and brothers (all of them) had gone before him, and he expected soon to go himself. His granddaughter Eleanor told Lewis Mumford that in his waning years, Melville liked to grow roses on the patch of land behind the house; but beyond this sort of family lore, if we look for evidence of the writer's mood in his old age, there is little to be found outside the gnomic texts of the late poems.

In one of them, Melville recounted a church experience in which, fallen asleep to the preacher's droning, the speaker describes a vision of paradise:

> *The preacher took from Solomon's Song*
> *Four words for text with mystery rife—*
> *The Rose of Sharon—figuring Him*
> *The Resurrection and the Life;*
> *And, pointing many an urn in view,*
> *How horrid a homily he drew.*
>
> *There, in the slumberous afternoon,*
> *Through minister gray, in lullaby rolled*
> *The hummed metheglin charged with swoon.*
> *Drowsy, my decorous hands I fold*
> *Till sleep overtakes with dream to boon.*
>
> *I saw an Angel with a Rose*
> *Come out of Morning's garden-gate,*
> *And, lamp-like hold the rose aloft.*
> *She entered a sepulchral Strait.*
> *I followed. And I saw the Rose*
> *Shed dappled down upon the dead;*
> *The shrouds and mort-cloths all were lit*
> *To plaids and checquered tartans red.*

> *I woke. The great Rose-window high,*
> *A mullioned wheel in gable set,*
> *Suffused with rich and soft in dye*
> *Where Iris and Aurora met;*
> *Aslant in sheaf of rays it threw*
> *From all its foliate round of panes*
> *Transfiguring light on dingy stains,*
> *While danced the motes in dusty pew.*

We get another glimpse of the old man who wrote this delicate dream-poem in a touching little memoir by a New York bookdealer and antiquarian, Oscar Wegelin, who in 1935 remembered seeing Melville forty-five years earlier in the Nassau Street bookshop where he had been an apprentice. Walking with "rapid stride and almost a sprightly gait," the old man struck the boy as a person of generosity and gentleness. Whenever books were to be delivered to the Melville home, Oscar was eager to take them, since he could always expect a kind word and a tip. To the boy's point of view, Melville cut a deliberately anachronistic figure (his "beard . . . impressive even for those hirsute days"), and though Oscar had heard people say that Mr. Melville was a disappointed and misanthropic man, he never saw him "permit his disappointment to come out into the open."

Melville was still welcome in certain quiet corners of New York's café society, but he mostly preferred to stay away from what he had once called "the party-giving city of New York." His house was close enough to the original Madison Square Garden (demolished in 1928) that he could hear the ruckus of the crowds and see from his second-floor windows the gilded statue of naked Diana (preserved today atop the grand staircase in the Philadelphia Museum of Art) that adorned the tower. It was an easy walk to Delmonico's, where every night the "dining salon was filled with beautiful women and men of national celebrity," but Melville visited these places mainly in his imagination—as when he set his poem "At the Hostelry" at Delmonico's, where he imagines a group of painters, including Tintoretto, Rubens, and Michelangelo, has gathered, having time-traveled to New York.

His brother Allan had belonged to the prestigious Century Association until his death in 1872, but Herman never joined, though not for lack of invitation. In 1882, the directors of the Century, perhaps under the impression that hefty dues were keeping prospective members away, created a subsidiary "Authors Club," which Melville was invited to join for a nominal fee. At first he accepted, then reconsidered, writing (in the club secretary's paraphrase) that "he had become too much of a hermit, saying his nerves could no longer stand huge gatherings and begged to rescind his acceptance."

In 1886, in a notice about some local literati, the New York *Commercial Advertiser* remarked that Herman Melville, "after all his wanderings, loves to stay at home." But Oscar Wegelin knew better. The old man "would take long walks in those latter months, voyaging as far afield as Central Park—a promenade which I doubt if many residents of East Twenty-sixth Street indulge in today." Almost to the end, Melville was out and about in the great city that he had always found both enlarging and enervating. Broadway was not far from his house, and there he still "found some relief," as he had written (about Pierre) nearly forty years earlier, in walking "through the greatest thoroughfare of the city [where] the utter isolation of his soul might feel itself the more intensely from the incessant joggling of his body against the bodies of the hurrying thousands." A British admirer, who thought Melville "the one great imaginative writer fit to stand shoulder to shoulder with Whitman," had the impression that in New York "no one seemed to know anything of him," while another reported that "it was difficult to get more than a passing glimpse of his 'tall, stalwart figure' and grave, preoccupied face." He was, as the scholar Alan Trachtenberg remarks, an "internal exile within the nervous city."

When he did venture out, he stepped into his own past, and would sometimes accept an invitation to talk about it. There are reports that he would drop in "for an hour or two" when asked to this or that literary gathering, and one old acquaintance from sailing days remarked that he "never denied himself to his friends," though "he sought no one" of his own accord. He seemed to know that he would not live to see his genius affirmed, and when he went out "voyaging," he went, as he had always done, alone. He suffered increasingly frequent and virulent infections, from each of which he would emerge weaker than before—portents of death, which he had once called "the King of Terrors," but by which he had never been terrified. In his copy of Hawthorne's story "The Birthmark," which he had first read in 1850, and to which he refers in *Billy Budd,* he underlined a passage in which Hawthorne reflects that to live much beyond the span of three-score years and ten would be to "produce a discord in Nature which all the world, and chiefly the quaffer of the immortal nostrum, would find cause to curse."

Melville did not live long enough to curse himself for outliving his time—though he had survived Hawthorne by more than a quarter century. By the summer of 1891 he was clearly failing, and in the early hours of September 28 he died at home in his iron-framed bed. The doctor wrote "cardiac dilatation" on the death certificate. There was little public awareness (a posthumous reference on October 6 in the *New York Times* garbled Melville's first name), and a private funeral service was held in the house the next day, at which the pastor of All Souls Church spoke briefly. After the house was sold the following

ity, forming an organized body of nearly 1000 men, entered the convict stockade at that place, and set 160 prisoners free; at other mining camps they released, within the next two days, about 300 more. Liberal rewards were promptly offered by the Governor for the arrest of the leaders in this movement, and for the return of the released convicts.

An official statement, published November 10th, showed the public debt of Canada to be $235,000,000 —a considerable increase over the figures of last year.

The Right Hon. Arthur James Balfour, Chief Secretary for Ireland, was appointed, October 17th, to succeed the late William Henry Smith as First Lord of the Treasury in the British cabinet.—On the 23d of October William L. Jackson was appointed to succeed Mr. Balfour as Chief Secretary for Ireland.

The death of Charles Stewart Parnell, on the 7th of October, far from leading to the union of the two Irish political factions, seemed to widen the breach between them. Great bitterness of feeling was exhibited, and several riots occurred. At an election held in Cork November 7th, to choose Mr. Parnell's successor in Parliament, the opposition or McCarthyite candidate received a plurality of votes.

On the 30th of October the French Senate agreed to rescind the law prohibiting the importation of American pork. A similar action was taken by the Italian government a few days earlier.

During the first week in September festivities were held throughout Chili in celebration of the restoration of peace. The provisional government was recognized by the leading European powers.—On the 19th of September General Balmaceda, ex-President of the republic, who since the triumph of the revolutionists had remained in concealment, committed suicide at the Argentine Legation in Santiago. Elections were held October 22d for Presidential electors and members of the Senate and Chamber of Deputies, resulting in a complete victory for the Liberals.—In Valparaiso, October 16th, a mob of Chilians killed two of the crew of the United States cruiser *Baltimore*, and seriously injured several others. Thirty-five of the crew were arrested by the police of Valparaiso, and detained in custody without due cause being shown. The United States government, upon ascertaining the particulars, courteously demanded an explanation or reparation from the Chilian junta. An unfavorable and somewhat defiant reply was made to this demand, but assurances were given that the affair was being investigated.—On the 10th of November the revolutionary junta surrendered its power to the newly elected Congress, and the cabinet which had been appointed by its authority resigned.

A revolt against the government was attempted in Paraguay October 21st, but was promptly quelled, and the insurgents driven into the Argentine Republic, where they were disarmed.

Another revolution was inaugurated in Brazil on the 4th of November. By proclamation of President De Fonseca the Congress was dissolved, martial law was declared, and a dictatorship established, with De Fonseca himself as dictator. This action of the chief magistrate, which was supported by the army and navy, was said to have been provoked by the efforts of the monarchist party in Congress to overthrow republican institutions. The national capital was declared to be in a state of siege for two months, a government censorship over telegraphic despatches was ordered, and it was an-

nounced that an election of new representatives to Congress would be held. Much dissatisfaction existed, especially in the province of Rio Grande do Sul.

Famine prevailed in twenty-one provinces of Russia. Twenty million rubles was expended by the government in buying seed-corn for the peasants in the stricken districts.

Eleven thousand Mohammedan pilgrims to Mecca, Arabia, died of cholera during the summer.

DISASTERS.

September 16th.—Accounts were received of extensive floods in the south of Spain. In the provinces of Toledo and Almeria 2000 persons were drowned, and great destitution prevailed throughout the flooded districts. The damage done to property was estimated at $4,000,000.—In a gale off Labrador three fishing-vessels were wrecked and thirteen persons drowned.

September 25th.—In a railroad accident near Burgos, Spain, fourteen persons were killed and many others injured.

October 26th.—In a railroad accident near Moirans, France, fifteen persons were killed and more than fifty others injured.—The British bark *Charlwood* collided with the steamer *Boston* near the Eddystone Rocks, and immediately foundered. Sixteen persons were drowned.

October 29th.—The steamboat *Oliver Bierne* was burned on the Mississippi River at Milliken's Bend, and twenty lives were lost.

October 30th.—Particulars were received of a terrible earthquake in the island of Hondo, Japan. It was estimated that 7000 persons were killed and nearly 30,000 houses destroyed.

November 8th.—By an explosion of gas in a mine at Nanticoke, Pennsylvania, twelve miners were killed.

November 11th.—A cylone in the Andaman Islands, in the Bay of Bengal, caused the loss of nearly 150 lives. Many vessels at anchor near Calcutta were wrecked.

OBITUARY.

September 25th.—At Saratoga, New York, the Rev. Samuel D. Burchard, D.D., aged seventy-nine years. —In New York city, Henry Kiddle, ex-Superintendent of Public Schools, aged seventy years.

September 27th.—In New York city, Herman Melville, aged seventy-three years.

September 30th.—At Brussels, Belgium, General George Ernest Jean Marie Boulanger, French ex-Minister of War, aged fifty-four years.

October 6th.—In London, England, William Henry Smith, First Lord of the Treasury, Warden of the Cinque Ports, and the Conservative leader in the House of Commons, aged sixty-six years.—In Stuttgart, Germany, King Charles of Würtemberg, aged sixty-eight years.

October 7th.—In Brighton, England, Charles Stewart Parnell, the Irish leader, aged forty-five years.

October 17th.—At Newburyport, Massachusetts, James Parton, author and journalist, aged seventy years.

November 3d.—In Rome, Italy, Prince Louis Lucien Bonaparte, nephew of Napoleon I., aged seventy-eight years.

November 6th.—At St. Albans, Vermont, John Gregory Smith, ex-Governor of Vermont, aged seventy-three years.

*Elizabeth Shaw
Melville, 1894*

spring, Lizzie Melville moved from East Twenty-sixth Street into an apartment hotel eight blocks south, where she did her best to replicate the furnishings of her late husband's study. She took the portrait painted by Joseph Eaton twenty years earlier that had hung in the back parlor and placed it over the mantel in her new library, whose shelves she filled with Herman's books.

In one of them, Isaac Disraeli's *The Literary Character*, Lizzie marked the following passage by Disraeli's widow: "My ideas of my husband . . . are so much associated with his *books*, that to part with them would be as it were breaking some of the last ties which still connect me with so beloved an object. The being in the midst of books he has been accustomed to read, and which contain his *marks* and *notes*, will still give him *a sort of existence* with *me*." On Herman's desk she placed the precious bread box containing his unpublished manuscripts, from which she would extract a poem or two, or a few pages of *Billy Budd*, to show to some interested guest.

Some thirty years later, soon after *Billy Budd* was finally in print, its almost unbearable beauty was recognized not only in Melville's own country but also by such twentieth-century European masters as W. H. Auden, E. M. Forster, and Albert Camus. When Thomas Mann, close to death, came to read it, he called it "the most beautiful story in the world" and, expressing the pardonable envy of one great artist for another, exclaimed: "O could I have written that!" During the second half of the twentieth century, *Billy Budd* was scored for opera by Benjamin Britten and adapted for film by Peter Ustinov, and today it continues to exert an emotional and intellectual force attained by only a very few works of art.

For some readers, the Melville who speaks most directly to the mind and heart is the chastened author of *Billy Budd*. For others, the true Melville will always be the boisterous young author of *Moby-Dick*. Still others have found, with replenished gratitude, that there is a season in life for each.

NOTES

These notes are intended primarily as an aid for locating quoted passages, but I have also elaborated on points where a footnote in the text would have distracted from the narrative. Though I have tried to give some sense here of what I owe to previous scholars, anyone writing about Melville incurs a debt too large to be fully enumerated. For guides to the vast range of Melville scholarship and interpretation, the reader may wish to consult the bibliographies in John Bryant, ed., *A Companion to Melville Studies* (Westport, CT: Greenwood Press, 1986), and Robert Levine, ed., *The Cambridge Companion to Herman Melville* (New York: Cambridge University Press, 1998). For more recent work, a good resource is JSTOR, a continually updated electronic database of journal articles.

With the exception of *Billy Budd*, all quotations from Melville's prose works are cited in the standard Northwestern–Newberry Library edition. Because of their editorial scrupulosity and deeply researched historical commentaries, these volumes are of inestimable value. So that readers using other editions can readily locate quoted passages, I have included chapter numbers as well as page numbers for each reference. In the case of *Billy Budd*, not yet published in the Northwestern–Newberry series, citations are to the Library of America edition, abbreviated as *BB*. Reliable texts of Melville's poems other than *Clarel* can be found in *Collected Poems of Herman Melville*, ed. Howard P. Vincent (Chicago: Hendricks House, 1947), or in *The Poems of Herman Melville*, ed. Douglas Robillard (Kent, OH: Kent State University Press, 2000), and are cited here by individual title.

Melville's works in the Northwestern–Newberry Library edition, and the indispensable chronological sourcebook *The Melville Log*, edited by the pioneering scholar Jay Leyda, are abbreviated as follows:

> T   *Typee: A Peep at Polynesian Life,* ed. Harrison Hayford, Hershel Parker, and G. Thomas Tanselle (1968)
>
> O   *Omoo: A Narrative of Adventures in the South Seas,* ed. Harrison Hayford, Hershel Parker, and G. Thomas Tanselle (1968)
>
> Mardi   *Mardi and A Voyage Thither,* ed. Harrison Hayford, Hershel Parker, and G. Thomas Tanselle (1970)
>
> R   *Redburn, His First Voyage: Being the Sailor-Boy Confessions and Reminiscences of the Son-of-a-Gentleman, in the Merchant Service,* ed. Harrison Hayford, Hershel Parker, and G. Thomas Tanselle (1969)
>
> WJ   *White-Jacket, or the World in a Man-of-War,* ed. Harrison Hayford, Hershel Parker, and G. Thomas Tanselle (1970)

MD *Moby-Dick, or the Whale,* ed. Harrison Hayford, Hershel Parker, and G. Thomas Tanselle (1988)

P *Pierre, or the Ambiguities,* ed. Harrison Hayford, Hershel Parker, and G. Thomas Tanselle (1971)

PT *The Piazza Tales and Other Prose Pieces, 1839–1860,* ed. Harrison Hayford, Alma A. MacDougall, G. Thomas Tanselle, et al. (1987)

IP *Israel Potter: His Fifty Years of Exile,* ed. Harrison Hayford, Hershel Parker, and G. Thomas Tanselle (1982)

CM *The Confidence-Man, His Masquerade,* ed. Harrison Hayford, Hershel Parker, and G. Thomas Tanselle (1984)

Clarel *Clarel: A Poem and Pilgrimage in the Holy Land,* ed. Harrison Hayford, Alma A. MacDougall, Hershel Parker, and G. Thomas Tanselle (1991)

Journals *Journals,* ed. Howard C. Horsford with Lynn Horth (1989)

Correspondence *Correspondence,* ed. Lynn Horth (1993)

Log *The Melville Log: A Documentary Life of Herman Melville, 1819–1891,* Volumes I and II, ed. Jay Leyda (New York: Gordian Press, 1969)

PREFACE

XXI "no materials exist": "Bartleby," in *PT,* p. 13.

XXI "vile habit": HM to Sophia Van Matre, December 10, 1863, in *Correspondence,* p. 387. See *Log,* I, xiii–xv, for a speculative account of several bonfires in which Melville's papers may have been consumed.

XXI The "business" of the biographer: Henry James, *Hawthorne* (1879; New York: St. Martin's Press, 1967), p. 51.

XXI a featureless silhouette: This photograph, first published in *Melville Society Extracts* 116 (February 1999), was discovered by Mel Hardin, then a curator at Sailors' Snug Harbor, founded in 1831 on Staten Island as a home for retired seamen. I am grateful to Mr. Hardin for supplying me with a print of this photograph. Thomas Melville, Herman's younger brother, was governor of Snug Harbor when the photograph was taken, c. 1878, and at first Mr. Hardin believed that Thomas was the figure at the center of the photo. But closer study convinced him, as well as other scholars, that it was his brother Herman, who often went out to the island in summer to escape the heat of Manhattan.

XXI "fabulous shadow": Hart Crane, "At Melville's Tomb" (1925).

XXI Madison Square Park: In an essay entitled "Herman Melville Through a Child's Eyes"—*Bulletin of the New York Public Library* 69 (December 1965)—Melville's granddaughter Frances recalled the day in 1887 when, after running among the tulips while her grandfather rested on a bench, she could no longer find him. "Perhaps," she wrote, ". . . he was off in some distant land, or on a rolling ship at sea with nothing to distract his thoughts. Wherever he was, there was no little granddaughter with him. She had ceased to exist." Frances Thomas's essay is reprinted in Merton M. Sealts, Jr., *The Early Lives of Melville: Nineteenth-*

Century Biographical Sketches and Their Authors (Madison: University of Wisconsin Press, 1974), pp. 179–85.

XXII   "on a personal interview": "Hawthorne and His Mosses," in *PT*, p. 240.

XXII   "isolatoes": *MD*, ch. 27, p. 121.

XXII   "deliberately [to] drag up the ladder": *MD*, ch. 8, p. 39.

XXII   hang a towel over the doorknob: In chapter 5 of *Redburn*, the narrator writes that he "hung a towel over the knob, so that no one could peep through the keyhole." In her copy of that novel, Melville's granddaughter Eleanor noted beside this passage that her mother, Frances Melville Thomas, "told her that H.M. used to do this at times in his own home." Eleanor's copies of her grandfather's works (the Constable edition, published in England, 1922–24) are in the Berg Collection of the New York Public Library.

XXIII   "black-letter volume": HM to Nathaniel Hawthorne, April 16, 1851, in *Correspondence*, p. 185.

XXIII   "home-feeling with the past": Nathaniel Hawthorne, *The Scarlet Letter* (1850; Boston: Houghton Mifflin, 1960), p. 11.

XXIII   "wrote from a sort of dream-self": D. H. Lawrence, *Studies in Classic American Literature* (1923; New York: Viking, 1964), p. 134.

XXIII   "Most of us": Richard Poirier, *The Renewal of Literature: Emersonian Reflections* (New York: Random House, 1987), pp. 111–12.

XXIII   "I actually shade my eyes": Emerson, journal entry, December 7[?], 1835, in Joel Porte, ed., *Emerson in His Journals* (Cambridge, MA: Harvard University Press, 1982), p. 145.

INTRODUCTION. MELVILLE: FROM HIS TIME TO OURS

3   "the moral law ... incarnation of God": Emerson, *Nature* (1836), in Stephen E. Whicher, ed., *Selections from Ralph Waldo Emerson* (Boston: Houghton Mifflin, 1957), pp. 39, 50.

4   "lawless, Godless ... soil to the sky": William Dean Howells, *A Hazard of New Fortunes* (1890; New York: New American Library, 1965), p. 160.

4   "until I was twenty-five": HM to Nathaniel Hawthorne, June 1[?], 1851, in *Correspondence*, p. 193.

4   "his own generation has long thought": *New York Press*, September 29, 1891, quoted in *Log*, II, 836.

5   "labial melody": *T*, ch. 31, p. 227.

5   "indulgent captivity"; *O*, Introduction, p. 3.

5   "the tornadoed Atlantic": *MD*, ch. 87, p. 389.

6   "depths ... that compel a man to swim": Hawthorne to Evert Duyckinck, August 29, 1850, quoted in *Log*, I, 391.

6   a "moody stricken" captain: *MD*, ch. 28, p. 124.

6   "like a revolving Drummond light": *CM*, ch. 44, p. 239.

6   "This whole book": *MD*, ch. 32, p. 145.

6   "monomania": HM uses this term (and its adjectival form, "monomaniac") fifteen times in *Moby-Dick* to describe Ahab; the first use comes in ch. 41, p. 184.

6   "frantic morbidness . . . spiritual exasperations": *MD,* ch. 41, p. 184.

7   "He has lost his prestige": G. W. Curtis to Joshua A. Dix, January 2, 1856, quoted in Historical Note to *PT,* p. 458.

8   "the unavoidable centerpiece": Michael T. Gilmore, *Surface and Depth: The Quest for Legibility in American Culture* (New York: Oxford University Press, 2003), p. 87.

8   More recently, Melville's personal copy: See David A. Randall, *Dukedom Large Enough: Reminiscences of a Rare Book Dealer, 1929–1956* (New York: Random House, 1969), p. 208, for an account of the discovery of Melville's copy of Beale's book among some "miscellaneous maritime books" that came into the shop of the famous New York book dealer Max Harzof. "Someone had erased most of [HM's] writing" in the book, "probably the Brooklyn dealer who bought it—to make it a 'clean copy.' " In 1969, Randall looked forward to the day when "modern technology could find means to recover most of the erasures."

9   At Yale, students refer: Alvin Kernan, *In Plato's Cave* (New Haven: Yale University Press, 1999), p. 175.

9   "Moby Dick coupon": *New York Post,* September 24, 2004.

9   "floor-length periwinkle Grecian gown": *New York Magazine,* double issue, July 29–August 5, 2002, p. 57, recommends the dress ("we're wild" for it), designed by Behnaz Sarafpour and available at Barneys New York for $1,740.

9   "then all collapsed": Emily Yoffe, "Things Fall Apart: Pamela Anderson's Breasts Cannot Hold," Slate.com, May 13, 1999.

10   "literary text acts as a kind of mirror": Wolfgang Iser, "The Reading Process: A Phenomenological Approach," in Jane P. Tompkins, ed., *Reader-Response: From Formalism to Post-Structuralism* (Baltimore: Johns Hopkins University Press, 1980), p. 56.

10   "The firm tower": *MD,* ch. 99, p. 431.

10   "an Elizabethan force": Archibald MacMechan, quoted in Michael Zimmerman, "Herman Melville in the 1920s: A Study in the Origins of the Melville Revival" (Ph.D. diss., Columbia University, 1963), p. 18.

11   "sinned blackly against": Raymond Weaver, *Herman Melville: Mariner and Mystic* (New York: George H. Doran, 1921), p. 18.

11   "like eating hasheesh": Frank Jewett Mather, Jr., "Herman Melville," *Review* 1 (August 1919); reprinted in Hershel Parker, ed., *The Recognition of Herman Melville* (Ann Arbor: University of Michigan Press, 1967), p. 156.

11   "a futurist . . . of the elements": Lawrence, *Studies in Classic American Literature,* p. 146.

11   "Melville desires": Frank Lentricchia, *Lucchesi and the Whale* (Durham: Duke University Press, 2001), p. 62.

11   "only the haters": Walker Percy, *The Moviegoer* (1961; New York: Vintage Books, 1998), p. 100.

11   "prophetic song . . . revenge": E. M. Forster, *Aspects of the Novel* (New York: Harcourt Brace, 1927), p. 200.

11 "in battling against evil": Lewis Mumford, *Herman Melville* (New York: Harcourt Brace, 1929), p. 186.

12 "That inscrutable thing": *MD,* ch. 36, p. 164.

12 "dusky phantoms": *MD,* ch. 47, p. 216.

12 "the biography of the last days": C. L. R. James, *Mariners, Renegades and Castaways: The Story of Herman Melville and the World We Live In* (1953; London: Allison & Busby, 1985), p. 68.

12 "I hate goodies": Emerson, journal entry, June 23, 1838, in Porte, ed., *Emerson in His Journals,* p. 191.

12 "to devour" a woodchuck raw: *Walden* (1854), "Higher Laws" chapter, in Henry David Thoreau, *A Week on the Concord and Merrimack Rivers, Walden, The Maine Woods, Cape Cod* (New York: Library of America, 1985), p. 490.

12 many writers are good for thinking about: Dominic LaCapra, "Canon, Texts, and Contexts," in *Learning History in America: Schools, Cultures, and Politics,* ed. Lloyd Kramer, Donald Reid, and William L. Barney (Minneapolis: University of Minnesota Press, 1994), p. 123.

13 "Osama bin Laden's name": *The Observer* (London), September 16, 2001.

13 "demagogue [who] can fuse": Andrew Delbanco, "Melville Has Never Looked Better," *New York Times Book Review,* October 28, 2001, p. 14.

13 One scholar has enumerated: Samuel Otter, "Blue Proteus: *Moby-Dick* and the World We Live In," unpublished paper.

13 Gary Hart . . . Richard Gere: Cited ibid. In the spring of 2003, with preparations under way for the invasion of Iraq, the Chilean writer Ariel Dorfman took note that Americans wondered if Saddam Hussein might be a modern-day Ahab, obsessed with hatred of the United States. "But what if Saddam is not Ahab?" Dorfman asked; what if "Saddam might be the whale and . . . George Bush might in fact be an Ahab whose search for the monster in the oceans of sand and oil could end up with the ruin, not of the monster, but of those who were bent on its extermination?"—www.opendemocracy.net, March 20, 2003.

13 "tender-minded" faith in "the great universe of God": William James, *Pragmatism* (1907; New York: Meridian, 1955), pp. 22, 35.

13 "Odyssey beneath . . . foam and night": Albert Camus, "Herman Melville" (1952), in *Lyrical and Critical Essays,* trans. Ellen Conroy Kennedy (New York: Knopf, 1968), pp. 291, 294.

14 "voids and immensities": *MD,* ch. 42, p. 195.

14 "neither believe, nor be comfortable": Hawthorne, journal entry, November 20, 1856, quoted in *Journals,* p. 628.

14 "calmly and fixedly gaze away": *MD,* ch. 87, p. 388.

14 "I love all men who *dive*": HM to Evert Duyckinck, March 3, 1849, in *Correspondence,* p. 121.

14 "[As] far as any geologist": *P,* bk. 21, p. 285.

15 "cannibal of a craft . . . bones of her enemies": *MD,* ch. 16, p. 70.

15 "red hell": *MD,* ch. 96, p. 423.

15 "We Americans are the peculiar, chosen people": *WJ,* ch. 36, p. 151.

16 "repositories . . . the yes and no of their culture": Lionel Trilling, *The Liberal Imagination* (New York: Harcourt Brace, 1950), p. 9.

CHAPTER 1. CHILDHOOD AND YOUTH

17 "like sieves . . . barbarity to the utmost": Robert Middlekauff, *The Glorious Cause: The American Revolution, 1763–1789* (New York: Oxford University Press, 1982), p. 507.

17 "wielding the stock": *IP,* ch. 3, p. 13.

17 "exhibiting in magnificent terms": Timothy Dwight, *Travels in New England and New York,* 4 vols. (1822; Cambridge, MA: Harvard University Press, 1969), III, 134.

17 "Sir:—In answer": Pomroy Jones, *Annals and Recollections of Oneida County* (Rome, NY, 1851), p. 355.

19 in Indian garb and warpaint: This anecdote was first reported by Alexander Young in his newspaper column "Here in Boston," quoted in Sealts, *Early Lives of Melville,* p. 22.

19 "grand old Pierre . . . their heads": *P,* bk. 2, pp. 29–30.

19 "deluxe Mr. Micawber": James Wood, *The Broken Estate: Essays on Literature and Belief* (New York: Modern Library, 1999), p. 43.

19 *"confidential Connexion . . .* eventual success": *Log,* I, 29.

20 "Fancy Hdfks. and Scarfs": *Log,* II, 905.

21 "ambassador extraordinary": *WJ,* ch. 6, p. 22.

21 "element in which we move": *BB,* ch. 21, p. 1414. For a discussion of Melville's dense biblical references, see H. Bruce Franklin, *The Wake of the Gods* (Stanford: Stanford University Press, 1963), pp. 126–36, and Dan McCall, *The Silence of Bartleby* (Ithaca: Cornell University Press, 1989), p. 5.

21 "he could smell the burning of Gomorrah": Nathalia Wright, *Melville's Use of the Bible* (Durham: Duke University Press, 1949), p. 27.

22 "Ah, fathers and mothers!": *P,* bk. 4, p. 70.

22 "shadowy reminiscences": *R,* ch. 1, p. 4.

22 the miniature glass ship: There was evidently such a glass ship in Thomas Melvill's Boston home. See Sealts, *Early Lives,* p. 22.

22 "children are . . . utmost of your power": J. M. Mathews, quoted in T. Walter Herbert, Jr., *Moby-Dick and Calvinism* (New Brunswick: Rutgers University Press, 1977), p. 28.

23 "In this republican country": *The House of the Seven Gables* (1851), in Nathaniel Hawthorne, *Novels* (New York: Library of America, 1983), ch. II, pp. 383–84.

23 "I am destitute . . . daily expences": Allan Melvill to Thomas Melvill, December 4, 1830, ms. letter. (By permission of the Houghton Library, Harvard University—call number bMS Am 188[116]).

23 "I had learned . . . almost strangles me": *R,* ch. 7, p. 36.

23 "lying in his berth": *MD,* ch. 9, p. 45.

23 "ambiguous condition": Elizabeth Hardwick, *Herman Melville* (New York: Penguin, 2000), p. 17.

24 "a pauper . . . pity alone could reach him": "Jimmy Rose" (1855), in *PT,* p. 342.

24 "Hope is no longer permitted": Thomas Melvill to Lemuel Shaw, January 15, 1832, in *Log,* I, 52.

24 "raving in his hammock": *MD*, ch. 41, p. 185.

25 "tenacious memory . . . slow in comprehension": Allan Melvill to Peter Gansevoort, Jr., September 22, 1827, and August 9, 1826, quoted in *Log*, I, 25.

26 the Connecticut clergyman Timothy Dwight: Dwight, *Travels in New England and New York*, III, 296, and see Laurie Robertson-Lorant, *Melville: A Biography* (New York: Clarkson-Potter, 1996), p. 65.

26 "In our cities": *P*, bk. 3, p. 9.

26 "palm upon the public . . . disappointed of its prey": Quoted in William H. Gilman, *Melville's Early Life and Redburn* (New York: New York University Press, 1951), pp. 257–58.

27 "one long, long kiss": *PT*, p. 204.

27 "Cursing the ignus fatuus": *PT*, p. 198.

27 "Absurd conceits": *PT*, p. 200.

27 "Herman is happy": Maria Melville to Gansevoort Melville, June 1, 1839, quoted in *Log*, I, 86.

28 "says he would give all the sights": Maria Melville to Allan Melville, September 25, 1839, quoted in *Log*, I, 92.

28 "Now our ship": Norman Knox Wood, *Sea Journal: N.Y. to Liverpool* (1838), ms. (By permission of the Houghton Library, Harvard University—call number MS Am 889.340).

29 "Let to rove": *Clarel*, pt. 1, 1, ll. 109–10.

29 "Talk not of the bitterness": *R*, ch. 2, p. 11.

30 "a whaleship was my Yale College": *MD*, ch. 24, p. 112.

30 "with the most painful feelings": *Log*, I, 96.

30 "family post-man": HM's aunt Helen Melvill Souther (January 5, 1840), quoted in Hershel Parker, *Herman Melville: A Biography, 1819–1851*, Vol. 1 (Baltimore: Johns Hopkins University Press, 1996; cited hereafter as Parker, I), p. 159.

30 "strangely docile": *P*, bk. 1, p. 16.

31 "an old negro": *WJ*, ch. 74, p. 311.

31 "How is you?": HM to Allan Melville, December 7, 1839, quoted in *Log*, I, 98. Robertson-Lorant, *Melville*, p. 79, hypothesizes that HM had been subject to "racist barbs about his suntan."

31 "Money has not for many years": Peter Gansevoort to Maria Melville, October 18, 1839, in *Log*, I, 97.

31 "thinks of going far-west": Maria Melville to Peter Gansevoort, May 16, 1840, in *Log*, I, 104.

31 "that laziness which consists": Gansevoort Melville to Allan Melville, January 21, 1840, in *Log*, I, 103.

31 "Agathe believed": Wilson Walker Cowen, "Melville's Marginalia," 11 vols. (Ph.D. diss., Harvard University, 1965), II, 213–14. Leon Howard, *Herman Melville: A Biography* (Berkeley: University of California Press, 1967), p. 334, asserts that as a child and young adult, Herman "played second fiddle to the brilliant Gansevoort."

32 "a little heterodox": Hawthorne, journal entry, November 20, 1856, quoted in *Journals*, p. 628.

32 "Posted like silent sentinels": *MD*, ch. 1, p. 4.

33 "billiard-room and bar-room . . . ocean-like expansiveness": *MD*, ch. 54, pp. 248–49.

34 "In their interflowing aggregate": *MD*, ch. 54, p. 244.

34 "in the groggeries": *BB*, ch. 1, p. 1354.

34 "if you travel away inland": "Hawthorne and His Mosses" (1850), in *PT*, p. 249.

35 "Rosebeefrosegoosemuttonantaters!": Parker, I, 181.

35 "far inland": HM, "A Thought on Bookbinding," review of Cooper's *The Red Rover*, in *The Literary World*, March 16, 1850, reprinted in *PT*, p. 238.

35 "tied and welded": HM to Richard Henry Dana, Jr., May 1, 1850, in *Correspondence*, p. 160. Michael Rogin, *Subversive Genealogy: The Politics and Art of Herman Melville* (New York: Knopf, 1983), p. 5, suggests that Cooper's "romance may have influenced his decision to abandon his family for the sea."

35 "The Melville family": Julia Maria Melvill to Allan Melville (HM's brother), quoted in Robertson-Lorant, *Melville*, p. 91.

35 "It is a great consolation . . . no use to a sailor": Gansevoort Melville to Allan Melville, January 14, 1841, ms., Berkshire Athenaeum, Pittsfield, Massachusetts.

36 "Last week I received": Maria Melville to Augusta Melville, January 8, 1841, quoted in *Correspondence*, p. 24.

CHAPTER 2. GOING NATIVE

37 "another West, prefigured in the Plains": Charles Olson, *Call Me Ishmael* (1947; San Francisco: City Lights Books, 1958), p. 13.

37 the most satisfying husbands: Nathaniel Philbrick, *In the Heart of the Sea: The Tragedy of the Whaleship Essex* (New York: Viking, 2000), p. 13. Philbrick writes (p. 17) that the women of Nantucket referred to their dildoes as "he's-at-homes" in honor of their absent husbands. In his *Letters from an American Farmer* (1782), Hector St. Jean de Crèvecoeur reports that Nantucket women followed "the Asiatic custom of taking a dose of opium every morning," perhaps as an aid in facing the trials of solitude.

37 These were meager wages: Lee A. Craig and Robert M. Fearn, "Wage Discrimination and Occupational Crowding in a Competitive Industry: Evidence from the American Whaling Industry," *Journal of Economic History* 53, no. 1 (March 1993): 123–38.

38 "You will find": Benjamin Franklin to Susanna Wright, November 21, 1751, in Leonard Labaree et al., *The Papers of Benjamin Franklin*, 21 vols. (New Haven: Yale University Press, 1959–), IV, 211.

38 "in raptures with her": Margaret S. Creighton, *Rites and Passages: The Experience of American Whaling, 1830–1870* (Cambridge: Cambridge University Press, 1995), pp. 175–78.

38 "Where's your girls . . . bursting grapes": *MD*, ch. 40, pp. 174, 176. Some critics read HM's references in chapter 42 of *White-Jacket* to sailors "polishing [their] bright-work" and "embracing . . . *monkey-tails* . . . screws, *prickers*, little irons and other things" as coded language for the widespread practice of masturbation

aboard ship. On the evidence of a surviving diary kept by one American whaleman, B. R. Burg (in Burg, ed., *An American Seafarer in the Age of Sail: The Intimate Diaries of Philip C. Van Buskirk, 1851–1870* [New Haven: Yale University
Press, 1994], p. 26) concludes that mutual masturbation may also have been
fairly common.

39 "the deprivations peculiar to whalemen": *The Life and Remarkable Adventures
of Israel Potter* (1824; New York: Corinth, 1962), p. 12.

39 "New England mothers": Gregory Gibson, *Demon of the Waters,* quoted in *New
York Times Book Review,* May 19, 2002, p. 11.

40 "clannish commitment to the hunt": Philbrick, *In the Heart of the Sea,* p. 13.

40 "there were still skippers": Olson, *Call Me Ishmael,* p. 21.

40 "Yankees in one day": *MD,* ch. 53, p. 239.

40 a survey published in *Hunts' Merchants' Magazine:* February 1849, p. 182.

40 "The native American . . . ends of the earth": *MD,* ch. 27, p. 121.

40 Captain E. C. Williams: Pamphlets sold at these shows survive. See E. C.
Williams, *History of the Whale Fisheries* (New York, 1862). An example of a
roughly contemporaneous book with the image of a whaleman (in this case a
South Seas islander) on the cover is James Montgomery, *Poetical Works* (Philadelphia, 1846).

41 Dispersed among villages: See John Bryant, Introduction to *Typee* (New York:
Penguin, 1996).

42 Captain David Porter: See T. Walter Herbert, Jr., *Marquesan Encounters: Melville and the Meaning of Civilization* (Cambridge, MA: Harvard University
Press, 1980), esp. ch. 4.

42 "cordial detestation": *T,* ch. 5, p. 32.

42 "Leaning . . . dry, sarcastic humor": *T,* ch. 5, pp. 33, 32.

42 "Jack Nastyface . . . MacAdamized road": Quoted in Parker, I, 200.

42 "one of that class of rovers": *T,* ch. 5, p. 32.

43 "who had resided on the Island": "Toby's Own Story," *Buffalo Commercial
Advertiser,* July 11, 1846, quoted in Parker, I, 217.

44 "small, slatternly looking craft": *O,* ch. 1, p. 5.

44 "a twang . . . beginning with one": *O,* ch. 53, p. 204. From an account by one of
their earlier employees, William G. Libbey ("Autobiography of a Quondam
Sailor," published in 1878 in the *Shaker Manifesto*), Zeke has been identified as
James Martin and Shorty as one "Edward by name"—whether first name or surname is unknown. See Parker, I, 228.

44 the ship's library was stocked with wholesome books: Wilson L. Heflin, *New
Light on Herman Melville's Cruise in the Charles and Henry* (Glassboro, NJ:
The Melville Society, 1977), and see Parker, I, 232–33.

45 "ten-stroke": *WJ,* ch. 23, p. 94.

45 "a man of any education": *O,* ch. 30, p. 113.

45 "On Board the Lucy Ann": HM, letter to George Lefevre, for Henry Smyth,
September 25, 1842, in *Correspondence,* pp. 25–26.

46 "students versed more in their tomes": *Clarel,* pt. II, 5, ll. 13–14.

47 "the olden voyagers": *T,* ch. 1, p. 5.

47 "naked houris": *T,* ch. 1, p. 5.

47 "lovely houris": See the List of Textual Expurgations in the Penguin edition of *Typee*, ed. Bryant, pp. 275–87.

47 "groves of cocoa-nut . . . strangely jumbled anticipations": *T*, ch. 1, p. 5.

47 "the contrast between 'savagery' and 'civilization' ": Michael P. Rogin, *Fathers and Children: Andrew Jackson and the Subjugation of the American Indian* (New York: Knopf, 1975), p. 166.

47 "pseudo . . . civilized": George Featherstonhaugh, quoted in John Ehle, *Trail of Tears: The Rise and Fall of the Cherokee Nation* (New York: Anchor Books, 1988), p. 315.

47 "their lives . . . in their baggage": Greg Dening, *Islands and Beaches: Discourse on a Silent Land, Marquesas 1774–1880* (Chicago: Dorsey Press, 1980), p. 23.

47 "the wondrous custom": Robert Beverly, quoted in Roy Harvey Pearce, *Savagism and Civilization* (Baltimore: Johns Hopkins University Press, 1965), p. 43.

48 displaying the severed hands: *WJ*, ch. 64, pp. 226–67.

48 "to be found in any of his savage grandeur": Cooper, *Notions of the Americans*, 2 vols. (1828), I, 245.

48 "Indians' bones must enrich the soil": James Farnham, quoted in Pearce, *Savagism*, p. 65.

48 "already established": Quoted in Ehle, *Trail of Tears*, p. 324.

49 "it is impossible to conceive": Quoted ibid., p. 273.

49 "the superior ideas . . . the cannon": Theodore Parker, "Sermon on War," in Michael Warner, ed., *American Sermons: The Pilgrims to Martin Luther King, Jr.* (New York: Library of America, 1999), p. 622.

49 According to the most advanced students: See Bruce Dain, *A Hideous Monster of the Mind: American Race Theory in the Early Republic* (Cambridge, MA: Harvard University Press, 2002), pp. 180–85.

49 "implement in the hand": Simms, quoted in George M. Fredrickson, *The Black Image in the White Mind: The Debate on Afro-American Character and Destiny, 1817–1914* (New York: Harper & Row, 1972), p. 55.

49 "nature has plainly assigned": Emerson, journal entry, November 8, 1822, in *Journals and Miscellaneous Notebooks,* ed. William H. Gilman et al., 16 vols. (Cambridge, MA: Harvard University Press, 1961), II, 43.

50 "Tahitians . . . can hardly be said": *O*, ch. 45, p. 174.

50 "a wild race": Horace Bushnell, "Barbarism the First Danger" (1864), in *Work and Play* (New York: Scribner's, 1910), pp. 231–32.

50 "fireside stories . . . human tongue": Francis Parkman, *The Conspiracy of Pontiac,* 2 vols. (1851; Boston, 1883), I, 37.

51 "attached to us no more merit": Porter, quoted in Herbert, *Marquesan Encounters,* p. 80.

51 "First, we see men living together": James Monboddo, *Of the Origin and Progress of Language,* 8 vols. (Edinburgh, 1773), I, 240–43.

52 "frugivore to a cannibal": Geoffrey Sanborn, "Invented Appetites: Cannibalism in Melville's Pacific Fiction" (Ph.D. diss., UCLA, 1992), p. 39.

52 "Let a philosophic observer commence": Jefferson, letter to William Ludlow, September 6, 1824, quoted in Pearce, *Savagism*, p. 155.

53   "The friendly and flowing savage": Whitman, "Song of Myself" (sect. 39, 1855 version).

53   speculated that sedentary life leads: Benjamin Rush, *Medical Inquiries and Observations upon the Diseases of the Mind* (Philadelphia, 1812), pp. 17–27.

53   "constitutional affinity": Higginson, journal entry, November 21, 1863, in Christopher Looby, ed., *The Complete Civil War Journal and Selected Letters of Thomas Wentworth Higginson* (Chicago: University of Chicago Press, 2000), p. 175.

53   "primitiveness and freshness": Schoolcraft, quoted in *The Literary World*, vol. 2, November 13, 1848.

53   "sententious fulness": James Fenimore Cooper, *The Last of the Mohicans* (1826), in Cooper, *The Leatherstocking Tales*, 2 vols. (New York: Library of America, 1985), I, 473. For a discussion of these themes, see Helen Carr, *Inventing the American Primitive: Politics, Gender, and the Representation of Native American Literary Traditions* (New York: New York University Press, 1996).

53   "children and savages use only nouns": Emerson, *Nature*, in Whicher, ed., *Selections*, pp. 31–32.

54   "Prone, prone": *Clarel*, pt. II, 8, ll. 39–40.

54   The German scholar . . . morality and wisdom: Barbara Packer, "The Transcendentalists," in Sacvan Bercovitch, ed., *The Cambridge History of American Literature*, Vol. 2: *Prose Writing, 1820–1865* (New York: Cambridge University Press, 1995), pp. 344–46.

54   "called what revolted him": Newton Arvin, *Herman Melville* (New York: William Sloane, 1950), p. 54.

54   "What a contrast": Emerson, "Self-Reliance" (1840), in Whicher, ed., *Selections*, p. 165.

55   "Among savages": *Mardi*, ch. 24, p. 77.

55   "A Parisian will be surprised": Abner Kneeland, *Review of the Trial, Conviction and Final Imprisonment . . . of Abner Kneeland* (Boston, 1838), pp. 13–14.

55   "savages we call them": Franklin, *Remarks Concerning the Savages of North America* (1782), quoted in Pearce, *Savagism*, 139.

55   "[Wooloo] seemed a being": *WJ*, ch. 28, p. 118.

56   "the science of the age": Quoted in Reginald Horsman, *Race and Manifest Destiny: The Origins of American Racial Anglo-Saxonism* (Cambridge, MA: Harvard University Press, 1981), p. 139.

56   a gallery on Chambers Street: John J. M. Gretchko, "Melville at the New York Gallery of the Fine Arts," *Melville Society Extracts* 82 (September 1990): 7–8.

56   "a mass of bones and ashes": Dwight, quoted in Catherine Hoover Voorsanger and John K. Howat, *Art and the Empire City: New York, 1825–1861* (New York and New Haven: Metropolitan Museum of Art and Yale University Press, 2000), p. 124.

56   "The prairie-wolf": William Cullen Bryant, "The Prairies" (1831).

57   " 'A harree ta fow' ": *O*, ch. 49, p. 192.

57   "until I was twenty-five": Parker (I, 842), points out that Melville may have "used 'twenty-fifth' year accurately" to designate the year that began in August 1843, after his twenty-fourth birthday—a year spent at sea.

57   "He was mad": Lawrence, *Studies in Classic American Literature*, p. 134.

58   "gallant rascally epicurean": Ibid., p. 140.

CHAPTER 3. BECOMING A WRITER

59   "swinging half round . . . can't help you now!": Richard Henry Dana, *Two Years
      Before the Mast* (1840; New York: Airmont, 1965), p. 84.

60   "St. Domingo melodies . . . against the metal": *WJ*, ch. 15. p. 58.

60   "dunderfunk"; "burgoo": *WJ*, ch. 32, p. 132.

60   "Sailors, even in the bleakest weather": *WJ*, ch. 9, p. 36.

60   "airy perch": *WJ*, ch. 4, p. 15. For the debate over whether Melville actually
      served in the maintop, see Charles Anderson, "A Reply to Herman Melville's
      White-Jacket by Rear-Admiral Thomas O. Selfridge, Sr.," *American Literature*
      7 (May 1935): 123–44.

60   "spacious and cosy"; "a kind of balcony": *WJ*, ch. 4, p. 15.

61   "Jack had read": *WJ*, ch. 4, p. 14.

61   "man-of-war hermit": *WJ*, title of ch. 13, p. 50.

61   "scoured all the prairies": *WJ*, ch. 13, p. 51.

61   "Never mind, my boy": *WJ*, ch. 45, p. 192.

62   "peep from below": *T*, ch. 11, p. 86.

62   "lingering or malingering": Hardwick, *Herman Melville*, p. 41.

62   "the social and political respectabilities": Dana, quoted in *Log*, II, 514. For
      Shaw's career, see Frederic Hathaway Chase, *Lemuel Shaw: Chief Justice of the
      Supreme Judicial Court of Massachusetts, 1830–1860* (Boston: Houghton Mif-
      flin, 1928).

63   "bearded lips": Parker, I, 311.

63   "The flood-gates of the wonder world": *MD*, ch. 1, p. 7.

63   "scanned the page": Helen Melville, letter of September [?], 1841, to Augusta
      Melville, quoted in Robertson-Lorant, *Melville*, p. 132.

63   "beguiled the long winter hours": Willis, review of *Redburn, New York Home
      Journal*, November 24, 1849, quoted in Brian Higgins and Hershel Parker, eds.,
      Herman Melville: The Contemporary Reviews (New York: Cambridge Univer-
      sity Press, 1995; cited hereafter as *Contemporary Reviews*), p. 283.

63   "vague prophetic thought": *R*, ch. 1, p. 7.

64   "the odor . . . *maladie de mer*": Cooper, Preface (1849) to *The Pilot* (orig. pub.
      1823; New York: Putnam's, n.d.), p. vi.

64   "he managed . . . a detailed description": William Charvat, "Melville and the
      Common Reader," in *Studies in Bibliography*, ed. Fredson Bowers, *Papers of the
      Bibliographical Society of the University of Virginia*, vol. 12 (1959), p. 43.

64   "If he meets a native": Review of *Typee* in the New Haven *New Englander*, July
      1846, quoted in Higgins and Parker, eds., *Contemporary Reviews*, p. 52.

64   Polynesian girls applying tropical oil: This passage, from the fragment of the
      Typee manuscript discovered in 1984 in a trunk in an upstate New York barn, was
      never printed in full in Melville's lifetime. See the discussion in Parker, I, 365,

and the Penguin edition of *Typee*, ed. Bryant, p. 310, for a transcription of the ms. fragment. The expurgated passage appears in *T*, ch. 4, p. 110.

64 "have held forth": Hardwick, *Herman Melville*, p. 43.

64 "who is wise, will expect appreciative recognition": HM to Nathaniel Hawthorne, November 17[?], 1851, in *Correspondence*, p. 212.

65 "a man of humorous desperation": Lawrence, *Studies in Classic American Literature*, p. 140.

65 "unfortunate affair": *O*, ch. 2, p. 12.

65 "life is a pic-nic": *CM*, ch. 24, p. 133.

65 "low musical voice": *BB*, ch. 10, p. 1380.

65 "difficult art": *WJ*, ch. 47, p. 199.

65 "when he describes any thing": Sophia Hawthorne, letter to her mother, October 24, 1852, quoted in Hershel Parker, *Herman Melville: A Biography, 1851-1891*, Vol. 2 (Baltimore: Johns Hopkins University Press, 2002; cited hereafter as Parker, II), p. 141.

66 "a fight which he had seen": Julian Hawthorne, *Nathaniel Hawthorne and His Wife*, 2 vols. (Boston, 1884), I, 407.

66 "a man with a true warm heart . . . if it were anywhere": Sophia Hawthorne, quoted in *Log*, I, 393.

66 "With his cigar": Willis, quoted in Hershel Parker, "Herman Melville," *American History Illustrated*, September–October 1991, p. 36.

66 "a lounging circle": *MD*, ch. 54, p. 243.

66 "Tell me": *MD*, ch. 54, p. 258.

66 "writing something": Allan Melville, quoted in Parker, I, 378.

66 "it was impossible": Recollections of Frederick Saunders, Spring[?], 1845, quoted in *Log*, I, 196.

66 "gas and glory": Horace Greeley, editorial in the *New York Tribune*, October 12, 1844, quoted in *Log*, I, 186.

67 "Young Hickory": Hershel Parker, Introduction to *Gansevoort Melville's 1846 London Journal* (New York: New York Public Library, 1966), p. 9.

67 "scented the forbidden thing": Murray, quoted in *Log*, I, 200.

67 "kept him from church": Gansevoort Melville, diary entry, January 11, 1846, quoted in *Log*, I, 202.

68 "Get it and read it": Reprinted in Higgins and Parker, eds., *Contemporary Reviews*, p. 36. The review appeared on April 1, 1846.

68 Hawthorne expressed delight: *Salem Advertiser*, March 25, 1846, reprinted ibid., pp. 22–23.

68 "sensitive and alive all over": Hazlitt's essay, first published in the *Examiner*, May 26, 1816, is reprinted in W. J. Bate, ed., *Criticism: The Major Texts* (New York: Harcourt Brace Jovanovich, 1970), pp. 301–3.

69 "tacking . . . somewhere off Buggery Island": *T*, ch. 4, p. 23.

69 "Do not suffer your hand": Catherine Beecher, *A Treatise on Domestic Economy For the Use of Young Ladies At Home, And At School* (1841), quoted in Barbara Goldsmith, *Other Powers: The Age of Suffrage, Spiritualism, and the Scandalous Victoria Woodhull* (New York: Knopf, 1998), p. 127.

69   "a radiant and tender smile": Hawthorne, *The Scarlet Letter,* ch. 18, p. 201.

69   "free pliant figure": *T,* ch. 11, p. 85.

69   "inconceivably smooth and soft": *T,* ch. 11, p. 86.

69   "Her complexion was a rich and mantling olive": *T,* ch. 11, p. 85.

70   though in some underground fictions: See Michael Mason, *The Making of Victorian Sexuality* (New York: Oxford University Press, 1994), pp. 202–3; David S. Reynolds, *Beneath the American Renaissance: The Subversive Imagination in the Age of Emerson and Melville* (New York: Knopf, 1982), pp. 215–18; David S. Reynolds, *Walt Whitman's America: A Cultural Biography* (New York: Knopf, 1995), p. 202; and Carl N. Degler, "What Ought to Be and What Was: Women's Sexuality in the Nineteenth Century," *American Historical Review* 79, no. 5 (December 1974): 1467–90.

70   "exactly what the American Victorian lady": Ann Douglas, *The Feminization of American Culture* (New York: Knopf, 1977), p. 297.

70   a "warm, wild" reception: *MD,* ch. 40, p. 176.

70   "I have more than one reason": *T,* ch. 26, p. 191.

70   "on the very best terms possible": *T,* ch. 18, p. 133.

70   "peculiar favorite": *T,* ch. 11, p. 85.

70   "dance all over": *T,* ch. 20, p. 152.

70   "like a woman roused": *O,* ch. 16, p. 58.

70   "spreading overhead": *O,* ch. 31, p. 120.

71   "plunged into the recesses . . . upon my ear": *T,* ch. 4, p. 28.

71   "protuberance in front": *T,* ch. 6, p. 36.

71   "You dear creature": Quoted in Parker, I, 464. The phrase occurs in an October 1846 letter to HM's sister Augusta from Ellen Astor Oxenham, who addresses HM in the second person.

71   "Oh! ye state-room sailors": *T,* ch. 1, p. 3.

71   Before the end of the year: See Amy Elizabeth Puett, "Melville's Wife: A Study of Elizabeth Shaw Melville" (Ph.D. diss., Northwestern University, 1969), pp. 44–45. Parker, I, 450, suggests that they were engaged by the end of August 1846.

71   "And Lemuel said": Elizabeth Shaw, ms., n.d. (By permission of the Houghton Library, Harvard University—call number bMS Am 188 [160]).

73   Yet he had no illusions: Parker points out (I, 483) that Murray hoped Melville's second book would stimulate new interest in his first book, which had not yet paid its expenses.

73   "brood of unfortunates": Charles F. Briggs, in the *Broadway Journal,* January 4, 1845, quoted in Kenneth Silverman, *Edgar A. Poe: Mournful and Never-Ending Remembrance* (New York: HarperCollins, 1991), p. 245.

73   an incentive to push sales: See William Charvat, *Literary Publishing in America* (Philadelphia: University of Pennsylvania Press, 1959), p. 49. There is an irresistible, if inexact, analogy to be made here with today's distinction between a trade book and an academic book: when a bookstore buys a trade book, it typically gets a discount of approximately 50 percent, but if it buys a scholarly book, the discount may be only 20 percent, which means less incentive to display and sell it. Behind this distinction, of course, lies the publisher's estimate of the size of the book's potential audience.

73   "sixpence . . . International Copyright": Fred Kaplan, *Dickens: A Biography* (New York: William Morrow, 1988), pp. 124, 127.

73   developments that eventually worked: Michael Davitt Bell, "Conditions of Literary Vocation," in Bercovitch, ed., *Cambridge History of American Literature,* vol. 2, pp. 16–17.

74   "Here have I a choice of books": Charles Brockden Brown, "A Sketch of American Literature," published in *The American Register* (1806), quoted in James D. Wallace, *Early Cooper and His Audience* (New York: Columbia University Press, 1986), p. 61.

74   why authorship in America remained more a hobby: As Washington Irving wrote in 1813, "In America, the man of letters is almost an insulated being, with few to understand, less to value, and scarcely any to encourage his pursuits." Quoted in Bell, "Conditions of Literary Vocation," p. 17.

74   "Literature is not yet a distinct profession": Jefferson, quoted in Harold Laski, *The American Democracy* (New York: Viking, 1948), p. 393.

74   "the old evangelical hostility": Henry James, "The Art of Fiction" (1888), in Leon Edel, ed., *Henry James: Selected Fiction* (New York: Dutton, 1964), p. 587.

74   Hawthorne imagines: Hawthorne, "The Custom House," preface to *The Scarlet Letter,* p. 12.

74   "were merely slight transformations": Kenneth Silverman, *A Cultural History of the American Revolution* (New York: Crowell, 1976), p. 15.

74   "You know I am apt to swing my arms": Hope Savage Shaw to Lem Shaw, May 25, 1852, quoted in Parker, II, 109.

75   "Who reads an American book?": Sidney Smith, writing in the *Edinburgh Review,* 1820.

75   "wide-awake youngster": Jacques Barzun, *From Dawn to Decadence: Five Hundred Years of Western Culture* (New York: HarperCollins, 2000), p. 91.

75   "satirically said to have thought": *P,* bk. 15, p. 218.

76   "small number of men": Alexis de Tocqueville, *Democracy in America,* 2 vols. (1835–40; New York: Vintage, 1990), II, 55–56.

76   "Long enough . . . have we been skeptics": *WJ,* ch. 36, p. 151.

76   "an original comedy": The prize was sponsored by the comic actor James H. Hackett. I owe this reference to Matthew Rebhorn.

76   Between 1820 and 1830: Samuel Goodrich, cited in James D. Hart, *The Popular Book: A History of America's Literary Taste* (New York: Oxford University Press, 1950), pp. 67–68, 90.

76   "the peculiar nature": William Gilmore Simms, *Views and Reviews* (1845; Cambridge, MA: Harvard University Press, 1962), p. 13.

77   "Believe me, . . . literary flunkeyism toward England": "Hawthorne and His Mosses," in *PT,* p. 245.

77   "the expression of [the] nation's mind": William Ellery Channing, "On National Literature" (1830), in *Works,* 6 vols. (Boston, 1848), I, 243.

77   "literary sin . . . in sinning": *BB,* ch. 4, p. 1365.

78   they could have run along a raw coral beach: See the Historical Note by Leon Howard in *T,* p. 292.

78   "no ear . . . exclaimed the last": Stevenson, quoted in the Explanatory Notes by

Harrison Hayford and Walter Blair in *Omoo* (New York: Hendricks House, 1969), p. 344.

78   "He gets up voluptuous pictures": Review by George Washington Peck, *American Whig Review,* July 6, 1847, in Higgins and Parker, eds., *Contemporary Reviews,* p. 137.

79   which, he claimed, he had declined to join: Hershel Parker believes that Melville, worried about contracting venereal disease, abstained until he got "inland, where the sexual welcome would be as enthusiastic and where the brown girls, if Providence were kind, would never have been touched by men from whaleships"—Parker, I, 213.

79   "These swimming nymphs": *T,* ch. 2, pp. 14–15.

80   "penalty of the Fall": *T,* ch. 26, p. 195.

80   "There was not a padlock": *T,* ch. 27, p. 201.

80   "social acerbities": *MD,* ch. 94, p. 416.

80   "bathing in company with troops of girls": *T,* ch. 18, p. 131.

80   "We dream all night": Henry David Thoreau, "Walking" (1862), in *Walden and Other Writings,* ed. Brooks Atkinson (New York: Modern Library, 1950), p. 609.

81   "At first, Kory-Kory goes to work": *T,* ch. 14, p. 111.

82   "long exile from Christendom": *MD,* ch. 57, p. 270.

82   "We can't go back": Lawrence, *Studies in Classic American Literature,* p. 137.

82   "down into the bosom": *T,* ch. 7, p. 49.

82   "to concentrate all my capabilities": *T,* ch. 8, p. 53.

83   "Robinson Crusoe . . . could not have been more startled": *T,* ch. 7, p. 44.

83   "partly hidden by the dense foliage": *T,* ch. 10, p. 68.

83   "a struggling child": *T,* ch. 11, p. 80.

84   "fiction . . . of the nervous white mind": Sanborn, "Invented Appetites," p. 10. Caleb Crain, "Lovers of Human Flesh: Homosexuality and Cannibalism in Melville's Novels," *American Literature* 66, no. 1 (March 1994): 25–53, argues that fear of cannibalism in antebellum America was a deflected expression of anxiety about the equally scandalous practice of homosexual sex. For an informative and amusing survey of the debate among modern anthropologists as to whether cannibalism has ever existed in human culture or is merely a matter of "culturally malicious hearsay," see Lawrence Osborne, "Does Man Eat Man?: Inside the Cannibalism Controversy," *Lingua Franca,* April–May 1997, pp. 28–38.

84   "the disordered members": *T,* ch. 32, p. 238.

84   "green winding sheets": *T,* ch. 32, p. 235.

84   "in leaves of the hibiscus": Ellis, *Polynesian Researches,* 2 vols. (New York, 1833), I, 276.

84   "remembered of the Islands of the Pacific": Anonymous review in *The New Englander* (July 1846), in Parker, ed., *The Recognition,* p. 4.

84   "I must throw a veil": John Coulter, *Adventures in the Pacific* (Dublin, 1845), p. 232.

85   "every Author, as far as he is great": See Thomas Heffernan, "Melville and Wordsworth," *American Literature* 49, no. 3 (1977): 350.

86   "when between sheets": *MD,* ch. 11, p. 54.

86   "a painter of his own face": Hardwick, *Herman Melville*, p. 36.

86   "if you rightly look for it": "Hawthorne and His Mosses," in *PT*, p. 249.

86   "laced chapeau"; "tattooed savage": *T*, ch. 4, p. 29.

CHAPTER 4. ESCAPE TO NEW YORK

87   a familiar presence in the office: See Parker, I, 355.

87   "his countenance spoke": Augusta Whipple to Augusta Melville, January 14, 1846, quoted in Robertson-Lorant, *Melville*, p. 137, and Parker, I, 381.

87   "I would to God Shakspeare had lived later": HM to Evert Duyckinck, March 3, 1849, in *Correspondence*, p. 122.

87   "I don't know how it is precisely . . . merry little walk?": HM to Catherine Melville, January 20, 1845, ibid., pp. 27–30.

88   "the country is tired": Willis, quoted in Benjamin T. Spencer, *The Quest for Nationality: An American Literary Campaign* (Syracuse: Syracuse University Press, 1957), p. 85.

88   "intoxicating way of crushing her eyes up": Willis, quoted in Vera Brodsky Lawrence, *Strong on Music*, Vol. 1: *Resonances, 1836–1850* (New York: Oxford University Press, 1988), p. 325.

89   "And I have felt": These lines appear in Willis's poem "The Lady in the White Dress, Whom I Helped into the Omnibus," first collected (along with "City Lyric") in his *Poems, Sacred, Passionate, and Humorous* (New York, 1844).

89   "pulled up stakes somewhere": E. B. White, *Here Is New York* (New York: Little Bookroom, 1999), p. 19.

89   "fills up [his] mouth": Charles F. Briggs, *The Adventures of Harry Franco: A Tale of the Great Panic*, 2 vols. (New York, 1839), I, 24.

90   "threw up [her] . . . skirts": *T*, ch. 1, p. 8.

90   "utterly incredible": Review in the *Morning Courier and New York Enquirer*, April 17, 1846, in Higgins and Parker, eds., *Contemporary Reviews*, pp. 46–47.

90   "opera-dancers, and voluptuous prints": Review in the *New York Evangelist*, April 9, 1846, ibid., p. 46.

90   "*Typee* is a true narrative": HM's comments were published as a letter to the editor of the *Albany Argus* (April 21, 1846), which had reviewed *Typee* favorably in its issue of March 26. The reviewer praised the book, but expressed some incredulity by attributing to it the "charm of a beautiful novel." See the review in Higgins and Parker, eds., *Contemporary Reviews*, p. 23, and HM's reply in *Correspondence*, p. 35.

90   "I sometimes fear": Gansevoort Melville to HM, April 3, 1846, in *Correspondence*, p. 576.

90   "I . . . think I see you": HM to Gansevoort Melville, June 29, 1846, ibid., pp. 40–41.

90   "No doubt, two years ago": *Journals*, p. 28.

91   " 'How my heart thumped' ": *WJ*, ch. 59, p. 245.

91   "exceedingly embarrassed circumstances": HM to Secretary of State James Buchanan, June 6, 1846, in *Correspondence*, p. 43.

91   The *Sunday Times:* May 2, 1847, in Higgins and Parker, eds., *Contemporary Reviews,* p. 98.

91   "racy lightness": Greeley, in the *Tribune,* June 26, 1847, ibid., p. 130.

91   "restless and . . . lonely": Maria Gansevoort Melville to Augusta Melville, May 30, 1847, quoted in Parker, I, 522.

91   "continued from, tho' wholly independent of": HM to John Murray, October 29, 1847, in *Correspondence,* pp. 98–99.

91   "BREACH OF PROMISE SUIT": *New-York Daily Tribune,* August 7, 1847, in *Log,* I, 256.

92   "half Bostonian": Parker, I, 497.

92   "the capital of the universal Yankee nation": New York *Independent,* December 28, 1848, quoted in Edward K. Spann, *The New Metropolis: New York City, 1840–1857* (New York: Columbia University Press, 1981), p. 7.

92   "it somehow or other happens": Briggs, *Harry Franco,* II, 104.

92   "without a background": Yvor Winters, Foreword to *Maule's Curse,* reprinted in Winters, *In Defense of Reason* (Chicago: Swallow Press, n.d.), p. 173.

93   not "*fleshy* . . . exactly": Willis, "Miss Albina McLush," first published in *American Monthly Magazine* (July 1830); reprinted in Kendall B. Taft, *Minor Knickerbockers: Representative Selections* (New York: American Book Company, 1947), p. 294.

93   "dallying with her grass fan . . . the carnal part": *O,* ch. 46, p. 178.

93   "cross-lights of a druggist's window": *P,* bk. 16, p. 237.

93   "very clerical looking": Whitman, quoted in Edward L. Widmer, *Young America: The Flowering of Democracy in New York City* (New York: Oxford University Press, 1999), p. 21.

93   "Ay, ay, *Arcturion!*": *Mardi,* ch. 1, p. 5.

94   "elegant inutilities": The friend was Joann Miller. See Donald Yannella, "Writing the '*Other Way*': Melville, the Duyckinck Crowd, and Literature for the Masses," in Bryant, ed., *Companion to Melville Studies,* p. 66. For an evocative account of the Duyckincks, see Perry Miller, *The Raven and the Whale: The War of Words and Wits in the Era of Poe and Melville* (New York: Harcourt Brace, 1956), p. 72.

95   when that day of which every author dreams: Leonard Cassuto, in his introduction to *Edgar Allan Poe: Literary Theory and Criticism* (Mineola, NY: Dover, 1999), p. vii, remarks that antebellum American writers faced "a Catch-22—their work could get published only if it were popular, and they could become popular only if their work were published."

95   "The most 'popular' ": Poe's essay, first published in installments from May to October 1846 in *Godey's Lady Book,* is excerpted in Cassuto, *Edgar Allan Poe,* pp. 111–24. Duyckinck described Melville at this time "agitating the conscience" of John Wiley while simultaneously "tempting the pockets of the Harpers" with the manuscript of *Omoo.* See the Historical Note in *PT,* p. 464.

95   "From the proprietors of the Magazines": *P,* bk. 17, p. 253.

96   the Duyckincks' request: See Yannella, "Writing the '*Other Way,*' " p. 65.

96   "petitioning and remonstrating": *P,* bk. 17, p. 255.

96   the "wide-spread and disastrous" fire: *P*, bk. 22, p. 300.

96   "If there is *la jeune France*": Cooper, *Home as Found* (1838), quoted in Widmer, *Young America*, p. 59.

96   "world capital of invective": Miller, *Raven and the Whale*, p. 186.

96   "Horace Greeley, BA and ASS": Bennett (April 20, 1841), quoted in Hans Bergmann, *God in the Street: New York Writing from the Penny Press to Melville* (Philadelphia: Temple University Press, 1995), p. 32.

97   "the only way of securing exemption": James Silk Buckingham, "Metropolis and Summer Watering-Place" (1841), in Allan Nevins, ed., *American Social History as Recorded by British Travellers* (New York: Henry Holt, 1923), p. 319.

97   "superannuated dust-box": George Sanders, quoted in John Stafford, *The Literary Criticism of "Young America"* (Berkeley: University of California Press, 1952), p. 20.

97   "country town of litterateurs": Evert Duyckinck, "Traits of American Authorship," first published April 17, 1847, in *The Literary World;* reprinted in Kay S. House, *Reality and Myth in American Literature* (New York: Fawcett, 1966), p. 157.

97   "Eat sh—t!": Evert Duyckinck, quoted in Miller, *Raven and the Whale*, p. 74. Miller points out that Duyckinck used dashes even when recording this bit of medical advice in his private diary.

97   "He's in joke half the time": James Russell Lowell, "A Fable for Critics" (1848), quoted ibid., p. 49.

97   "You Gothamites strain hard": Lowell to Briggs, quoted ibid.

98   "New York the empress queen": Allan Melvill to Lemuel Shaw, January 16, 1819. (By permission of the Houghton Library, Harvard University—call number *93M-70.) I am grateful to Dennis Marnon for calling to my attention his recent discovery of this unpublished letter.

98   the same shops that sold libretti: Lorenzo Da Ponte, *Memoirs* (1823–1830), trans. Elisabeth Abbott (New York: New York Review Books, 2000), p. 436.

98   "clapper-clawed" her rival: George Templeton Strong, quoted in Miller, *Raven and the Whale*, p. 16.

98   one observer posted himself: Joel Ross, *What I Saw in New York* (1851), quoted in Spann, *The New Metropolis*, p. 3.

98   "A more ingenious contrivance": Poe (1844), quoted in Luc Sante, *Low Life: Lures and Snares of Old New York* (New York: Farrar, Straus & Giroux, 1991), p. 47. Asphalt was not introduced as a paving material until after the Civil War.

98   "high above the city's din": *The Knickerbocker*, February 1840, p. 139.

99   "made considerable noise . . . other delicacies": Thomas DeVoe, *The Market Book*, 2 vols. (New York, 1862), I, 369.

99   "wading through puddles": Friedrich Engels, *The Condition of the Working Class in England* (1844; Stanford: Stanford University Press, 1968), p. 58.

99   "hurried through the streets": Briggs, *Harry Franco*, II, 59.

99   "babylonish brick-kiln": HM to Nathaniel Hawthorne, June 29, 1851, in *Correspondence*, p. 195.

99   "as natural . . . wideness of the world": Mumford, *Herman Melville*, p. 11.

99   "satisfaction that the constant flicker": F. Scott Fitzgerald, *The Great Gatsby* (1925; New York: Scribner's, 1953), p. 57.

99   "Pinkster's Day": See Sterling Stuckey, "The Tambourine in Glory: African Culture in Melville's Art," in Levine, ed., *Cambridge Companion to Herman Melville,* pp. 38-40.

99   "bright silks and sparkling faces": "Bartleby," in *PT,* p. 28.

100   "pallidly neat": "Bartleby," in *PT,* p. 19.

100   "men are but men": Briggs, *Harry Franco,* I, 17.

101   "crowded hotels . . . city's soul and body": "The New York Park" (1851), in A. J. Downing, *Rural Essays* (New York, 1890), pp. 147-48.

101   "crowds, pacing straight for the water": *MD,* ch. 1, p. 4.

101   "insular city": *MD,* ch. 1, p. 3.

101   "an unobstructed view": Philip Hone, *Diary,* 2 vols. (New York, 1899), I, 380.

101   guided toy boats: Elizabeth Hone Smith, *Newsboy* (1854), quoted in Bergmann, *God in the Street,* p. 101.

102   "The gorgeous rainbow": Greeley, quoted in Spann, *The New Metropolis,* p. 73. For the prevalence of scavenging and prostitution, see Christine Stansell, *City of Women: Sex and Class in New York, 1789–1860* (Urbana: University of Illinois Press, 1987), p. 50.

102   "creep into a safe retreat": Margaret Fuller (March 25, 1846), in Judith Bean and Joel Myerson, eds., *Margaret Fuller, Critic: Writings from the New York Tribune, 1844–1846* (New York: Columbia University Press, 2000), p. 376.

102   "worthless foreigners": Report of the Philadelphia Guardians of the Poor (1827), quoted in Michael Katz, *In the Shadow of the Poorhouse: A Social History of Welfare in America* (New York: Basic Books, 1996), p. 17.

102   "the inmates of [Europe's] Alms-Houses": R. C. Waterston, *An Address on Pauperism* (Boston, 1844), p. 21.

102   "a sort of common sewer for the filth": Lydia Maria Child (1863), *Selected Letters, 1817–1880,* ed. Milton Meltzer and Patricia G. Holland (Amherst: University of Massachusetts Press, 1982), p. 434.

102   "old men, tottering with age": *R,* ch. 33, p. 168.

103   "one of the out & out *Reds*": Browning, quoted in Larry J. Reynolds, *European Revolutions and the American Literary Renaissance* (New Haven: Yale University Press, 1988), p. 50.

103   "every shop was shut": George Duyckinck, quoted ibid., p. 8.

103   "divine equality": *MD,* ch. 26, p. 117.

104   "to be a born American citizen": *R,* ch. 41, p. 202.

104   "safety-valve": The phrase was used by Michigan senator Lewis Cass in a speech to the Senate on February 10, 1847, reprinted in Norman Graebner, ed., *Manifest Destiny* (New York: Bobbs-Merrill, 1968), pp. 156–59.

104   secretly urging New York Democrats: Parker, Introduction to Gansevoort Melville, *London Journal* (New York: New York Public Library, 1966), p. 10.

104   "class . . . who . . . hedge themselves round": William Leggett, in the *New York Evening Post,* November 4, 1834, reprinted in Joseph Blau, ed., *Social Theories of Jacksonian Democracy* (New York: Bobbs-Merrill, 1954), p. 68.

104   "Americanos! Conquerors!": Whitman, "Starting from Paumanok."

105 "slavery in the South": *Democratic Review* (May 1848), quoted in Frank Luther Mott, *A History of American Magazines, 1741–1850* (Cambridge, MA: Harvard University Press, 1957), p. 681.

105 "the seat in his ample pants": HM, "Authentic Anecdotes of Old Zack," first published in *Yankee Doodle*, July 24, 1847; reprinted in *PT*, p. 215. See the Historical Note in *PT*, p. 467, for discussion of Melville's opposition to the Mexican War.

106 "the best kind of conquest": Whitman, editorial in the *Brooklyn Eagle*, September 23, 1847, in Graebner, *Manifest Destiny*, p. 209.

106 "in that age": *Clarel*, pt. I, 4, ll. 11–13.

106 "romance . . . see whether": Preface to *Mardi*, p. xvii.

106 "proceeding in my narrative of *facts*": HM to John Murray, March 25, 1848, in *Correspondence*, p. 106.

106 "Antarctic tenor": HM to John Murray, June 19, 1848, ibid., p. 109.

106 "peculiar thoughts & fancies": HM to Richard Bentley, June 5, 1849, ibid., p. 131.

106 "the Island of Delights . . . valve of a shell": *Mardi*, ch. 43, p. 147.

107 "pursuers and pursued flew on": *Mardi*, ch. 195, p. 654.

107 "a walk in Broadway to-day . . . en rapport with the Revolution": Evert Duyckinck to George Duyckinck, March 18, 1848, quoted in Merrell R. Davis, *Melville's Mardi: A Chartless Voyage* (New Haven: Yale University Press, 1952), p. 82.

107 a "wondrous" man: Whitman, quoted in Reynolds, *European Revolutions*, p. 20.

107 "great whale the French revolution": Evert Duyckinck to George Duyckinck, March 24, 1848, quoted in Davis, *Melville's Mardi*, p. 83.

108 "What if the Kings": *Clarel*, pt. II, 4, ll. 99–102.

108 "Evil . . . is the chronic malady": *Mardi*, ch. 161, p. 529. Compare Thoreau, "Higher Laws," in *Walden*, p. 498: "When the reptile is attacked at one mouth of his burrow, he shows himself at another." On Dana, see Reynolds, *European Revolutions*, ch. 3.

108 "the world of mind . . . if wreck I do": *Mardi*, ch. 169, p. 557.

108 "radiant young" muse: *Mardi*, ch. 43, p. 138.

108 "far to the South": *Mardi*, ch. 119, p. 366.

109 "rubbishing rhapsody": *Blackwood's*, August 1849, in Higgins and Parker, eds., *Contemporary Reviews*, p. 241.

109 a long, respectful review: The review, by Philarete Chasles, was originally published on May 15, 1849, in Paris in *Revue des deux mondes,* and appeared in translation in *The Literary World* in the issues of August 4 and August 11, 1849.

109 "stabbed *at*": HM (writing from London) to Evert Duyckinck, December 14, 1849, in *Correspondence*, p. 149.

109 "an onward development": From Evert Duyckinck review of *Mardi* in *Literary World,* April 7, 1849, quoted in Higgins and Parker, eds., *Contemporary Reviews*, p. 206.

109 "Like a frigate": *Mardi*, ch. 119, p. 367.

109 "We breakfast at 8 o'clock": Elizabeth Melville to Hope Shaw, December 23, 1847, quoted in Eleanor Melville Metcalf, *Herman Melville: Cycle and Epicycle* (Cambridge, MA: Harvard University Press, 1953), pp. 48–49.

110   "duns all round him": HM to Evert Duyckinck, December 14, 1849, in *Correspondence*, p. 149.

110   "the necessity of bestirring himself": *Mardi*, ch. 180, p. 592.

110   "When old Zack heard of it": HM to Allan Melville, February 20, 1849, in *Correspondence*, p. 116. See Hennig Cohen and Donald Yannella, *Herman Melville's Malcolm Letter: "Man's Final Lore"* (New York: Fordham University Press, 1992), for a detailed study of the family context at the time this letter was written.

111   "two *jobs* which I have done": HM to Lemuel Shaw, October 6, 1849, in *Correspondence*, p. 138.

111   "I, the author": Journal entry, November 6, 1849, in *Journals*, p. 13.

111   "pestilent lanes and alleys": *R*, ch. 39, p. 191.

111   "very much such a place": *R*, ch. 41, p. 202. In *Melville's City* (New York: Cambridge University Press, 1996), p. 125, Wyn Kelley remarks that Liverpool, as Melville rendered it in *Redburn*, "appears a faithful portrait of New York."

111   his "lady-like" friend: *R*, ch. 56, p. 281.

111   "impressed every column": *R*, ch. 31, p. 151.

111   "priory or castle": *R*, ch. 31, p. 159.

111   "two shrunken things": *R*, ch. 37, p. 180.

112   "It's none of my business": *R*, ch. 37, p. 181.

112   "caught . . . convulsively": *R*, ch. 37, p. 182.

112   With an infant mortality rate among the poor: James Walvin, *English Urban Life, 1776–1851* (London: Hutchinson, 1984), p. 24.

112   "not a Paradise then": *R*, ch. 33, p. 169.

112   "suffer more in mind": "Poor Man's Pudding and Rich Man's Crumbs," in *PT*, p. 296.

112   "dog-kennels": *R*, ch. 47, p. 239.

112   whom she likened to dogs: Child, letter to Maria Chapman, April 26, 1842, in *Selected Letters*, pp. 169–70.

113   "America must have seemed": *R*, ch. 51, p. 260.

113   "Let us waive": *R*, ch. 58, p. 292.

113   "elbowing, heartless-looking crowd": *R*, ch. 41, p. 202.

113   "going thro' the press": HM to Richard Bentley, July 20, 1849, in *Correspondence*, p. 134.

113   the amazingly short span of two months: See Willard Thorp, Historical Note, in *WJ*, p. 404.

114   "a polite, courteous way": *WJ*, ch. 4, p. 14.

114   "Nestor of the crew": *WJ*, ch. 86, p. 363.

114   "Troglodite . . . goggle-eyes": *WJ*, ch. 30, p. 125.

114   "curling his fingers . . . an insulted and unendurable existence": *WJ*, ch. 67, p. 280.

115   "our Revolution was in vain": *WJ*, ch. 35, p. 144.

115   "What, to the American slave": Douglass, "What to the Slave is the Fourth of July?" in the *Norton Anthology of American Literature*, 6th ed. (New York: Norton, 2003), p. 2003.

115   "*Head-bumping* . . . an especial favorite": *WJ*, ch. 66, p. 275.

115   "I . . . permit you to *play*": *WJ*, ch. 66, p. 276.

116   "I have swam through libraries": *MD*, ch. 32, p. 136.

116   "crack'd Archangel": See Merton M. Sealts, Jr., *Melville's Reading* (Columbia: University of South Carolina Press, 1988), pp. 38–39.

116   "Like a grand, ground swell": *Mardi*, ch. 119, p. 367.

116   "soul-becalmed": *WJ*, ch. 92, p. 393.

116   "placental": The word is Howard P. Vincent's, in *The Tailoring of Melville's White-Jacket* (Evanston: Northwestern University Press, 1970), p. 223.

116   "up and down": *WJ*, ch. 92, p. 394.

116   "metropolitan magnificence": *R*, ch. 46, p. 234.

117   "distinct and original signature": Warner Berthoff, *The Example of Melville* (Princeton: Princeton University Press, 1962), p. 5.

117   "Like a good wife": *Mardi*, ch. 121, p. 376.

117   "Where does any novelist": *CM*, ch. 44, p. 238.

117   "fantastic, incorrect, overburdened": Tocqueville, *Democracy in America*, II, 62.

117   "fire flames on my tongue": *Mardi*, ch. 119, p. 368.

119   the nineteenth-century equivalent: David Henkin, *City Reading: Written Words and Public Space in Antebellum New York* (New York: Columbia University Press, 1998), p. 74.

119   "our blood is as the flood": *R*, ch. 33, p. 169.

120   "vagabonding thro' the courts": Journal entry, November 10, 1849, in *Journals*, p. 16.

120   "The mob was brutish": Journal entry, November 13, 1849, ibid., p. 17.

120   Charles Dickens was present, too: Howard Horsford, "Melville and the London Street Scene," *Essays in Arts and Sciences* 16 (May 1987): 23–35.

120   "struggling to understand": Dennis Berthold, "Class Acts: The Astor Place Riots and Melville's 'The Two Temples,' " *American Literature* 71, no. 3 (1999): 453. Berthold's article gives a fine overview of Melville's developing political ambivalence in his New York years.

120   "Herman by birth": Augusta Melville to Peter Gansevoort, Jr., April 15, 1857, in *Log*, II, 572.

120   "in the fields and in the study": Evert Duyckinck and George Duyckinck, *Cyclopedia of American Literature* (1855), reprinted in Sealts, *Early Lives*, p. 95.

120   "feeling of loneliness . . . tether us to history": "With Ishmael in the Island City," *New York Times*, October 18, 2001, p. E1.

121   "In towns there is . . . soaring out of them": "I and My Chimney," in *PT*, p. 354.

121   "barbaric yawp": Whitman, "Song of Myself."

CHAPTER 5. HUNTING THE WHALE

122   "half way" into "a strange sort of book": HM to R. H. Dana, May 1, 1850, in *Correspondence*, p. 162.

122   "watery part of the world": *MD*, ch. 1. p. 3.

122   "howling infinite": *MD*, ch. 23, p. 107.

122   "unaccountable masses": *MD,* ch. 3, p. 12.

122   "pictures of nothing": Hazlitt, quoted in Robert K. Wallace, *Melville and Turner: Spheres of Love and Fright* (Athens: University of Georgia Press, 1992), p. 36.

122   "Turner's pictures of whalers": Cowen, "Melville's Marginalia," II, 275.

123   "unvarnished facts": HM, review of Browne, first published in *The Literary World,* March 6, 1847, in *PT,* p. 205.

123   "Blubber is blubber": HM to R. H. Dana, May 1, 1850, in *Correspondence,* p. 162.

123   "a romance of adventure": HM to Richard Bentley, June 27, 1850, ibid., p. 163.

123   signed up as a boatsteerer: See Howard, *Herman Melville,* pp. 63–64.

123   "rose cold": Puett, "Melville's Wife," p. 71.

123   "unrivalled either for the beauty": Robert Melville, advertisement in the *Pittsfield Sun,* quoted in Parker, I, 595.

124   "Don't you buy it": HM to Sarah Morewood, September [12 or 19?], 1851, in *Correspondence,* p. 206.

125   "Glorious place": Quoted in *Log,* I, 379.

125   "grounds would satisfy an English nobleman": Duyckinck, quoted in Luther Stearns Mansfield, "Melville and Hawthorne in the Berkshires," in Howard P. Vincent, ed., *Melville and Hawthorne in the Berkshires: A Symposium* (Kent, OH: Kent State University Press, 1968), p. 17.

125   Melville moved quickly toward a deal: Parker, I, 778.

125   "as ridiculous a fanfaronade . . . Eternal Quiet": Miller, *Raven and the Whale,* pp. 82–83.

125   "The Poets have made no mistake": Quoted in Parker, I, 743.

125   Melville's sister Kate: Puett, "Melville's Wife," p. 80.

125   "Quite a piece . . . tea party in the harbor": Quoted in Parker, I, 743.

126   "to seat himself . . . merry shouts and laughter": *Log,* I, 384.

126   "One day it chanced": J. E. A. Smith, *Taghconic* (1879), quoted in Sealts, *Early Lives of Melville,* p. 198.

126   "on the new hay in the barn": Sophia Hawthorne to Evert Duyckinck, August 29, 1850, in *Log,* I, 391. Melville's books were sent to Hawthorne by Duyckinck; see *Correspondence,* p. 166.

126   "dropped germinous seeds": "Hawthorne and His Mosses," in *PT,* p. 250.

126   "truth . . . finds its way": Hawthorne, "The Birthmark," in Hawthorne, *Tales* (New York: Library of America, 1982), p. 767.

127   "Melville has a new book": Evert Duyckinck to George Duyckinck, August 7, 1850, in *Log,* I, 385.

127   "Revision" is too slight a term: The hypothesis that *Moby-Dick* underwent radical revision was first advanced by Leon Howard, "Melville's Struggle with the Angel," *Modern Language Quarterly* 1 (1940): 195–206, and was elaborated by Olson (*Call Me Ishmael*) and by George R. Stewart, "The Two *Moby-Dicks*," *American Literature* 25 (January 1954): 417–48. James R. Barbour, " 'All my books are botches': Melville Struggles with *The Whale,*" in James Barbour and Tom Quirk, eds., *Writing the American Classics* (Chapel Hill: University of North Carolina Press, 1990), pp. 25–52, argues that *Moby-Dick* went through not two but three distinctive phases: first came a straightforward story of the "whale fisheries"; then, after August 1850, the "cetological" chapters were added; and

finally, the story of Ahab and his quest took shape in the early months of 1851. Perhaps the most cogent assessment of what can be known about how HM wrote the work is Robert Milder, "The Composition of *Moby-Dick:* A Review and a Prospect," *ESQ* 23 (1977): 203-16. Also valuable is Walter Bezanson, "*Moby-Dick:* Document, Drama, Dream," in Bryant, ed., *Companion*, pp. 176-83.

127   "You must have plenty of sea-room": "Hawthorne and His Mosses," in *PT*, p. 246.

127   "to future generations": "Hawthorne and His Mosses," in *PT*, p. 249.

127   "Nathaniel of Salem": "Hawthorne and His Mosses," in *PT*, p. 246.

127   "soft ravishments": "Hawthorne and His Mosses," in *PT*, p. 241.

127   "genius, all over the world": "Hawthorne and His Mosses," in *PT*, p. 249.

127   "better to fail in originality": Satan's speech in *Paradise Lost* occurs at bk. I, l. 263, an echo of Homer's *Odyssey*, bk. 11, ll. 489-91, where Achilles, visited in Hades by Odysseus, declares that he would rather be a slave on earth than a king in Hades. For the impact of Milton on Melville, see Henry F. Pommer, *Milton and Melville* (Pittsburgh: University of Pittsburgh Press, 1950). HM's letters are full of Miltonic references, such as one to Duyckinck of August 16, 1850, where he speaks of "thrones and dominations" (a mistake for "dominions"), echoing the phrase from *Paradise Lost* at bk. 3, l. 320. See the headnote in *Correspondence*, p. 166.

127   "Virgil my minstrel": *Mardi*, ch. 119, p. 368.

128   "Mecaenas listening to Virgil": *WJ*, ch. 11, p. 41.

128   "safety, comfort, hearthstone": *MD*, ch. 23, p. 106.

128   "New Bedford rose in terraces of streets": *MD*, ch. 13, pp. 59-60.

129   "that direst of storms": *MD*, ch. 119, p. 503.

129   "through that transparent air": *MD*, ch. 35, p. 159.

129   "clos'd his Swimming Eyes": *Aeneid* (Dryden translation), bk. 5, l. 1113.

129   plunges into the ocean and drowns: Anthony Hecht, in *Melodies Unheard: Essays on the Mysteries of Poetry* (Baltimore: Johns Hopkins University Press, 2003), pp. 219-37, compares Melville's short-lived Bulkington to Virgil's helmsman Palinurus. Hecht's essay is richly suggestive of Melville's indebtedness to Homeric as well as Virgilian epics. A helpful resource devoted to this subject is Gail H. Coffler, *Melville's Classical Allusions: A Comprehensive Index and Glossary* (Westport, CT: Greenwood Press, 1985), and see, more generally, Mary K. Bercaw Edwards, *Melville's Sources* (Evanston: Northwestern University Press, 1987).

129   While in London, Melville had acquired: Sealts, *Melville's Reading*, p. 214.

129   "marvellously endowed": Cowen, "Melville's Marginalia," VII, 180.

129   "Are you then so easily turned": Mary Shelley, *Frankenstein* (1818; Oxford: Oxford University Press, 1980), p. 214.

130   "What say ye men": *MD*, ch. 36, p. 163.

130   the idea of Captain Ahab: See the invaluable explanatory notes to the edition of *Moby-Dick* edited by Luther S. Mansfield and Howard P. Vincent (New York: Hendricks House, 1962), esp. pp. 648ff. for discussion of many possible influences on HM's conception of Ahab.

130   "revenge, immortal hate": *Paradise Lost*, bk. I, ll. 106-8. Sources have also been suggested in Byron, Goethe, Carlyle, Bulwer-Lytton, and many other writers.

130   "every copy that was come-atable": HM to Evert Duyckinck, February 24, 1849, in *Correspondence*, p. 119.

130 "painted hideously"; "very pretty": Journal entry, November 19, 1849, in *Journals,* p. 22.

130 "Richard-the-third-humps": "Hawthorne and His Mosses," in *PT,* p. 244.

130 "if another Messiah ever comes": HM to Evert Duyckinck, February 24, 1849, in *Correspondence,* p. 119.

131 "dark characters" as "Hamlet, Timon": "Hawthorne and his Mosses," in *PT,* p. 244.

131 "with a crucifixion in his face": *MD,* ch. 28, p. 124.

131 "a long, limber, portentous, black mass ": *MD,* ch. 3, p. 12.

131 "chief mates, and second mates": *MD,* ch. 3, p. 22.

131 "This young fellow's healthy cheek": *MD,* ch. 5, pp. 29–30.

131 "could show a cheek": *MD,* ch. 5, p. 30.

131 "an island far away": *MD,* ch. 12, p. 55.

131 "is a dangerous man": *MD,* ch. 3, p. 19.

132 "bosom friend": *MD,* title of ch. 10, p. 49.

132 "the color of a three-days' old Congo baby": *MD,* ch. 3, p. 22.

132 "The departure from home": William Cox, "Traveling—Mentally and Bodily" (first pub. in *New York Mirror,* January 19, 1833), in Taft, ed. *Minor Knickerbockers,* p. 279.

132 "thrown over me . . . I had been his wife": *MD,* ch. 4, p. 25.

133 "similar circumstance . . . longest day in the year": *MD,* ch. 4, pp. 25–26.

133 "Instantly I felt a shock": *MD,* ch. 4, p. 26.

133 takes up residence in his own psyche: Mansfield and Vincent (Hendrick House edition of *Moby-Dick,* p. 609) suggest that Melville had in mind Thomas De Quincey's "The Vision of Sudden Death" (published in *Blackwood's Magazine* in December 1849 and briefly excerpted in *The Literary World,* January 5, 1850). De Quincey describes a child's dream of temptation and fear: "Perhaps not one of us escapes that dream; perhaps, as by some sorrowful doom of man, that dream repeats for every one of us, through every generation, the original temptation of Eden. Every one of us, in this dream, has a bait offered to the infirm places of his own individual will; once again a snare is made ready for leading him into captivity to a luxury of ruin; again, as in aboriginal Paradise, the man falls from innocence. . . . Even so in dreams, perhaps, under some secret conflict of the midnight sleeper, lighted up to the consciousness at the time, but darkened to the memory as soon as all is finished, each several child of our mysterious race completes for himself the aboriginal fall."

133 "whether it was a reality or a dream": *MD,* ch. 4, p. 25.

134 "how elastic our stiff prejudices grow": *MD,* ch. 11, p. 54.

134 "No more my splintered heart": *MD,* ch. 10, p. 51.

134 "perfect prodigy": HM to Allan Melville, February 20, 1849, in *Correspondence,* p. 116.

134 "Mirth and a heavy heart": Rush, letter to John Coakely Lettsom, April 21, 1788, in *Letters of Benjamin Rush,* ed. L. H. Butterfield, 2 vols. (Princeton: Princeton University Press, 1951), I, 458.

134 "currents of the Universal Being": Emerson, *Nature,* in Whicher, ed., *Selections,* p. 24.

134 "In reading some of Goethe's sayings . . . upon your head": HM to Nathaniel Hawthorne, June 1[?], 1851, in *Correspondence*, pp. 193-94.

135 "When conversing": Sophia Hawthorne to her mother, September 3, 1850, in *Log*, I, 393-94.

135 "Mr. Noble Melancholy": In *Log*, I, 383.

135 "The freshness of primeval nature": Sophia Hawthorne to Evert Duyckinck, August 29, 1850, quoted in Metcalf, *Herman Melville: Cycle and Epicycle*, p. 90.

135 "ocean-experience has given sea-room": Sophia Hawthorne to her mother, Elizabeth Palmer Peabody, quoted in Brenda Wineapple, *Hawthorne: A Life* (New York: Knopf, 2003), p. 227.

135 "was very careful not to interrupt": Sophia Hawthorne to Elizabeth Palmer Peabody, October [?], 1850, quoted in *Log*, II, 925.

135 "ontological heroics": HM to Nathaniel Hawthorne, June 29, 1851, quoted in *Log*, I, 415.

135 "lasted pretty deep into the night": Hawthorne's journal, August 1, 1851, quoted in *Log*, I, 419.

136 "evasive and enigmatic": Martin Green, "Herman Melville," in *Penguin History of American Literature to 1900*, ed. Marcus Cunliffe (New York: Penguin, 1993), p. 202.

136 But Hawthorne was different: Many scholars have made the point that Hawthorne succeeded HM's late brother Gansevoort and the limited Evert Duyckinck as his mentor and confidant. See Widmer, *Young America*, p. 112; Barbour, " 'All my books are botches,' " p. 36; and Edwin Haviland Miller, who remarks in *Melville: A Biography* (New York: Perseus Books, 1975), p. 246, that Hawthorne was "a father and a brother come to life."

136 "Whenever . . . it is a damp, drizzly November": *MD*, ch. 1, p. 3.

136 "the first person": Sophia Hawthorne to Evert Duyckinck, August 29, 1850, in *Log*, I, 391.

137 "up to the present day": "Hawthorne and His Mosses," in *PT*, p. 253.

137 "by-gone days": Henry F. Chorley, review of *Twice-Told Tales* in the *Athenaeum*, August 23, 1845, in J. Donald Crowley, ed., *Hawthorne: The Critical Heritage* (New York: Barnes & Noble, 1970), p. 96.

137 "spite of all the Indian-summer sunlight": "Hawthorne and His Mosses," in *PT*, p. 243.

137 "time and eternity": Hawthorne's journal, August 1, 1851, quoted in *Log*, I, 419.

137 "dig a deep hole": HM to Nathaniel Hawthorne, July 22, 1851, in *Correspondence*, p. 200.

137 "Whence come you, Hawthorne? . . . both in God's": HM to Nathaniel Hawthorne, November [17?], 1851, ibid., p. 212.

137 "let no man": *WJ*, ch. 63, p. 260.

138 "great power of blackness": "Hawthorne and His Mosses," in *PT*, p. 243.

138 "You should see the maples": HM to Evert Duyckinck, October 6, 1850, in *Correspondence*, p. 170.

138 "imperial muse tosses the creation": Emerson, *Nature*, in Whicher, ed., *Selections*, p. 44.

138   Eastern tales of dervishes: See Dorothee Finkelstein, *Melville's Orienda* (New Haven: Yale University Press, 1961).

138   "the remotest spaces of nature": Emerson, *Nature,* in Whicher, ed., *Selections,* p. 44.

138   "all the generations of whales": *MD,* ch. 104, p. 456.

139   "candidate for an archbishoprick": *MD,* ch. 95, p. 420.

139   "Perseus, St. George, Hercules": *MD,* ch. 82, p. 363.

139   "Towards thee I roll": *MD,* ch. 135, pp. 571–72.

139   "heroes, saints, demigods": *MD,* ch. 82, p. 363.

139   "at once masculine and feminine": Richard Slotkin, *Regeneration Through Violence* (Middletown: Wesleyan University Press, 1973), p. 547.

139   "A gentle joyousness": *MD,* ch. 133, p. 548.

139   "grand hooded phantom": *MD,* ch. 1, p. 7.

139   "All men live enveloped in whale-lines": *MD,* ch. 60, p. 281.

140   "Herman, I hope returned home safe": Maria Melville to Augusta Melville, March 1851, quoted in Parker, I, 820.

140   her nephew Robert: For the incident with Robert, see Parker, I, 733.

140   "spring begins to open": HM to Evert Duyckinck, March 26, 1851, in *Log,* I, 408.

140   "shaping out the gigantic conception": Nathaniel Hawthorne, quoted in *Log,* I, 416.

140   "at his desk all day": *Log,* I, 412.

140   "in a sort of mesmeric state": HM to Evert Duyckinck, December 13, 1850, in *Correspondence,* p. 174.

140   "a sort of sea-feeling . . . rig in the chimney": HM to Evert Duyckinck, December 13, 1850, ibid., p. 173.

140   "everlasting terra incognita": *MD,* ch. 58, p. 273.

141   "those dreary regions . . . too thick for me to master them": HM to Evert Duyckinck, August 16, 1850, in *Correspondence,* pp. 167–68.

141   "driven forth": HM to Evert Duyckinck, February 21, 1850, ibid., p. 154.

141   "matters of course": HM to Lemuel Shaw, April 23, 1849, ibid., p. 130.

141   "to regard my literary affairs": HM to John Murray, October 29, 1847, ibid., p. 99.

141   felt compelled to borrow $2,000 more: See G. Thomas Tanselle, Historical Note, in *MD,* p. 660.

141   "Though I wrote the Gospels . . . holding the door ajar": HM to Nathaniel Hawthorne, [June 1?], 1851, in *Correspondence,* pp. 192, 191.

142   "This country is at present": HM to Richard Bentley, July 20, 1851, ibid., p. 198.

142   "in full blast": HM to Evert Duyckinck, November 7, 1851, ibid., p. 210.

142   "each silent worshipper": *MD,* ch. 7, p. 34.

142   "drooped and fell away": *MD,* ch. 9, p. 48.

142   "happiness . . . of the artist discovering": Walker Percy, *Signposts in a Strange Land* (New York: Farrar, Straus & Giroux, 1991), p. 201.

143   "did not build himself in with plans": *Mardi,* ch. 180, p. 595.

143   "A good half of writing": Norman Mailer, *The Armies of the Night* (New York: New American Library, 1968), p. 28.

143   "Nantucket! Take out your map": *MD,* ch. 14, p. 63.

144   "Give me a condor's quill!": *MD,* ch. 104, p. 456.

144   "shallow and scanty": Hawthorne, notebook entry, July 27, 1844, in *The American Notebooks,* ed. Claude M. Simpson (Columbus: Ohio State University Press, 1972), p. 250.

145   "taking a book off the brain": HM to Evert Duyckinck, December 13, 1850, in *Correspondence,* p. 174.

145   "possible and impossible matters": Hawthorne's journal, August 1, 1851, in *Log,* I, 419.

145   "When we see how little we can express": Hawthorne, notebook entry, July 27, 1844, in *American Notebooks,* ed. Simpson, p. 250.

145   "gathering up and piecing together": Hawthorne, *The Marble Faun* (1860), ch. 11, in *Novels,* p. 929.

145   "send me about fifty fast-writing youths": HM to Evert Duyckinck, December 13, 1850, in *Correspondence,* p. 174.

145   "George Washington cannibalistically developed": *MD,* ch. 10, p. 50.

145   "the exact embodiment": *MD,* ch. 16, p. 75.

145   "so utterly lost": *MD,* ch. 27, p. 119.

145   "with a chest like a coffer-dam": *MD,* ch. 3, p. 16.

145   and then, twenty chapters later, summarily dismisses: See Harrison Hayford's discussion in the Historical Note to *MD,* p. 657.

146   "two books . . . being writ": *P,* bk. 22, p. 304.

146   "ebullition of mind": Melville marked this passage in Hazlitt's essay "On Application to Study," published in the 1845 American edition of *Table Talk.* See Wallace, *Melville and Turner,* p. 111.

146   "in mental life": Freud, *Civilization and Its Discontents* (1930; New York: Norton, 1961), p. 16.

146   "noble shoulders . . . dazzling by contrast": *MD,* ch. 3, p. 16.

147   "there is but one planet": *CM,* ch. 44, p. 239.

147   "Brave as he might be": *MD,* ch. 26, p. 117.

147   But that he changed his ideas: See the Editorial Appendix in *MD,* p. 832, where G. Thomas Tanselle remarks that "Bulkington seems best explained as a vestigial character from an earlier stage in the book's composition, in which he was to be Ishmael's 'comrade,' a role subsequently assigned to Queequeg." Parker (II, 933) accepts Geoffrey Sanborn's suggestion that "Melville based Queequeg on Tupai Cupa, a Maori described in George Lillie Craik's *The New Zealanders* (1830)," and surmises that HM "had progressed some distance into his manuscript with Bulkington as Ishmael's special comrade before he picked up *The New Zealanders,*" which gave him the idea for a new character.

147   "Some chapters back": *MD,* ch. 23, p. 106.

148   "Take heart, take heart": *MD,* ch. 23, p. 107.

148   "introduces a character": Stewart, "The Two *Moby-Dicks,*" p. 424.

148   "the idea of a connected and collected story": Review by Henry F. Chorley, *Athenaeum,* October 25, 1851, in Watson G. Branch, ed., *Melville: The Critical Heritage* (London: Kegan Paul, 1985; cited hereafter as *Critical Heritage*), p. 253.

148   "intellectual chowder": Duyckinck, review in *The Literary World,* November 15 and 22, 1851, ibid., p. 265.

148   "there are some enterprises": *MD,* ch. 82, p. 361.

148   "This man interested me at once": *MD,* ch. 3, p. 16.

148   a short, "six-inch chapter": *MD,* ch. 23, p. 106.

148   "the unconscious mind": John Freeman, *Herman Melville* (London and New York: Macmillan, 1926), p. 176.

148   "of romance, philosophy, natural history": Evert Duyckinck, review of *Moby-Dick* in *The Literary World,* November 22, 1851, in Higgins and Parker, eds., *Contemporary Reviews,* p. 384.

CHAPTER 6. CAPTAIN AMERICA

149   "It seems a golden Hell!": *Mardi,* ch. 166, p. 547.

149   "The United States will conquer Mexico": Emerson, quoted in Bernard De Voto, *The Year of Decision, 1846* (Boston: Little, Brown, 1943), p. 492.

149   In his copy of the works of William D'Avenant: See Steven Olsen-Smith and Dennis C. Marnon, "Melville's Marginalia in *The Works of William D'Avenant*," *Leviathan* 6, no. 1 (March 2004): 86.

150   "Let slavery take care of itself": Evert Duyckinck to George Duyckinck, May 23, 1848, quoted in Davis, *Melville's Mardi,* p. 88.

150   "the unacknowledged ghost": Charles M. Wiltse, *The New Nation, 1800–1845* (New York: Hill & Wang, 1961), p. 156.

150   "He looked like a man cut away": *MD,* ch. 28, p. 123. For a survey of contemporary descriptions of Calhoun as a man "at once repulsive and fascinating," see Alan Heimert, "*Moby-Dick* and American Political Symbolism," *American Quarterly* 15 (1963): 523.

150   "exclusive power of controlling the Government": Calhoun, speech in the United States Senate, March 4, 1850, in *Calhoun: Basic Documents,* ed. John M. Anderson (State College, PA: Bald Eagle Press, 1952), p. 300.

150   "cannot . . . be saved by eulogies": Ibid., p. 312.

150   "I wish to speak today": Webster, speech in the United States Senate, March 7, 1850, in *The Great Speeches of Daniel Webster* (Boston, 1894), p. 600.

151   "Every member of every Northern legislature": Ibid., p. 617.

151   "nothing to propose": Ibid., p. 623.

151   "We have the wolf by the ears": Jefferson, letter to John Holmes, April 22, 1820, in Merrill D. Peterson, ed., *Thomas Jefferson: Writings* (New York: Library of America, 1984), p. 1434.

152   only a few crackpot dreamers: John Stauffer, *The Black Hearts of Men: Radical Abolitionists and the Transformation of Race* (Cambridge, MA: Harvard University Press, 2002), offers portraits of four antebellum public figures—Gerrit Smith, John Brown, James McCune Smith, and Frederick Douglass—who envisioned a racially egalitarian society to be achieved, if necessary, by violence. But Stauffer rightly calls these men "in no way 'representative' " (p. 3) and celebrates them as unheralded prophets. Charles Sumner's unsuccessful argument before the Massachusetts Supreme Court in 1849 for desegregation of the Boston public schools has been recognized in retrospect as a forerunner

of *Brown v. Board of Education* more than a hundred years later. For a convenient gathering of antebellum writings envisioning a society organized on principles of racial justice, see William H. Pease and Jane H. Pease, *The Antislavery Argument* (New York: Bobbs-Merrill, 1965), ch. 10, "Arguments for Racial Equality."

152   "if they were all landed there in a day . . . not know what to do": Lincoln, "Speech on the Kansas-Nebraska Act" (October 16, 1854), in Don E. Fehrenbacher, ed., *Abraham Lincoln: Speeches and Writings,* 2 vols. (New York: Library of America, 1989), I, 316. Tocqueville (*Democracy in America,* I, 377–78) estimated that "in twelve years the Colonization Society has transported 2500 Negroes to Africa; in the same space of time about 700,000 blacks were born in the United States."

152   "What has the North to do with slavery?": *The Journals of Bronson Alcott,* ed. Odell Shepard (Boston: Houghton Mifflin, 1938), p. 243.

152   "Northern Representatives . . . are no better": Parker, "Sermon on War," in Warner, ed., *American Sermons,* p. 624.

153   "If our resistance to this law is not right": Emerson, "Address to the Citizens of Concord on the Fugitive Slave Law" (May 3, 1851), in Len Gougeon and Joel Myerson, eds., *Emerson's Antislavery Writings* (New Haven: Yale University Press, 1995), pp. 57–58.

153   Dr. Holmes, who signed a public circular: Louis Menand, *The Metaphysical Club* (New York: Farrar, Straus & Giroux, 2001), p. 16.

153   "slavery in its best and mildest form": Holmes, quoted in Carolyn L. Karcher, *Shadow over the Promised Land: Slavery, Race, and Violence in Melville's America* (Baton Rouge: Louisiana State University Press, 1980), p. 11.

153   John C. Hoadley: Parker, I, 801.

153   "dwelt together in greater peace and affection": Hawthorne, quoted in Karcher, *Shadow over the Promised Land,* p. 12.

153   "I hate to see the poor creatures": Lincoln, letter to Joshua Speed, August 24, 1855, in Fehrenbacher, ed., *Abraham Lincoln: Speeches and Writings,* I, 360.

154   "like a black squall": Richard Henry Dana, Jr., *Journal,* ed. Robert F. Lucid, 3 vols. (Cambridge, MA: Harvard University Press, 1968), II, 412.

154   "What a moment was lost": Emerson, quoted in Albert J. Von Frank, *The Trials of Anthony Burns: Freedom and Slavery in Emerson's Boston* (Cambridge, MA: Harvard University Press, 1998), p. 28. For the connection between *Uncle Tom's Cabin* and the Crafts, see Joan Hedrick, *Harriet Beecher Stowe: A Life* (New York: Oxford University Press, 1994), p. 212.

154   "pure, fearless, and upright": Frederic Hathaway Chase, *Lemuel Shaw: Chief Justice of the Supreme Judicial Court of Masschusetts* (Boston: Houghton Mifflin, 1918), p. 164.

154   "an owner of a slave": Quoted ibid., pp. 164–65.

154   "It is strange": Quoted in Von Frank, *Trials of Anthony Burns,* p. 30.

155   "abstains from doing downright ill": *P,* bk. 14, p. 214.

155   "NO UNION WITH SLAVEHOLDERS!": Garrison, in *The Liberator,* May 31, 1844, reprinted in George M. Fredrickson, ed., *William Lloyd Garrison* (Englewood Cliffs, NJ: Prentice-Hall, 1968), p. 52.

155 "I wake in the morning": Emerson, "Address to the Citizens of Concord," in Gougeon and Myerson, eds., *Emerson's Antislavery Writings,* p. 53.

156 "woe-begone figures of captives": *R,* ch. 31, p. 155.

156 "Thank God! I am a white": *WJ,* ch. 67, p. 277.

156 "each answering all": Whitman, "Salut au Monde!"

156 "superstitious, ignorant, and thievish race": Whitman, letter to his mother (1868), quoted in Newton Arvin, *Whitman* (New York: Macmillan, 1938),p. 33.

156 "so inferior a race": Emerson, journal entry, September 10, 1840, in Porte, ed., *Emerson in His Journals,* p. 245.

156 put the Negro just above: See Kenneth Silverman, *Lightning Man: The Accursed Life of Samuel F. B. Morse* (New York: Knopf, 2003), p. 401.

156 "the extent to which the Americans": Charles Lyell, *Travels in North America in the Years 1841-42* (New York, 1845), excerpted in Clement Eaton, *The Leaven of Democracy* (New York: George Braziller, 1963), p. 422.

156 "Seamen have strong prejudices": HM, "The 'Gees,' " in *PT,* p. 347.

156 "no distinction as to color": John Allan, quoted in James Farr, "A Slow Boat to Nowhere: The Multi-Racial Crews of the American Whaling Industry," *Journal of Negro History* 68, no. 2 (Spring 1983): 165.

156 Robert Lucas: See Brook Thomas, *Cross-Examinations of Law and Literature: Cooper, Hawthorne, Stowe, and Melville* (New York: Cambridge University Press, 1987), pp. 94-95.

156 "a man can be honest": *MD,* ch. 3, p. 21.

157 Mungo Park's *Travels:* "I . . . enter many nations," HM wrote in *Mardi* (ch. 119, p. 368), "as Mungo Park rested in African cots." See Sterling Stuckey, *Going Through the Storm So Long: The Influence of African American Art in History* (New York: Oxford University Press, 1994), pp. 154-56.

157 "to be short, then": *MD,* ch. 32, p. 137.

157 "Narwhale"; "Nostril whale": *MD,* ch. 32, p. 142.

157 "the Fin-Back is not gregarious": *MD,* ch. 32, p. 139.

157 "sentimental Indian eyes": *MD,* ch. 32, p. 144.

157 "a zestful-skeptical running commentary": Lawrence Buell, *Writing for an Endangered World: Literature, Culture, and Environment in the U.S. and Beyond* (Cambridge, MA: Harvard University Press, 2001), p. 212. See also Samuel Otter, *Melville's Anatomies* (Berkeley: University of California Press, 1999), who remarks that "Melville employs the whale's massive corpus as the revealing stage on which to play out the tragedy and comedy of nineteenth-century bodily investigations" (p. 132).

157 "It is in vain . . . repellingly intricate": *MD,* ch. 32, pp. 138-39.

157 "sin it is, no less": *Mardi,* ch. 162, p. 534.

157 "from the Southern States": *WJ,* ch. 34, p. 141.

158 "no hearts above the snow-line": *MD,* ch. 125, p. 522.

158 "humanity cries out": *Mardi,* ch. 162, p. 534.

158 "like a slave": *R,* ch. 13, p. 66.

158 "about to be dashed to pieces": Mississippi senator Henry Foote (1848), quoted in Heimert, "American Political Symbolism," p. 500.

158 "the ferocity and carnage": Thoreau, "Brute Neighbors," in *Walden,* p. 507.

158   "the American army": *MD,* ch. 27, p. 121.

158   "coal-black" harpooneer Daggoo: *MD,* ch. 27, p. 120.

159   "The sight of little Flask": *MD,* ch. 48, p. 221.

159   "Thy race is the undeniable dark side": *MD,* ch. 40, p. 177.

159   an "Alabama boy" and a native of Connecticut: Pip is identified as being from Alabama in *MD,* ch. 27, p. 121, and as a native of Tolland County, Connecticut, in ch. 93, p. 412.

159   "Beat thy belly": *MD,* ch. 40, p. 174.

160   "Stick to the boat . . . hurried traveller's trunk": *MD,* ch. 93, p. 413.

160   "ringed horizon . . . at least they said he was": *MD,* ch. 93, p. 414.

160   "Upon my soul . . . they look": *MD,* ch. 99, p. 434.

160   "white squalls": *MD,* ch. 40, p. 178.

160   "Will ye do one little errand for me?": *MD,* ch. 110, p. 479.

161   "Where sayest thou . . . Pip the coward?": *MD,* ch. 125, p. 522.

161   "strange sweetness of his lunacy": *MD,* ch. 110, p. 479.

161   "Come! I feel prouder": *MD,* ch. 125, p. 522.

161   "darkness . . . licked up by": *MD,* ch. 96, p. 422.

162   "spermaceti, oil, and bone": *MD,* ch. 98, p. 427.

162   "iron horse . . . breathing fire": Thoreau, "Sounds," in *Walden,* p. 415.

162   "With huge pronged poles": *MD,* ch. 96, p. 423.

163   "grand, ungodly . . . deeper wonders than the waves": *MD,* ch. 16, p. 79.

163   "ribbed bed . . . not before": *MD,* ch. 19, pp. 91–92.

163   a "lividly whitish" scar: *MD,* ch. 28, p. 123.

163   "Reality outran apprehension": *MD,* ch. 28, p. 123.

163   "erect" and "nervous" Ahab: *MD,* ch. 28, p. 124; ch. 36, p. 160. In *M,* ch. 162, p. 534, HM had portrayed Calhoun as the "hard-hearted" character "Nulli." See Heimert, "American Political Symbolism," p. 525.

163   "was the huge reservoir of rebellion": G. W. Curtis, *Orations and Addresses,* 2 vols. (New York, 1894), I, 128.

163   "like an anvil": *MD,* ch. 128, p. 532.

163   "to prevent excitement": Calhoun, *Basic Documents,* p. 299.

164   "violently agitated" and "clamorous crowd": *Mardi,* ch. 161, p. 524.

164   "the so-called democratic party": Parke Godwin, "Our New President," *Putnam's Monthly Magazine,* September 1853, pp. 304, 308.

164   "an incorrigible old hunks": *MD,* ch. 16, p. 74.

164   "hickory, with the bark": *MD,* ch. 113, p. 489.

164   these freighted political symbols: See Heimert, "American Political Symbolism," passim.

165   "destroys all sin": *MD,* ch. 9, p. 48.

165   "top-gallant delight": *MD,* ch. 9, p. 48.

165   the "higher law" of God: On Seward and other proponents of the "higher law" in the 1850s, see Gregg D. Crane, *Race, Citizenship, and Law in American Literature* (New York: Cambridge University Press, 2002), ch. 1.

165   the black abolitionist James McCune Smith: "Horoscope," *Frederick Douglass's Paper,* March 7, 1856. This early example of political interpretation of *Moby-Dick* was recently discovered by John Stauffer; see *Black Hearts,* p. 66.

165   Robert C. Winthrop as a likely model: See Charles H. Foster, "Something in
      Emblems: A Reinterpretation of *Moby-Dick,*" *New England Quarterly* 34 (1961),
      reprinted in Hershel Parker and Harrison Hayford, eds., *Moby-Dick as Dou-
      bloon* (New York: Norton, 1970), p. 283.

165   plausibly identified as Thomas Hart Benton: Heimert, "American Political Sym-
      bolism," p. 530.

165   William Lloyd Garrison: The identification of Ahab with Garrison was pro-
      posed by Willie T. Weathers, "*Moby-Dick* and the Nineteenth-Century Scene,"
      Texas Studies in Language and Literature 1, no. 4 (Winter 1960): 477–501.

165   "distortion of the 'political Messiah' ": Sacvan Bercovitch, *The American Jere-
      miad* (Madison: University of Wisconsin Press, 1978), p. 192.

166   "comprehensive, combining, and subtle": *MD,* ch. 74, p. 331.

166   "many myths and many men": Richard Chase, *Herman Melville: A Critical
      Study* (New York: Macmillan, 1949), p. 43. In his copy of Shelley's *Essays,*
      Melville underscored a passage in which Satan is described as "far superior to
      God . . . one who perseveres . . . in spite of adversity and torture"; see F. O.
      Matthiessen, *American Renaissance* (New York: Oxford University Press, 1941),
      note at p. 450.

166   *Watson and the Shark:* Copley's painting was widely available in the form of
      engraved printed copies. The painting itself, which had been given by the artist's
      son "to a near relative in Boston," very likely hung through the first half of the
      nineteenth century in a Beacon Hill drawing room, where it may have been
      known to the Melvill and Shaw families. See Theodore Stebbins et al., *A New
      World: Masterpieces of American Painting, 1760–1910* (Boston: Museum of Fine
      Arts, 1983), p. 211.

166   "man of stone and iron": Emerson, "Napoleon," in *Representative Men* (Cam-
      bridge, MA: Harvard University Press, 1996), pp. 133–36.

166   "out-reaching comprehensiveness": *MD,* ch. 104, p. 456.

166   "original character . . . is like a revolving Drummond light": *CM,* ch. 44, p. 239.

167   "be careful in the hunt": *MD,* ch. 22, p. 105.

167   "athirst for human blood": *MD,* ch. 41, p. 181.

167   "His three boats": *MD,* ch. 41, p. 184.

167   "wondrous story": Owen Chase's narrative is reprinted in Nathaniel Philbrick
      and Thomas Philbrick, eds., *The Loss of the Ship Essex, Sunk by a Whale: First-
      Person Accounts* (New York: Penguin, 2000). Nathaniel Philbrick's *In the Heart
      of the Sea* (2000) is a highly readable retelling of the frightful events. For Mel-
      ville's annotations in his copy of Chase, see Sealts, *Melville's Reading,* pp. 23,
      69, and Cowen, "Melville's Marginalia," IV, 245–68.

167   "an old bull whale": See Howard P. Vincent, *The Trying-out of Moby-Dick*
      (Kent: Kent State University Press, 1980), pp. 169–75.

168   "for long months of days and weeks": *MD,* ch. 41, pp. 184–85.

168   "entire, and to all appearances lusty": *MD,* ch. 106, p. 463.

168   "the rare ambiguous monster": W. H. Auden, "Herman Melville."

168   Ahab, "dismasted": *MD,* ch. 28, p. 124; ch. 36, p. 163.

168   "so great a multitude": *MD,* ch. 87, p. 382.

168   expose "themselves to increased attack": Robert L. Pittman et al., "Killer Whale

Predation on Sperm Whales: Observations and Implications," *Marine Mammal Science* 17, no. 3 (July 2001): 494.

169   "Beheld through a blending atmosphere": *MD*, ch. 87, pp. 382–83.

169   "calmly and fixedly gaze away": *MD*, ch. 87, p. 388. See Elizabeth Schultz, "Melville's Environmental Vision in *Moby-Dick*," *Interdisciplinary Studies in Literature and Environment (ISLE)* 7 (2000): 97–113, and, for an early instance of "green" criticism, Robert Zoellner's *The Salt Sea-Mastodon: A Reading of Moby-Dick* (Berkeley: University of California Press, 1973), especially chapter 9, "Fraternal Congenerity: The Humanizing of Leviathan," in which Zoellner repeatedly refers to the aged dying whale of chapter 81 as "The Medicare Whale."

169   "Lost in . . . reminiscence sore": *Clarel*, pt. I, 11, ll. 25–26.

169   "I'd strike the sun": *MD*, ch. 36, p. 164.

169   "To accomplish his object": *MD*, ch. 46, p. 211.

170   "the waves curling and hissing . . . grazed by the iron, escaped": *MD*, ch. 48, p. 224.

170   "churned his long sharp lance . . . corpse he had made": *MD*, ch. 61, p. 286.

170   "vocal organ was in itself": Hawthorne, *The Scarlet Letter*, p. 241.

170   "an oral world in which the spoken word was central": Lawrence W. Levine, *Highbrow / Lowbrow: The Emergence of Cultural Hierarchy in America* (Cambridge, MA: Harvard University Press, 1988), p. 36.

171   "declaiming some stormy passage": Whitman, quoted ibid., p. 37.

171   "vague thoughts of becoming a great orator": *R*, ch. 7, p. 36.

171   "mount that might not be touched": Kenneth Cmiel, *Democratic Eloquence: The Fight over Popular Speech in Nineteenth-Century America* (New York: William Morrow, 1990), p. 23.

171   "animal sob": *MD*, ch. 36, p. 163.

171   "language of the screamer": Chase, *Herman Melville*, p. 91. See Constance Rourke, *American Humor: A Study of the National Character* (New York: Harcourt, Brace, 1931), for a penetrating discussion (pp. 195–96) of how "comedy remains in *Moby-Dick* like the strong trace of an irresistible mood." Reading Rourke on nineteenth-century American humor remains the best way to appreciate Ahab as a tall-tale braggart in the lineage of such folklore heroes as Sam Slick ("I am Sam Slick the Yankee peddler—I can ride on a flash of lightning and catch a thunderbolt in my fist," p. 73). Later scholars, notably Joel Porte, in an essay entitled "Melville: Romantic Cock-and-Bull; or, The Great Art of Telling the Truth" (*In Respect to Egotism: Studies in American Romantic Writing* [New York: Cambridge University Press, 1991], pp. 189–212), go so far as to argue that Ahab's speeches, in their "rhetorical overopulence," are "mere tinsel Shakespeare" (pp. 196–97) in the style of the worst melodramatic actors of the day, and that Melville wrote them at least in part in a parodic mood. See also Edward H. Rosenberry, *Melville and the Comic Spirit* (Cambridge, MA: Harvard University Press, 1955), and Jane Mushabac, *Melville's Humor: A Critical Study* (Hamden, CT: Archon Books, 1981).

171   "country gentlemen . . . 'T'will soon be out' ": *MD*, ch. 36, p. 160.

171   "bigotry of purpose . . . 'a stove boat!' ": *MD*, ch. 36, p. 161.

172   "whosoever of ye . . . call Moby Dick": *MD*, ch. 36, p. 162.

172   " 'Moby Dick?' shouted Ahab . . . 'Moby Dick!' ": *MD*, ch. 36, pp. 162–63.

173   " 'Captain Ahab,' said Starbuck": *MD*, ch. 36, p. 163.

173   "the moderate man": *CM*, ch. 21, p. 112.

173   " 'Captain Ahab . . . ye do look brave' ": *MD*, ch. 36, p. 163.

173   "he drilled deep down": *MD*, ch. 38, p. 169.

173   " 'Aye, aye!' shouted the harpooneers": *MD*, ch. 36, p. 163.

174   "lower layer . . . if it insulted me": *MD*, ch. 36, p. 164.

174   "a representation": W. H. Auden, *The Enchafèd Flood* (New York: Vintage, 1967), p. 134.

174   "comfort would be the destruction": Kierkegaard, *Sickness unto Death,* quoted ibid.

174   "All my means are sane": *MD*, ch. 41, p. 186.

174   "All that most maddens": *MD*, ch. 41, p. 184.

174   "every sufferer instinctively seeks": Friedrich Nietzsche, *The Genealogy of Morals* (1887), trans. Francis Golffing (New York: Anchor Books, 1956), pp. 263–64. I owe this reference to Roosevelt Montás.

175   "hatred becomes stronger": Julien Benda, *The Treason of the Intellectuals,* trans. Richard Aldington (1928; New York: Norton, 1969), p. 6.

175   *"homogeneous,* impassioned group": Ibid., p. 5.

175   "provided an ominous glimpse of what was to result": Matthiessen, *American Renaissance,* pp. 438, 459.

175   "as profoundly aware of the existence of radical evil": Mumford, review of William Ellery Sedgwick's *Herman Melville: The Tragedy of Mind,* in the *New York Times Book Review,* January 21, 1945, p. 103.

175   "prophecy of the essence of fascism": Henry Murray, Introduction to *Pierre* (New York: Hendricks House, 1949), p. xxxi.

175   "intense subjectivism": James, *Mariners, Renegades, and Castaways,* p. 56.

175   "a pliant, disciplined, committed": Leo Marx, *The Machine in the Garden* (New York: Oxford University Press, 1964), p. 287.

CHAPTER 7. "HERMAN MELVILLE CRAZY"

176   "Your letter was handed me . . . can't write what I felt": HM to Nathaniel Hawthorne, November [17?], 1851, in *Correspondence,* pp. 212–13.

177   "to bury myself": HM to Nathaniel Hawthorne, [June 1?], 1851, in *Correspondence,* p. 191.

177   The new title, he said, is "legitimate": The best short treatment of discrepancies between the English and American editions is G. Thomas Tanselle, Note on the Texts, in the Library of America edition of *Redburn, White-Jacket,* and *Moby-Dick* (New York: Library of America, 1983), pp. 1414–20. For a more detailed account of how *Moby-Dick* came into print, see Tanselle's discussion in *MD* (Northwestern–Newberry Library edition), pp. 659–89.

177   "The proofs . . . were replete with errors": *P,* bk. 25, p. 340.

178   "before them with a crucifixion": *MD*, ch. 28, p. 124.

178   "anonymous babies all over the world": *MD*, ch. 88, pp. 392, 393.

178   "miners in a pit": Review in the London *Spectator*, October 25, 1851, in Higgins and Parker, eds., *Contemporary Reviews*, p. 360.

178   there was someone who expressed respect: Such as the reviewer who credited HM in the London *Morning Advertiser* of October 24, 1851 (reprinted in Higgins and Parker, eds., *Contemporary Reviews*, p. 353), with "an unusual power . . . rising to the verge of the sublime."

178   "Try to get a living by the Truth": HM to Nathaniel Hawthorne, [June 1?], 1851, in *Correspondence*, p. 191.

178   Total earnings from the American sales: See G. Thomas Tanselle, "The Sales of Melville's Books," *Harvard Library Bulletin* 17 (April 1969): 195–215.

178   "The Fates . . . rural bowl of milk": HM to Sophia Hawthorne, January 8, 1852, in *Correspondence*, p. 219.

179   "unquestionable novelty": HM to Richard Bentley, April 16, 1852, ibid., p. 226.

179   "in too rapid succession": Richard Bentley to HM, March 4, 1852, ibid., p. 618.

179   At one point in the negotiations: Parker, II, 77, and see Parker, Introduction to *Pierre* (New York: HarperCollins, 1995).

179   "HERMAN MELVILLE CRAZY": *New York Day Book*, September 7, 1852, in Higgins and Parker, eds., *Contemporary Reviews*, p. 436.

179   "fancy is diseased": George Washington Peck, in *American Whig Review*, November 1852, ibid., pp. 441–51.

179   "Let Mr. Melville stay his step": *Putnam's Monthly Magazine*, February 1853, in Branch, ed., *Critical Heritage*, pp. 323–29.

179   "the burning out of Melville's volcano": Murray, Introduction to *Pierre*, p. xiv.

179   "runs a constant fever": John Updike, "Melville's Withdrawal," *The New Yorker*, May 10, 1982, p. 124.

180   "disappointment with the married state": W. S. Maugham, "Moby-Dick," *Atlantic Monthly*, June 1948, p. 102.

180   "English-looking woman . . . He wasn't": Quoted from Raymond Weaver papers in Hershel Parker, *Reading Billy Budd* (Evanston: Northwestern University Press, 1990), p. 45.

180   "only one condition . . . alienation from his family": Lewis Mumford, *Sketches from Life: The Autobiography of Lewis Mumford: The Early Years* (New York: Dial Press, 1982), p. 456. I owe this reference to my colleague Casey Blake.

180   "dear old crooked Boston": Elizabeth Shaw Melville to Samuel H. Savage, September 12–18, 1847, quoted in Parker, I, 554.

180   "as bewitchingly as possible": Elizabeth Shaw Melville to Hope Savage Shaw, December 23, 1847, in *Log*, I, 266.

180   "tone and look of love": John Hoadley to Augusta Melville, March 28, 1854, quoted in Parker, II, 215.

180   "Of all chamber furniture . . . in the mizzen-top": *WJ*, ch. 12, p. 46.

181   In the winter of 1852, while she was nursing Stanwix: Maria Gansevoort Melville to Augusta Melville, November 5, 1851, quoted in Parker, II, 31.

181   "Claggart could even have loved Billy": *BB*, ch. 17, p. 1394.

181   "the most desperate in our literature": Matthiessen, *American Renaissance*, p. 471.

181   "playfulness of . . . unclouded love": *P*, bk. 1, p. 5.

182 "much that goes to make up the deliciousness": *P,* bk. 1, p. 7.

182 "ardent sentiment": *P,* bk. 15, p. 218.

182 "the preliminary love-friendship": *P,* bk. 15, p. 217.

182 "Why hast thou made us": In *P,* bk. 2, p. 27, HM writes that bringing Pierre and Lucy together required "no maneuvering at all. The two Platonic particles, after roaming in quest of each other . . . came together before Mrs. Tartan's [Lucy's mother] own eyes; and what more could Mrs. Tartan do toward making them forever one and indivisible?"

183 "much more than cousinly attachment": *P,* bk. 15, p. 216.

183 "the letters of Aphroditean devotees": *P,* bk. 15, p. 217.

183 "uncertainty in regard . . . *inhibited development* ": Sigmund Freud, *Dora: An Analysis of a Case of Hysteria,* ed. Philip Rieff (New York: Simon & Schuster, 1963), p. 43.

183 "uncelestial" desires: *P,* bk. 1, p. 16.

183 "reverential, and most docile": *P,* bk. 1, p. 20.

183 "Methinks . . . one husbandly embrace": *P,* bk. 3, p. 58.

183 the pallor associated with female purity: See Hart, *The Popular Book,* p. 87.

183 "stiffness, formality . . . a milliner's doll": *T,* ch. 22, p. 161.

184 "passion for fat women": Willis, "Miss Albina McLush," in Taft, *Minor Knicker-bockers,* p. 293.

184 "skinny scrawny arms": Journal entry, November 20, 1849, in *Journals,* p. 23.

184 "flirtations with South Sea beauties": *Mrs. Longfellow: Selected Letters and Jour-nals of Fanny Appleton Longfellow,* ed. Edward Wagenknecht (New York: Long-mans, Green, 1956), p. 132.

184 "an early and most cherished friend": *P,* bk. 2, p. 25.

184 "dark-eyed haughtiness": *P,* bk. 1, p. 20.

184 "Yes, [Lucy is] a very pretty little pint-decanter": *P,* bk. 3, p. 60.

184 "contracting and expanding" velvet collar: *P,* bk. 3, p. 46.

185 "all too obvious emotion": *P,* bk. 3, p. 47.

185 Maurice Sendak is more explicit: See the illustrations in the HarperCollins edi-tion of *Pierre,* ed. Hershel Parker (1995).

185 "beneath the pendulous canopies": *P,* bk. 3, p. 61.

185 "was not the universe": Mumford, *Herman Melville,* p. 211.

185 "features [are] transformed": *P,* bk. 3, p. 62.

185 "two souls, alas": *Faust,* I, l. 1112.

185 "distinctly to feel two antagonistic agencies": *P,* bk. 3, p. 63.

186 "boundless expansion": *P,* bk. 3, p. 66.

186 "Dearest Pierre": *P,* bk. 3, p. 64.

186 "Not only was the long-cherished image": *P,* bk. 5, p. 88.

186 "scaly, glittering folds of pride": *P,* bk. 5, p. 90.

187 "the dark-haired 'forest girl' ": Sacvan Bercovitch, *The Rites of Assent: Transfor-mations in the Symbolic Construction of America* (New York: Routledge, 1993), p. 253.

187 "not yet . . . dropped his angle": *P,* bk. 21, p. 284.

187 "spiritual autobiography in the form": Murray, Introduction to *Pierre,* p. xxiv.

187 "Here [was] a sick man": Metcalf, *Herman Melville: Cycle and Epicycle,* p. 135.

187   One theory that has proven especially enduring: See Amy Puett Emmers, "Melville's Closet Skeleton: A New Letter About the Illegitimacy Incident in *Pierre*," in *Studies in the American Renaissance,* ed. Joel Myerson (Boston: Twayne, 1978), pp. 339-42; Henry Murray, "Allan Melvill's By-Blow," *Melville Society Extracts* 61 (February 1985): 1-6; and Philip Young, "History of a Secret Sister," in *The Private Melville* (University Park: Pennsylvania State University Press, 1993), pp. 9-26.

187   "Judging from what we know": Parker, I, 65.

188   "the heroic flourished": Thornton Wilder, "Toward an American Language," *Atlantic Monthly,* July 1952, p. 36.

188   "from ambiguity to ambiguity": Bercovitch, *The American Jeremiad,* p. 28.

189   "his eyes fixed upon": *P,* bk. 6, p. 119.

189   "The wild girl played on the guitar": *P,* bk. 6, p. 126.

189   the "image . . . of white-browed": *P,* bk. 5, p. 99.

190   "Mr. Falsgrave was just hovering": *P,* bk. 5, pp. 98-99.

190   "Heaven had given him": *P,* bk. 5, p. 98.

190   "In heaven's name, what is the matter": *P,* bk. 8, p. 162.

190   "For heaven's sake, . . . heartlessness of the world?": *P,* bk. 8, p. 163.

191   "the immense difficulty": Harold Bloom, *The American Religion* (New York: Simon & Schuster, 1992), p. 23.

191   "ultraism of all sorts": Joseph Story ("Literary Tendencies of the Times," 1842), quoted in Robert A. Ferguson, *Reading the Early Republic* (Cambridge, MA: Harvard University Press, 2004), p. 248.

191   "all a little wild": Emerson to Carlyle, October 30, 1940, in Joseph Slater, ed., *Correspondence of Emerson and Carlyle* (New York: Columbia University Press, 1964), pp. 283-84.

191   "I do not wish": Garrison, in *The Liberator,* January 1, 1831, in Fredrickson, ed., *William Lloyd Garrison,* p. 23. For an argument that HM gave Pierre the attributes of an abolitionist zealot, see Nancy F. Sweet, "Abolition, Compromise and 'The Everlasting Elusiveness of Truth' in Melville's *Pierre,*" *Studies in American Fiction* 26, no. 1 (Spring 1998): 3-28.

191   "formalist" who usurps the pulpit: Emerson, "Divinity School Address" (1838), in Whicher, ed., *Selections,* p. 109.

192   "intense and doating biasses": Dana (April 1856), quoted in *Log,* II, 514.

192   "almost infantile delicacy": *P,* bk. 5, p. 98.

192   "The Ch. Justice read the petition": Dana, *Journal,* II, 412.

193   "virtuous expediency": *P,* bk. 14, p. 214.

193   "the absolute [is] introduced": Hannah Arendt, *On Revolution* (New York: Penguin, 1963), p. 84.

194   Melville had purchased a set of literary illustrations: See Howard Schless, "Flaxman, Dante, and Melville's *Pierre,*" *Bulletin of the New York Public Library* 64, no. 2 (February 1960): 68-69.

194   "Francesca's mournful face": *P,* bk. 2, p. 42.

194   "long dark shower": *P,* bk. 6, p. 126.

194   "writhing from out the imprisoning earth": *P,* bk. 25, p. 345.

194   "gospelize the world anew": *P,* bk. 19, p. 273.

194   "sublime heaven of heroism": *P*, bk. 23, p. 310.

194   "frantic, diseased-looking men and women": *P*, bk. 16, p. 240.

195   "I will write such things": *P*, bk. 19, p. 273.

195   "From eight o'clock in the morning": *P*, bk. 22, pp. 303–4.

196   "unstinted fertilizations": *P*, Dedication to "Greylock's Most Excellent Majesty," p. vii.

196   "THE COMPLETE WORKS OF GLENDINNING": *P*, bk. 17, p. 247.

196   "According to Fichte": Quoted in Barbara L. Packer, "The Transcendentalists," in Bercovitch, ed., *The Cambridge History of American Literature*, Vol. 2: *Prose Writing, 1820–1865*, p. 363.

197   "I look for the new Teacher": Emerson, "Divinity School Address," in Whicher, ed., *Selections*, pp. 115–16.

197   "the priest departs": Whitman, *Democratic Vistas* (1870), in *Walt Whitman: Poetry and Prose*, ed. Justin Kaplan (New York: Library of America, 1982), p. 932.

197   "out-reaching comprehensiveness . . . placard capitals": *MD*, ch. 104, p. 456.

197   "pasteboard mask . . . naught beyond": *MD*, ch. 36, p. 164.

197   "Say what some poets will": *P*, bk. 25, p. 342.

197   "all-controlling and all-permeating wonderfulness": *P*, bk. 7, p. 139.

197   "almost a nun": *P*, bk. 23, p. 313.

198   "Never, never would he be able": *P*, bk. 7, p. 142.

198   "there is no sex": *P*, bk. 8, p. 149.

198   "He held her tremblingly": *P*, bk. 12, p. 192.

198   "tremendous displacing": *P*, bk. 26, p. 353.

198   "he 'fell' for the Face": Murray, Introduction to *Pierre*, p. lix.

198   "I am too full without discharge": *P*, bk. 6, p. 113.

198   "Oh, I am sick, sick, sick!": *P*, bk. 19, p. 273.

198   "O blood": Melville refers to Reni Guido's painting of the Cenci in *P*, bk. 26, p. 351.

199   "Oh, praised be the beauty of this earth": *P*, bk. 2, p. 32.

199   "Lo! . . . I strike through thy helm": *P*, bk. 3, p. 66.

199   "emotion is in excess": T. S. Eliot, "Hamlet and His Problems" (1919), in *Selected Essays* (New York: Harcourt Brace, 1932), pp. 121–26. Without alluding to Eliot, Mumford (*Herman Melville*, pp. 208–9) makes essentially the same argument about *Pierre*: since "Pierre's emotional reaction to Isabel is entirely out of proportion to the fact that he has found a sister," Melville's novel suffers from a "disproportion between stimulus and effect."

199   "married in order to combat inclinations": Maugham, *"Moby-Dick,"* p. 102.

199   impulses for which there was no established language: Robert K. Martin, *The Homosexual Tradition in American Poetry* (Austin: University of Texas Press, 1979), p. 51, writes that "prior to Whitman there were homosexual acts but no homosexuals."

200   the term "adhesiveness": See Michael Lynch, " 'Here is Adhesiveness': From Friendship to Homosexuality," *Victorian Studies* 29, no. 1 (Autumn 1985): 67–96.

200   "excessive adhesiveness": By the 1870s, the English classicist John Addington Symonds, who wrote appreciatively to Whitman, used interchangeably such

terms as "inversion," "paiderastia," and, occasionally, "homosexuality." See ibid., p. 93.

200 Though it is hard now to take seriously: See Peter Gay, *The Bourgeois Experience: Victoria to Freud,* Vol. 2: *The Tender Passion* (New York: Oxford University Press, 1986), p. 217; and Sally Satel, review of *The Cult of Personality* by Annie Murphy Paul, in the *New York Times Book Review,* October 10, 2004, p. 14.

200 "chickenship . . . all over his body if he don't": B. R. Burg, *An American Seafarer in the Age of Sail: The Erotic Diaries of Philip C. Van Buskirk, 1851–1870* (New Haven: Yale University Press, 1994), pp. 78–79.

201 "eye for masculine beauty": Maugham, *"Moby-Dick,"* p. 102.

201 "matchless symmetry of form": *T,* ch. 18, p. 135.

201 "never for one moment": *T,* ch. 14, p. 109.

201 "adjusting everything": *T,* ch. 14, p. 111.

201 "whole body": *T,* ch. 14, p. 110.

201 "a rich-cheeked . . . gushing from every rent": *R,* ch. 49, p. 247.

201 "in dreams Elysian": *R,* ch. 49, p. 251.

201 "pulling and twitching": *R,* ch. 49, p. 249.

201 "make, unmake me": *R,* ch. 49, p. 250.

202 "every positive depiction of sexuality": Martin, *Hero, Captain, and Stranger,* p. 63.

202 "circle jerk": Camille Paglia, *Sexual Personae: Art and Decadence from Nefertiti to Emily Dickinson* (New Haven: Yale University Press, 1990), p. 587.

202 "Squeeze! squeeze! squeeze!": *MD,* ch. 94, p. 416.

202 "androgynic personality": Murray, "In Nomine Diaboli," in *Moby-Dick: Centennial Essays,* ed. Tyrus Hilway and Luther S. Mansfield (Dallas: Southern Methodist University Press, 1953), p. 16.

202 "the expectation of sexual intercourse is more exciting": Maugham, *"Moby-Dick,"* p. 102. Mumford (*Herman Melville,* p. 219) read *Pierre* as evidence of Melville's sexual immaturity.

203 "Isabel is the personification . . . barred by culture": Murray, Introduction to *Pierre,* p. lii.

203 "such a creature as civilized, domestic people": *MD,* ch. 50, p. 231.

203 "odds and ends of strange nations": *MD,* ch. 50, p. 230.

203 "self-reciprocally efficient hermaphrodite": *P,* bk. 18, p. 259.

203 "felt himself emotionally trapped": Arvin, *Herman Melville,* p. 204.

203 "transferring his guilt": James Creech, *Closet Writing / Gay Reading: The Case of Melville's Pierre* (Chicago: University of Chicago Press, 1993), p. 122.

203 "the wink of homosexuality": Ibid., p. 95.

204 He never reduced the complexity of experience: The same cannot always be said for his readers, as when the homophobic Edward Dahlberg accused Melville in 1960 of "sodomy of the heart" and dismissed *Moby-Dick* as a book for "hermaphrodites and spados." Dahlberg complained that "after the blubber pots and love scenes of these corrugated mammoth Don Juans of the sea, what virile male reader does not yearn for . . . a sweet bosom that would set Ilium on fire?" Dahlberg, *"Moby-Dick:* A Hamitic Dream," in *The Edward Dahlberg Reader* (New York: New Directions, 1967), pp. 191, 194.

204   "for the deeper that some men feel": *P,* bk. 15, p. 224.

204   the "woman-soft" boy: *P,* bk. 26, p. 362.

204   "For Pierre is neuter now!": *P,* bk. 26, p. 360.

204   "Watch yon toddler . . . not without shrieks": *P,* bk. 22, p. 296. In light of such an indictment, one may question Mumford's judgment that "Melville identified himself with Pierre and defended his immaturity" (*Herman Melville,* p. 210).

205   "that an author can never": HM to Evert Duyckinck, December 14, 1849, in *Correspondence,* p. 149.

205   "in this world of lies": "Hawthorne and His Mosses," in *PT,* p. 244.

205   "we cannot pass without remark": Evert Duyckinck, review in *The Literary World,* August 21, 1852, in Higgins and Parker, eds., *Contemporary Reviews,* p. 431.

205   "the finest psychological novel": Hershel Parker, Introduction to *Pierre* (Harper-Collins, 1995), p. xii.

205   "short, quick probings": "Hawthorne and His Mosses," in *PT,* p. 244.

CHAPTER 8. SEEING TOO MUCH

206   "the Harpers think Melville is a little crazy": Elizabeth Barstow Stoddard, quoted in Parker, II, 125.

206   sold fewer than two thousand copies: See Tanselle, "The Sales of Melville's Books," p. 214.

206   "might be supposed to emanate": *Boston Post,* August 4, 1852, in Higgins and Parker, eds., *Contemporary Reviews,* pp. 419–20.

206   "loathsome": Simms, *Southern Quarterly Review,* October 1849, in Branch, ed., *Critical Heritage,* p. 187.

206   "gone 'clean daft' . . . the better": Simms, *Southern Literary Messenger,* October 22, 1852, in Higgins and Parker, eds., *Contemporary Reviews,* pp. 439–40.

206   "the solitary Crusoeish island": HM to Nathaniel Hawthorne, July 17, 1852, in *Correspondence,* p. 230.

206   "a wife (for a night) . . . all tender obligations": HM to Nathaniel Hawthorne, October 25, 1852, ibid., p. 240.

207   "the great patience, & endurance": HM to Nathaniel Hawthorne, August 13, 1852, ibid., p. 232.

207   Drawn to Agatha, perhaps: Leon Howard offers this hypothesis in his *Herman Melville,* p. 197.

207   "in this matter you would make a better hand": HM to Nathaniel Hawthorne, August 13, 1852, in *Correspondence,* p. 234.

207   "Supposing the story to open": HM to Nathaniel Hawthorne, August 13, 1852, ibid., p. 235.

208   "prevented from printing": HM to Harper & Brothers, November 24, 1853, ibid., p. 250.

208   "glorious" and "noble cock": "Cock-A-Doodle-Doo!" in *PT,* pp. 274, 275.

208   "looked underdone": "Cock-A-Doodle-Doo!" in *PT,* p. 268.

208   "any gentleman hereabouts": "Cock-A-Doodle-Doo!" in *PT,* p. 281.

208 "the constant in-door confinement": Maria Gansevoort Melville to Peter Gansevoort, April 20, 1853, in *Log*, I, 469.

209 He was drifting away from Duyckinck: Duyckinck's review of *Moby-Dick* (*The Literary World*, November 15 and 22, 1851) is in Branch, ed., *Critical Heritage*, pp. 264–68.

209 "There is something lacking . . . done rare": HM to Evert Duyckinck, February 12, 1851, in *Correspondence*, p. 181.

209 "Hawthorne has simply availed himself": "Hawthorne and His Mosses," in *PT*, p. 243.

209 "exclusively *imported*": James, *Hawthorne*, p. 67.

209 "This name of '*Hawthorne*' ": HM to Nathaniel Hawthorne, July 17, 1852, in *Correspondence*, p. 230.

210 "The divine magnet is in you": HM to Nathaniel Hawthorne, November [17?], 1851, ibid., p. 213.

210 "My breast is full of thee": Nathaniel Hawthorne to Sophia Peabody, quoted in Edwin Haviland Miller, *Salem Is My Dwelling Place: A Life of Nathaniel Hawthorne* (Iowa City: University of Iowa Press, 1991), p. 177.

210 "it is an age since thou hast been": Nathaniel Hawthorne to Sophia Peabody, August 22, 1841, in Henry W. Sams, ed., *Autobiography of Brook Farm* (Englewood Cliffs, NJ: Prentice-Hall, 1958), p. 31.

210 "self-centered, self-reproductive": Charles King Newcomb, quoted in Miller, *Salem Is My Dwelling Place*, p. 195.

210 "unsearchable eyes": Moncure Conway, quoted in Wineapple, *Hawthorne: A Life*, p. 270.

210 "Nothing pleases me more": Sophia Hawthorne to Elizabeth Palmer Peabody, May 7, 1851, in *Log*, II, 926.

210 "that queer monster, the artist": Henry James to Henry Adams, March 21, 1914, in *The Selected Letters of Henry James*, ed. Leon Edel (New York: Anchor Books, 1960), p. 169.

210 "on a personal interview": "Hawthorne and His Mosses," in *PT*, p. 240.

210 "Under cheer": *Clarel*, pt. I, 29, ll. 31–33. Walter Bezanson discusses the affinities of Hawthorne and Vine in his introduction to his great edition of *Clarel* (New York: Hendricks House, 1960), pp. xcii–xciii.

211 "there appears to be a certain": *CM*, ch. 30, pp. 171–72.

211 "could lure / Despite reserve": *Clarel*, pt. I, 17, ll. 19–21.

211 "dryness and tiredness": Arvin, *Herman Melville*, pp. 205–6.

211 an apparently "unperplexed" man: James, *Hawthorne*, p. 43.

211 "a fountain sealed": *Clarel*, pt. II, 17, l. 22.

211 Some scholars speculate: See, for example, Philip Young, *Hawthorne's Secret: An Untold Tale* (Boston: David Godine, 1984), which argues that Hawthorne felt and may have acted upon incestuous desire for his sister Elizabeth.

211 "hiddenly reside": "Hawthorne and His Mosses," in *PT*, p. 253.

211 "negative capability": John Keats to his brothers, December 21, 1817, in Bate, ed., *Criticism: The Major Texts*, p. 349.

212 "constant brain labor": Edwin Croswell to Caleb Cushing, April 29, 1853, in *Log*, I, 471.

212   "perhaps the craziest fiction extant": *Boston Post* review, August 4, 1852, in Higgins and Parker, eds., *Contemporary Reviews*, pp. 419–20.

212   "much the best Mag.": Thackeray, quoted in the Historical Note to *PT*, p. 513.

212   *Putnam's* was broadly anti-slavery: See Frank Luther Mott, *A History of American Magazines, 1850–1865* (Cambridge, MA: Harvard University Press, 1938), pp. 420–23.

212   "Herman has always been a firm Democrat": Peter Gansevoort, quoted in Miller, *Raven and the Whale*, p. 321.

213   "pent up in lath and plaster": *MD*, ch. 1, p. 4.

213   nicknamed Turkey and Nippers: Hans Bergmann, *God in the Street*, suggests (p. 161) that "Turkey" is a slang word meaning drunk and "Nippers" may be slang for a thief or pickpocket.

213   "afternoon devotions": "Bartleby," in *PT*, p. 16.

213   "twitching in his chair": "Bartleby," in *PT*, pp. 22–23.

213   "an eminently *safe* man": "Bartleby," in *PT*, p. 14.

213   "The Business Man": First published in the *Broadway Journal*, August 2, 1845; reprinted in *Edgar Allan Poe: Poetry and Tales* (New York: Library of America, 1984), pp. 373–81. Parker (II, 176) notes the affinity between Poe's tale and Melville's, which was written seven years later.

213   "I was not unemployed": "Bartleby," in *PT*, p. 14.

214   "dull business": Briggs, *Harry Franco*, II, 99.

214   one enterprising penmanship teacher: *Hunt's Merchants' Magazine & Commercial Review*, April 1852, p. 522.

214   "the prudent, penniless beginner": Abraham Lincoln, "Address to the Wisconsin State Agricultural Society," September 30, 1859, in Fehrenbacher, ed., *Abraham Lincoln: Speeches and Writings*, II, 2, 97–98.

214   The glut in the Manhattan labor supply: See Allan S. Horlick, *Country Boys and Merchant Princes: The Social Control of Young Men in New York* (Lewisburg, PA: Bucknell University Press, 1975).

214   "an unobstructed view": "Bartleby," in *PT*, p. 14.

215   In his "cadaverous" gloom: "Bartleby," in *PT*, p. 30.

215   his "advent": "Bartleby," in *PT*, p. 15.

215   "I would prefer not to": First appearance is in "Bartleby," *PT*, p. 20.

215   "the least uneasiness": "Bartleby," in *PT*, p. 21.

215   " '*Why* do you refuse?' ": "Bartleby," in *PT*, pp. 21–22.

215   "I burned . . . Windsor soap": "Bartleby," in *PT*, p. 24.

215   " 'Bartleby,' said I": "Bartleby," in *PT*, p. 25.

216   "Nippers's ugly mood": "Bartleby," in *PT*, p. 22.

216   " 'Say now you will help' ": "Bartleby," in *PT*, pp. 30–31.

216   "Bartleby moved not a limb": "Bartleby," in *PT*, p. 31.

217   "It is not seldom the case": "Bartleby," in *PT*, p. 22.

217   "sole spectator . . . friendlessness and loneliness": "Bartleby," in *PT*, p. 27.

217   "For the first time in my life": "Bartleby," in *PT*, p. 28.

218   "not-unpleasing" representations: "Bartleby," in *PT*, p. 28.

218   "making merry in the house of the dead": *R*, ch. 37, p. 184.

218 "all that is solid melts into air": Karl Marx and Friedrich Engels, *The Communist Manifesto* (1848).

218 " 'I'll take odds he doesn't' ": "Bartleby," in *PT*, p. 34.

218 "entertain . . . with your conversation?": "Bartleby," in *PT*, p. 41.

218 his "motionless" vagrant: "Bartleby," in *PT*, p. 39.

218 "You are responsible": "Bartleby," in *PT*, p. 39.

219 "the pathetic and the ludicrous": Dana, letter to Evert Duyckinck, January 25, 1854, quoted in *Log*, I, 484.

219 "opulent in withheld replies": *Clarel*, pt. IV, 5, l. 67.

219 "great sacks, locked and sealed": Article in the September 23 issue of the *Albany Daily State Register*, quoted in Parker, II, 138.

220 One suit, brought against the Boston & Worcester Railroad in 1842: Frederick Wertheim, "Slavery and the Fellow Servant Rule: An Antebellum Dilemma," *New York University Law Review* 61, no. 6 (December 1986): 1127–28. See also Lawrence M. Friedman, *A History of American Law* (New York: Simon & Schuster, 1985), pp. 468–75, and Morton Horwitz, *The Transformation of American Law, 1780–1860* (Cambridge, MA: Harvard University Press, 1977), for arguments that American law in the antebellum period tended to defend corporate interests.

220 "a bit of wreck": "Bartleby," in *PT*, p. 32.

220 "the things I had seen disqualified me": "Bartleby," in *PT*, p. 29.

220 "not only . . . the business of Sabbath days": Jonathan Edwards, *A Treatise Concerning Religious Affections* (1746; New Haven: Yale University Press, 1959), pp. 383–84.

221 "the old Adam of resentment": "Bartleby," in *PT*, p. 36.

221 "the limits of moral responsibility": Thomas Haskell, "Capitalism and the Origins of the Humanitarian Sensibility," in *Objectivity Is Not Neutrality: Explanatory Schemes in History* (Baltimore: Johns Hopkins University Press, 1998), p. 252.

CHAPTER 9. THE MAGAZINIST

222 "ejaculatory prose": Matthiessen, *American Renaissance*, p. 426.

222 "the nicer strings": Dana, Sr., letter to Evert Duyckinck, January 25, 1854, in *Log*, I, 484.

222 "Take five-and-twenty heaps of cinders": *Encantadas*, in *PT*, p. 126.

223 "bandit birds": *Encantadas*, in *PT*, p. 135.

223 "prostrate trunks": *Encantadas*, in *PT*, p. 129.

223 "mass of rubbish": *New York Herald*, December 11, 1853, quoted in Parker, II, 187.

223 "Before Hunilla's eyes they sank": *Encantadas*, in *PT*, p. 154.

224 "trod the cindery beach": *Encantadas*, in *PT*, p. 155.

224 "fat-paunched, beadle-faced": "The Two Temples," in *PT*, p. 303.

225 "pungent" satire risked "offending": Charles F. Briggs to HM, May 12, 1854, in *Correspondence*, p. 636; and see James Duban, "Transatlantic Counterparts:

The Diptych and Social Inquiry in Melville's 'Poor Man's Pudding and Rich Man's Crumbs,'" *New England Quarterly* 66 (1993): 274–86.

225 "undulatory as an anaconda": "The Paradise of Bachelors and the Tartarus of Maids," in *PT*, p. 325.

225 "in case I serve up": Journal entry, December 18, 1849, in *Journals*, p. 43.

226 "harassed by night and day": *Israel Potter, Life and Adventures*, ed. Leonard Kriegel (New York: Corinth Books, 1962), p. 43.

226 "exile as a lifetime experience": Alfred Kazin, Introduction to *Israel Potter* (New York: Warner Books, 1974), p. 5.

226 "before hastening to one duty": *IP*, ch. 3, p. 13.

226 "sturdy farmer": *R*, ch. 56, p. 281.

227 "primeval orientalness": *IP*, ch. 8, p. 46.

227 "jaunty barbarian in broadcloth": *IP*, ch. 11, p. 63.

227 "sour fruit . . . doors have been cut": *IP*, ch. 19, p. 126.

227 "in view of this battle": *IP*, ch. 19, p. 130.

227 "Desperate with want": *IP*, ch. 23, p. 154.

227 "spavined-looking old men": *IP*, ch. 25, p. 165.

227 "ridged and mottled sky": *IP*, ch. 23, p. 156.

227 "himself home into the mists": *IP*, ch. 25, p. 165.

228 "to get a glimpse of his father's homestead": *IP*, ch. 26, p. 168.

228 "certain caprices of law": *IP*, ch. 26, p. 169.

228 "brace of fowl": HM to Harper & Bros., September 18, 1854, in *Correspondence*, p. 269.

228 "I should have sent": Helen Griggs to HM, May 29, 1854, ibid., pp. 640–41.

229 "so bad that he was helpless": See Elizabeth Shaw Melville, notes on her husband, in Sealts, *Early Lives*, p. 169.

229 "rather gruff taciturn man": Holmes, Jr., quoted in *Log*, II, 936.

229 "half a (½) dozen lb": Maria Gansevoort Melville, letter to Elizabeth Shaw Melville, June 7, 1855, quoted in Parker, II, 253.

229 "does everything too hurriedly now": G. W. Curtis to J. A. Dix, April 20, 1855, in *Log*, II, 501.

229 "decline any novel from Melville": G. W. Curtis to J. A. Dix, mid-April 1855[?], in *Log*, II, 500.

229 "arthritically clumsy": Warner Berthoff, headnote to "The Bell-Tower," in *Great Short Works of Herman Melville* (New York: Harper, 1969), p. 223.

229 "Who does not feel his faith": Thoreau, *Walden*, p. 587.

229 "small shining beetle or bug": "The Apple-Tree Table," in *PT*, p. 389.

229 "anxious to see": G. W. Curtis to J. A. Dix, April 17, 1855, in *Log*, II, 500.

230 "a skeleton of actual reality": HM to Nathaniel Hawthorne, April 13, 1852, in *Correspondence*, p. 237.

230 "a little spun out": G. W. Curtis to J. A. Dix, April 19, 1855, in *Log*, II, 501.

230 "to dance upon . . . cross wires": "Our New President," *Putnam's*, September 1853, pp. 308, 303.

230 "the leading review": *DeBow's Review* (February 1857), quoted in Mott, *History of American Magazines*, p. 423.

230 "the suicide of slavery . . . marauders of Missouri": "The Kansas Question," *Putnam's*, October 1855, pp. 427–28.

231 "who kept constantly at the elbows . . . confidant and companion": Amasa Delano, *A Narrative of Voyages and Travels in the Northern and Southern Hemispheres* (Boston, 1817), p. 324; reprinted in *PT*, p. 818.

231 "human treachery": Mumford, *Herman Melville*, p. 246.

231 Sterling Brown: *The Negro in American Fiction* (Washington, DC: Association of Negro Folk Education, 1937), pp. 12–13; reprinted in Robert Burkholder, *Critical Essays on Herman Melville's "Benito Cereno"* (New York: G. K. Hall, 1992), pp. 24–25.

231 "blindness to evil": Benjamin Barber, *Fear's Empire: War, Terrorism, and Democracy* (New York: Norton, 2003), p. 53.

231 "the African Diaspora": Russell Banks, "Who Will Tell the People?" *Harper's*, June 2000.

232 "tie up a lame young woman": Frederick Douglass, *Narrative of the Life of an American Slave* (Cambridge, MA: Harvard University Press, 1960), pp. 29–30.

232 "to mutilate . . . a powder magazine": Theodore Parker, "A Sermon on the Dangers That Threaten the Rights of Man in America," July 2, 1854, in Pease and Pease, *The Antislavery Argument*, p. 255.

232 Two years after the *Amistad* incident: See Howard Jones, *Mutiny on the Amistad* (New York: Oxford University Press, 1987), and, for the *Creole* case, Maurice G. Baxter, *One and Inseparable: Daniel Webster and the Union* (Cambridge, MA: Harvard University Press, 1984), pp. 327–28.

233 "Depravity in the oppressed": *WJ*, ch. 34, p. 142.

233 "strange sail . . . showed no colors": *Benito Cereno*, in *PT*, p. 46.

233 "shreds of fog here and there": *Benito Cereno*, in *PT*, p. 48.

233 "Delano continued . . . to be dropped": *Benito Cereno*, in *PT*, p. 47.

233 "shield-like stern-piece": *Benito Cereno*, in *PT*, p. 49.

233 "captain, mate, people": Delano, *Narrative of Voyages and Travels*, p. 322; reprinted in *PT*, p. 816.

234 "Climbing the side . . . object about him": *Benito Cereno*, in *PT*, p. 49.

234 "a shepherd's dog": *Benito Cereno*, in *PT*, p. 51.

234 "master and man . . . before him": *Benito Cereno*, in *PT*, p. 57.

234 "for some unknown purpose": *Benito Cereno*, in *PT*, p. 87.

235 "singularly undistrustful . . . nature": *Benito Cereno*, in *PT*, p. 47.

235 "childlike, affectionate, docile": Orville Dewey, *A Discourse on Slavery and the Annexation of Texas* (1844), quoted in Fredrickson, *The Black Image in the White Mind*, p. 102. "Romantic Racialism" is the subject of chapter 4 of Fredrickson's important book.

235 "Delano could not but bethink": *Benito Cereno*, in *PT*, p. 94.

235 the "whole story": *Benito Cereno*, in *PT*, p. 54.

235 "He is like one flayed alive": *Benito Cereno*, in *PT*, p. 93.

235 reverts to "tranquilizing" thoughts: *Benito Cereno*, in *PT*, p. 70.

236 "an apprehensive twitch": *Benito Cereno*, in *PT*, p. 59.

236 some "low-born" impostor: *Benito Cereno*, in *PT*, p. 64.

236   "he leaned against the carved balustrade": *Benito Cereno,* in *PT,* p. 74.
236   "If a man be told a thing wholly new": *P,* bk. 14, p. 209.
237   "There is something in the negro": *Benito Cereno,* in *PT,* p. 83. For the occupations of free blacks, see Joe William Trotter, Jr., *River Jordan: African American Urban Life in the Ohio Valley* (Lexington: University Press of Kentucky, 1998).
237   "low down under the throat": *Benito Cereno,* in *PT,* p. 84.
237   "Setting down his basin": *Benito Cereno,* in *PT,* pp. 84–85.
238   "castle in a blood-red field diagonal . . . a man at the block": *Benito Cereno,* in *PT,* p. 85.
238   "which stained the creamy lather": *Benito Cereno,* in *PT,* p. 86.
238   "with comb, scissors and brush": *Benito Cereno,* in *PT,* p. 87.
238   "Ah, ah, ah . . . nothing had happened": *Benito Cereno,* in *PT,* p. 88.
239   "Adieu, my dear": *Benito Cereno,* in *PT,* p. 97.
239   "Don Benito sprang over the bulwarks . . . desperate fidelity": *Benito Cereno,* in *PT,* p. 98.
239   "most unique collection": Journal entry, December 5, 1849, in *Journals,* p. 33.
239   "larger, darker, deeper part": *MD,* ch. 41, p. 185.
239   a delicately carved ivory mirror case: This artifact is illustrated in Alain Erlande-Brandenburg et al., *Musée Nationale du Moyen Age Thermes de Cluny: Guide to the Collections* (Paris: Réunion des Musées Nationaux, 1993), p. 135.
239   Especially striking were several alabaster carvings: For illustrations, see Christiane Prigent, *Les Sculptures Anglaises d'Albatre: Musée Nationale du Moyen Age, Thermes de Cluny* (Paris: Musée de Cluny, 1998).
240   "dark satyr in a mask": *Benito Cereno,* in *PT,* p. 49. I am grateful to Dawn Delbanco for pointing out the Christian iconography implicit in *Benito Cereno.*
240   "prostrate Negro": *Benito Cereno,* in *PT,* p. 99.
241   "Captain Delano . . . whole story": *Benito Cereno,* in *PT,* p. 99.
241   "with upthrown gestures": *Benito Cereno,* in *PT,* p. 100.
242   "the long, mild voyage": *Benito Cereno,* in *PT,* p. 114.
242   " 'you are saved' ": *Benito Cereno,* in *PT,* p. 116.
242   "the story that a community": Ferguson, *Reading the Early Republic,* p. 132.
242   "American innocence so opaque": Barber, *Fear's Empire,* p. 53.
242   "spoil *Benito Cereno*": Mumford, *Herman Melville,* p. 245.
243   "had managed . . . to work on more than one level ": Sealts, Historical Note, in *PT,* p. 513.

CHAPTER 10. ADRIFT

244   "black years": Arvin, *Herman Melville,* p. 210.
244   "feel that the author is capable": *London Weekly Chronicle,* June 2, 1855, quoted in Higgins and Parker, eds., *Contemporary Reviews,* p. 465.
244   After deductions for advances: Parker, II, 268.
244   "should do something higher and better": *New York Times,* June 27, 1856, in Branch, ed., *Critical Heritage,* p. 357.

244   "after an ecstasy of a courtship": Lawrence, *Studies in Classic American Literature*, p. 141.

244   "proved no fulfillment": Arvin, *Herman Melville*, p. 203.

244   "if [Lizzie] had breasts": De Voto, *The Year of Decision, 1846*, p. 36. I owe this reference to Katherine Barger.

244   "winter's folic skirmisher . . . oblation of old": "To Winnefred," in Robert C. Ryan, "Weeds and Wildings Chiefly, with a Rose or Two, by Herman Meville: Reading Text and Genetic Text, Edited from the Manuscripts, with Introduction and Notes" (Ph.D. diss., Northwestern University, 1967), p. 6. "To Winnefred" is also printed in Vincent, ed., *Collected Poems of Herman Melville*, pp. 481-83. Hershel Parker, in *Reading Billy Budd*, p. 39, dates its composition to August 1891, a month before HM's death.

245   "surgical operation": "I and My Chimney," in *PT*, p. 356.

245   "humbly bowing over it": "I and My Chimney," in *PT*, p. 353.

245   "maxim is, Whatever is": "I and My Chimney," in *PT*, p. 360.

245   "is desirous that . . . I should retire": "I and My Chimney," in *PT*, p. 362.

245   "My wife . . . cares not a fig": "I and My Chimney," in *PT*, p. 376.

245   "all this about the wife": Quoted in Arvin, *Herman Melville*, p. 204.

245   "ugly attacks": Sam Shaw to Lemuel Shaw and Hope Savage Shaw, July[?] 1856, quoted in Parker, II, 286.

245   "great anxiety": Judge Lemuel Shaw to Sam Shaw, September 1, 1856, describing Lizzie's concern, in *Log*, II, 521.

245   "even when she was a prisoner": Cowen, "Melville's Marginalia," VII, 193-94.

245   "the recluse life": Sarah Morewood to George Duyckinck, December 28, 1851, quoted in *Log*, I, 441.

246   "imaginative, voluptuously inclined": HM to Evert Duyckinck, April 5, 1849, in *Correspondence*, p. 128.

246   *Don Quixote,* which he had acquired: Tom Quirk, *Melville's Confidence Man: From Knave to Knight* (Columbia: University of Missouri Press, 1982), p. 13.

246   "a series of conversations": Arvin, *Herman Melville*, p. 250.

246   "Who can forever resist": *WJ*, ch. 44, p. 188.

246   "at a loss to determine": *CM*, ch. 41, p. 223.

247   "Martin Takemthrough": *Hunt's Merchants' Magazine,* July 1852, p. 137.

247   "swindling was raised": Joseph Baldwin, *The Flush Times of Alabama and Mississippi: A Series of Sketches* (1853; Baton Rouge: Louisiana State University Press, 1987), p. 85.

247   "elaborate machinery": Ibid., p. 93.

247   "let the public believe": Ibid., p. 82.

247   "decidedly the worst": *Cincinnati Enquirer,* February 3, 1858, quoted in Higgins and Parker, eds., *Contemporary Reviews*, p. 506.

247   "We began the book": London *Illustrated Times,* April 25, 1857, quoted ibid., pp. 498-99.

247   "pages of crude theory": Lem Shaw to Sam Shaw, April 21, 1857, in *Log*, II, 574.

248   "holds up a mirror": Walter McDougall, *Freedom Just Around the Corner: A New American History, 1585-1828* (New York: HarperCollins, 2004), pp. 1-2.

248   The amiable Mark Winsome: The first scholar to connect Winsome with Emer-

son, and Egbert with Thoreau, was Egbert S. Oliver, "Melville's Picture of Emerson and Thoreau," *College English* 8 (November 1946): 61–72. A recent elaboration of Oliver's argument is to be found in Jonathan A. Cook, *Satirical Apocalypse: An Anatomy of Melville's "The Confidence-Man"* (Westport, CT: Greenwood Press, 1996), pp. 160–69.

248   Charlie Noble: On Charlie Noble as Hawthorne, see Cook, *Satirical Apocalypse*, pp. 144–60. On Poe, see Harrison Hayford, "Poe in *The Confidence-Man*," *Nineteenth-Century Fiction* 14 (December 1959): 207–18; for Abbott Lawrence, see William Norris, "Abbott Lawrence in *The Confidence-Man*: American Success or American Failure," *American Studies* 17 (Spring 1976): 25–38, and Helen Trimpi, *Melville's Confidence Men and American Politics in the 1850s* (Hamden, CT: Archon Books, 1987), pp. 103–5. Cook, *Satirical Apocalypse*, pp. 95–106, makes an alternative case for the "Man in Gold Buttons" as a portrait of Lemuel Shaw (and for another character, the college sophomore, as Lemuel Shaw, Jr.). For the "Man in Gray" as Parker, see Trimpi, *Melville's Confidence Men*, pp. 94–102. The satire of Fanny Kemble Butler is discussed in the Historical Note by Watson Branch, Hershel Parker, Harrison Hayford, and Alma A. MacDougall, in *CM*, p. 290. These are only a few of the many interpretations of Melville's intricate satire. For a case that the book resists interpretation, and that any attribution to it of intentional coherence ought to be suspect, see Peter J. Bellis, "Melville's *Confidence-Man*: An Uncharitable Interpretation," *American Literature* 59, no. 4 (December 1987): 548–69.

248   "latent benignity": *CM*, ch. 36, p. 190.

248   "had she not, on unimpeachable authority": HM to Evert Duyckinck, February 24, 1849, in *Correspondence*, pp. 119–20.

248   "allusiveness that only adds": Jean-Christophe Agnew, *Worlds Apart: The Market and the Theater in Anglo-American Thought, 1550–1750* (Cambridge: Cambridge University Press, 1986), p. 197. Agnew goes on to remark that "the novel's many clues lead everywhere and nowhere" (p. 198).

248   "I do not jumble them": *CM*, ch. 28, p. 157.

249   "poets send out the sick spirit": *CM*, ch. 21, p. 107.

249   "Machines for me": *CM*, ch. 22, p. 116.

249   "the mystery of human subjectivity": *CM*, ch. 23, p. 129.

249   "haters have at bottom": *CM*, ch. 27, p. 154.

249   "Cain afloat": *R*, ch. 22, p. 104.

249   "He was just entering upon manhood": *CM*, ch. 27, p. 153.

250   "straggling thoughts of other outrages": *CM*, ch. 26, pp. 149–50.

250   With full settlement of principal and interest: See Parker, II, 289.

250   "dispirited and ill": Lemuel Shaw, Jr., to Samuel Shaw, April 21, 1857, quoted in *Log*, I, 574.

250   "authors . . . who have written out": Emerson, "The American Scholar" (1837), in Whicher, ed., *Selections*, p. 71.

250   "fresh from his mountain": Evert Duyckinck, diary entry, October 1, 1856, quoted in *Log*, II, 523.

251   "the most silent man . . . East India religions and mythologies": Maunsell Field, *Memories of Many Men* (1874), quoted in *Log*, II, 506.

251 "good story from the Decameron . . . indecency and blasphemy": Evert Duyc-kinck, in his diary, October 1, 1856, in *Log*, II, 523.

251 "picture of one of the old masters": *Journals*, 1856–1857, p. 49.

251 "like flamingoes among the cliffs": *Journals*, 1856–1857, p. 50.

251 "depressed and aimless": Julian Hawthorne, writing in the *Dearborn Independent*, September 24, 1927, quoted in Parker, II, 343.

251 "An agreeable day": Journal entry, November 13, 1856, in *Journals*, p. 51.

252 "*November 20th, Thursday*" [and on to page 253]: Hawthorne, journal entry, November 20, 1856, in *Journals*, pp. 628–33.

253 "Art thou the first soul?": *Clarel*, pt. II, 27, ll. 124–25.

254 "peeps of villages . . . covered with bird lime": Journal entry, November 26, 1856, in *Journals*, p. 52.

254 "warren of stone houses": Journal entry, December 2, 1856, ibid., p. 53.

254 "terrible nest . . . a peice [*sic*] of old root": Journal entry, December 2, 1856, ibid., p. 54.

254 "It was a coy disclosure": Journal entry, December 12, 1856, ibid., p. 58.

254 "nature feeding on man": Journal entry, January 3, 1857, ibid., p. 74.

254 "a new grave . . . haunt me horribly": Journal entry, December 14, 1856, ibid., p. 62.

254 "would make a noble ball room": Journal entry, December 13, 1856, ibid., p. 60.

254 "a kind of dented appearance": Journal entry, December 17, 1856, ibid., p. 67.

254 "rascally priests": Journal entry, December 13, 1856, ibid., p. 59.

254 "old . . . intense, verbally inventive bandinage": Parker, II, 512.

254 "From his long curved and crain-like neck": Journal entry, December 20, 1856, in *Journals*, p. 69.

255 "flies on the eyes at noon": Journal entry, January 3, 1857, ibid., p. 74.

255 "dead calm of masonry": Journal entry, January 3, 1857, ibid., p. 78.

255 "stony mountains & stony plains . . . figure in the Bible": Journal entry, January 26, 1857, ibid., p. 90.

255 "foam on beach . . . these waters of Death": Journal entry, January 26, 1857, ibid., p. 83.

256 "blank, blank towers": *Clarel*, pt. I, 1, l. 61.

256 ". . . 'tis here": *Clarel*, pt. I, 3, ll. 7–11.

256 "*Talk of the guides*": Journal entry, January 26, 1857, in *Journals*, p. 89.

256 "cross-legged & smoking . . . like a butcher's slab": Journal entry, January 26, 1857, ibid., p. 87.

256 "the eaves of": *Encantadas*, in *PT*, p. 134.

256 "the Turk permits the tribes to creep": *Clarel*, pt. I, 16, ll. 94–95.

256 "again afflicted with the great curse . . . robbed us of the bloom": Journal entry, February 5, 1857, in *Journals*, p. 97.

257 "bravadoing mischievousness": *CM*, ch. 30, p. 172.

257 "grated nutmeg": *MD*, ch. 134, p. 559.

257 "man could have undergone amputation": *WJ*, ch. 25, p. 101.

257 "This day saw nothing": Journal entry, March 15, 1857, in *Journals*, p. 112.

257 "amity of art & nature": Journal entry, May 2, 1857, ibid., p. 128.

257   "not going to write any more": Lem Shaw to Sam Shaw, June 2, 1857, in *Log*, II, 580.

257   "name the day": HM to Phillips, Sampson & Co., August 19, 1857, in *Correspondence*, p. 310.

258   "had begun to suffer": Metcalf, *Herman Melville: Cycle and Epicycle*, p. 159.

258   "instantaneously previous": *P*, bk. 15, p. 223.

258   "a disappointed man": John Thomas Gulick, journal entry, April 20, 1859, in *Log*, II, 605.

258   "My dear darling Herman": Maria Gansevoort Melville to Augusta Melville, quoted in Walter Bezanson, Historical Supplement, in *Clarel*, pp. 644–45.

258   "low purse": *P*, bk. 20, p. 281.

258   "A lecturer," Holmes declared: Henry Gansevoort, diary entry, May 27, 1857, quoted in *Log*, II, 579.

258   "My lectures are written to be read as lectures": Emerson to Elizur Wright, January 7, 1852, quoted in Joel Myerson, ed., *The Selected Letters of Ralph Waldo Emerson* (New York: Columbia University Press, 1997), p. 366.

259   "daily progress of man": HM to G. W. Curtis, September 15, 1857, in *Correspondence*, p. 314.

259   they can only be very roughly reconstructed: Such reconstructions have been expertly done by Merton M. Sealts, Jr., in *Melville as Lecturer* (Cambridge, MA: Harvard University Press, 1957).

259   "justness of vision": Review of HM's initial lecture, Lawrence, MA, *Courier*, November 25, 1857, quoted ibid., p. 22.

259   "articulated so feebly": *Auburn Daily Advertiser*, January 6, 1858, quoted ibid., p. 29.

259   "not his forte": Rockford *Republican*, March 3, 1859, quoted in *Log*, II, 603.

259   "some nervous people": *Bunker Hill Aurora*, February 13, 1858, quoted in *Log*, II, 592.

259   "vivid stories": Henry Gansevoort, quoted in Stanton Garner, *The Civil War World of Herman Melville* (Lawrence: University of Kansas Press, 1993), p. 40.

259   "make the gallows as glorious": Emerson, quoted in Robert D. Richardson, Jr., *Emerson: The Mind on Fire* (Berkeley: University of California Press, 1995), p. 545.

260   "never was a man so justly hanged": Hawthorne, quoted in Miller, *Salem Is My Dwelling Place*, p. 473.

260   "through his moustache": *Auburn Advertiser*, quoted in Sealts, *Melville as Lecturer*, p. 29.

260   he spoke, for instance, of how people tend to confuse: My understanding of Melville's lectures has been greatly influenced by an unpublished seminar paper by William Deresiewicz.

260   "lion of the platform": Sealts, *Melville as Lecturer*, p. 113.

260   "countenance [was] slightly flushed": J. T. Gulick, in *Log*, II, 605.

260   In three seasons, he earned roughly $1,200: Sealts, *Melville as Lecturer*, p. 117.

260   "in the unmanning position": Garner, *Civil War World*, p. 51.

261   "Mrs. Melville planned to leave Herman twice": Weaver, quoted in Clare Spark,

Hunting Captain Ahab: Psychological Warfare and the Melville Revival (Kent, OH: Kent State University Press, 2001), p. 212.

261   "solar optimism": Peter Conrad, *Imagining America* (New York: Oxford University Press, 1980), p. 222.

261   "restore me the power": *CM,* ch. 16, p. 82.

261   "Horrible snowy mountains": Journal entry, August 7, 1860, in *Journals,* p. 133.

261   "I . . . read & think": Journal entry, August 10, 1860, ibid., pp. 134–35.

261   "at a given word . . . a good-for-nothing one": HM to Malcolm Melville, September 1 and 16, 1860, in *Correspondence,* pp. 347–49.

262   "big as chickens . . . middle of the ocean": HM to Elizabeth Melville, September 2, 1860, ibid., pp. 350–54.

262   "in pursuit of health": *Daily Evening Bulletin,* quoted in *Log,* II, 627.

262   "Herman Melville, the author of 'Omoo' ": *Daily Evening Bulletin,* quoted in *Log,* II, 628.

262   "gloomy lull": This is Melville's phrase in his note to his poem "The Conflict of Convictions," published in *Battle-Pieces and Other Aspects of the War* (1866): "The gloomy lull of the early part of the winter of 1860–1, seeming big with final disaster to our institutions, affected some minds that believed them to constitute one of the great hopes of mankind, much as the eclipse which came over the promise of the first French Revolution affected kindred natures, throwing them for the time into doubts and misgivings universal."

264   "take the oath on the Capitol steps": Richard T. Greene to HM, January 4, 1861, in *Correspondence,* p. 679.

265   "working hard . . . Thine, My Dearest Lizzie": HM to Elizabeth Shaw Melville, March 24–25, 1861, ibid., pp. 365–67.

265   Among the papers found in Shaw's wallet: See Parker, II, 467.

265   "Yes, my dear friend": Undated ms. letter from Nancy Wroe Melvill to Lemuel Shaw (Collection of the Social Law Library, Boston).

CHAPTER 11. SEASON OF DEATH

266   "Come, Shepherd": HM to Daniel Shepherd, July 6, 1859, in *Correspondence,* pp. 336–39.

266   "Not magnitude, nor lavishness": "Greek Architecture" was first published in the section entitled "Fruit of Travel Long Ago" in Melville's *Timoleon, etc.,* privately printed in the year of his death, 1891. The date of its composition is uncertain.

267   "If we are completely to understand": Robert Penn Warren, Introduction to *Selected Poems of Herman Melville* (1970; New York: Barnes & Noble, 1998), p. 4. Warren's introduction is a brilliant assessment of Melville's poetry, and one of the best general essays about Melville ever written. More recently, HM's merits as a poet have been vigorously asserted by Helen Vendler, "Desert Storm," *The New Republic,* December 7, 1992, pp. 39–42; William Spengemann, "Melville the Poet," *American Literary History* 11, no. 4 (Winter 1999): 569–609; and Lawrence Buell, "Melville the Poet," in Levine, ed., *Cambridge Companion to Herman Melville,* pp. 135–56.

267   "Pray do not mention to *any* one": Elizabeth Shaw Melville to Hope Savage Shaw, March 9, 1875, in *Log,* II, 741.

267   " 'No seeing here' ": "Donelson. (February, 1862)."

267   "Bridegroom Dick": First published in *John Marr and Other Sailors* (1888), this was probably composed around 1875. A convenient modern edition of Melville's poetry is Douglas Robillard, *The Poems of Herman Melville* (Kent, OH: Kent State University Press, 2000), which reprints *John Marr* on pp. 263–301.

268   "Obscure as the wood": "The Armies of the Wilderness, 1863–4."

268   "baffled, humiliated": Whitman, *Specimen Days,* in *Walt Whitman: Complete Poetry and Collected Prose* (New York: Library of America, 1982), p. 708.

268   "chronicle . . . of the patriotic feelings": Edmund Wilson, *Patriotic Gore* (New York: Oxford University Press, 1962), p. 479.

268   "saw various battlefields": Elizabeth Shaw Melville, notes about her husband, in Sealts, *Early Lives,* p. 172.

269   "when we will be able to talk": HM to Gansevoort Melville, May 29, 1846, in *Correspondence,* p. 41. This is the letter that Gansevoort never received.

269   "disordered . . . decks of a whaleship": *MD,* ch. 24, p. 109.

269   "How should they dream": "Ball's Bluff. *A Reverie* (October, 1861)."

269   "One noonday": "Ball's Bluff."

270   "thousands of vivid images": Warren, Introduction to *Selected Poems,* p. 7.

270   "rosy clime": "Ball's Bluff."

270   "starry heights": "The Conflict of Convictions (1860–1)."

270   "gladsome air": "America."

270   "War shall yet be": "A Utilitarian View of the Monitor's Fight."

270   "carding machines, horse-shoe machines": *CM,* ch. 22, p. 117.

270   "Perish their Cause!": "Rebel Color-Bearers at Shiloh."

270   "He hears the drum": "The Released Rebel Prisoner."

270   "rhyme's barbaric cymbal": "A Utilitarian View."

270   "bearing the brunt": Whitman, *Democratic Vistas,* in *Complete Poetry and Collected Prose,* p. 944.

271   "We are coming—thanks to the war": Emerson, "Fortune of the Republic" (December 1, 1863), in Gougeon and Myerson, eds., *Emerson's Antislavery Writings,* p. 144.

271   "Strange to say": Hawthorne to Horatio Bridge, May 26, 1861, in William Charvat et al., eds., *The Centenary Edition of the Works of Nathaniel Hawthorne,* 23 vols. (Columbus: Ohio State University Press, 1962–   ), XVIII, 380.

271   "I am too old": Hawthorne, quoted in James Mellow, *Nathaniel Hawthorne in His Times* (Boston: Houghton Mifflin, 1980), p. 541.

271   Union troops had dug a tunnel: See David Cody, " 'So then, Solidity's a Crust': Melville's 'The Apparition' and the Explosion of the Petersburg Mine," *Melville Society Extracts* 78 (September 1989): 1–8.

272   "the cause of the war": Lincoln, "Second Inaugural Address," March 4, 1865, in Fehrenbacher, ed., *Abraham Lincoln: Speeches and Writings,* II, 686.

273   "Is it possible": Howells, *Atlantic Monthly,* February 1867, quoted in Higgins and Parker, eds., *Contemporary Reviews,* p. 527.

273   All survived, though Guert: He was acquitted, but never recovered his reputa-

tion; see Parker, II, 518–19. For an assessment of Guert's career and its impact on Melville, see Eric Homberger, "Melville, Lt. Guert Gansevoort and Authority: An Essay in Biography," in Faith Pullin, ed., *New Perspectives on Melville* (Edinburgh: Edinburgh University Press, 1978), pp. 255–74.

273 "was much attached . . . much shocked": Maria Gansevoort Melville to Peter Gansevoort, May 24, 1864, in *Log*, II, 669.

273 Melville's horse bucked in panic: *Berkshire County Eagle*, November 13, 1862, in *Log*, II, 655.

274 "This recovery . . . is flattering": HM to Samuel S. Shaw, December 10, 1862, in *Correspondence*, p. 381.

274 "If I venture to displace": Poe, *Eureka* (1848), in W. H. Auden, ed., *Edgar Allan Poe: Selected Prose, Poetry, and Eureka* (New York: Holt, Rinehart, and Winston, 1950), p. 512.

274 "I have a voice": *WJ*, ch. 75, p. 321.

274 "insinuation, that had he lived in those days": HM to Evert Duyckinck, March 3, 1849, in *Correspondence*, p. 121.

274 "square, old-fashioned": Stanwix Melville to Augusta Melville, September 30, 1862, quoted in Parker, II, 520.

275 "As for scribbling anything about it": HM to Evert Duyckinck, December 31, 1863, in *Correspondence*, p. 389.

275 "bards . . . love wine, mead": Emerson, "The Poet" (1840), in Whicher, ed., *Selections*, p. 234.

275 "I won't believe in a Temperance Heaven": HM to Nathaniel Hawthorne, June [1?], 1851, in *Correspondence*, p. 191. Hawthorne had written to G. W. Curtis on April 25, 1851, that Melville "is an admirable fellow, and has some excellent old port and sherry wine" (*Log*, I, 410).

275 "keep some Champagne or Gin": HM to Nathaniel Hawthorne, October 25, 1852, in *Correspondence*, p. 240.

275 "have ready a bottle . . . morning till night": HM to Nathaniel Hawthorne, June 29, 1851, ibid., p. 196.

275 "attach the screw of your hose-pipe": *P*, bk. 22, p. 301.

275 "I could drink a great deal": *P*, bk. 22, pp. 299–300.

275 "periodically violent to his wife": Olson, *Call Me Ishmael*, p. 92. See Elizabeth Renker, "Wife Beating and the Written Page," in *Strike Through the Mask: Herman Melville and the Scene of Writing* (Baltimore: Johns Hopkins University Press, 1996), pp. 49–68. Renker believes that Melville may have beaten Lizzie in response to her threat to leave him (p. 50).

275 "His moods he had": *Clarel*, pt. II, 4, ll. 140–41.

276 "convinced that her husband is insane": Samuel S. Shaw, letter to Henry Whitney Bellows, May 6, 1867, first published in Walter D. Kring and Jonathan S. Carey, "Two Discoveries Concerning Herman Melville," *Proceedings of the Massachusetts Historical Society* 87 (1975): 140.

276 "whatever further trial": Elizabeth Shaw Melville, letter to Henry Whitney Bellows, May 10, 1867, ibid., p. 141. Eleven responses to the discovery of the two letters bearing on the Melvilles' marital crisis are gathered in Donald Yannella and Hershel Parker, eds., *The Endless, Winding Way in Melville: New Charts by*

Kring and Carey (Glassboro, NJ: The Melville Society, 1981). One respondent, Paul Metcalf (Melville's great-grandson), reports that Charles Olson told him that Melville had come home "smashed on brandy" and thrown his wife down the stairs. Metcalf surmised that his mother, Eleanor Melville Metcalf, had been privy to the "dirt" and had shared it with Henry Murray and Howard P. Vincent; but, according to a footnote, neither Murray nor Vincent recalled such a conversation. Other respondents interpret the letters as nothing more than confirmation that "most serious authors are trials to their wives" (Leon Howard, in *Endless, Winding Way*, p. 23).

276   "purity . . . gentleness": Hoadley, quoted in Parker, II, 640.

276   According to Sam Shaw's account: Sam Shaw to Hope Savage Shaw, September 12, 1867, in *Log*, II, 688.

276   "And there were the children": Paul Metcalf, *Genoa: A Telling of Wonders* (Albuquerque: University of New Mexico Press, 1991), p. 73.

277   "no motive having appeared": New York *Evening Post*, September 16, 1867, quoted in Parker, II, 643–44.

277   "I wish you could have seen him": HM to John C. Hoadley, between September 14 and September 18, 1867, extract printed in *Correspondence*, pp. 399–400.

277   "He's a perfect prodigy": HM to Allan Melville, February 20, 1849, ibid., p. 116.

277   There is a poem, "Monody": See Harrison Hayford, *Melville's "Monody": Really for Hawthorne?* (Evanston: Northwestern University Press, 1990). Douglas Robillard, in *The Poems of Herman Melville* (Kent, OH: Kent State University Press, 2000), p. 341, suggests that HM more likely had Malcolm in mind.

278   "fairly devour": Augusta Melville to Helen Melville, December 31, 1850, in *Correspondence*, p. 605.

278   "little round curls": Stanwix Melville to Hope Savage Shaw, July 11, 1861, ms. (By permission of the Houghton Library, Harvard University—call number bMS Am 188 [239]).

278   "fearlessness of an old equestrian": Hawthorne, *American Notebooks*, ed. Simpson, p. 448.

278   "loved Mr. Melville": Ibid., pp. 467–68.

278   "I am very happy": HM to Julian Hawthorne, February [9?], 1852, in *Correspondence*, p. 221.

278   "So good, so young": Quoted in Parker, II, 649.

278   "one representing him . . . speak of Mackie": HM to Maria Melville (HM's niece), October 22, 1867, in *Correspondence*, pp. 400–401.

279   "barrenness of Judea": Journal entry, January 26, 1857, in *Journals*, p. 83.

279   "innate and incurable disorder": "Bartleby," in *PT*, p. 29.

279   "the mind is ductile": *CM*, ch. 4, p. 20.

280   "a metrical affair": HM to James Billson, October 10, 1884, in *Correspondence*, p. 483.

280   "dreadful *incubus* of a book": Elizabeth Shaw Melville to Catherine Lansing, February 2, 1876, in *Log*, II, 747.

280   "philosophical verse-novel": Daniel Aaron, *The Unwritten War: American Writers and the Civil War* (Madison: University of Wisconsin Press, 1987), p. 88.

280   "Frost believed": Joseph Brodsky, Seamus Heaney, and Derek Walcott, *Homage to Robert Frost* (New York: Farrar, Straus & Giroux, 1996), p. 63.

280   "whitish mildew pervading whole tracts": Journal entry, "Barrenness of Judea," January 1857, in *Journals*, p. 83.

280   "blind arches . . . sealed windows": *Clarel*, pt. I, 1, ll. 163–64.

280   "The student mused": *Clarel*, pt. I, 25, ll. 81–84.

280   "How . . . be derived from things": *Clarel*, pt. I, 34, ll. 16–17.

281   "Hand is amputated now": Emily Dickinson, poem #1581.

281   "Men have come to speak": Emerson, "Divinity School Address," in Whicher, ed., *Selections*, p. 107.

281   "to feed only on inspirations": Orestes Brownson, "Introduction," *Brownson's Quarterly Review* 1 (January 1844): 10.

281   "the divine *aura*": Emerson, "The Poet," in Whicher, ed., *Selections*, p. 233.

281   "floods of life stream around": Emerson, *Nature*, ibid., p. 26.

281   "as young today as when it was created": "Hawthorne and His Mosses," in *PT*, p. 246.

281   "Every happy little wave": *R*, ch. 13, p. 64.

282   "I could not see": *R*, ch. 16, p. 78.

282   "departed the last hope": Frank Kermode, *The Classic: Literary Images of Permanence and Change* (Cambridge, MA: Harvard University Press, 1983), p. 97.

282   "the craving of the heart": William James, "The Will to Believe" (1896), in *The Will to Believe and Other Essays in Popular Philosophy* (New York: Dover, 1956), p. 40.

282   "Shall Science then": *Clarel*, pt. II, 25, ll. 154–57.

282   "The abbot and the palmer rest": *Clarel*, pt. I, 35, ll. 108–11.

283   "Won men to look for solace there": *Clarel*, pt. I, 13, l. 43.

283   "hands, nailed down": *Clarel*, pt. II, 3, ll. 155–57.

283   "last adopted style": *Clarel*, pt. II, 1, ll. 35–36.

283   "Yea, long as children feel affright": *Clarel*, pt. I, 31, ll. 187–90.

283   "nothing but a simple cavity" Arthur Penrhyn Stanley, *Sinai and Palestine in Connection with Their History* (1863), quoted in the explanatory notes by Walter Bezanson in the Hendricks House edition of *Clarel*, p. 584. Bezanson's notes to this edition of *Clarel* constitute a monumental work of scholarship.

283   "faces, yet defacements too": *Clarel*, pt. I, 26, l. 4.

283   "Dim showed across the prairie green": *Clarel*, pt. I, 17, ll. 58–60.

284   "Alone, and at Doubt's freezing pole": *Clarel*, pt. I, 17, ll. 193–95.

284   "a source that well might claim": *Clarel*, pt. I, 17, ll. 198–99.

284   "bigoted Hebrew nationality": *R*, ch. 33, p. 169.

284   "looking for [the Messiah]": Hawthorne and His Mosses," in *PT*, p. 246.

284   "the mind infertile of the Jew": *Clarel*, pt. I, 17, l. 25.

284   "The Hebrew seers announce in time": *Clarel*, pt. I, 17, ll. 261–64.

284   "deliberately hobbled his muse": Gay Wilson Allen, Foreword to Vincent Kenny, *Herman Melville's Clarel: A Spiritual Autobiography* (Hamden, CT: Archon Books, 1973), pp. xii–xiii.

284   "dark quarries": *Clarel*, pt. I, 16, l. 34.

284   "Slant on the shore": *Clarel*, pt. II, 39, ll. 15–18.

285 "He's gone": *Clarel,* pt. II, 39, ll. 67-70.

285 "One he perceived": *Clarel,* pt. I, 17, ll. 157-67.

285 "while pacing the floor": Metcalf, *Herman Melville: Cycle and Epicycle,* p. 76.

286 "Sands immense": *Clarel,* pt. II, 12, ll. 38-50.

286 "Herman . . . is in such a frightfully nervous state": Elizabeth Shaw Melville to Catherine Lansing, February 2, 1876, in *Log,* II, 747.

287 "There's none so far astray": *Clarel,* pt. II, 4, ll. 148-56.

287 "well-kept secret of one's self": Cowen, "Melville's Marginalia," I, 116.

287 of which about a third were sold: See the Historical Note in *Clarel,* pp. 539-40, 659.

287 When Lewis Mumford, in 1925: Mumford, *Sketches from My Life* (New York: Dial Press, 1982), p. 456.

CHAPTER 12. THE QUIET END

288 "there are no second acts": F. Scott Fitzgerald, *The Last Tycoon* (New York: Scribner's, 1941), p. 189.

288 "Melville Medal": John Updike, *Bech Is Back* (New York: Knopf, 1982), p. 167. I owe this reference to Lee Siegel.

288 "My vigor sensibly declines": HM to Archibald MacMechan, December 5, 1889, in *Correspondence,* p. 519.

289 "More than once": Harrison Hayford and Merton M. Sealts, Jr., eds., *Melville's Billy Budd: The Genetic Text* (Chicago: University of Chicago Press, 1962), p. 1.

289 "whoever . . . dost seek happiness": Quoted in Wallace, *Melville and Turner,* p. 11.

290 "the sparkle, the verve": Raymond Weaver, *Herman Melville: Mariner and Mystic* (New York: George H. Doran, 1921), p. 381.

290 "songful passages": Edward Said, interview, in Carola Kaplan, Peter Mallios, and Andrea White, eds., *Conrad in the Twenty-first Century* (London: Routledge, 2004), p. 285.

290 "reaches straight back into the universal": Forster, *Aspects of the Novel,* p. 206.

291 "clinging like a weary but tenacious barnacle": George Parsons Lathrop to Horace Scudder, October 20, 1890, quoted in *Log,* II, 826.

291 "Towards the end he sailed": Auden, "Herman Melville."

291 Later, he was assigned to an East River pier: Elizabeth Shaw Melville, notes on her husband, in Sealts, *Early Lives,* p. 170.

291 wearing a brass-buttoned woolen coat: Larry Reynolds, "*Billy Budd* and American Labor Unrest: The Case for Striking Back," in Donald Yannella, ed., *New Essays on Billy Budd* (New York: Cambridge University Press, 2002), p. 38.

291 It was not savory work: See Stanton Garner, "Melville in the Customhouse, 1881-1882: A Rustic Beauty Among the Highborn Dames of Court," *Melville Society Extracts* 35 (September 1978): 12-14; and Parker, II, 694.

291 "surrounded . . . by low venality": Hoadley to George Boutwell, January 9, 1873, in *Log,* II, 730-31.

292 "unprotected . . . were debauched": Dorman B. Eaton, *The "Spoils" System*

and Civil Service Reform in the Custom-House and Post-Office at New York, Publications of the Civil Service Reform Association, 3 (New York, 1881), quoted in Garner, "Melville in the Customhouse," p. 12.

292 "For a year or so past": Elizabeth Shaw Melville to Catherine Lansing, January 10, 1886, in *Log,* II, 796.

292 "man of genius": *Log,* II, 832. Arthur Stedman, who assisted Lizzie Melville as her husband's literary executor, reports in his introduction to an 1892 edition of *Typee* that Melville was reading Schopenhauer during his final illness. Between February 5 and 12, 1891, HM borrowed Schopenhauer's *Counsels and Maxims* from the New York Society Library and later purchased a copy of the work, along with *Religion: A Dialogue, Studies in Pessimism, The Wisdom of Life,* and *The World as Will and Idea.* See Sealts, *Melville's Reading,* pp. 129–30.

292 "within a very short distance": Frederick Busch, *The Night Inspector* (New York: Harmony Books, 1999), p. 23.

292 "You are young . . . I aint crazy": HM to John C. Hoadley, March 31, 1877, in *Correspondence,* pp. 451–54.

293 Later that year, Melville's behavior: Metcalf, *Herman Melville: Cycle and Epicycle,* p. 259.

293 "*morbidly* sensitive": Elizabeth Shaw Melville to Catherine Lansing, February 25, 1877, in *Log,* II, 759.

293 "Yet Ah, that Spring should vanish": Cowen, "Melville's Marginalia," VIII, 72.

293 "Like tides that enter creek or stream": *John Marr.* For Melville's use of *Omar Khayyám,* see Robert K. Wallace, "Melville's Prints: David Metcalf's Prints and Tile," *Harvard Library Bulletin* 8, no. 4 (Winter 1997): 23.

293 "cries decrease—": *Clarel,* pt. IV, 15, ll. 60–62.

294 "I have been recently improving": HM to Catherine Melville Hoadley (HM's sister Kate), December 28, 1881, in *Correspondence,* p. 477.

294 "Melville, whose magic drew Typee": *Log,* II, 792.

294 "vein of true poetical feeling": *New York Mail and Express,* November 20, 1888, in Higgins and Parker, eds., *Contemporary Reviews,* p. 545.

294 "unique merits": Archibald MacMechan to HM, November 21, 1889, in *Correspondence,* p. 752.

294 "Putnam's group": Henry James, June 11, 1898, in Leon Edel, ed., *Henry James: Literary Criticism—Essays on Literature, American Writers, English Writers* (New York: Library of America, 1984), p. 683.

294 "as for Herman Melville": Edith Wharton, *A Backward Glance* (New York: Scribner's, 1934), p. 68.

295 "it is hard enough to get along": Elizabeth Shaw Melville to Hope Savage Shaw, March 9, 1875, in *Log,* II, 741.

295 "topped by strange plaster heads": Metcalf, *Herman Melville: Cycle and Epicycle,* p. 283.

295 "I could play with anything . . . palish blue color": Frances C. T. Osborne (HM's granddaughter), "Herman Melville Through a Child's Eyes," in Sealts, *Early Lives,* p. 184.

295 There was a back porch: Hershel Parker, "The Melville House at 104 East 26th Street," *Harvard Library Bulletin* 8, no. 4 (Winter 1997): 38.

295   "pale, sombre, nervous": *Log*, II, 782.

296   "bowel trouble": Elizabeth Shaw Melville to Hope Savage Shaw, July 20, 1875, in *Log*, II, 742.

296   "the most profitable business": Elizabeth Shaw Melville to Hope Savage Shaw, March 14, 1874, in *Log*, II, 736.

296   "serious obsticle": Stanwix Melville to Hope Savage Shaw, April 25, 1873, in *Log*, II, 732-33.

296   "unable to find solace": Helen Griggs to Catherine Lansing, May 5, 1886, in *Log*, II, 800.

297   "As the growing sense of his environment": See Merton M. Sealts, Jr., "Innocence and Infamy: *Billy Budd, Sailor*," in Bryant, ed., *Companion*, p. 411.

298   "the consciousness of having done my duty": Mary Ann Gansevoort to Peter Gansevoort, January 2, 1843, in *Log*, I, 161.

298   A prose work began to grow: The best account of the genesis and development of *Billy Budd* is Hayford and Sealts, eds., Editors' Introduction, in *Melville's Billy Budd: The Genetic Text*, reprinted in Hayford and Sealts, eds., *Billy Budd, Sailor* (Chicago: University of Chicago Press, 1962), pp. 1-39.

298   "tarry hand": *BB*, ch. 30, p. 1434.

298   "unworldly servers": *John Marr*, l. 37, in Robillard, ed., *Poems*, p. 268.

298   Melville noted in the manuscript on April 19, 1891: See Hayford and Sealts, eds., *Billy Budd: The Genetic Text*, p. 425.

299   "ragged edges": *BB*, ch. 28, p. 1431.

299   "and despite his all but fully developed frame": *BB*, ch. 2, p. 1359.

299   "rueful reproach . . . Sorry": *BB*, ch. 1, p. 1356.

299   "in the time before steamships": *BB*, ch. 1, p. 1353.

299   "A virtue went out of him . . . at the *Bellipotent* ": *BB*, ch. 1, pp. 1356-57.

300   "in a terrible breach . . . Down, sir!": *BB*, ch. 1, p. 1358.

300   "The will to it": *BB*, ch. 1, pp. 1358-59.

300   "A novice in the complexities": *BB*, ch. 2, p. 1360.

300   "to deal in double meanings": *BB*, ch. 1, p. 1359.

300   "the contact of one man with another": *Mardi*, ch. 3, p. 14.

300   "of self-consciousness . . . composer of his own song": *BB*, ch. 2, p. 1361.

301   "which the Greek sculptor . . . gave to his heroic strong man": *BB*, ch. 2, p. 1360.

301   "expression of sweet and divine gravity": Thomas Mann, *Death in Venice* (1912), trans. David Luke (New York: Bantam Books, 1988), p. 216.

301   the "Me" and the "Not-Me": Emerson, *Nature*, in Whicher, ed., *Selections*, p. 22.

301   "became . . . disunited with himself": Ibid., p. 55.

301   "a period prior to Cain's city": *BB*, ch. 2, p. 1362.

301   "Who was your father?": *BB*, ch. 2, p. 1361.

301   "Men may seem detestable": *MD*, ch. 26, p. 117.

301   "Under sudden provocation": *BB*, ch. 2, p. 1362.

302   "master-at-arms": In *WJ*, ch. 6, p. 26, HM had described the master-at-arms as "a sort of high constable and schoolmaster . . . whom all sailors hate."

302   "hue of time-tinted marbles": *BB*, ch. 8, p. 1373.

302   "peculiar ferreting genius": *BB*, ch. 8, p. 1375.

302   "The two men . . . come, socially speaking": Arendt, *On Revolution,* p. 83.

302   "He looked like a man . . . in the sky": *BB,* ch. 8, pp. 1373-75.

302   "Jemmy Legs is down . . . Baby Budd": *BB,* ch. 15, p. 1392.

303   "His portrait I essay": *BB,* ch. 8, p. 1372.

303   "What was the matter": *BB,* ch. 11, p. 1381.

303   "motiveless malignity": Coleridge, *Lectures, 1808–1819, on Literature,* ed. R. A. Foakes (Princeton: Princeton University Press, 1987), p. 315.

303   "the death of Satan": Wallace Stevens, "Esthetique du Mal."

303   "elemental evil": *BB,* ch. 12, p. 1385.

304   "the opinion of the million": Emerson, "Fate" (1860), in Whicher, ed., *Selections,* p. 345.

304   "chief of police": *BB,* ch. 8, p. 1372.

304   "To the British empire": *BB,* ch. 3, p. 1363.

304   "stand with drawn swords": *BB,* ch. 5, p. 1368.

304   "workmen are denied the right of organization": Ignatius Donnelly, Preamble to the platform of the First National Convention of the People's Party at Omaha, July 4, 1892, quoted in Walter Rideout's introduction to Donnelly, *Caesar's Column: A Story of the Twentieth Century* (1890; Cambridge, MA: Harvard University Press, 1960), p. xi. For an argument that *Billy Budd* is Melville's direct commentary on contemporary events, see Larry J. Reynolds, "*Billy Budd* and American Labor Unrest," in Yannella, ed., *New Essays on Billy Budd;* and for a broader interpretation in the context of Gilded Age capitalism, see Alan Trachtenberg, *The Incorporation of America: Culture and Society in the Gilded Age* (New York: Hill & Wang, 1982), pp. 201–7.

304   "the one way to deal with a mob": *New York Independent,* quoted in Edwin G. Burrows and Mike Wallace, eds., *Gotham: A History of New York City to 1898* (New York: Oxford University Press, 1999), p. 1036.

304   In March 1886, in a violent strike: See ibid., p. 1095.

305   Eighteen months later, four self-avowed anarchists: Robert K. Wallace suggests that HM had these events in mind; see his "*Billy Budd* and the Haymarket Hangings," *American Literature* 47 (March 1975): 108–13.

305   "a young horse fresh from the pasture": *BB,* ch. 15, p. 1390.

305   "divine equality": *MD,* ch. 26, p. 117.

305   "free Republic": Howells to his father, quoted in Frederick Anderson, William M. Gibson, and Henry Nash Smith, eds., *Selected Mark Twain–Howells Letters* (Cambridge, MA: Harvard University Press, 1967), p. 275.

305   "the seed is sown": *R,* ch. 33, p. 169.

305   "Mammonite freebooters": *Clarel,* pt. IV, 9, l. 122.

306   "Past is dead": *WJ,* ch. 36, p. 150.

306   "Come, thou who makest such hot haste": *Clarel,* pt. II, 4, ll. 67–68.

306   "old imagined America": Trachtenberg, *Incorporation of America,* p. 206.

306   "bias toward those books": *BB,* ch. 7, p. 1371.

306   "like live cinders": *BB,* ch. 3, p. 1364.

306   "a dike against those invading waters": *BB,* ch. 7, p. 1371.

306   "With mankind": *BB,* ch. 27, p. 1430.

307   "tool for laying little traps": *BB,* ch. 13, p. 1386.

307   "D—d—damme": *BB*, ch. 14, p. 1389.
307   "it never entered [Billy's] mind": *BB*, ch. 15, p. 1391.
307   "deferentially . . . with the air of a subordinate": *BB*, ch. 18, pp. 1397–98.
307   "repellent distaste . . . Master-at-arms?": *BB*, ch. 18, p. 1397.
307   "who had entered . . . something clandestine": *BB*, ch. 18, p. 1398.
307   "William Budd . . . ruddy-tipped daisies": *BB*, ch. 18, p. 1400.
307   "Stay . . . heed what you speak": *BB*, ch. 18, p. 1401.
307   "practically [to] test the accuser": *BB*, ch. 18, p. 1402.
307   "exceptional moral quality": *BB*, ch. 18, p. 1401.
308   "With the measured step": *BB*, ch. 19, pp. 1403–4.
308   "an expression like that . . . touching Billy's heart": *BB*, ch. 19, p. 1404.
308   " 'Fated boy' . . . till thence summoned": *BB*, ch. 19, p. 1405.
309   "Catching the surgeon's arm . . . the angel must hang!": *BB*, ch. 19, p. 1406.
309   The answers lie in the crystal clarity: The question of whether Vere acts legally has been much debated. Richard H. Weisberg, *The Failure of the Word: The Protagonist as Lawyer in Modern Fiction* (New Haven: Yale University Press, 1984), pp. 131–76, is a brief against Vere for "gross violations" (p. 155) of British naval procedure. Richard A. Posner, *Law and Literature: A Misunderstood Relation* (Cambridge, MA: Harvard University Press, 1988), pp. 155–65, defends Vere's actions as consistent with precedent and appropriate under war conditions. In *WJ*, ch. 71, p. 299, Melville describes the Articles of War as "tyrannical ordinances," but this comment refers specifically to the practice of flogging. With respect to Vere's citation of the Articles of War, Hayford and Sealts argue in their edition of *Billy Budd* (p. 176) that "Melville simply had not familiarized himself with statutes of the period concerning administration of British naval justice," and did not intend to imply that Vere was conducting an illegitimate judicial action. Sealts modified this conclusion in a later essay on *BB* in Bryant, *Companion*, pp. 417–418. The relevant section of the Articles (Article XXII, prescribing execution for striking an officer) is quoted on p. 180 of the Hayford and Sealts edition. A study of judicial morality that links Vere to Judge Shaw is Robert Cover, *Justice Accused: Antislavery and the Judicial Process* (New Haven: Yale University Press, 1975).
309   "matter should be referred to the admiral": *BB*, ch. 20, p. 1407.
309   "In the jugglery of circumstances": *BB*, ch. 21, p. 1408.
310   "How can we adjudge": *BB*, ch. 21, p. 1414.
310   "the ship's company . . . that alone we have to do": *BB*, ch. 21, p. 1412.
310   "the monotonous blank": *BB*, ch. 21, p. 1413.
310   "critical ocean": *MD*, ch. 26, p. 116.
310   "it is Nature": *BB*, ch. 21, p. 1414.
310   "But do these buttons": *BB*, ch. 21, pp. 1414–15.
311   "*Why?* they will ruminate": *BB*, ch. 21, p. 1416.
311   "Who in the rainbow can draw": *BB*, ch. 21, p. 1407.
311   "we carve out groups of stars": James, *Pragmatism*, p. 164.
312   "what sometimes happens": See Hayford and Sealts, eds., *Billy Budd: The Genetic Text*, p. 8.
312   "strong patriotic impulse": *BB*, ch. 29, p. 1433.
313   (from E. M. Forster . . . and many others): There is a broad consensus among

these writers and critics that, as Camus puts it, Captain Vere "submits his heart to the law . . . so that an order may be maintained, and the ship of men continue to move forward towards an unknown horizon" (Camus, *Lyrical and Critical Essays*, p. 292). The critical history of *Billy Budd* is reviewed in Peter Shaw, "The Fate of a Story," *American Scholar* 62 (Autumn 1993): 591–601, and Geraldine Murphy, "The Politics of Reading *Billy Budd*," *American Literary History* 1, no. 2 (Summer 1989): 361–82.

313 "however pitilessly": *BB*, ch. 21, p. 1415.

313 "tragedy of Spirit in the world of Necessity": Lionel Trilling, *The Middle of the Journey* (1947; New York: New York Review Books, 2002), p. 181.

313 "awesome responsibility": Posner, *Law and Literature*, p. 161. For an argument that Vere is the agent of an oppressive legal system that serves the rich, see Thomas, *Cross-Examinations of Law and Literature*, pp. 201–50. Thomas rejects Weisberg's "focus on technicalities" in favor of a broader argument that Melville attacks "the entire legal system" (p. 212) as an instrument of class oppression. Thomas is one of several critics who, following Robert Cover (see note to p. 309 above), identifies Vere with Judge Lemuel Shaw. He suggests (p. 226), as does Tom Quirk—in "The Judge Dragged to the Bar: Melville, Shaw, and the Webster Murder Trial," *Melville Society Extracts* 84 (February 1991): 1–8—that HM had in mind not only Shaw's role in the Fugitive Slave cases, but also in the sensational 1850 murder trial of a Harvard professor accused of murdering an eminent Bostonian over a financial dispute.

313 To intrude would be to violate: Melville had likely read Dryden's *Essay of Dramatic Poesy*, in which Dryden declares that it would be unseemly to allow "the undecent appearance . . . on the stage" of "actions which by reason of their cruelty, will cause aversion in us."

313 "the condemned one . . . covers all at last": *BB*, ch. 23, p. 1419.

314 "shot through with a soft glory": *BB*, ch. 26, p. 1427. See Nathalia Wright's discussion, in *Melville's Use of the Bible*, p. 163, of HM's combination of imagery from Acts 1:9 (the ascension of Christ) and Rev. 7:9 (the lamb on the throne).

314 "God Bless Captain Vere": *BB*, ch. 26, p. 1426.

314 "that strange transition": *P*, ch. 15, p. 218.

315 It has become skeletal: Many critics have noted HM's painterly prose and his special affection for the Dutch masters. See the essays in Christopher Sten, ed., *Savage Eye: Melville and the Visual Arts* (Kent, OH: Kent State University Press, 1991), especially Dennis Berthold, "Melville and Dutch Genre Painting" (pp. 218–45); and see also Douglas Robillard, *Melville and the Visual Arts: Ionian Form, Venetian Tint* (Kent, OH: Kent State University Press, 1997), who describes HM's style as "literary pictorialism" (p. 99).

315 "umbrageous shade": *T*, ch. 12, p. 91.

315 "outreaching comprehensiveness": *MD*, ch. 104, p. 456.

315 "arbitrary enlistment": *BB*, ch. 3, p. 1363.

315 "enforced enlistment": *BB*, ch. 1, p. 1359.

315 "sinister dexterity": *BB*, ch. 1, p. 1358. It is apparent from the *Billy Budd* ms. that HM added the word "sinister" after writing "dexterity." See Hayford and Sealts, eds., *Billy Budd: The Genetic Text*, p. 291.

315   "holds the action at a remove": Berthoff, *The Example of Melville*, p. 174.

316   "Can you tell me . . . the evanescence": HM to Maria Gansevoort Melville, May 5, 1870, in *Correspondence*, p. 412.

316   "seemed to wander": Henry James, "The Beast in the Jungle" (1903), in Edel, ed., *Henry James: Selected Fiction*, p. 532.

316   "the old people had mostly gone": Henry James, "The Jolly Corner" (1909), ibid., p. 549.

316   "no great and enduring volume": *MD*, ch. 104, p. 456.

316   *"Heart of autumn!"*: "The Chipmunk," in Vincent, ed., *Collected Poems*, p. 268.

317   In the final line, Melville changed "the hearth": See Hennig Cohen and Donald Yannella, *Herman Melville's Malcolm Letter: "Man's Final Lore"* (New York: Fordham University Press, 1992), pp. 79–85, and John Bryant, "Melville's Rose Poems: As They Fell," *Arizona Quarterly* 53 (Spring 1997): 49–84, for discussion of "The Chipmunk" and its relation to the death of Malcolm.

317   "The preacher took from Solomon's Song": "Rose Window," in Vincent, ed., *Collected Poems*, p. 299.

318   "rapid stride": Oscar Wegelin, "Melville as I Recall Him," *The Colophon: A Quarterly for Bookmen*, new ser. 1, no. 1 (Summer 1935): 22.

318   "beard . . . impressive even for those hirsute days": Ibid., pp. 21, 23.

318   "the party-giving city": "Jimmy Rose," in *PT*, p. 338.

318   "dining salon was filled": Henry Collins Brown, quoted in William B. Dillingham, *Melville and His Circle: The Last Years* (Athens: University of Georgia Press, 1996), p. 13.

318   "he had become too much of a hermit": Charles DeKay, *Reminiscences of the Authors Club*, in *Log*, II, 781.

319   "after all his wanderings": *New York Commercial Advertiser*, January 14, 1886, quoted in *Log*, II, 796.

319   "would take long walks": Wegelin, "Herman Melville as I Recall Him," p. 23.

319   "found some relief": *P*, bk. 25, p. 340.

319   "the one great imaginative writer": Robert Buchanan, quoted in Sealts, *Early Lives*, p. 23.

319   "it was difficult to get more than a passing glimpse": Ernest Rhys, quoted ibid., p. 24.

319   "internal exile": Trachtenberg, *The Incorporation of America*, p. 202.

319   "for an hour or two": Brander Mathews, quoted in Sealts, *Early Lives*, p. 25.

319   "never denied himself": Titus Coan, quoted ibid., p. 27.

319   "produce a discord in Nature": Cowen, "Melville's Marginalia," V, 331.

321   did her best to replicate the furnishings: Puett, "Melville's Wife," p. 170.

321   "My ideas of my husband": Sealts, *Melville's Reading*, p. 4.

321   On Herman's desk she placed: Metcalf, *Herman Melville: Cycle and Epicycle*, p. 289.

321   "the most beautiful story in the world": Thomas Mann, quoted in Anthony Heilbut, *Exiled in Paradise: German Refugee Artists and Intellectuals in America from the 1930s to the Present* (Berkeley: University of California Press, 1997), p. 496.

ACKNOWLEDGMENTS

During my years of thinking and writing about Melville, my family and friends have shown me more kindness than can possibly be acknowledged here, but I would like to thank a few people and institutions who were directly helpful to this work.

Ginger Barber and Jennifer Rudolph Walsh supported this book enthusiastically all along the way from proposal to final draft. At Knopf, I am very grateful to Gary Fisketjon for his sensitive and rigorous editing, his graciousness, and his unflagging commitment. Ellen Feldman and Liz Van Hoose made the whole process of moving from manuscript to finished book less a trial than a pleasure.

With the support of the American Council of Learned Societies, I spent eight months in 1999–2000 in residence at the Dorothy and Lewis Cullman Center for Scholars and Writers at the New York Public Library. My colleagues there, especially Ada Louise Huxtable, Allen Kurzweil, and Howard Markel, helped me to get my thoughts in focus. Three years later, when I was ready to start writing, I spent nearly a year in North Carolina at the National Humanities Center, where conversations with Charles Capper, Harriet Ritvo, Paul Griffiths, Lloyd Kramer, Kalman Bland, and James Knowlson were particularly helpful. I owe warm thanks to Joel Elliott for keeping my computer running, and to the incomparable library staff of the Humanities Center—Liza Robertson, Betsy Dain, and Jean Houston—for filling the shelves in my study with the books and articles I needed.

In the intervening years, I had the pleasure of teaching Melville to many insightful students at Columbia University. I am grateful to Columbia not only for helping to make possible the periods of leave during which I was able to concentrate on writing, but for giving me the chance to try out ideas in the atmosphere of freedom and challenge that prevails in its classrooms. I also want to thank my former student and current colleague Roosevelt Montás, who gave me indispensable help in the final stages of manuscript preparation.

One of the great good fortunes of my life was to have been mentored in my own student days by the late Alan Heimert, and, when I was a fledgling teacher, by Steven Marcus, each of whom inspired me in different ways to undertake and see this work through. Many years ago, Bernard Malamud took an interest in a young student who imagined someday writing a book about Melville. I wish I could thank him for his interest and encouragement, which have always stayed with me.

I hope that my debt to the community of Melville scholars is at least hinted at in the notes. Like all students of Melville, I am keenly aware of, and especially grateful for, the prodigious scholarship of Hershel Parker, whose discoveries have immeasurably deepened our knowledge of Melville's life. I must also add particular thanks to Samuel Otter for sharing his unpublished work on the reception history of *Moby-Dick,* and to Robert

K. Wallace for helping me track down some elusive materials. Many other readers of Melville—among them colleagues and friends whom I thank individually in the notes— called my attention over the years to aspects of Melville's writing or references to him that eventually found their way into this book.

Over time, one becomes increasingly aware of the blessing of friends. In connection with this book, I think especially of Rochelle Gurstein, who, at a moment when I needed a boost, wrote me a generous response to something I had written that sent me in a new direction, and Eric Himmel, who took time from his busy schedule to help me with the illustrations, and whose critical interest in my writing has always challenged me.

I am grateful as well to many other institutions and individuals. Barbara Epstein, Leon Wieseltier, Richard Poirier, and Caroline Herron invited essays or reviews that gave me the chance to formulate initial thoughts about some of the themes that are more fully addressed in this book. For help in locating manuscripts, images, and other relevant items, I am especially grateful to Ruth Carr at the New York Public Library; Michael Stoller at New York University; Dennis Marnon, Leslie Morris, Vicki Denby, and Thomas Ford at the Houghton Library; Ann-Marie Harris and Kathleen Reilly at the Berkshire Athenaeum; Sara Holliday at the New York Society Library; Rebecca Akan at the Metropolitan Museum of Art; and Bert Saul at the Boston Social Law Library. I also wish to thank Catherine Reynolds, curator of Arrowhead, who came out on a wintry Saturday morning to show me around Melville's home.

I am grateful to Ray Bradbury and Don Congdon Associates for permission to reprint a portion of "Ahab at the Helm," to Maurice Sendak and Michael Di Capua for agreeing to allow reproduction of one of Mr. Sendak's illustrations for *Pierre,* to Bruce Grivetti and HBO for permission to print my transcription of season 4, episode 12 of *The Sopranos,* and to Paul Romano and Natalie Rauch at Relapse Records for permission to reproduce Mr. Romano's artwork for the Mastodon CD *Leviathan.*

My children, Ben and Yvonne, have been appropriately eager to see the work completed, and have helped to keep me at it with their wonderful good humor and irreverence. As for my wife, Dawn, only she knows how much she means to my ability to write or do anything at all.

INDEX

Page numbers in *italics* refer to illustrations.

Grateful acknowledgment is made to the following for permission to reprint previously published material.

Don Congdon Associates, Inc.: Excerpt from *Ahab at the Helm* by Ray Bradbury. Copyright © 1964 by Ray Bradbury. Reprinted by Don Congdon Associates, Inc.

Harcourt, Inc.: Excerpts from *The Melville Log: A Documentary Life of Herman Melville, 1819–1891, Volume I and II.* Copyright 1951 and renewed 1979 by Jay Leyda. Reprinted by permission of Harcourt, Inc.

Northwestern University Press and The Newberry Library: Excerpts from *The Writings of Herman Melville: Journals* by Herman Melville, edited by Howard C. Horsford and Lynn Horth. Excerpts from *The Writings of Herman Melville: Correspondence* by Herman Melville, edited by Lynn Horth. Reprinted by permission of Northwestern University Press and The Newberry Library.

Random House, Inc.: "Herman Melville" copyright 1940 and renewed 1968 by W. H. Auden, from *Collected Poems* by W. H. Auden. Reprinted by permission of Random House, Inc.

University of New Mexico Press: Excerpt from *Genoa: A Telling of Wonders* by Paul Metcalf. Reprinted by permission of University of New Mexico Press.

Several errors of typography, fact, and omission in the first printing of the cloth edition have been corrected for the Vintage edition. I am grateful to the readers who pointed them out.